THE KEY

DIPLOMA PREPARATION GUIDE

Biology 30

THE KEY

THE KEY series of student study guides is specifically designed to assist students in preparing for unit tests, provincial achievement tests, and diploma examinations. Each ***KEY*** includes questions, answers, detailed solutions, and practice tests. The complete solutions show problem-solving methods, explain key concepts, and highlight potential errors.

TABLE OF CORRELATIONS

Castle Rock Research has designed ***THE KEY*** by correlating every question and its solution to Alberta Learning's curriculum outcomes. Each unit of review begins with a Table of Correlations that lists the General and Specific Outcomes from the Alberta curriculum along with Related Questions that correspond to the outcomes. Usually the emphasis placed on outcomes, concepts, and skills within each unit varies. Students and teachers can quickly identify the relevant importance of each outcome and concept in the unit as determined by the number of related questions provided in ***THE KEY***.

For grades 3, 6, 9, and 12, the weighting of each unit and concept is determined by analyzing the blueprint for the respective provincial achievement tests and diploma examinations. Based on this analysis, the Related Questions for outcomes and concepts are organized on a proportionate basis. For grades other than 3, 6, 9, and 12, the breakdown of each course is determined by consulting with experienced teachers and by reviewing curriculum guides and textbooks.

The Table of Correlations is a critical component of ***THE KEY***. For students, it offers a visual cue for effectively organizing study time. For teachers, the Table of Correlations indicates the instructional focus for each content strand, serves as a curriculum checklist, and focuses on the outcomes and concepts that are the most important in the unit and the particular course of study. Students become "test wise" by becoming familiar with exam and question formats used most often in provincial examinations.

Canadian Cataloguing in Publication Data

Rao, Gautam, 1961 –
THE KEY – Biology 30   (2008 Edition)

1.   Science – Juvenile Literature. I. Title

Published by:
Castle Rock Research Corp.
2340 Manulife Place
10180 – 101 Street
Edmonton, AB T5J 3S4

5 6 7 FP 07 06 05

Printed in Canada

Pb
Gautam Rao

Cb
Robin Hill
Dan Merrills
Simonne Longerich

Dedicated to the memory of Dr. V. S. Rao

THE KEY – BIOLOGY 0

THE KEY is a student study guide specifically designed to assist students in preparing for unit tests, final exams, and diploma examinations. It is a compilation of questions and answers from previous diploma examinations, complete with detailed solutions for all questions. Questions have been grouped by concepts so that students can use the resource throughout the year to study for all unit tests and to prepare for their diploma exams. An overview of the main sections of **THE KEY** follows.

I   ***Key Factors Contributing to School Success*** provides students with examples of study and review strategies. Information is included on learning styles, study schedules, and developing review notes.

II   ***Unit Review*** with *Challenger Questions*, includes questions from the 2001 (January) and 2000 (January and June) diploma exams. All questions are classified according to the units studied in class and are correlated to the specific concept(s) being tested. In *Unit Review*, questions considered to be more difficult are labelled as *Challenger*. **THE KEY provides detailed solutions for all qestions.**

III ***Unit Tests*** have been created for each unit to provide students with a sample test that covers the breadth of the curriculum. These tests are comprised of the relevant diploma exam questions from January and June 1999.

IV   ***Key Strategies for Success on Exams*** explores topics such as common exam question formats and strategies for responding, directing words most commonly used, how to begin the exam, and managing test anxiety.

V   ***Diploma Examinations Preparation*** section contains the diploma examinations that were administered in June 2001 and January 2002. The questions presented here are distinct from the questions in the previous section. It is **recommended** that students work through these exams carefully as they are reflective of the exam format and level of difficulty that students are likely to encounter on their final. **Complete solutions are provided for all qest ions in th section.**

THE KEY *Study Guides* are available for English 30-1, English 30-2, Biology 30, Chemistry 30, Physics 30, Applied Mathematics 30, Pure Mathematics 30 , Social Studies 30, and Social Studies 33. A complete list of **THE KEY** *Study Guides,* available for Grades 3 to 12, is included at the back of this book.

For information about any of our resources or services, please call Castle Rock Research at 780.448.9619 or visit our web site at http://www.castlerockresearch.com

At Castle Rock Research, we strive to produce a resource that is error-free. If you should find an error, please contact us so that future editions can be corrected.

CONTENTS

KEY FACTORS CONTRIBUTING TO SCHOOL SUCCESS

NOTES

KEY FACTORS CONTRIBUTING TO SCHOOL SUCCESS

You want to do well in school. There are many factors that contribute to your success. While you may not have control over the number or types of assignments and tests that you need to complete, there are many factors that you can control to improve your academic success in any subject area. The following are examples of these factors.

- **REGULAR CLASS ATTENDANCE** – helps you to master the subject content, identify key concepts, take notes and receive important handouts, ask your teacher questions, clarify information, use school resources, and meet students with whom you can study

- **POSITIVE ATTITUDE AND PERSONAL DISCIPLINE** – helps you to come to classes on time, prepared to work and learn, complete all assignments to the best of your ability, and contribute to a positive learning environment

- **SELF-MOTIVATION AND PERSONAL DISCIPLINE** – helps you to set personal learning goals, take small steps continually moving toward achieving your goals, and to "stick it out when the going gets tough"

- **ACCESSING ASSISTANCE WHEN YOU NEED IT** – helps you to improve or clarify your understanding of the concept or new learning before moving on to the next phase

- **MANAGING YOUR TIME EFFICIENTLY** – helps you to reduce anxiety and focus your study and review efforts on the most important concepts

- **DEVELOPING 'TEST WISENESS'** – helps to increase your confidence in writing exams if you are familiar with the typical exam format, common errors to avoid, and know how the concepts in a subject area are usually tested

- **KNOWING YOUR PERSONAL LEARNING STYLE** – helps you to maximize your learning by using effective study techniques, developing meaningful study notes, and make the most efficient use of your study time

📖 KNOW YOUR LEARNING STYLE

You have a unique learning style. Knowing your learning style – how you learn best – can help you to maximize your time in class and during your exam preparation. There are seven common learning styles. Read the following descriptions to see which one most closely describes your learning preferences.

- **LINGUISTIC LEARNER** (sometimes referred to as an auditory learner) – learns best by saying, hearing and seeing words; is good at memorizing things such as dates, places, names and facts

- **LOGICAL/MATHEMATICAL LEARNER** – learns best by categorizing, classifying and working with abstract relationships; is good at mathematics, problem solving and reasoning

- **SPATIAL LEARNER** (sometimes referred to as a visual learner) – learns best by visualizing, seeing, working with pictures; is good at puzzles, imaging things, and reading maps and charts

- **MUSICAL LEARNER** – learns best by hearing, rhythm, melody, and music; is good at remembering tones, rhythms and melodies, picking up sounds

- **BODILY/KINESTHETIC LEARNER** – learns best by touching, moving, and processing knowledge through bodily sensations; is good at physical activities

- **INTERPERSONAL LEARNER** – learns best by sharing, comparing, relating, cooperating; is good at organizing, communicating, leading, and understanding others

- **INTRAPERSONAL LEARNER** – learns best by working alone, individualized projects, and self-paced instruction

(Adapted from http://snow.utoronto.ca/Learn2/mod3/mistyles.html)

Your learning style may not fit "cleanly" into one specific category but may be a combination of two or more styles. Knowing your personal learning style allows you to organize your study notes in a manner that provides you with the most meaning. For example, if you are a spatial or visual learner, you may find mind mapping and webbing are effective ways to organize subject concepts, information, and study notes. If you are a linguistic learner, you may need to write and then "say out loud" the steps in a process, the formula, or actions that lead up to a significant event. If you are a kinesthetic learner you may need to use your finger to trace over a diagram to remember it or to "tap out" the steps in solving a problem or "feel" yourself writing or typing the formula.

📖 SCHEDULING STUDY TIME

Effective time management skills are an essential component to your academic success. The more effectively you manage your time the more likely you are to achieve your goals such as completing all of your assignments on time or finishing all of the questions on a unit test or year-end exam. Developing a study schedule helps to ensure you have adequate time to review the subject content and prepare for the exam.

You should review your class notes regularly to ensure you have a clear understanding of the new material. Reviewing your lessons on a regular basis helps you to learn and remember the ideas and concepts. It also reduces the quantity of material that you must study prior to a unit test or year-end exam. If this practice is not part of your study habits, establishing a study schedule will help you to make the best use of your time. The following are brief descriptions of three types of study schedules.

- **LONG-TERM STUDY SCHEDULE** – begins early in the school year or semester and well in advance of an exam; is the **most effective** manner for improving your understanding and retention of the concepts, and increasing self-confidence; involves regular, nightly review of class notes, handouts and text material

- **SHORT-TERM STUDY SCHEDULE** – begins **five to seven days prior to an exam**; must organize the volume of material to be covered beginning with the most difficult concepts; each study session starts with a brief review of what was studied the day before

- **CRAMMING** – occurs the night before an exam; is the **least effective** form of studying or exam preparation; focuses on memorizing and reviewing critical information such as facts, dates, formulas; do not introduce new material; has the potential to increase exam anxiety by discovering something you do not know

Regardless of the type of study schedule you use, you may want to consider the following to maximize your study time and effort:

- establish a regular time and place for doing your studying

- minimize distractions and interruptions during your study time

- plan a ten minute break for every hour that you study

- organize the material so you begin with the most challenging content first

- divide the subject content into smaller manageable "chunks" to review

- develop a marking system for your study notes to identify key and secondary concepts, concepts that you are confident about, those that require additional attention or about which you have questions

- reward yourself for sticking to your schedule and/or completing each review section

- alternate the subjects and type of study activities to maintain your interest and motivation

- make a daily task list with the headings "must do", "should do", and "could do"

- begin each session by quickly reviewing what you studied the day before

- maintain your usual routine of eating, sleeping, and exercising to help you concentrate for extended periods of time

KEY STRATEGIES FOR REVIEWING

Reviewing textbook material, class notes, and handouts should be an ongoing activity and becomes more critical in preparing for exams. You may find some of the following strategies useful in completing your review during your scheduled study time.

READING OR SKIMMING FOR KEY INFORMATION

- Before reading the chapter, preview it by noting headings, charts and graphs, chapter questions.

- Turn each heading and sub-heading into a question before you start to read.

- Read the complete introduction to identify the key information that is addressed in the chapter.

- Read the first sentence of the next paragraph for the main idea.

- Skim the paragraph noting key words, phrases, and information.

- Read the last sentence of the paragraph.

- Repeat the process for each paragraph and section until you have skimmed the entire chapter.

- Read the complete conclusion to summarize each chapter's contents.

- Answer the questions you created.

- Answer the chapter questions.

CREATING STUDY NOTES

Mind Mapping or Webbing

- Use the key words, ideas or concepts from your reading or class notes to create a *mind map or web* (a diagram or visual representation of the information). A mind map or web is sometimes referred to as a knowledge map.

- Write the key word, concept, theory or formula in the centre of your page.

- Write and link related facts, ideas, events, and information to the central concept using lines.

- Use colored markers, underlining, or other symbols to emphasize things such as relationships, information of primary and secondary importance.

- The following example of a mind map or web illustrates how this technique can be used to develop an essay.

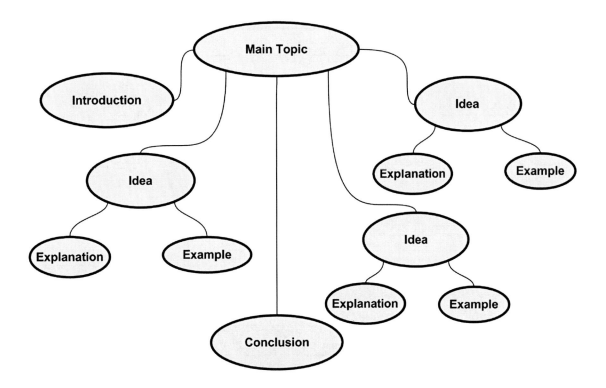

Charts

♦ Use charts to organize your information and relate theories, concepts, definitions, applications and other important details.

♦ Collect and enter the information in key categories.

♦ Use the completed chart as a composite picture of the concept or information.

The following is an example of how a chart can be used to help you organize information when exploring an issue in subjects such as Social Studies, the Sciences, or Humanities.

Define Key Words		
1.		
2.		
3.		
Explore the Issue		
Yes to the Issue	**No** to the Issue	**Maybe** to the Issue
1.	1.	1.
2.	2.	2.
3.	3.	3.
Case Studies and **Examples**		
1.	1.	
2.	2.	
3.	3.	
Defense of Your Point of View		
1.		
2.		
3.		

Index Cards

◆ Write a key event, fact, concept, theory, word or question on one side of the index card.

◆ On the reverse side, write the date, place, important actions and key individuals involved in the event, significance of the fact, salient features of the concept, essence and application of the theory, definition of the word or answer to the question.

◆ Use the cards to quickly review important information.

International System of Units (SI)

International System of Units (SI)

SI base unit

Base quantity	Name	Symbol
length	metre	m
mass	kilogram	kg
time	second	s
amount of substance	mole	mol

Derived Measures

Measures	Unit	Symbol
Volume	cubic metre	m^3

SI Prefixes

Factor	Name	Symbol
10^6	mega	M
10^3	kilo	k
10^{-2}	centi	c
10^{-3}	milli	m
10^{-6}	micro	μ

Symbols

◆ Develop your own symbols to use when reviewing your material to identify information you need in preparing for your exam. For example, an exclamation mark (!) may signify something that "must be learned well" because it is a key concept that is likely to appear on unit tests and the year-end exam. A question mark (?) may identify something you are unsure of while a star or asterisk (*) may identify important information for formulating an argument. A check mark (✓) or an (✕) can be used to show that you agree or disagree with the statement, sentence or paragraph.

Crib Notes

- Develop brief notes that are a critical summary of the essential concepts, dates, events, theories, formulas, supporting facts, or steps in a process that are most likely to be on the exam.

- Use your crib notes as your "last minute" review before you go in to write your exam. You can not take crib notes into an exam.

MEMORIZING

- **ASSOCIATION** relates the new learning to something you already know. For example, in distinguishing between the spelling of 'dessert' and 'desert', you know 'sand' has only one 's' and so should desert.

- **MNEMONIC DEVICES** are sentences you create to remember a list or group of items. For example, the first letters of the words in the sentence "**E**very **G**ood **B**oy **D**eserves **F**udge" helps you to remember the names of the lines on the treble clef staff
(E, G, B, D, and F) in music.

- **ACRONYMS** are words formed from the first letters of the words in a group. For example, **HOMES** helps you to remember the names of the five Great Lakes (**H**uron, **O**ntario, **M**ichigan, **E**rie, and **S**uperior).

- **VISUALIZING** requires you to use your mind's eye to "see" the chart, list, map, diagram, or sentence as it exists in your textbook, notes, on the board, computer screen or in the display.

BIOLOGY 30

Unit Review has been developed to aid students in their study throughout the term. Students can prepare for unit exams while gaining exposure to previous diploma exam questions. This section of *THE KEY* is a compilation of questions from the diploma exams that were administered in 2000 (January and June) and 2001 (January). All questions have been organized by content strand to correspond to the units in Biology 30. Students will find questions for *Nervous and Endocrine Systems*, *Reproductive Systems*, *Cell Division and Genetics*, and *Population Genetics and Interactions*.

A Table of correlations at the beginning of each unit lists the curriculum outcomes and the *Multiple Choice, Numerical-Response*, and *Written Response* questions that specifically test those concepts. To help students understand the curriculum, *THE KEY* provides explanations of the *key* concepts for each unit. After each explanation, students are directed to questions from previous diploma exams that are related to the underlying concepts. Sample unit tests are included at the end of each unit. The Unit Tests include the relevant questions from diploma exams administered in 1999 (January and June).

THE KEY **contains detailed solutions for all questions**. Solutions show the processes and/or ideas used in arriving at the correct answers and may help students gain a better understanding of the concepts that are being tested.

In the *Unit Review*, certain have been categorized as *Challenger Questions*. *Challenger Questions* represent the more difficult questions that a student is likely to face, as illustrated in the following example.

CHALLENGER QUESTION	DIFFICULTY: 43.2

> **2.** In a large population of randomly breeding Drosophila, 1% of the population exhibits burgundy eye-colour, an autosomal recessive trait. According to the Hardy-Weinberg equilibrium, what percentage of the population is expected to be heterozygous?
>
> Answer: _____ %

The difficulty rating is based on the percentage of students that answered the question correctly when it appeared on the diploma exam. In the example above, only 43.2% of students answered correctly (Source: *Alberta Education Examiner's Reports*.) *Challenger questions* for Biology 30 include those with under 60% achievement (as indicated by the difficulty rating.)

NERVOUS AND ENDOCRINE SYSTEMS

Table of Correlations		
General Outcome	**Specific Outcome**	**Related Questions**
	Students are expected to:	
demonstrate an understanding that the human organism, like other organisms, maintains control over its internal environment with neural systems by extending from Science 10, Unit 1, energy systems, Science 10, Unit 2, cell processes, and Biology 20, Unit 4, the biological systems that maintain the organism's equilibrium with the environment, and by:	1.1.1.1 describing the structure and function of a neuron and myelin sheath, explaining the formation and transmission of an action potential and the transmission of a signal across a synapse or neuromuscular junction and the main chemicals and transmitters involved; i.e., norepinephrine, acetylcholine, and the enzyme that breaks them down	1, 2, 3, 4, 5, 6 7, 8, 9
	1.1.1.2 describing the composition and function of a simple reflex arc and the organization of neurons into nerves	NR1, 16
	1.1.1.3 identifying the principal structures of the central and peripheral nervous systems and explaining their functions in regulating the voluntary (somatic) and involuntary (autonomic) systems of the human organism; e.g., cerebral hemispheres, cerebellum, pons, medulla, hypothalamus, pituitary, spinal cord, sympathetic and parasympathetic nervous systems	10, 11, 12, 13, 14, 15, 17, 18
	1.1.1.4 explaining how human organisms sense their environment and their spatial orientation in it; e.g., auditory, visual, skin receptors, olfactory, proprioceptors	19, 20, 21, 22, 23, 24 25
demonstrate an understanding of how endocrine systems coordinate other organ systems through feedback to maintain internal homeostasis, as well as the organism's equilibrium with the environment, by extending from Biology 20, Unit 4, the maintenance of metabolic equilibrium, and by:	1.2.1.1 identifying the principal endocrine glands of the human organism; e.g., the hypothalamus/pituitary complex, thyroid and adrenal glands, pancreas islet cells	29
	1.2.1.2 describing the hormones of the principal endocrine glands; i.e., TSH/thyroxine, ACTH/cortisol glucagon/ insulin, HGH, ADH, epinephrine, norepinephrine, aldosterone	26, 27, 28, 30, 31, 32, 33, NR2
	1.2.1.3 explaining the metabolic roles hormones play in homeostasis; i.e., thyroxine to metabolism, insulin to blood sugar regulation, HGH to growth, ADH to water regulation	
	1.2.1.4 explaining how the endocrine system allows human organisms to sense their internal environment and respond appropriately; e.g., sugar metabolism	
	1.2.1.5 comparing the endocrine and neural control systems and explaining how they act together; eg., stress and the adrenal gland	34
	1.2.1.6 describing, using an example, the physiological consequences of hormone imbalances	

NERVOUS AND ENDOCRINE SYSTEMS

1.1.1.1   Describing the structure and function of a neuron and myelin sheath, explaining the formation and transmission of an action potential and the transmission of a signal across a synapse or neuromuscular junction and the main chemicals and transmitters involved; i.e. norepinephrine, acetylcholine, and the enzyme that breaks them down

A neuron is a nerve cell specialized for conducting nerve signals. It has long cell extensions called fibres, which consist of cytoplasm covered with cell membrane. These fibres are either dendrites, which carry signals toward the cell body, or axons, which carry signals away from the cell body. Neurons that carry signals from sensory organs to the central nervous system (spinal cord and brain) are called sensory neurons. Those that carry signals from the CNS to the muscles are called motor neurons, and neurons that transmit signals within the CNS are called interneurons. Some fibres are covered in a neurilemma, which is a membrane that helps the fibre repair itself should there be an injury. Many of the fibres are also covered with a white myelin sheath composed of Schwann cells. Between the Schwann cells is a small space where the fibre is exposed, called a node of Ranvier.

A Neuron

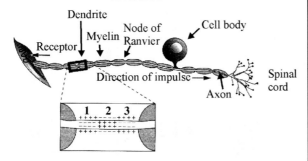

When the fibre is not transmitting a signal, a sodium/potassium pump maintains the resting potential that involves keeping sodium ions of the fibre and potassium ions inside the fibre. There are also large organic ions inside the fibre – the resting potential can be measured at about –60mV.

That is, more negative inside the fibre than outside. If a fibre is stimulated strongly enough to reach a stimulus threshold, an action potential occurs in which sodium gates open and sodium ions rush in, making the inside of the fibre more positive. When this happens, the potassium ions rush out, restoring the negative potential inside. This is referred to as depolarization. At this point, the sodium/potassium pump moves the sodium back out and the potassium back in. If the fibre is non-myelinated, this change at one spot stimulates an action potential at the next adjacent spot. In this manner, action potentials flow in a wave along the fibre. If the fibre is myelinated, the action potentials only occur at the nodes, so the signal skips from node to node. A signal travels faster in a myelinated fibre than in a non-myelinated fibre and requires far less energy. If a signal in an individual fibre cannot be strong or weak, we say it is all-or-none. If a fibre carries many signals in quick succession, it may have all the sodium inside and all the potassium outside, and the sodium/potassium pump is then unable to work quickly enough to restore the resting potential. This results in weakened stimulation known as neural fatigue.

A synapse is the space between the end of an axon and the next neurons dendrite or cell body. When a signal arrives at the end of the axon, calcium ions rather than sodium ions, enter the fibre. The calcium stimulates vesicles of neurotransmitter to be released into the synapse. The neurotransmitter diffuses across the synapse and binds with receptor sites on the postsynaptic membrane, thus causing depolarization in the next neuron. One such neurotransmitter is acetylcholine. Immediately after acetylcholine is released, cholinesterase is released into the synapse. The cholinesterase breaks down the acetylcholine to stop the depolarization. Other common neurotransmitters are norepinephrine, seratonin, and dopamine.

Related Questions: 1, 2, 3, 4, 5, 6, 7, 8, 9

1.1.1.2   describing the composition and function of a simple reflex arc and the organization of neurons into nerves

1.1.1.3   identifying the principal structures of the central and peripheral nervous systems and explaining their functions in regulating the voluntary (somatic) and involuntary (autonomic) systems of the human organism; e.g. cerebral hemispheres, cerebellum, pons, medulla, hypothalamus, pituitary, spinal cord, sympathetic and parasympathetic nervous systems

During a reflex response, a signal travels along a sensory neuron, into the CNS where interneurons coordinate a response that is sent out of the CNS via motor neurons to effect a motor response.
The somatic nervous system regulates skeletal muscles that a person can consciously control.

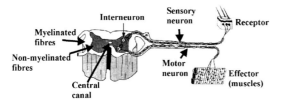

The autonomic nervous system regulates muscles of the glands and internal organs of which a person has no conscious control. The sympathetic component of the autonomic system prepares the body for action by diverting blood from internal organs to skeletal muscles, heart, and brain. As well, the sympathetic system increases blood pressure and breathing rate. The parasympathetic component of the autonomic system normalizes body functions.
The neurotransmitter for the sympathetic system is norepinephrine, and the neurotransmitter for the parasympathetic system is acetylcholine. The top of the brain is composed of the two cerebral hemispheres of the cerebrum that control conscious thought. The cerebrum can be divided into the frontal lobes that are responsible for our personality traits, the occipital lobes at the back where visual stimuli are coordinated, the temporal lobes at the bottom sides that control language and hearing stimuli, and, above the temporal lobes, the parietal lobes, that regulate touch sensations. Beneath the cerebrum is the corpus callosum, a band of myelinated fibres that transmit information between the right and left hemispheres. The cerebellum at the back of the skull coordinates muscular movements. The pons in front of the cerebellum is a relay centre for information moving to and from the cerebrum. The medulla oblongata controls basic functioning such as breathing, heart rate, and digestive functions. The hypothalamus and the pituitary control the endocrine system.

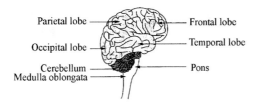

Related Questions: NR1, 10, 11, 12, 13, 14, 15, 16, 17, 18

1.1.1.4 explaining how human organisms sense their environment and their spatial orientation in it; e.g., auditory, visual, skin receptors, olfactory, propioceptors

Sensory organs are all the same in that they all stimulate sensory nerves that carry information to the CNS. The eye converts light signals into action potentials in the optic nerve. The eye is a sac that has three layers. The outer layer, the sclera, is white except for the front transparent part that is called the cornea. The middle layer is the choroid. It is mostly black to ensure that light that is not used to make a nerve signal is absorbed and does not bounce around in the eye. The front part of the choroid is modified into the lens and the ciliary muscles that adjust the shape of the lens.

The iris is the coloured part of the eye. The retina is the sensory membrane that lines the eye, contains the rods, receptors that work well in low light but do not detect colour, and the cones, which require more light and allow us to see in colour. There are three types of cones – red, green, and blue. The fovea is a spot directly at the back of the retina. It contains tightly packed cones and is where a person can see with most precision. Inside the eye is fluid: a watery aqueous humour in front of the lens and a thicker vitreous humour behind the lens.

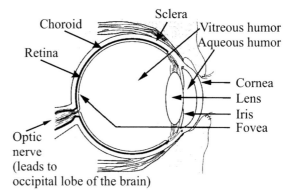

Nearsighted people cannot focus on distant objects because the image focuses in front of the retina instead of directly on it. Farsighted people cannot see close objects because the image is not yet focussed when the light arrives at the retina.
The problem with astigmatism is that the cornea does not have a smooth curve so that without corrective glasses one part of the visual field is in focus while other parts are not. A cataract is a lens that has become cloudy. Glaucoma is damage to the retina caused by excessive pressure from fluid in the eye.

The ear consists of an outer ear (the pinna and auditory canal), the middle ear (starting with the eardrum or tympanic membrane), and the fluid-filled inner ear. Air pressure inside the middle ear is kept equal to air pressure in the auditory canal by the Eustachian tube, which allows air to pass between the middle ear and the back of the mouth. Sound is transmitted from the eardrum through the tiny middle ear bones – the hammer (malleus), anvil (incus), and stirrup (stapes). Vibrations of the stirrup cause the oval window of the inner ear cochlea to vibrate, causing vibrations in the fluid of the inner ear which pass out the round window. The vibrations of the inner ear fluid cause hair cells of the organ of Corti to stimulate the auditory nerve. The inner ear also contains the utricle and saccule for stationary balance and the semicircular canals for movement balance.

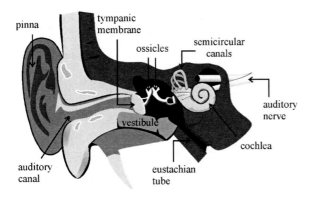

Related Questions: 19, 20, 21, 22, 23, 24, 25

1.2.1.1 identifying the principal endocrine glands of the human organism; e.g., the hypothalamus/pituitary complex, thyroid and adrenal glands, pancreas islet cells

1.2.1.2 describing the hormones of the principal endocrine glands; i.e., TSH/thyroxine, ACTH/cortisol glucagon/insulin, HGH, ADH, epinephrine, norepinephrine, aldosterone

The endocrine system involves endocrine glands and the hormones they produce.

Gland	Hormone	Target Tissues	Effects
hypo-thalamus	ADH	Kidney tubules	Increased reabsorption of water, thereby diluting blood
	oxytocin	Myometrium of uterus and mammary glands	Stimulates contractions of the uterus for birth; stimulates the release of milk during breast-feeding
Anterior pituitary	Thyroid stimulating horomone (TSH)	Thyroid gland	Stimulates the thyroid to release thyroxin
	Adreno-cortic-orophic horomone (ACTH)	Adrenal cortex	Stimulates the adrenal cortex to release horomones such as cortisol
	Growth horomone (HGH)	various tissues, chiefly the long bones	Causes mitosis to stimulate growth
Thyroid	Thyroxin	All body cells	Increases the rate of metabolic activity
Pancreas (beta cells)	Insulin	Liver, muscles	Stimulates uptake of glucose (thereby lowering blood glucose) and storage of glucose as glycogen
Pancreas (Alpha cells)	Glucagon	Liver	Stimulates the breakdown of glycogen and the release of glucose, thereby raising blood glucose

Adrenal cortex	Cortisol	All tissues	Initiates healing – reduces swelling, releases glucose and other compounds needed for repair of tissues
	Aldosterone	Kidney tubules	Increases rcadsorption of water and salts thereby increasing the water volume of the body
Adrenal medulla	Epinephrine/ norepine-phrine	Blood vessels, heart, brain, muscles, lungs	Increased blood pressure; increased blood flow to skeletal muscles, heart and brain, away from internal organs; dilation of pupils, increased breathing rate

Sex hormones – testosterone, estrogen, progesterone, HCG, LH, prolactin, relaxin – will be dealt with in the reproduction section.

Related Questions: 29, 26, 27, 28, 30, 31, 32, 33, NR2

1.2.1.3 explaining the metabolic roles hormones play in homeostasis; i.e., thyroxine to metabolism, insulin to blood sugar regulation, HGH to growth, ADH to water regulation

1.2.1.4 explaining how the endocrine system allows human organisms to sense their internal environment and respond appropriately; e.g., sugar metabolism

1.2.1.5 comparing the endocrine and neural control systems and explaining how they act together; e.g., stress and the adrenal gland

1.2.1.6 describing, using an example, the physiological consequences of hormone imbalances.

Control of hormone levels in the blood is usually accomplished through negative feedback.

To illustrate with thyroxin: a high thyroxin level is detected by the hypothalamus which then stops stimulating the anterior pituitary to secrete TSH, therefore the thyroid gland stops producing thyroxin.

Hypothyroidism – too little thyroxin – causes a lower metabolic rate, resulting in tiredness, apathy, and weight gain. In children, hypothyroidism causes slowed mental and physical development.

The reverse can also happen if a low thyroxin level is detected by the hypothalmus. Hyperthroidism – too much thyroxin – causes a higher metabolic rate which results in high blood pressure, sweating, irritability, and weight loss.

The inability to produce an adequate supply of insulin as a child is called type I diabetes mellitus. The blood glucose level can become dangerously high and glucose is excreted with urine. Type II diabetes mellitus usually affects older adults and is often caused by an inadequate supply of insulin receptors. It can usually be controlled with diet.

The endocrine system provides a slower, more generalized form of control than the nervous system.

Related Question: 34

Use the following information to answer the next question.

Movement of hair cells in normal ears opens tiny pores called ion channels in the nerve cell membrane. This process begins impulse transmission along the auditory nerve.

1. Nerve impulse transmission continues along the nerve cell membrane as

   A. a wave of depolarization

   B. a negative feedback loop

   C. a diffusing wave of summation

   D. the active transport of an electrical potential

   Source: January 2000

Use the following information to answer the next question.

Yaws, bejel, and syphilis are three diseases known to be caused by strains of bacteria in the genus *Treponema*. Syphilis is a sexually transmitted disease, whereas yaws and bejel are not sexually transmitted. Studies of 800-year-old to 1 600-year-old skeletons from Florida, Equador, and New Mexico show that these people suffered from syphilis. Studies on 6 000-year-old skeletons from Illinois, Virginia, and Ohio show that these people suffered from yaws.

The symptoms of untreated syphilis usually disappear within 12 weeks of the initial infection. However, new symptoms may appear many years later. These include damage to neurons of the central nervous system.

– from Zabludoff, 1996

CHALLENGER QUESTION   **56.1**

2. The neurons damaged by syphilis are

   A. interneurons

   B. sensory neurons

   C. somatic motor neurons

   D. autonomic motor neurons

   Source: January 2000

Use the following information to answer the next question.

Research has shown that although interneurons in the spinal cord make proteins that inhibit regeneration of damaged axons, peripheral nerve axons can regenerate.

3. The structure that allows neurons of peripheral nerves to regenerate is the

   A. axon

   B. dendrite

   C. neurilemma

   D. node of Ranvier

   Source: June 2000

Use the following information to answer the next three questions.

Serotonin is a naturally occurring neurotransmitter that plays an important role in a person's mood and emotions. A shortage of serotonin has been associated with phobias, schizophrenia, aggressive behaviour, depression, uncontrolled appetite, and migraine headaches. Synthetic drugs have been developed to enhance or hinder the performance of serotonin in the brain. Some of these drugs include

I   Prozac and Zoloft, which cause serotonin to remain in the brain for longer periods of time

II   Drugs, such as Clozapine, that prevent serotonin from binding to post-synaptic membranes

III   Diet drugs, such as Redux and Fenfluramine, that stimulate nerve cells to release more serotonin

IV   Hallucinogens, such as LSD and Ecstasy, that react directly with serotonin receptors to produce the same effect as serotonin

– from Lemonick, 1997

4. The drugs numbered above that would act as competitive inhibitors to serotonin and the drugs that would slow down the rate of removal of serotonin from the synapse are, respectively,

   A. I and III

   B. II and I

   C. II and III

   D. III and IV

   Source: June 2000

5. If a person were suffering from clinical depression, which of the following drugs would not reduce the symptoms of depression?

   A. LSD

   B. Zoloft

   C. Clozapine

   D. Fenfluramine

   Source: June 2000

Use the following additional information to answer the next question.

Two Neurons and a Synapse

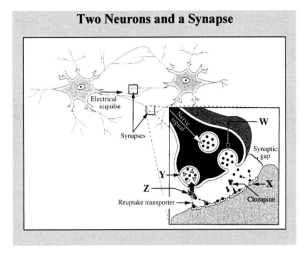

6. Which of the following rows identifies the structure that releases serotonin and the section of the neuron that this structure is found in?

Row	Released from structure	Found in
A.	W	axon terminal
B.	X	dendrite
C.	Y	axon
D.	Z	dendrite

Source: June 2000

Use the following information to answer the next question.

A Motor Neuron

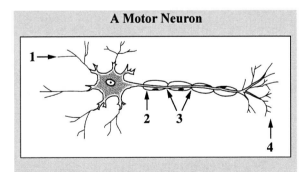

7. The part of the motor neuron that may release acetylcholine is labelled

A. 1   B. 2

C. 3   D. 4

Source: January 2001

8. What would happen if acetylcholine was released at a synapse, but no cholinesterase was present?

A. The acetylcholine would fail to stimulate the postsynaptic neuron.

B. The acetylcholine would diffuse more rapidly across the synaptic cleft.

C. A single nerve impulse would be generated in the postsynaptic neuron.

D. The postsynaptic neuron would remain in a constant state of depolarization.

Source: January 2001

Use the following information to answer the next question.

The brain neurotransmitter dopamine is linked to the good feelings associated with actions such as receiving a friendly hug. When cocaine is present in synapses, it binds with dopamine transporters producing similar emotional effects. Normally, dopamine transporters carry dopamine back into the cells where it was formed.

– from *Page*, 1997

9. Dopamine transmission is affected when dopamine transporters, which normally carry dopamine back to the cell that formed it, are occupied by cocaine. The effects of cocaine occur because dopamine

A. is produced in increased concentration

B. remains in the synapse in high concentration

C. levels drop rapidly as the molecules react with cocaine

D. is transported very effectively to the postsynaptic neuron

Source: January 2001

Use the following diagram to answer the next question.

A Reflex Arc

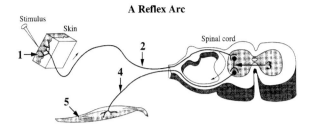

CHALLENGER QUESTION   55.9

Numerical Response

1. Identify the structure, as numbered above, that performs each of the functions given below.

Structure:	_____	_____	_____	_____
Function:	Transmits impulses to the central nervous system	Receives sensory stimulation	Carries out instructions from the central nervous system; is a muscle	Transmits impulses from the central nervous system to the effector

Source: January 2000

Use the following information to answer the next two questions.

A group of psychologists wondered if inhaling pure oxygen could enhance a person's mental capacity. They tested forty-five students. These students breathed through a face mask for one minute. They were given either pure oxygen or normal air, but they did not know which. Those receiving pure oxygen could recall twice as many words as those receiving normal air.

– from *Mihill*, 1996

10. The part of the brain that is directly responsible for the recall of previously learned words is the

   A. cerebrum

   B. cerebellum

   C. pituitary gland

   D. medulla oblongata

Source: January 2000

11. The part of the brain that controls the unconscious rate of breathing is the

   A. cerebrum

   B. cerebellum

   C. pituitary gland

   D. medulla oblongata

Source: January 2000

12. Jogging will cause heart rate to change because of

   A. increased sympathetic and decreased parasympathetic impulses

   B. decreased sympathetic and increased parasympathetic impulses

   C. increased sympathetic and decreased central nervous system impulses

   D. decreased sympathetic and increased central nervous system impulses

Source: January 2000

Use the following information to answer the next two questions.

A man was injured in an automobile accident. There appeared to be damage to his back, his arm, and his head.

A doctor examined the man, noted some symptoms, and hypothesized that nerve damage had occurred.

Some Possible Locations of Nerve Damage

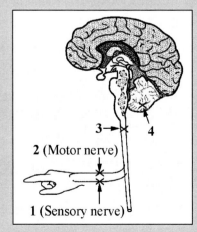

13. Which of the following rows correctly correlates possible observations about the accident victim with locations of nerve damage?

Row	Possible Observations	Locations of Nerve Damage
A.	The man could not move his wrist and could not feel sensations from his hand.	1 and 2
B.	The man could move his wrist normally but could not feel sensations from his hand.	1 and 4
C.	The man could not move his wrist but could feel sensations from his hand.	2 and 3
D.	The man could move his wrist normally and could feel sensations in his hand.	2 and 4

Source: June 2000

14. If, following the accident, the man exhibited a marked change in personality, the doctor would suspect damage to the

A. medulla

B. cerebrum

C. cerebellum

D. hypothalamus

Source: June 2000

Use the following information to answer the next question.

Researchers have been studying the connection between maternal care and stress in rats. Those rats that received more licking and grooming as babies release lower levels of ACTH in response to stress as adults. In humans, high levels of stress hormones are linked to an increase in heart disease, diabetes, depression, and alcoholism.

– from *Strauss*,1997

15. When a person, or a rat, is exposed to stressful situations, the response of the nervous system is the activation of the

A. sympathetic nervous system and the release of epinephrine by post-ganglionic fibres

B. sympathetic nervous system and the release of acetylcholine by post-ganglionic fibres

C. parasympathetic nervous system and the release of epinephrine by post-ganglionic fibres

D. parasympathetic nervous system and the release of acetylcholine by post-ganglionic fibres

Source: June 2000

Use the following information to answer the next question.

After accidentally hitting your thumb with a hammer, you immediately withdraw your hand. You do not feel pain for a short period of time.

16. This sequence of events may be explained by the fact that the

A. threshold of the receptor has been so greatly exceeded that the neuron does not pass the message to the brain

B. neural impulse is so large that the brain is unable to interpret the signal because it is beyond the range of tolerance

C. neural processing occurred in the spinal cord first, which caused you to quickly remove your thumb from further damage

D. sensory receptors in the thumb were damaged by the blow and are unable to initiate a stimulus to the sensory nerve

Source: January 2001

CHALLENGER QUESTION   **50.8**

17. Stimulation of an individual's sympathetic nervous system in response to imminent danger leads to all of the following responses **except**

     A. dilation of the pupils of the eye

     B. constriction of the bronchioles of the lungs

     C. constriction of the arterioles of the intestines

     D. dilation of the arterioles of the skeletal muscles

Source: January 2001

Use the following information to answer the next question.

Morphine is a drug obtained from the opium plant. It is routinely given to postoperative patients on a short-term basis for pain. At high doses, it causes breathing and heart contraction to become suppressed.

18. What area of the brain is affected by high doses of morphine?

     A. Pituitary

     B. Cerebrum

     C. Cerebellum

     D. Medulla oblongata

Source: January 2001

Use the following information to answer the next question.

Movement of hair cells in normal ears opens tiny pores called ion channels in the nerve cell membrane. This process begins impulse transmission along the auditory nerve.

19. The part of the ear **directly** responsible for stimulating the nerve endings that transmit sound impulses from the ear to the brain is the

     A. cochlea

     B. eardrum

     C. Eustachian tube

     D. semicircular canal

Source: January 2000

Use the following information to answer the next two questions.

Many predatory birds such as eagles have two foveas in each eye. The fovea in predatory birds is similar in structure and function to the fovea in humans. In addition, these birds have strong powers of near and far accommodation.

– from Curtis, 1983

20. If an eagle's brain were similar in structure to a human brain, impulses that begin in the retina of the eagle's eye would travel first to the

     A. frontal lobe

     B. parietal lobe

     C. occipital lobe

     D. temporal lobe

Source: January 2000

21. Strong near and far accommodation in the eye requires

     A. small blind spots

     B. a large number of rods

     C. a large number of cones

     D. highly developed ciliary muscles

Source: January 2000

Use the following information to answer the next two questions.

Human Ear

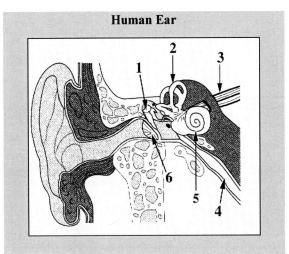

22. After riding the Tilt-A-Turn at an amusement park, people are often dizzy. Which of the structures numbered on the diagram above is initially stimulated to cause the sensation of dizziness?

    A. Structure 1

    B. Structure 2

    C. Structure 3

    D. Structure 5

    Source: June 2000

23. Which of the structures numbered on the diagram function together to convert sound waves to mechanical vibrations, and then to amplify these vibrations?

    A. Structures 6 and 1

    B. Structures 5 and 2

    C. Structures 6 and 3

    D. Structures 5 and 4

    Source: June 2000

Use the following information to answer the next question.

Many scientists believe that sleep cycles are influenced by the hormone melatonin. Two scientists have shown that the retinas in hamsters are involved in maintaining a 24-hour cycle. Their research shows that impulses sent from the retina to the brain after exposure to light influence the secretions of melatonin. Melatonin is normally produced in greater amounts at night when the eyes are exposed to less light. In humans, melatonin produces drowsiness.

– from *Raloff*, 1996

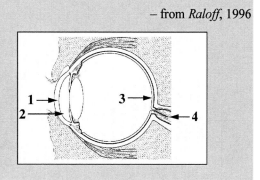

24. Melatonin secretion decreases when light stimulates receptors found in the structure labelled

    A. 1

    B. 2

    C. 3

    D. 4

    Source: June 2000

Use the following information to answer the next question.

A high percentage of purebred dogs have genetic defects. Some examples of these defects follow.

1. Hip dysplasia, a defect in the hip joints that can cripple a dog, occurs in 60% of golden retievers.

2. Hereditary deafness, due to a recessive autosomal disorder, occurs in 30% of Dalmatians.

3. Retinal disease, which may cause blindness, occurs in 70% of collies.

4. Hemophilia, an X-linked recessive disorder, is common in Labrador retrievers. Dwarfism is also common in this breed of dog.

– from *Lemonick*, 1994

Cross-Section of a Normal Eye

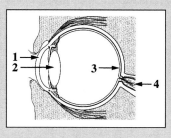

25. The structure that degenerates and causes blindness in collies is

    A. 1

    B. 2

    C. 3

    D. 4

    Source: January 2001

Use the following information to answer the next question.

Oxytocin and ADH are synthesized by neurosecretory cells in the hypothalamus.
These hormones are stored in the posterior pituitary. They can then be released into the bloodstream where they circulate to target cells.

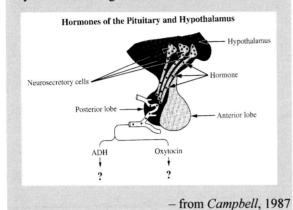

Hormones of the Pituitary and Hypothalamus

– from *Campbell*, 1987

26. In a human female, where are the target cells for ADH and oxytocin?

   A. In the kidney tubules and ovaries

   B. In the Bowman's capsule and the ovaries

   C. In the kidney tubules and uterine muscles

   D. In the Bowman's capsule and the uterine muscles

Source: January 2000

Use the following information to answer the next question.

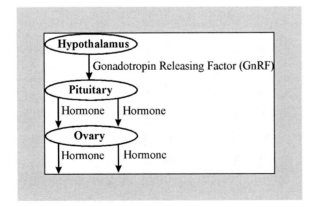

27. In humans, high levels of GnRF cause the pituitary to release

   A. LH and FSH

   B. LH and estrogen

   C. progesterone and FSH

   D. estrogen and progesterone

Source: January 2000

Use the following information to answer the next question.

Responses Stimulated by Hormones

1 Release of thyroxine
2 Development of bones and muscles
3 Water reabsorption by kidneys
4 Development of follicle and sperm
5 Ovulation and maintenance of the corpus luteum
6 Milk production

Numerical Response

2. Identify the response, as numbered above, that would be stimulated by each of the hormones given below.
Response: _____, _____, _____, _____
Hormone: STH LH TSH FSH
         (HGH)

Source: January 2000

Use the following information to answer the next question.

Although most strains of the bacterial species *Vibrio cholera* are harmless, the 01 strain produces a toxin that binds to cells of the small intestine, causing rapid depletion of salts and water, which, if not replaced, can be lethal in humans. This disease is known as cholera.

The transformation from harmless to harmful bacterial strains is thought to be caused by a virus that transfers the cholera toxin gene (CTX) from one bacterial strain and places it into another.
Researchers can mimic this process by using current technologies.

– from *Glausiusz*, 1996

28. The overall effects of cholera toxin are opposite to the physiological effects of which of the following hormones?

   A. Oxytocin

   B. Thyroxine

   C. Aldosterone

   D. Epinephrine

Source: January 2000

Use the following information to answer the next question.

Researchers have been studying the connection between maternal care and stress in rats. Those rats that received more licking and grooming as babies release lower levels of ACTH in response to stress as adults. In humans, high levels of stress hormones are linked to an increase in heart disease, diabetes, depression, and alcoholism.

– from *Strauss*, 1997

Some Endocrine Glands

29. Humans, as well as rats, release ACTH in response to stress. Which of the following rows identifies the gland that secretes ACTH and the target gland of ACTH in humans?

Row	Secreting Gland	Target Gland
A.	1	2
B.	1	3
C.	2	4
D.	2	5

Source: June 2000

Use the following information to answer the next two questions

A laboratory technician was asked to set up an experiment to determine the effect of thyroxine on metabolic rate. Four groups of adult male laboratory rats were used. Each group was placed in the same type of cage, which was designed to provide room for physical activity. Each of the four groups was given an adequate supply of water and one of the four diets listed below.

Diet W: rat chow, a preparation of rat food containing all essential nutrients

Diet X: rat chow containing a chemical that counteracts the effect of thyroxine in the body

Diet Y: rat chow containing dried thyroid tissue, which contains thyroxine

Diet Z: rat chow deficient in iodine

The technician was not aware of which diet she was feeding to each group of rats. The following data were obtained.

Group	Average Initial Weight (g)	Average Final Weight After Two Weeks (g)	Final Average Oxygen Consumption (mL/kg. min)
I	323	392	2.5
II	328	287	10.5
III	330	400	2.0
IV	315	320	4.0

30. According to the data table, which group of rats was **most likely** the control group?

   A. I   B. II

   C. III   D. IV

Source: June 2000

31. Which of the following rows correctly identifies two groups of laboratory rats and the diets they were most probably fed?

Row	Group	Diet	Group	Diet
A	I	Z	II	W
B	I	W	IV	X
C	II	Y	III	X
D	III	Z	IV	Y

Source: June 2000

Use the following information to answer the next question.

Many scientists believe that sleep cycles are influenced by the hormone melatonin. Two scientists have shown that the retinas in hamsters are involved in maintaining a 24-hour cycle. Their research shows that impulses sent from the retina to the brain after exposure to light influence the secretions of melatonin. Melatonin is normally produced in greater amounts at night when the eyes are exposed to less light. In humans, melatonin produces drowsiness.

– from Raloff, 1996

Scientists have discovered that, in many mammals, light exposure affects schedules of reproduction. Decreased light exposure in early winter results in a decrease in fertility in these mammals.

– from Norman and Litwack, 1997

32. Increased melatonin release due to decreased light exposure would reduce fertility in female mammals if it

   A. caused an increase in the secretion of LH

   B. caused an increase in the secretion of FSH

   C. stimulated the release of hormones from the pituitary

   D. prevented the release of gonadotropin-releasing hormones from the hypothalamus

   Source: June 2000

Use the following information to answer the next question.

Researchers have been studying the connection between maternal care and stress in rats. Those rats that received more licking and grooming as babies release lower levels of ACTH in response to stress as adults. In humans, high levels of stress hormones are linked to an increase in heart disease, diabetes, depression, and alcoholism.

– from Strauss, 1997

33. Which of the following rows gives the manipulated variable, responding variable, and a possible fixed (controlled) variable for this study?

Row	Manipulated Variable	Responding Variable	Fixed Variable
A	amount of licking by mother rats	amount of ACTH released in adult rats	rats' cage size
B	amount of ACTH released in adult rats	amount of licking by mother rats	age of mother
C	amount of stress in environment	amount of ACTH released in adult rats	amount of licking by mother rats
D	amount of licking by mother rats	heart disease in adult rats	amount of ACTH released in adult rats

Source: June 2000

34. Damage to which of the following endocrine glands would **most affect** the reaction of the body to an emergency that stimulates the sympathetic nervous system?

   A. Thyroid gland

   B. Adrenal gland

   C. Anterior pituitary gland

   D. Posterior pituitary gland

   Source: January 2000

UNIT TEST 1 – NERVOUS AND ENDOCRINE SYSTEMS

Use the following information to answer the next question.

In an experiment, four stimuli of increasing strengths were applied to the membrane of an axon. The graph below illustrates the change measured in the membrane potential of the neuron for each stimulus.

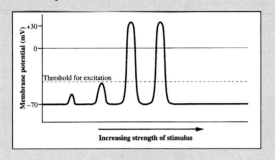

1. Which of the following statements gives an accurate interpretation of the results of this experiment?

   A. Most stimuli produce a nerve impulse.

   B. A nerve impulse has a variety of strengths.

   C. A stimulus must reach a threshold level to initiate a nerve impulse.

   D. The greater the stimulus, the greater the strength of the nerve impulse produced.

Use the following information to answer the next question.

Nerve Impulse Transmission

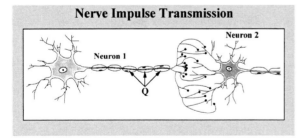

2. If the structures labelled **Q** were absent, what effect on neural transmission would be expected?

   A. The axon would not release acetylcholine.

   B. The axon would be not become depolarized.

   C. The speed of transmission would be reduced.

   D. Cholinesterase would not be secreted to deactivate acetylcholine.

Use the following information to answer the next question.

The disease myasthenia gravis causes a person to experience muscular weakness because of the failure of neuromuscular junctions to transmit signals from nerve fibres to muscle fibres. The weakness is due to a reduced sensitivity to acetylcholine, which is necessary to stimulate the muscle fibre. People suffering from this disease are often treated with neostigmine, an anticholinesterase drug, which can result in some normal muscular activity within minutes.

—from *Guyton and Hall*, 1996

3. Neostigmine is effective in treating this disease because it

   A. binds with cholinesterase to form acetylcholine

   B. binds with cholinesterase to increase acetycholine production

   C. reduces the amount of active cholinesterase, thereby increasing the amount of acetylcholine available to stimulate muscle contraction

   D. increases the amount of active cholinesterase, thereby increasing the amount of acetylcholine available to stimulate muscle contraction

Use the following information to answer the next question

Observations About a Synapse and Synaptic Transmission

1. Only axon terminals release neurotransmitters.

2. A neurotransmitter diffuses from an axon terminal across the synapse to the dendrites or cell body.

3. Many transmissions across a synapse in a short time may cause fatigue of synaptic transmission.

4. Electron micrographs of a synapse show that there is no direct connection between the axon terminal of a presynaptic neuron and the dendrites or cell body of a postsynaptic neuron.

4. The assumption that axon terminals contain a limited amount of neurotransmitter could account for observation

   A. 1   B. 2

   C. 3   D. 4

Use the following information to answer the next two questions.

"It begins in your gut and quickly spreads to your heart and head. Your confidence is swept away with dark foreboding as your heart races and your stomach becomes nauseous."

This description was given by a person experiencing a "panic attack" induced by the injection of cholecystokinin (CCK). CCK is a molecule with different functions in different parts of the body. In the brain, it acts as a neurotransmitter that normally regulates memory and recall. It also arouses the emotional and motivational regions of the brain. A gene that encodes CCK has been located.

—from *Hall*, 1996

5. *Persons affected by panic attacks appear to be "sensitive" to CCK.* This hypothesis would be supported if such persons were found to have

   A. low levels of CCK

   B. impaired production of CCK

   C. CCK inhibitors at these synapses

   D. excess postsynaptic receptors for CCK

6. Injections of CCK produce responses **similar** to those produced by the stimulation of

   A. interneurons

   B. sensory neurons

   C. sympathetic motor neurons

   D. parasympathetic motor neurons

Use the following information to answer the next two questions

Two symptoms of Parkinson's disease are lack of muscular coordination and tremors, both caused by inadequate amounts of dopamine. Symptoms of Alzheimer's disease include the deterioration of memory and mental abilities, possibly caused by a decrease in acetylcholine production.

Dopamine and acetylcholine are excitatory neurotransmitters in various parts of the brain.

7. For the neurotransmitters dopamine and acetylcholine, the releasing sites and the receptor sites are, respectively,

   A. cell bodies and dendrites

   B. dendrites and Schwann cells

   C. axon terminals and dendrites

   D. axon terminals and Schwann cells

CHALLENGER QUESTION	44.8

8. What role do both dopamine and acetylcholine have when they function as excitatory neurotransmitters?

   A. They make the presynaptic membrane more permeable to K^+ ions.

   B. They make the presynaptic membrane more permeable to Na^+ ions.

   C. They make the postsynaptic membrane more permeable to K^+ ions.

   D. They make the postsynaptic membrane more permeable to Na^+ ions.

Use the following additional information to answer the next question.

Damage to neurons in different parts of the brain appears to cause Parkinson's and Alzheimer's diseases. Nerve growth factor (NGF), a chemical produced by peripheral nerves, promotes axon regeneration. Studies show that neurons of the CNS are capable of regeneration when NGF is produced by genetically engineered cells that are transplanted in the CNS.

—from *Greene*, 1993

CHALLENGER QUESTION	53.9

9. Would it be reasonable to use NGF to regenerate neurons in which nuclei had been destroyed?

   A. Yes, because not all cells require a nucleus to function

   B. Yes, because organelles other than the nucleus cause growth

   C. No, because the nucleus controls protein synthesis and homeostasis

   D. No, because without the nucleus to actively transport ions, the cell would die

Use the following information to answer the next question.

For hundreds of years, Chinese folk doctors have known an intriguing but mysterious fact. Drinking herbal tea brewed with a type of club moss (*Huperzia serrata*) can improve a person's memory.

About ten years ago, researchers at the Shanghai Institute of Materia Medica isolated a compound from the tea that is a strong inhibitor of cholinesterase. The compound, called huperzine A, and its effect on acetylcholine are the subjects of intense research. Researchers hope to use huperzine A as an over-the-counter drug and as a potential medication for Alzheimer's disease.

—from *Cheng, Ren, and Tang,* 1996

10. If huperzine A were present in synapses between motor neurons and muscles, it would

    A. prevent the breakdown of acetylcholine

    B. prevent the contraction of skeletal muscles

    C. cause the release of sodium ions from axon terminals

    D. cause the secretion of acetylcholine from axon terminals

Use the following information to answer the next question.

A Simple Reflex Arc

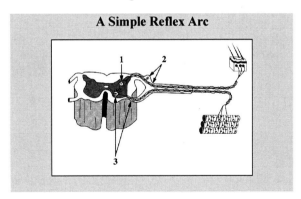

11. Structure 1 is an interneuron. Structures 2 and 3 are, **respectively**, a

    A. sensory neuron and a motor neuron

    B. motor neuron and a sensory neuron

    C. non-myelinated neuron and a myelinated neuron

    D. myelinated neuron and a non-myelinated neuron

12. Which of the following situations illustrates that simple reflexes can be controlled through learned behaviour or conscious effort?

    A. A student cries "ouch" after pulling his hand away from a sharp pin.

    B. A knee jerk occurs when the patellar ligament below the kneecap is tapped.

    C. While clenching a textbook against his chest, a student has an exaggerated knee jerk.

    D. Even though she is burned, a mother does not drop a pot of boiling water when her child is standing at her side.

13. Returning involuntary body functions to normal after a period of stress is the function of which division of the nervous system?

    A. Central

    B. Somatic

    C. Sympathetic

    D. Parasympathetic

Use the following information to answer the next question.

Mercury poisoning causes neurological damage, which leads to a deterioration of short-term memory and an inability to coordinate muscle movements.

14. The areas of the brain affected by mercury poisoning as indicated by the above symptoms are, respectively, the

    A. cerebrum and medulla

    B. cerebellum and cerebrum

    C. cerebrum and cerebellum

    D. hypothalamus and cerebellum

Use the following information to answer the next question.

The Human Eye

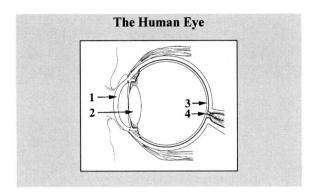

15. An area of the eye where sensory reception of light is most acute and an area where there is no such sensory reception are labelled, respectively,

   A. 1 and 2

   B. 2 and 3

   C. 3 and 4

   D. 4 and 1

Use the following information to answer the next question.

Some people experience motion sickness when they travel in a boat, airplane, or automobile. Symptoms include nausea, vomiting, dizziness, and headache. A drug can be taken to reduce these symptoms.

16. It is most likely that this drug inhibits the transmission of information from the

   A. cochlea to the brain

   B. organ of Corti to the brain

   C. basilar membrane to the brain

   D. semicircular canals to the brain

Use the following information to answer the next question.

Age and Eye Accommodation	
Age in Years	Near Point Accommodation* (cm)
10	7.5
20	10.0
30	11.5
40	17.2
50	65.9
60	90.0

* The shortest distance between the eye and an object where focus of the object is achieved.

—from *Schmidt and Thews*, 1983

17. After studying the data, a student stated, "From age 10 to age 60, the eye has an ever-increasing ability to focus on nearby objects."
This statement represents

   A. a restatement of the data

   B. a theory supported by the data

   C. an interpretation supported by the data

   D. an interpretation contradicted by the data

Use the following information to answer the next question.

The graph below illustrates the effects of different temperatures on the responses of four different nerve fibres in the skin.

Receptors:
W – a pain receptor stimulated by cold
X – a cold receptor
Y – a heat receptor
Z – a pain receptor stimulated by heat

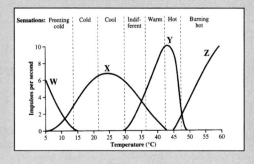

–from *Guyton and Hall*, 1996

18. Which of the following statements presents a valid interpretation of the information on the graph?

   A. A temperature of 5°C is less painful than a temperature of 50°C.

   B. A sensation of coolness is interpreted only when two types of receptors are stimulated.

   C. The threshold level of stimulation is higher for temperature receptors than it is for pain receptors.

   D. Temperature sensations are determined by the number of impulses per second and the specific type of receptors.

19. During an emergency situation, the adrenal gland is stimulated to release a hormone that **directly** causes an increase in

   A. insulin levels

   B. blood glucose levels

   C. parasympathetic stimulation

   D. conversion of glucose to glycogen

Use the following information to answer the next question.

The following procedures and observations were used to determine the function of secretions from an animal organ suspected of being an endocrine gland.

- The suspected endocrine gland was surgically removed from the animal.
- Symptoms in the animal were observed.
- A chemical mixture was extracted from the suspected endocrine gland.
- The chemical mixture was injected into the animal.
- Symptoms in the animal were no longer observed.
- Normal female rats injected with the chemical mixture showed accelerated body growth and increased estrogen production.

20. Based on these observations, the organ was

   A. an ovary

   B. the pancreas

   C. an adrenal gland

   D. the pituitary gland

Use the following information to answer the next question.

A tumor of the adrenal medulla is called Phenochromocytoma. This tumor causes hypersecretion of epinephrine and norepinephrine, and a number of other symptoms.

21. Possible symptoms of phenochromocytoma include

   A. increased heart rate, increased blood sugar, increased metabolic rate

   B. decreased heart rate, increased blood sugar, increased metabolic rate

   C. increased heart rate, decreased blood sugar, decreased metabolic rate

   D. decreased heart rate, decreased blood sugar, decreased metabolic rate

CHALLENGER QUESTION   30.2

22. A hormone that regulates glucose levels in the blood and a hormone that regulates Na^+ in the blood and, indirectly, water reabsorption by the kidneys are, respectively,

   A. aldosterone and insulin

   B. glucagon and aldosterone

   C. epinephrine and glucagon

   D. insulin and antidiuretic hormone

23. A condition that results in an enlargement of the thyroid gland may be caused by a diet deficient in

   A. iron

   B. iodine

   C. sodium

   D. potassium

Use the following information to answer the next question.

Mercury poisoning causes neurological damage, which leads to a deterioration of short-term memory and an inability to coordinate muscle movements. Mercury poisoning also affects the pituitary gland in such a way that frequent urination results.

24. Mercury compounds **most likely** affect the level of the hormone

    A. LH

    B. FSH

    C. ADH

    D. ACTH

Use the following information to answer the next question.

During stressful experiences, interactions between the nervous and endocrine systems prepare the body to defend itself or to handle injury.

25. Which hormone is released as a direct result of sympathetic motor neuron stimulation?

    A. HGH

    B. Thyroxine

    C. Aldosterone

    D. Epinephrine

Use the following additional information to answer the next two questions.

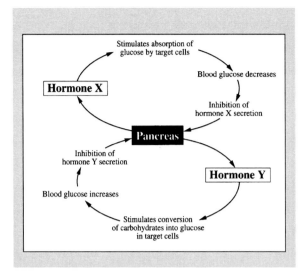

26. The names of hormones **X** and **Y** are, respectively,

    A. insulin and glucagon

    B. glucagon and insulin

    C. glycogen and insulin

    D. insulin and glycogen

27. If blood glucose levels change, the pancreas will

    A. stop hormone secretions because the target cells are not working

    B. produce a more active form of the hormone that stimulates the target cells.

    C. cause other endocrine glands to secrete hormones that stimulate the target cells

    D. increase the secretion of the appropriate hormone that stimulates the target cells

REPRODUCTIVE SYSTEMS, HORMONES, DIFFERENTIATION, AND DEVELOPMENT

Table of Correlations		
General Outcome	**Specific Outcome**	**Related Questions**
	Students are expected to:	
demonstrate an understanding that human organisms have evolved a specialized series of ducts and tubes to facilitate the union of an egg and sperm. They will demonstrate this understanding by:	2.1.1.1 describing hormonal and chromosomal factors and explaining the physiological events resulting in the formation of the primary (gonads) and secondary (associated structures) reproductive organs in the female and male fetus	1, 2, 3, 5, 6, 8, 10
	2.1.1.2 identifying the structures and describing their functions in female (e.g., ovaries, fallopian tubes, uterus, cervix, vagina) and male (e.g., testes, epididymis, vas deferens, seminal vesicles, prostate gland, penis) reproductive systems	
	2.1.1.3 explaining how sexually transmitted diseases can interfere with the passage of eggs and sperm; e.g., chlamydia, gonorrhea	4
demonstrate an understanding that the development of sexual anatomy and sexual functioning is influenced by hormones. They will demonstrate this understanding by:	2.2.1.1 describing the role of hormones in the regulation of primary and secondary sex characteristics in females and males	7, 11
	2.2.1.2 identifying the principal reproductive hormones in the female and explaining their interactions in the maintenance and functioning of the female reproductive system; e.g., estrogen, progesterone, LH, FSH, prolactin, oxytocin	9, 12, 13, 14, 15, 16, 17
	2.2.1.3 identifying the principal reproductive hormones in the male and explaining their interactions in the maintenance and functioning of the male reproductive system; e.g., testosterone, luteinizing hormone (LH), follicle stimulating hormone (FSH)	NR1
demonstrate an understanding that events following conception are governed by a combination of genetic, endocrine, and environmental influences, by extending from Biology 20, Unit 4, the human organism as a system, and by:	2.3.1.1 tracing the processes of fertilization, implantation, extraembryonic membrane formation (e.g., amnion, chorion, yolk sac, placenta), embryo development, parturition and lactation, and the control mechanisms of those events; e.g., progesterone, LH, chorionic gonadotropin, oxytocin, prolactin	18, 19, 20, 21, 22, 23, NR2, 24, 25, 26
	2.3.1.2 describing fetal development from implantation to full term in the context of the main physiological events that occur in the development of organ systems during each major stage (trimester) and the influence of environmental factors on the development of these systems; e.g. alcohol, drugs, pathogens	27, 28, NR3, NR4, NR5, 29
	2.3.1.3 describing the physiological or mechanical basis of different reproductive technology methods; e.g., conception control, in vitro fertilization, infertility reversal	30, 31, 32

REPRODUCTIVE SYSTEMS, HORMONES, DIFFERENTIATION, AND DEVELOPMENT

2.1.1.1 *describing hormonal and chromosomal factors and explaining the physiological events resulting in the formation of the primary (gonads) and secondary (associated structures) reproductive organs in the female and male fetus*

2.1.1.2 *identifying the structures and describing their functions in female (e.g., ovaries, fallopian tubes, uterus, cervix, vagina) and male (e.g., testes, epididymis, vas deferens, seminal vesicles, prostate gland, penis) reproductive systems*

2.1.1.3 *explaining how sexually transmitted diseases can interfere with the passage of eggs and sperms; e.g., chlamydia, gonorrhea*

In males, sperm are produced in the seminiferous tubules of the testes. In the spaces between the seminiferous tubules, there are the interstitial cells that respond to LH from the anterior pituitary and produce testosterone. Within the seminiferous tubules are the Sertoli cells that respond to FSH from the anterior pituitary. They stimulate meiosis in spermatocytes in order to form sperm. The sperm mature in the epididymis and are stored in the vas deferens. Upon ejaculation, the sperm are moved through the vas deferens past the three sets of glands (the seminal vesicles, the prostate gland and the Cowper's glands) that add fluid to the semen. Of primary interest are the fructose (sugar) that the sperm can use for nourishment and the buffer that neutralizes the acidity of the woman's vagina. (The acidity helps to resist infections.) As well, the prostate gland secretes a prostaglandin that stimulates the woman's uterine muscles to contract, thus drawing up the semen. The semen is ejaculated out of the urethra of the penis. In a male fetus, testosterone causes the penis to form and causes the testes to develop and descend into the scrotum. At the onset of puberty, testosterone causes the development of primary and secondary male sexual characteristics.

Related Questions: 1, 2, 3, 4, 5, 6, 8, 10

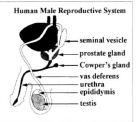

Human Male Reproductive System
- seminal vesicle
- prostate gland
- Cowper's gland
- vas deferens
- urethra
- epididymis
- testis

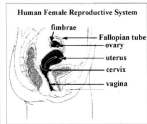

Human Female Reproductive System
- fimbrae
- Fallopian tube
- ovary
- uterus
- cervix
- vagina

2.2.1.1 *describing the role of hormones in the regulation of primary and secondary sex characteristics in females and males*

2.2.1.2 *identifying the principal reproductive hormones in the female and explaining their interactions in the maintenance and functioning of the female reproductive system; e.g., estrogen, progesterone, LH, FSH, prolactin, oxytocin*

2.2.1.3 *identifying the principal reproductive hormones in the male and explaining their interaction in the maintenance and functioning of the male reproductive system; e.g., testosterone, luteinizing hormone (LH), follicle stimulating hormone(FSH)*

In females, eggs are produced in the ovaries. FSH stimulates follicular cells that, in turn, stimulate meiosis in oocytes. The follicular cells also produce estrogen, which is secreted into the blood and stimulates thickening of the endometrium (the inner layer of the uterus.) Within 10 days, the oocyte and its supportive follicular cells are a fluid-filled sphere called a mature follicle. At about that time, an increase in the secretion of LH from the anterior pituitary causes ovulation to occur a few days later. The egg and some of the follicular cells burst out of the ovary and fimbriae sweep to draw the egg into the Fallopian tube.

The follicular cells that didn't leave with the egg reform into the corpus luteum, which begins the secretion of progesterone. The progesterone causes the endometrium to become vascularized (full of blood vessels) and secretory (full of glands). If no fertilization occurs, the high level of estrogen in the blood has a negative feedback effect on the hypothalamus, so that FSH production drops. The high level of progesterone has a negative feedback effect on the hypothalamus, so that LH production drops. As a result, the corpus luteum degenerates to the non-functional corpus albicans. The egg has also died by now, so production of estrogen and progesterone have dropped off. Without estrogen and progesterone to support it, the endometrium falls away (menstruation) starting at the end of the cycle (about day 28).

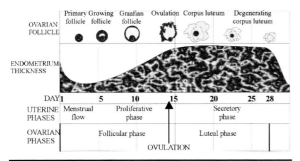

Related Questions: 7, 9, 11, 12, 13, 14, 15, 16, 17, NR1

2.3.1.1 tracing the processes of fertilization, implantation, extraembryonic membrane formation (e.g., amnion, chorion, yolk sac, placenta) embryo development, partition and lactation, and the control mechanisms of those events; e.g., progesterone, LH, chorionic gomadotropin, oxytocin, prolactin

2.3.1.2 describing fetal development from implantation to full term in the context of the main physiological events that occur in the development of organ systems during each major stage (trimester) and the influence of environmental factors on the development of these systems; e.g., alcohol, drugs, pathogens

If fertilization does occur in the Fallopian tube, the zygote quickly begins mitosis to increase the number of cells. Within a few days, it has become a hollow sphere of cells called a blastocyst, and has arrived at the uterus. The outer layer of the blastocyst is called the chorion. Cells of the chorion produce human chorionic gonadotropin (HCG). HCG is a hormone that maintains the corpus luteum so that there continues to be a supply of progesterone to support the endometrium. Meanwhile, the blastocyst implants into the endometrium and continues rapid development. Within a month, the embryo is a tube composed of three layers of tissues. The outer layer, the ectoderm, will become the skin and nervous system. The middle layer, the mesoderm, becomes the muscles, bones, kidneys, and sex organs. The inner layer, the endoderm, becomes the lining of the digestive system, including the liver and pancreas. By two months, the embryo floats in a fluid-filled sac surrounded by two membranes. The outer membrane, the chorion, forms the placenta. The inner membrane is the amnion. The fluid around the embryo is called amniotic fluid. The chorion forms folds, called villi, that increase surface area for more efficient exchange of materials between mother and fetus. Nutrients, oxygen, wastes, hormones, and drugs cross the placenta. Cells including disease-causing bacteria, cannot cross the placenta. Some viruses, however, are small enough to cross the placenta. Some of mother's antibodies can also cross the placenta.

The placenta also produces estrogen and progesterone to maintain the endometrium, so there is no longer a need for the corpus luteum. The production of HCG drops off, and the corpus luteum degenerates. Close to birth the level of progesterone drops quickly as the level of relaxin and the level of oxytocin increase. Relaxin causes the woman's ligaments to loosen. Oxytocin stimulates muscles of the uterus to contract at birth.

During birth (parturition), the cervix dilates, muscles of the uterus contract to expel the baby, and the uterus contracts further to pinch the placenta from the endometrium. Following birth, prolactin from the anterior pituitary stimulates the synthesis of milk. Oxytocin from the posterior pituitary stimulates the release of milk when the baby suckles.

Related Questions: 18, 19, 20, 21, 22, 23, NR2, 24, 25, 26, 27, 28, NR3, NR4, NR5, 29

2.3.1.3 describing the physiological or mechanical basis of different reproductive technology methods; e.g., conception control, in vitro fertilization, infertility reversal

Ultrasound, amniocentesis, and chorionic villus sampling (CVS) are all technologies that provide information about a fetus. Ultrasound involves bouncing sound waves off the fetus to produce a rough image of the fetus. Amniocentesis involves using a hypodermic needle to draw a sample of amniotic fluid. The fluid will have chemicals and cells that have come from the fetus. The cells can be used for DNA analysis or to construct a karyotype. CVS provides the same information as amniocentesis by removing a sample of chorionic cells. It has the advantage of being able to be done earlier and seems less dangerous for the fetus. There are several means of birth control. A condom or a diaphragm serve as a barrier for the sperm. Birth control pills, a combination of estrogen and progesterone, have a negative feedback effect on the hypothalamus so that ovulation does not occur. The pill RU 486 prevents a blastocyst from implanting in the uterus.

A vasectomy (male) or tubal ligation (female) involves closing off the vas deferens or Fallopian tubes to block sperm or eggs. In vitro fertilization means that fertilization takes place in a petri dish. A resulting embryo can be implanted into a woman's uterus.

Related Questions: 30, 31, 32

Use the following information to answer the next two questions.

The spermicide nonoxynol-9, which is applied to contraceptive devices such as diaphragms and condoms, has been linked to increased urinary tract infections in women. Although nonoxynol-9 is helpful in fighting the herpes virus and HIV, it also destroys beneficial bacteria (lactobacilli) that moderate the acidity of a woman's vagina. As a woman's vagina and external genitalia become more acidic, another bacterium, *Escherichia coli* (*E. coli*), increases in number and invades her urethra. This overpopulation of *E. coli* causes a bladder infection.

– from *Vergano*, 1996

1. Which of the following rows gives the site of sperm production and the gland that produces an alkaline secretion that neutralizes the acidity of the vagina?

Row	Site of Sperm Production	Gland that Produces an Alkaline Secretion
A.	seminiferous tubules	testis
B.	seminiferous tubules	prostate gland
C.	seminal vesicles	testis
D.	seminal vesicles	prostate gland

Source: January 2000

2. Testes are responsible for the production of sperm and testosterone. Cutting and tying the vas deferens (vasectomy) blocks the passage of sperm. After a vasectomy, the hormone testosterone

A. reaches all the body tissues because it comes from exocrine tissue

B. reaches all the body tissues because it comes from endocrine tissue

C. does not reach all the body tissues because it comes from exocrine tissue

D. does not reach all the body tissues because it comes from endocrine tissue

Source: January 2000

3. Cryptorchidism is the failure of one or both of the testes to descend from the abdominal cavity into the scrotum during human fetal development. Sterility results if both testes fail to descend. In this case, the likely cause of sterility is that

A. lack of oxygen inhibits testosterone function

B. gonadotropic hormones cannot stimulate the testes

C. the testes are not connected to the external environment

D. normal sperm do not readily develop at body temperature

Source: January 2000

Use the following information to answer the next question.

Yaws, bejel, and syphilis are three diseases known to be caused by strains of bacteria in the genus *Treponema*. Syphilis is a sexually transmitted disease, whereas yaws and bejel are not sexually transmitted. Studies of 800-year-old to 6 000-year-old skeletons from Florida, Equador, and New Mexico show that these people suffered from syphilis. Studies on 6 000-year-old skeletons from Illinois, Virginia, and Ohio show that these people suffered from yaws.

– from *Zabludoff*, 1996

4. Which of the following conclusions can be made about these related diseases?

A. A person can easily contract syphilis in warm climates.

B. The syphilis strain of *Treponema* may have mutated from the yaws strain.

C. Non-sexually transmitted diseases have developed from sexually transmitted diseases.

D. Older people tend to suffer from yaws, and younger victims develop syphilis when exposed to *Treponema*.

Source: January 2000

Use the following information to answer the next question.

A series of experiments initially designed to study the effects of fathers' drinking habits on fetal development produced some unexpected results. Seventy-five male rats were injected with enough alcohol to produce a 0.2% concentration of alcohol in their blood. After 24 hours, these male rats were mated with 75 female rats not treated with alcohol. A control group of 75 untreated male rats were also mated with untreated female rats. Both sets of males copulated normally and with the same vigour. The pregnancy rate of female rats mated with the alcohol-treated male rats was 50% lower than the pregnancy rate of female rats mated with untreated rats.

Also, pup litters in the group with alcohol-treated males appeared to be smaller and individual pups weighed less. Repetition of these experiments produced similar results.

– from *Fackelmann*, 1994

5. Fluids in rat semen bathe the egg and sperm for several days after fertilization. This fluid contains secretions from the

   A. prostate gland only

   B. seminal vesicles only

   C. urethra and seminal vesicles

   D. Cowper's glands, prostate gland, and seminal vesicles

   Source: June 2000

Use the following information to answer the next two questions.

A rare defect inherited by 19 descendants of a Dominican man named Altagracia Carrasco caused genetically male children to be considered female until age 12. At this age, hormone levels increased dramatically and caused the testes to descend from the abdomen to the scrotum and male primary and secondary sexual characteristics to develop.

In their Dominican Republic village, these people were given the name "guevedoces," which means "penis at 12 years of age."

– from *Pringle*, 1992

6. The "guevedoces" might have reduced fertility because the late descent of their testes would cause

   A. high production of testosterone

   B. high production of progesterone

   C. cell development problems in their follicular cells

   D. cell development problems in their seminiferous tubules

   Source: June 2000

7. The sex hormone that increased in these individuals at age 12 and a secondary sexual characteristic the individuals would develop as a result are, respectively,

   A. FSH and decreased body fat

   B. testosterone and decreased breast size

   C. testosterone and increased larynx size

   D. FSH and increased muscle development

   Source: June 2000

Use the following information to answer the next question.

A male is having fertility problems. His sperm are not making their way to the oocyte in time to fertilize it. Analysis of his seminal fluid determines two insufficiencies.

8. The two insufficiencies in semen that would affect sperms' ability to travel to the oocyte are the lack of

   A. FSH and testosterone

   B. fructose and testosterone

   C. FSH and alkaline buffers

   D. fructose and alkaline buffers

   Source: January 2001

Use the following information to answer the next question.

The spermicide nonoxynol-9, which is applied to contraceptive devices such as diaphragms and condoms, has been linked to increased urinary tract infections in women. Although nonoxynol-9 is helpful in fighting the herpes virus and HIV, it also destroys beneficial bacteria (lactobacilli) that moderate the acidity of a woman's vagina. As a woman's vagina and external genitalia become more acidic, another bacterium, *Escherichia coli* (*E. coli*), increases in number and invades her urethra. This overpopulation of *E. coli* causes a bladder infection.

– from *Vergano*, 1996

9. Another contraceptive, the birth control pill, causes negative feedback on the pituitary, which prevents the release of eggs. Typically, the hormones in the birth control pill are similar to

   A. FSH and LH

   B. oxytocin and prolactin

   C. estrogen and progesterone

   D. relaxin and gonadotropins

   Source: January 2000

10. For the processes of spermatogenesis and oogenesis, respectively, which of the following rows identifies the hormone that stimulates the process, the location where the process occurs, and the number of gametes produced per germ cell?

Row	Spermatogenesis			Oogenesis		
	Hormone	Location of process	Number of gametes produced	Hormone	Location of process	Number of gametes produced
A.	FSH	semi-niferous tubules	4	FSH	ovaries	1
B.	LH	epidi-dymis	8	LH	pituitary	1
C.	testos-terone	interstitial cells	4	estrogen	follicle	4
D.	FSH	testes	8	proges-terone	corpus luteum	4

Source: January 2001

Use the following information to answer the next two questions.

A diagram of the feedback mechanism for lactation (milk production) follows.

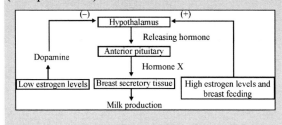

CHALLENGER QUESTION   53.8

11. The reason that males do not lactate even though they have breast tissue is that

   A. estrogen levels in males are too low to overcome the inhibiting action of dopamine

   B. males do not need to produce milk, thus the breast tissue in males is not designed to produce milk

   C. males have a Y chromosome, which has a gene that prevents the breast secretory tissue from producing milk

   D. males have high levels of testosterone, which inhibits the pituitary from releasing the hormone that stimulates lactation

   Source: June 2000

12. Hormone X, which initiates and maintains milk production in females, is

   A. estrogen

   B. oxytocin

   C. prolactin

   D. progesterone

   Source: June 2000

Use the following information to answer the next three questions.

In order to initiate *in vitro* fertilization, a woman must undergo hormonal therapy to release numerous mature eggs and to prepare the uterine lining. The eggs are removed using a laparoscope and fertilized in a petri dish. The developing embryos are inserted back into the woman for implantation to take place.

13. What hormone changes would cause a female to develop and release a large number of mature eggs?

A. Increased FSH and LH

B. Decreased FSH and LH

C. Increased estrogen and progesterone

D. Decreased estrogen and progesterone

Source: June 2000

Use the following information to answer the next question.

Female Reproductive Systems

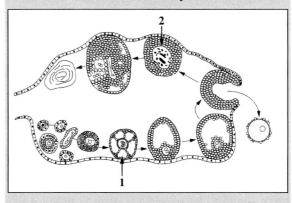

Prior to *in vitro fertilization* (IVF), oocytes must be obtained from a donor female.

14. To obtain oocytes for *in vitro* fertilization, the structure numbered above that must be hormonally stimulated is

A. 1

B. 2

C. 3

D. 4

Source: June 2000

Use the following additional information to answer the next question.

Changes That Occur in a Human Ovary Over One Ovarian Cycle

15. In order for artificial implantation to be successful, what hormone would a female need to take to maintain the uterine lining for implantation, and which of the structures of the ovary numbered above would naturally produce this hormone?

A. Estrogen and structure 1

B. Estrogen and structure 2

C. Progesterone and structure 1

D. Progesterone and structure 2

Source: June 2000

Use the following information to answer the next two questions.

Clomiphene citrate is a fertility drug used to induce ovulation in women. Clomiphene citrate, generally taken daily from day 3 to day 7 of the menstrual cycle, decreases the naturally circulating estrogen. The pituitary responds by increasing production of two gonadotropic hormones that then stimulate the ovary to ripen and release an egg.
Follicle development and ovulation are usually monitored with a combination of home urine tests (on day 11 or 12) and a follow-up ultrasound examination. About 70% of women using clomiphene citrate will ovulate and 40% of those will become pregnant. The risk of multiple pregnancy (usually twins) increases by 6% to 7%.

– from *Bay Area Fertility and Gynecology Medical Group*

16. Without the negative feedback that results from increasing amounts of naturally circulating estrogen, the body responds by secreting more

   A. FSH

   B. HCG

   C. prolactin

   D. progesterone

   Source: January 2001

CHALLENGER QUESTION   **46.9**

17. Following clomiphene citrate treatments, patients are advised to monitor their urine for the presence of a hormone that will signal ovulation. This hormone is

   A. LH

   B. FSH

   C. HCG

   D. estrogen

   Source: January 2001

Use the following information to answer the next question.

Some Endocrine Glands and Hormones
1. pituitary
2. estrogen
3. testosterone
4. hypothalamus
5. FSH
6. seminal vesicle
7. LH
8. testis

Numerical Response

1. To complete this statement, select the gland or hormone numbered above that best fills each blank. The production of sperm in the male is directly stimulated by the hormone_____, which is produced in the_____ , and by the hormone_____ , which is produced in the _____

   Source: June 2000

Use the following information to answer the next question.

The spermicide nonoxynol-9, which is applied to contraceptive devices such as diaphragms and condoms, has been linked to increased urinary tract infections in women. Although nonoxynol-9 is helpful in fighting the herpes virus and HIV, it also destroys beneficial bacteria (lactobacilli) that moderate the acidity of a woman's vagina. As a woman's vagina and external genitalia become more acidic, another bacterium, *Escherichia coli* (*E. coli*), increases in number and invades her urethra. This overpopulation of *E. coli* causes a bladder infection.

–from *Vergano*, 1996

Female Reproductive Structures

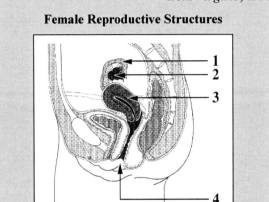

18. Some contraceptives, such as condoms, prevent fertilization. Fertilization usually occurs in the structure labelled

   A. 1

   B. 2

   C. 3

   D. 4

   Source: January 2000

Use the following information to answer the next four questions.

Research on sheep might explain what stimulates pregnant mammals, including humans, to give birth. Through research on pregnant sheep, scientists have developed the following scheme to explain normal events as birth begins.

Influence of Fetal Hormones on the Maternal Reproductive Systems

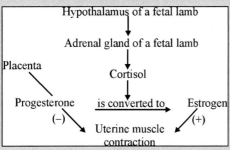

Note: The placenta produces progesterone throughout the pregnancy, but activation of the fetal hypothalamus only occurs as birth begins.

– from *Discover*, 1992

19. According to this diagram, the birth of a lamb is linked to

    A. increasing levels of estrogen in pregnant sheep

    B. decreasing production of cortisol by the fetal lamb

    C. increasing levels of progesterone in pregnant sheep

    D. decreasing activity of the hypothalamus by the fetal lamb

    Source: January 2000

20. To maintain a pregnancy for a normal gestation period, the contraction of uterine muscles is inhibited. According to the diagram, this inhibition is brought about by

    A. high levels of estrogen from the placenta

    B. low levels of progesterone from the uterus

    C. high levels of cortisol from the adrenal gland

    D. high levels of progesterone from the placenta

    Source: January 2000

CHALLENGER QUESTION   **45.8**

21. Which of the following statements concerning human reproduction is supported by the findings of this research?

    A. Developments within the fetus determine when birth will begin.

    B. The production of fetal cortisol delays birth until gestation is complete.

    C. During early fetal development, fetal hormones do not pass into the mother.

    D. High levels of progesterone in the mother's blood are essential for birth to begin.

    Source: January 2000

Use the following additional information to answer the next question.

Ingestion of a plant called skunk cabbage by pregnant sheep has been found to cause severe birth defects and to delay birth for several weeks.

22. A reasonable hypothesis is that skunk cabbage contains a chemical that

    A. increases uterine sensitivity to estrogen

    B. decreases placental production of progesterone

    C. inhibits the fetal hypothalamus or adrenal gland

    D. increases conversion of progesterone to estrogen

    Source: January 2000

Use the following diagram to answer the next question.

Chromosome Content of Human Cells During a Series of Events

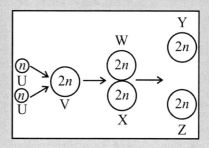

23. In humans, what process occurs between **U** and **V**?

A. Mitosis

B. Meiosis

C. Fertilization

D. Differentiation

Source: January 2000

Use the following information to answer the next question.

In order to initiate in *vitro* fertilization, a woman must undergo hormonal therapy to release numerous mature eggs and to prepare the uterine lining. The eggs are removed using a laparoscope and fertilized in a petri dish. The developing embryos are inserted back into the woman for implantation to take place.

In vitro Fertilization

Covered petri dish

1 2 3 4 5

Numerical Response

2. Match the parts of the diagram numbered above that represents the terms given below.
Number: ___ ___ ___ ___
Term: Oocyte   Blastocyst   First mitotic division   Fertilization

Source: June 2000

Use the following information to answer the next question.

The picture below shows how sperm is injected into an egg. This technology may be used to overcome infertility problems caused by sperm that are unable to penetrate an egg, or by sperm that lack a proper flagellum (tail).

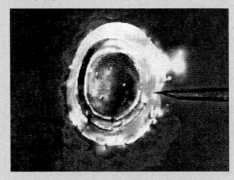

24. Sperm are normally able to penetrate an egg by

A. fusing their nuclei with the nucleus of the egg

B. releasing hydrolytic enzymes from the acrosome found in the head of the sperm

C. dissolving the covering of the egg with alkaline secretions from the prostate gland

D. dissolving the covering of the egg using the hydrolytic enzymes secreted from Cowper's gland

Source: January 2001

CHALLENGER QUESTION	59.5

25. During the first three days of development, the human embryo obtains nutrients and energy from the

A. HCG

B. amniotic fluid

C. cytoplasm of the mother's egg

D. mitochondria of the father's sperm

Source: January 2001

CHALLENGER QUESTION   34.7

26. The presence of a particular hormone in urine indicates that pregnancy has occurred. This hormone is secreted by the

A. ovary

B. amnion

C. chorion

D. pituitary

Source: January 2001

Use the following information to answer the next two questions.

A series of experiments initially designed to study the effects of fathers' drinking habits on fetal development produced some unexpected results. Seventy-five male rats were injected with enough alcohol to produce a 0.2% concentration of alcohol in their blood. After 24 hours, these male rats were mated with 75 female rats not treated with alcohol. A control group of 75 untreated male rats were also mated with untreated female rats. Both sets of males copulated normally and with the same vigour.

The pregnancy rate of female rats mated with the alcohol-treated male rats was 50% lower than the pregnancy rate of female rats mated with untreated rats. Also, pup litters in the group with alcohol-treated males appeared to be smaller and individual pups weighed less. Repetition of these experiments produced similar results.

– from *Fackelmann*, 1994

27. Reduction in pregnancy rates for rodent couples in the study group could have been caused by

A. alcohol-treated males' inability to copulate normally

B. alcohol in the females' blood affecting egg production

C. alcohol in the males' blood increasing pituitary hormone secretions

D. alcohol in the semen fluids producing a poisonous environment for fertilization

Source: June 2000

28. Prolonged high concentrations of alcohol in the male would likely affect male fertility in all of the following ways **except** by

A. reducing the rate of meiosis

B. preventing the maturation of sperm

C. depressing motility in sperm by damaging cells

D. stimulating motility in sperm by increasing metabolism

Source: June 2000

Use the following information to answer the next question.

Stages in Development

1 Fetus has a beating heart
2 Embryo differentiates into three layers (gastrulation)
3 Blastocyst implants in endometrium
4 Cleavage (mitosis) leads to a large number of cells without growth

CHALLENGER QUESTION   43.1

Numerical Response

3. Match each of the developmental stages numbered above with the time period in which it occurs, as given below.

Stage: _____   _____   _____   _____

Time   week 1 week 2 week 3 week 4
Period:

Source: June 2000

Use the following information to answer the next question.

Human Embryo Six Weeks After Fertilization

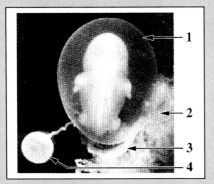

Descriptions of Embryonic Structures' Functions

A Transports embryonic blood

B Provides protection

C Is the site of exchange between embryonic and maternal blood

D Is used for nourishment in vertebrates other than mammals

– from Nilsson, 1990

CHALLENGER QUESTION   **41.7**

Numerical Response

4. Match each embryonic structure, as numbered above, with the letter that represents its function, as listed above.

Structure: _____   _____   _____   _____

Function: **A**   **B**   **C**   **D**

Source: January 2001

Use the following information to answer the next question.

Some Events in Labour

1. Uterine contractions increase in force.
2. Oxytocin travels through the bloodstream.
3. Nervous impulses are sent to the hypothalamus.
4. Oxytocin is released from the posterior pituitary.

Numerical Response

5. At the onset of labour, a baby's head pushes on the cervix. Following this, the events given above, listed in the order in which they occur, are _____, _____, _____, and _____.

Source: January 2001

Use the following information to answer the next question.

Premature infants born at 24-weeks gestation face a wide spectrum of physiological problems.

29. These problems arise because prior to the third trimester of pregnancy, fetuses

   A. have organs that are underdeveloped

   B. have not yet begun cell specialization

   C. depend upon amniotic fluid for oxygen

   D. depend upon amniotic fluid for nutrients

Source: January 2001

Use the following information to answer the next question.

The 42 000 wild horses and donkeys that live in the American West are reproducing at such a high rate that they could severely damage range lands in the future. In an effort to prevent overpopulation, some mares (females) are rounded up and injected with porcine zona pellucida (PZP), a long-lasting contraceptive. U.S. Food and Drug Administration guidelines prohibit the use of PZP until after a wild mare has had at least one successful pregnancy.

– from McInnis, 1996

30. If the effect of PZP on horses is like the effect of the birth control pill on women, pregnancy is prevented because

   A. ovulation does not occur

   B. implantation does not occur

   C. sperm cannot enter the uterus

   D. sperm cannot enter the oviducts

Source: June 2000

Use the following information to answer the next question.

The following picture shows how sperm is injected into an egg. This technology may be used to overcome infertility problems caused by sperm that are unable to penetrate an egg, or by sperm that lack a proper flagellum (tail).

Intracytoplasmic Sperm Injection (ICSI)

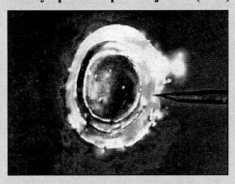

CHALLENGER QUESTION	56.5

31. If, during the ICSI process, more than one sperm head were injected into the egg's cytoplasm,

   A. fraternal twins would be formed

   B. identical twins would be formed

   C. the zygote would develop into a male child since more male chromosomes would be present

   D. the zygote would likely not develop because more than a diploid set of chromosomes would be present

   Source: January 2001

Use the following information to answer the next question.

Clomiphene citrate is a fertility drug used to induce ovulation in women. Clomiphene citrate, generally taken daily from day 3 to day 7 of the menstrual cycle, decreases the naturally circulating estrogen. The pituitary responds by increasing production of two gonadotropic hormones that then stimulate the ovary to ripen and release an egg. Follicle development and ovulation are usually monitored with a combination of home urine tests (on day 11 or 12) and a follow-up ultrasound examination. About 70% of women using clomiphene citrate will ovulate and 40% of those will become pregnant. The risk of multiple pregnancy (usually twins) increases by 6% to 7%.

– from *Bay Area Fertility* and *Gynecology Medical Group*

32. The incidence of multiple births increases in women who use clomiphene citrate because high levels of

   A. progesterone may stimulate the release of more than one egg

   B. FSH may stimulate the fertilized egg cell to divide and separate

   C. FSH may stimulate the complete development of more than one follicle

   D. progesterone may stimulate the fertilized egg cell to divide and separate

   Source: January 2001

UNIT TEST 2 – REPRODUCTIVE SYSTEMS, HORMONES, DIFFERENTIATION, AND DEVELOPMENT

Use the following information to answer the next question.

The Male Reproductive System and Accessory Structures

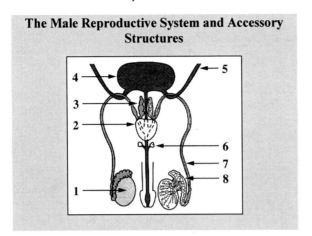

Numerical Response

1. Identify the three structures, as numbered above, that produce the fluid secretions that make up semen. (Record your **three-digit answer in lowest-to-highest numerical order.**)

Answer: _____ _____ _____

1. In humans, the temperature within the scrotum is usually

   A. above body temperature

   B. below body temperature

   C. the same as body temperature

   D. the same as room temperature

Use the following information to answer the next question.

Functions of the Four Main Reproductive Hormones in Human Females

1. Stimulation of egg development
2. Inhibition of ovulation and uterine contractions
3. Stimulation of the development of secondary sex characteristics
4. Stimulation of ovulation and information of the corpus luteum

Numerical Response

2. Identify the major functions, as numbered above, of each of the hormones given below.

Function: _____ _____ _____ _____
Hormone: FSH   LH   Estrogen Progesterone

Use the following diagrams to answer the next question.

Human Male and Female Reproductive Systems.

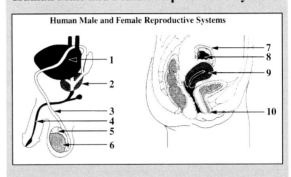

Human Male and Female Reproductive Systems

2. Reproductive structures that have similar functions in males and females are, respectively,

   A. 1 and 9

   B. 2 and 8

   C. 3 and 7

   D. 4 and 10

3. Collectively, the seminal vesicles, prostate gland, and Cowper's glands contribute to which of the following functions?

   A. Produce testosterone

   B. Stimulate spermatogenesis

   C. Help sperm survive in the female body

   D. Signal the pituitary to release gonadotropins

Use the following information to answer the next question.

In male and female embryos, the development of the genital ridge influences gender determination.
The male and female genotypes (sex chromosomes) differ in that they cause the release of different hormones from the genital ridge in males and females during development.

4. Which of the following statements about normal embryonic hormone secretion is correct?

    A. The X chromosome secretes estrogen in a female embryo.

    B. The Y chromosome secretes testosterone in a male embryo.

    C. The genital ridge produces estrogen in a potential female embryo.

    D. The genital ridge produces testosterone in a potential female embryo.

CHALLENGER QUESTION   **55.0**

5. The development of secondary sexual characteristics in the female is due to the secretion of

    A. LH, followed by the secretion of estrogen

    B. LH, followed by the secretion of progesterone

    C. FSH and LH, followed by the secretion of estrogen

    D. FSH and LH, followed by the secretion of progesterone

6. The hormone that stimulates sex-cell production in both males and females is

    A. LH

    B. FSH

    C. testosterone

    D. progesterone

7. Hormones that stimulate the production of testosterone are transported by the

    A. blood

    B. vas deferens

    C. seminiferous tubules

    D. ducts from the gland secreting the hormones

Use the following information to answer the next question.

Compared with premenopausal women, women entering menopause have increased levels of FSH and LH. These women can choose to undergo estrogen and/or progesterone hormone replacement therapy to alleviate the symptoms of menopause.

8. If a menopausal woman takes hormone replacement therapy, the levels of her FSH and LH will

    A. remain the same because her ovaries no longer respond to estrogen

    B. cause the ovary to produce eggs, and the woman will again be fertile

    C. drop because of the negative-feedback effect of progesterone and estrogen

    D. rise as estrogen and progesterone levels stimulate the production of FSH and LH

Use the following information to answer the next question.

Reseachers have developed a birth control vaccine that would be given once a year. This vaccine is made from a fragment of HCG attached to a protein. The vaccine causes a woman to manufacture antibodies that bind to HCG molecules (when present) in the blood. The antibodies prevent HCG from functioning and thereby affect the implantation of a blastocyst (embryo).

9. The vaccine affects the permanent implantation of a blastocyst by indirectly causing

    A. disintegration of the endometrium

    B. increased progesterone production

    C. development of new follicles in the ovary

    D. inhibition of the movement of cilia in the Fallopian tubes

Use the following information to answer the next question.

In vitro fertilization techniques can enable postmenopausal women (those who have gone through menopause) to have babies. Eggs are removed from a female donor and then fertilized in a culture dish. The early embryo is inserted into the uterus of the postmenopausal woman.
The postmenopausal woman requires hormone supplements in order for implantation and development to succeed.

10. During the first trimester of a pregnancy, an extraembryonic membrane secretes HCG. In a pregnancy resulting from *in vitro* fertilization of a postmenopausal woman, HCG would **not** function normally because the

   A. placenta would not be permeable to hormones

   B. woman would not have a corpus luteum

   C. placenta would not produce FSH or LH

   D. woman's pituitary would not respond

11. Which of the steps of human development occurs **after** chorion development?

   A. Fertilization

   B. Implantation

   C. Cleavage (division of the zygote by mitosis)

   D. Organogenesis (the formation of body organs and systems)

12. Which part of the brain regulates male or female reproductive behaviour by directly controlling the release of gonadotropins from the pituitary gland?

   A. Hypothalamus

   B. Pituitary gland

   C. Medulla oblongata

   D. Frontal lobe of the cerebrum

Use the following information to answer the next question.

In rare cases, human males develop functioning mammary glands. Hormone levels are known to affect the development and function of mammary glands in both males and females.

13. In order for human males to produce milk and to eject milk, high levels of which two hormones, respectively, must be present?

   A. Prolactin and relaxin

   B. Relaxin and prolactin

   C. Prolactin and oxytocin

   D. Oxytocin and prolactin

Use the following information to answer the next question.

Some Events in the Human Reproductive Cycle

1. Pre-embryo releases HCG, which maintains hormone levels.
2. A hormone signals the follicle to rupture.
3. Blastocyst is implanted
4. The egg is fertilized to form a zygote.

CHALLENGER QUESTION	54.6

Numerical Response

3. Listed in the sequence in which they occur during the reproductive cycle, the above events are _____, _____, _____, and _____.

14. The onset of labour at the end of pregnancy is caused partly by a decreased level of

   A. LH

   B. FSH

   C. estrogen

   D. progesterone

Use the following information to answer the next two questions.

In vitro fertilization techniques can enable postmenopausal women (those who have gone through menopause) to have babies. Eggs are removed from a female donor and then fertilized in a culture dish. The early embryo is inserted into the uterus of the postmenopausal woman.
The postmenopausal woman requires hormone supplements in order for implantation and development to succeed.

15. After *in vitro* fertilization, hormone supplements are administered until the fourth month of pregnancy. At this time, the hormone supplements may be discontinued because the

   A. placenta produces oxytocin to inhibit uterine contraction

   B. pituitary produces oxytocin to inhibit uterine contraction

   C. placenta produces progesterone and estrogen to maintain the uterine lining

   D. pituitary produces progesterone and estrogen to maintain the uterine lining

16. To increase the chance of successful implantation of an embryo produced by *in vitro* fertilization, the postmenopausal woman must receive

   A. FSH and LH to promote the development of the follicle

   B. FSH and LH to promote the development of the endometrium

   C. estrogen and progesterone to promote the development of the follicle

   D. estrogen and progesterone to promote the development of the endometrium

Use the following information to answer the next question.

Mercury poisoning causes neurological damage, which leads to a deterioration of short-term memory and an inability to coordinate muscle movements.

Certain mercury compounds are able to cross the placenta and thereby affect embryological development.

– from *Hedegard*, 1993

CHALLENGER QUESTION   41.9

17. Exposure to mercury compounds during embryological development would *most likely* disrupt the

   A. production of amniotic fluid

   B. development of the neural tube

   C. production of ovarian hormones

   D. development of the umbilical cord

Use the following information to answer the next question.

Reproductive Events in a Mature Human Female
1. Ovulation occurs
2. Placenta forms
3. Fertilization occurs
4. Implantation takes place

Numerical Response

4. Listed in the sequence in which they occur, the events above are
_____, _____, _____, and _____.

Use the following information to answer the next question.

William Hunter was born without vas deferens. Despite surgery and attempts at artificial insemination and conventional *in vitro* fertilization, William and his wife were unable to conceive.

– from *Shirk*, 1994

18. A new technology that may help William involves sperm extraction followed by sperm injection to produce a fertilized egg. This technology must involve

   A. LH therapy

   B. testosterone therapy

   C. extraction of sperm from the male's urethra

   D. extraction of sperm from the male's epididymis

Use the following information to answer the next question.

The genital tract of both females and males can play host to many disease-causing microbes. The sexually transmitted diseases (STDs) that can result include gonorrhea, syphilis, herpes, AIDS, genital warts, and chlamydia. These diseases, if untreated, can lead to brain and nervous system deterioration, circulatory system damage, cancer, and infertility. Microbes may pass from mother to child during pregnancy and birth.

CHALLENGER QUESTION   38.7

19. STD microbes may be transmitted to a (an)

   A. child in the vagina

   B. zygote in the endometrium

   C. embryo through the ingestion of amniotic fluid

   D. fetus through the entry of blood from the uterine veins

CELL DIVISION, MENDELIAN GENETICS, AND MOLECULAR GENETICS

Table of Correlations		
General Outcome	**Specific Outcome**	**Related Questions**
	Students are expected to:	
demonstrate an understanding that: genetic information in chromosomes is translated into protein structure; that the information may be manipulated; and that the manipulated information may be used to transform cells, by:	3.1.1 summarizing the historical events that led to the discovery of the structure of the DNA molecule, as described by Watson and Crick	1, 2, NR1, 5, 6, 7, 8
	3.1.2 describing, in general, how genetic information is contained in the sequence of bases in DNA molecules in chromosomes; how the DNA molecules replicate themselves; how the information is transcribed into sequences of bases in RNA molecules and is finally translated into sequences of amino acids in proteins	
	3.1.3 explaining, in general, how restriction enzymes and ligase may cut DNA molecules into smaller fragments and reassemble them with new sequences of bases	
	3.1.4 explaining, in general, how cells may be transformed by inserting new DNA sequences into their genomes	3
	3.1.5 explaining how a random change (mutation) in the sequence of bases provides a source of genetic variability	
	3.1.6 explaining how information in nucleic acids contained in the nucleus, mitochondria, and chloroplasts gives evidence for the relationships among organisms of different species	4
	3.1.7 predicting the general arrangement of genes in a chromosome from analysis of data on crossing over between genes in a single pair of chromosomes; designing and constructing models of DNA to demonstrate the general structure and base arrangement; performing simulations to demonstrate the replication of DNA and the transcription and translation of its information; designing and performing an experiment to demonstrate how an environmental factor can cause a change in the expression of genetic information of an organism; performing simulations to demonstrate the use of restriction enzymes and ligases in creating new DNA sequences (e.g., electrophoresis); analyzing and inferring, from published data, the relationship between human activities and changes in genetic information that leads to inheritable mutations and cancer; understanding how DNA structure and function can explain classical genetics; explaining DNA manipulation, mutations, and DNA evidence for organism relationships; predicting gene sequences; designing and constructing DNA models; performing experiments to demonstrate DNA expression; and analyzing and inferring the relationship between human activities and mutations	9, 10, 11, 12, 13, 14
demonstrate an understanding that chromosomes are duplicated before cells divide; daughter cells get one complete set of chromosomes; chromosome number must be reduced before fertilization; and that variations in the combination of genes on a chromosome can occur during that reduction, by.	3.2.1 explaining, in general, the events of the cell cycle, including cytokinesis, and chromosomal behaviour in mitosis and meiosis	15, NR2, 19, 20, 21
	3.2.2 describing the processes of spermatogenesis and oogenesis and the necessity for chromosomal number reduction in meiosis	16, 22, 25, 26
	3.2.3 describing the processes of nondisjunction and crossing over; and evaluating their significance on organism development	
	3.2.4 comparing the processes of mitosis and meiosis	23, 24, 27, 28
	3.2.5 comparing the formation of fraternal and identical offspring in a single birthing event	
	3.2.6 describing the diversity of reproductive strategies by comparing the alternation of generations in a range of plants and animals; e.g., pine, bee, mammal	17 18, NR3

demonstrate an understanding that chromosomes consist of a sequence of genes and their alleles, and that during meiosis and fertilization, these genes become combined in new sequences, by extending from Biology 30, Unit 2, fertilization and development in the human organism, and by:	3.3.1	describing the evidence for the segregation of genes and the independent assortment of genes on different chromosomes, as investigated by Mendel	29, 35, 50
	3.3.2	explaining the influence of crossing over on the assortment of genes on the same chromosome; e.g., gene linkage	43
	3.3.3	explaining the significance of sex chromosomes compared with autosomes, as investigated by Morgan	37, 44
	3.3.4	performing experiments to investigate the relationships between chance and genetic inheritance	31, 32, 33, 38, NR4, NR5, 39, 40
	3.3.5	performing simulations to investigate monohybrid and dihybrid genetic crosses, by using Punnett squares	46
	3.3.6	designing a procedure and collecting data in peer groups or families to demonstrate the presence of single and multiple alleles in human inheritance	41
	3.3.7	drawing and interpreting pedigree charts from data on human single allele and multiple allele inheritance patterns; e.g., blood types	
	3.3.8	predicting, quantitatively, the probability of inheritance from monohybrid, dihybrid, and sex-linked inheritance data	
	3.3.9	designing and performing an experiment to demonstrate the inheritance pattern of a trait controlled by a single pair of genes	30, 34, 36, 42, NR6, NR7, NR8, NR9, 47, 48, 49, NR10, NR11
	3.4.	making STS Connection. Understanding how genetic characters are handed down by simple rules; describing evidence for gene segregation and explaining the significance of crossing over and sex chromosomes; drawing and interpreting pedigree charts; performing simulations or experiments to predict inheritance patterns, within the context of evaluating, from a variety of perspectives, the needs and interests of society and the role of genetic counselling in the identification and treatment of potentially disabling genetic disorders; e.g., phenylketonuria	45

NOTES

CELL DIVISION, MENDELIAN GENETICS AND MOLECULAR GENETICS

3.1.1   *summarizing the historical events that led to the discovery of the structure of the DNA molecule, as described by Watson and Crick*

3.1.2   *describing, in general, how genetic information is contained in the sequence of bases in DNA molecules in chromosomes; how the DNA molecules replicate themselves; how the information is transcribed into sequences of bases in RNA molecules and is finally translated into sequences of amino acids in proteins*

3.1.3   *explaining, in general, how restriction enzymes and ligase may cut DNA molecules into smaller fragments and reassemble them with new sequences of bases*

3.1.4   *explaining, in general, how cells may be transformed by inserting new DNA sequences into their genomes*

3.1.5   *explaining how a random change (mutation) in the sequence of bases provides a source of genetic variability*

3.1.6   *explaining how information in nucleic acids contained in the nucleus, mitochondria, and chloroplasts gives evidence for the relationships among organisms of different species*

3.1.7   *predicting the general arrangement of genes in a chromosome, from analysis of data on crossing over between genes in a single pair of chromosomes; designing and constructing models of DNA to demonstrate the general structure and base arrangement; performing simulations to demonstrate the replication of DNA and the transcription and translation of its information; designing and performing an experiment to demonstrate how an environmental factor can cause a change in the expression of genetic information of an organism; performing simulations to demonstrate the use of restriction enzymes and ligases in creating new DNA sequences (e.g., electrophoresis); analyzing and inferring, from published data, the relationship between human activities and changes in genetic information that leads to inheritable mutations and cancer; understanding how DNA structure and function can explain classical genetics; explaining DNA manipulation, mutations and DNA evidence for organism relationships; by predicting gene sequences; designing and constructing DNA models; performing experiments to*

demonstrate DNA expression; and analyzing and inferring the relationship between human activities and mutations

During the 1950s, Watson and Crick worked out the double helix model for the structure of DNA.

DNA is thought to consist of a twisted ladder. The sugar deoxyribose and phosphates make up the uprights of the ladder, and pairs of bases form the ladder rungs. The base pairs are adenine with thymine and guanine with cytosine.

Genetic information is stored in the bases according to the order in which they are arranged. Because three bases code for one amino acid, they are said to form a triplet code.

In the nucleus of any cell, there are many free nucleotides. A nucleotide consists of a base attached to a sugar and a phosphate. During the S phase of interphase, DNA replicates. A polymerase enzyme unzips the DNA, and nucleotides are fitted onto the exposed bases. As a result, there are two identical strands of DNA.

Protein synthesis has two steps: transcription and translation. During the first step, transcription, a message of messenger RNA (mRNA) is formed. RNA is similar to DNA, with three important differences. RNA is a single strand (half of a ladder), the sugar is ribose rather than deoxyribose, and in place of the DNA base thymine, RNA has the base uracil. The DNA unzips, and RNA nucleotides fit onto the coding side of the DNA.

The RNA nucleotides do not stay attached to the DNA, however. As the mRNA strand is formed, it falls away from the DNA and is transported out of the nucleus to the ribosomes. Ribosomes complete the second step of protein synthesis – translation. Ribosomes read the mRNA in groups of three bases called codons. As a codon is read, a molecule of transfer RNA (tRNA) with an anticodon site is attached to the complementary to the mRNA codon. At the other end of the tRNA is attached an amino acid, so the first amino acid has been put into position. As the next codon is read, the next tRNA is inserted into place and the next amino acid is lined up beside the first. The two amino acids then click together. In this way, a chain of amino acids or a polypeptide forms. The polypeptide then will coil into a functional shape as a completed protein.

T becomes U

G C
T

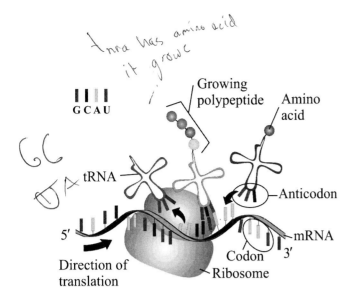

trna has amino acid it grows

GCAU

GC
UA

Growing polypeptide — Amino acid

tRNA

Anticodon

5′

mRNA

Codon 3′

Direction of translation — Ribosome

The strand of mRNA always begins with an initiator codon, and ends when the ribosome reads the terminator codon.

A structural gene is one that codes for the production of a protein, as described above. Regulator genes turn on or turn off structural genes. An oncogene is one that is responsible for cells becoming cancerous. All the genes that make up an organism are called the genome. A mutation alters the sequence of bases on the DNA, thus introducing a genetic variation. In recent years, altering the genome of an organism through recombinant DNA has become an important technology. Firstly, a restriction enzyme is used to cut out a needed gene and the same restriction enzyme is used to cut open a bacterial plasmid. A plasmid is a ring of DNA that a bacterium can take up from its environment. Then, the cut-open plasmids and the DNA containing the needed gene are mixed together, and ligase enzymes are used to fasten the new DNA into the plasmids. Then, the genetically altered plasmids are taken up by bacteria, which will then make the protein coded by the inserted gene.

The technology of gel electrophoresis also uses restriction enzymes. DNA is cut into fragments using restriction enzymes, and the DNA fragments are stained with a radioactive DNA marker. Then, the DNA fragments are placed in gel. An electrical current is used to draw the DNA through the gel. The smaller fragments move more quickly. After some time, the gel has bands corresponding to the DNA – a sort of DNA fingerprint.

Related Questions: 1, 2, NR1, 5, 6, 7, 8, 3, 4, 9, 10, 11, 12, 13, 14

3.2.1 explaining, in general, the events of the cell cycle, including cytokinesis, and chromosomal behavior in mitosis and meiosis

3.2.2 describing the processes of spermatogenesis and oogenesis and the necessity for chromosomal number reduction in meiosis

3.2.3 describing the processes of nondisjunction and crossing over; and evaluating their significance on organism development

3.2.4 comparing the processes of mitosis and meiosis

3.2.5 comparing the formation of fraternal and identical offspring in a single birthing event

3.2.6 describing the diversity of reproductive strategies by comparing the alternation of generations in a range of plants and animals; e.g., pine, bee, mammal

Cells typically move through a cell cycle. Most of the time is spent in interphase, during which the cell carries out its normal functions. Interphase can be divided into Gap 1 (G1), which involves some cell growth, Synthesis (S), during which the DNA replicates itself, and Gap 2 (G2), which involves more growth. The end of interphase is signaled by the start of mitosis.

The first phase of mitosis is prophase, during which chromatin condenses into visible chromosomes. At this point a chromosome is composed of two identical chromatids joined by a centromere. Also during prophase, the nuclear membrane and nucleolus disappear and the two centrioles begin to migrate toward the cell poles. As the centrioles move apart, asters of spindle fibres begin to form from them. Following prophase is metaphase, during which the centrioles, which are now situated at the poles, have formed a complete spindle and the spindle fibres have drawn the chromosomes to the equator.

The next phase is anaphase, in which the spindle fibres contract, drawing the chromatids toward the poles. Lastly, there is telophase. This is when the nuclear membrane and nucleolus begin to reform and the chromosomes uncoil. At the end of telophase, there is cytokinesis, during which the cell cytoplasm splits in two. In animal cells, cytokinesis occurs with the cell pinching in the middle (furrowing). In plant cells, the cytoplasm splits when a cell plate (cell wall) forms down the middle. Mitosis results in two genetically identical cells and is responsible for growth of organisms. Each of the trillions of cells of a human is genetically identical to each other cell because of mitosis.

Cloning involves placing the nucleus of one cell into an egg cell to produce an organism genetically identical to the donor organism. Cancer results from uncontrolled cell division. Radiation therapy is used to destroy cancerous tumors. Chemotherapy involves using drugs that destroy dividing cells. The idea is that since cancer cells are always dividing, the chemotherapy should effectively destroy the cancer cells. Unfortunately, the drugs also destroy normal cells that are dividing.

The production of gametes (sperm and eggs) requires the special cell division called meiosis, in which the chromosome number is halved (diploid to haploid). In the case of humans, the 46 chromosomes (23 pairs) of a somatic cell become 23 unpaired chromosomes of a gamete. Meiosis has two cell divisions that occur one after the other. In males, sperm formation is called spermatogenesis. It begins with the formation of a diploid primary spermatocyte. During prophase I of meiosis I, the chromosome pairs come together (synapsis) to form tetrads. Each tetrad consists of a homologous pair of chromosomes, or four chromatids. At this time, crossing over, in which sections of DNA are exchanged between adjacent chromatids, may occur. In metaphase I it is the tetrads that are pulled to the equator, and during anaphase I it is the homologous chromosomes that are pulled to the poles. (This is different from mitosis since in mitosis, it is chromatids that are pulled apart.)

This "pulling apart" that occurs in meiosis is called segregation, and it ensures that the two cells resulting from meiosis I will each have 23 chromosomes made up of two chromatids. These cells, called secondary spermatocytes, will not be genetically equal. Meiosis II takes place immediately after telophase I, with no interphase between. Meiosis II is just like mitosis, although the cells are haploid, not diploid. At the end of spermatogenesis, there are four haploid spermatids.

Genetic variation has been achieved by the crossing over during prophase I and by the random sorting of the chromosome pairs during anaphase I. Egg formation, or oogenesis, is similar to spermatogenesis, with two significant differences. Firstly, all the primary oocytes that a woman will ever have exist before she is born. Following puberty, a number of these begin meiosis each month, although usually only one completes meiosis to become an egg. Secondly, during telophase I and telophase II, cytoplasm division is unequal. At the end of meiosis I, there is a tiny first polar body that does not survive long and the very large secondary oocyte. As a result of the secondary oocyte undergoing meiosis, there is a tiny second polar body

that will die, and the large ootid. The ootid will swell to become the mature ovum. So, while spermatogenesis results in four small spermatids, oogenesis produces one large ootid. If a woman should produce two eggs at the same time, they may both be fertilized, and fraternal twins may result. However, sometimes one zygote will form and begin to undergo mitosis to form a cluster of cells only to split into two clusters that will eventually become identical twins. Nondisjunction is an error that occurs during anaphase of meiosis in which both members of the chromosome pair are pulled to one end. One of the resulting cells will have 24 chromosomes and the other 22. Following fertilization, a zygote may have 47 chromosomes (trisomy, because one pair contains three) or 45 (monosomy, because one pair contains one). Down syndrome results when a person has three chromosomes in pair number 21 (trisomy 21). A photograph can be taken of the chromosomes during mitosis. The chromosomes can be organized into pairs in order to observe for chromosomal abnormalities. This is called a karyotype.

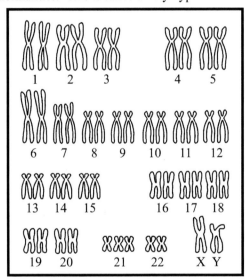

Plant life cycles are complex, with a diploid adult form called a sporophyte, and a haploid adult form called a gametophyte. The gametophyte (*1n*) produces *1n* gametes through mitosis. Two gametes fuse (fertilization) to form a zygote (*2n*) that undergoes mitosis to become the sporophyte (*2n*). The sporophyte undergoes meiosis to produce *1n* spores that undergo mitosis to create *1n* gametophytes again.

Related Questions: 15, NR2, 16, 17, 18, 19, 20, 21, 22, 23, 24, 25, 26, 27, 28, NR3

3.3.1 *describing the evidence for the segregation of genes and the independent assortment of genes on different chromosomes, as investigated by Mendel*

3.3.2 *explaining the influence of crossing over on the assortment of genes on the same chromosome; e.g., gene linkage*

3.3.3 *explaining the significance of sex chromosomes compared with autosomes, as investigated by Morgan*

3.3.4 *performing experiments to investigate the relationships between chance and genetic inheritance*

3.3.5 *performing simulations to investigate monohybrid and dihybrid genetic crosses, by using Punnett squares*

3.3.6 *designing a procedure and collecting data in peer groups or families to demonstrate the presence of single and multiple alleles in human inheritance*

3.3.7 *drawing and interpreting pedigree charts from data on human single allele and multiple allele inheritance patterns; e.g., blood types*

3.3.8 *predicting, quantitatively, the probability of inheritance from monohybrid, dihybrid, and sex-linked inheritance data*

3.3.9 *designing and performing an experiment to demonstrate the inheritance pattern of a trait controlled by a single pair of genes*

3.4 *STS Connections: Understanding how genetic characters are handed down by simple rules; describing evidence for gene segregation and explaining the significance of crossing over and sex chromosomes; drawing and interpreting pedigree charts; performing simulations or experiments to predict inheritance patterns, within the context of evaluating, from a variety of perspectives, the needs and interests of society and the role of genetic counselling in the identification and treatment of potentially disabling genetic disorders; e.g., phenylketonuria*

During the 1800s, the Austrian monk Gregor Mendel studied inherited traits of pea plants and developed laws to explain heredity. He discovered that in an organism, alleles (versions of a gene) existed in pairs, but during gamete formation, the allele pairs segregated so that a gamete contains unpaired alleles (law of segregation).

How an organism appears (such as brown eyes or blue eyes) is called its phenotype. What its genes are like (*BB*, *Bb* or *bb*) is called its genotype.
If the alleles of an organism are the same (*BB* or *bb*) it is called pure or homozygous. If the alleles are different (*Bb*) it is a hybrid or heterozygous.
B (brown eyes) dominates over, or prevents the expression, of *b* (blue eyes). Sometimes dominance is incomplete, as in the case of a red-flowered plant crossed with a white-flowered plant producing pink-flowered offspring.

Mendel discovered that he could determine if an organism showing the dominant trait was homozygous (*BB*) or heterozygous (*Bb*) by crossing it with an organism showing the recessive trait (*bb*).
If any of the offspring show the recessive trait, the organism in question had to be heterozygous. Mendel called this procedure a test cross.

A Punnett square is a convenient way to display a particular cross. To determine the probability of two independent events occurring, the probability of each is multiplied. For example, if a man and woman both heterozygous for eye colour have a child, the chance of it being a male is 0.5. The chance of the child having blue eyes is 0.25. The chance of them having a blue-eyed male child is $0.25 \times 0.5 = 0.125$. Probability has no memory. Even if a couple has 5 daughters, when they have their next child, the chance of it being a girl is still 0.5.

Mendel noted that when he observed two traits during a cross (for example, *BbRr* × *BbRr*), the alleles of the two traits segregated independently of each other. This he called his law of independent assortment. This law holds true only for genes that do not exist on the same chromosome (gene linkage). Many traits are the result of more than simply a dominant or recessive allele.

Traits that result from more than two possible alleles are called multiple allele traits. Human blood types are an example. The alleles I^A, I^B, and i produce the genotypes $I^A I^A$, $I^A i$ (phenotype A), $I^B I^B$ or $I^B i$ (phenotype B) or ii (phenotype O). I^A and I^B show incomplete dominance, and both dominate over i. Most traits from genes genes on the autosomes, but some are the result of genes on the sex chromosomes. These sex-linked traits normally affect males who inherit the trait from their mother. Colorblindness and hemophilia are two examples of sex-linked traits in humans. Both these traits are caused by a gene on the X chromosome. Females have two chances to get the correct allele because they are XX, but males, XY, have only one chance to get the proper allele. A pedigree is a diagram of a family tree that can show how a trait has passed from generation to generation.

Related Questions: 29, 35, 50, 43, 37, 44, 31, 32, 33, 38, NR4, NR5, 39, 40, 46, 41, 30, 34, 36, 42, NR6, NR7, NR8, NR9, 47, 48, 49, NR10, NR11, 45

Use the following information to answer the next question.

Erwin Chargaff found that the relative amount of each of the base pairs that make up DNA varies from species to species. He analyzed a sample of DNA from *Escherichia coli* (a bacterium) and found that 23.6% of the nitrogen base molecules present in this sample were thymine.

– from *Curtis*, 1983

1. In this sample of *Escherichia coli* DNA, the percentage of the nitrogen base molecules that would be adenine is

   A. 76.4%

   B. 38.2%

   C. 23.6%

   D. 11.8%

Source: January 2000

Use the following information to answer the next two questions.

Some people have condemned the use of food preservatives because they may cause cancer. A researcher has found contradictory evidence that suggests that two widely used food preservatives actually increase levels of natural cancer-fighting agents in laboratory animals. The preservatives BHA and BHT increase the activity of a gene that controls the production of an enzyme. This enzyme helps destroy cancer-causing substances (carcinogens) before they trigger the development of tumours.

– from *Pearson et al*, 1983

CHALLENGER QUESTION   50.1

2. The most **direct** relationship between a gene and an enzyme is that

   A. an enzyme causes a gene to destroy carcinogens

   B. the sequence of nucleotides in a gene determines the structure of an enzyme

   C. each gene contains the code needed to construct many different types of enzymes

   D. the sequence of amino acids in an enzyme is unrelated to nucleotide sequence in a gene

Source: January 2000

Use the following additional information to answer the next question.

Some Events that Occur Following Exposure to BHA or BHT

1 The polypeptide folds into an enzyme shape.
2 tRNAs transport amino acids to the ribosomes.
3 A polypeptide is released from the ribosomes.
4 mRNA leaves the nucleus and attaches to ribosomes in the cytoplasm.

CHALLENGER QUESTION   57.9

Numerical Response

1. The sequence of events that results in the production of the cancer-fighting enzyme is _____, _____, _____, and _____.

Source: January 2000

Use the following information to answer the next question.

Although most strains of the bacterial species *Vibrio cholera* are harmless, the 01 strain produces a toxin that binds to cells of the small intestine, causing rapid depletion of salts and water, which, if not replaced, can be lethal in humans. This disease is known as cholera.

The transformation from harmless to harmful bacterial strains is thought to be caused by a virus that transfers the cholera toxin gene (CTX) from one bacterial strain and places it into another. Researchers can mimic this process by using current technologies.

– from *Glausiusz*, 1996

3. The sequence of events that would enable researchers to incorporate the CTX gene into bacterial DNA would be to

   A. first open the bacterial DNA with ligase enzymes, then position the CTX gene in the DNA, and then join the DNA by restriction enzymes

   B. first open the bacterial DNA with restriction enzymes, then position the CTX gene in the DNA, and then join the DNA by ligase enzymes

   C. first position the CTX gene in the DNA, then open the DNA with ligase enzymes, and then join the DNA by restriction enzymes

   D. first position the CTX gene in the DNA, then open the DNA with restriction enzymes, and then join the DNA by ligase enzymes

Source: January 2000

Use the following information to answer the next question.

Portion of the Insulin Protein

Phenylalanine - Valine - Asparagine - Glutamate – Histidine

Assume that a mutation occurred in the strand of DNA that codes for the portion of protein shown above. The protein was altered in structure and no longer performed its function.

– from *Campbell*, 1987

4. Which of the following effects would this mutation have on an individual's body?

   A. A chronic increase in blood sugar after meals

   B. A chronic decrease in blood sugar after meals

   C. A decrease in the body's metabolic rate after meals

   D. An increase in the body's metabolic rate after meals

Source: January 2000

Use the following information to answer the next question.

A study published in the journal *Pediatrics* indicates that breast-fed infants have a substantially decreased risk of developing diarrhea compared with infants fed formula. Another study reported that although a majority of infants harbour populations of bacteria that would cause diarrhea in adults, breast-fed infants do not get sick. The bacterium *Clostridium difficile* produces a toxin that irritates the lining of the colon, causing diarrhea. Breast milk contains a protein called secretory component that binds to the toxin, thus causing the toxin to be ineffective.

– from *Science News*, 1997

5. The protein secretory component is produced in breast milk when

   A. DNA is translated

   B. DNA is replicated

   C. mRNA is translated

   D. mRNA is replicated

Source: June 2000

Use the following information to answer the next question.

Cystic fibrosis is a recessive Mendelian trait in the human population. A symptom of cystic fibrosis is the production of large amounts of mucin protein. New studies indicate that although the cystic fibrosis condition is present at birth, increased mucin production is preceded by an infection with the bacterium *Pseudomonas aeruginosa*. Individuals who are not affected by cystic fibrosis produce a natural antibiotic, defensin, that kills the *Pseudomonas* aeruginosa and eliminates the stimulus for increased mucin production. Defensin is destroyed by a high chloride content in the tissues of individuals with cystic fibrosis as a result of faulty chloride-channel proteins.

– from *Sternberg*, 1997

CHALLENGER QUESTION	50.9

6. The allele that causes cystic fibrosis most likely results in a faulty amino acid sequence for the

  A. channel proteins

  B. mucin molecules

  C. defensin molecules

  D. Pseudomonas bacteria

  Source: January 2000

7. Which of the following rows correctly describes a DNA molecule?

Row	Components	Backbone	Molecules that form the links between two strands
A.	amino acids, sugars, and bases	sugars and bases	amino acids
B.	amino acids, sugars, and bases	sugars and amino acids	bases
C.	phosphates, sugars, and bases	sugars and bases	phosphates
D.	phosphates, sugars, and bases	sugars and phosphates	bases

Source: January 2001

Use the following information to answer the next question.

A section of template DNA contains the following proportions of bases:
adenine–20%   thymine–30%
cytosine–10%   guanine–40%

8. The proportions of three of the mRNA nucleotides produced from this DNA are

  A. 20% adenine, 30% uracil, and 10% cytosine

  B. 40% cytosine, 20% adenine, and 30% uracil

  C. 20% uracil, 40% cytosine, and 10% guanine

  D. 20% thymine, 30% adenine, and 10% guanine

  Source: January 2001

Use the following information to answer the next question.

Tay-Sachs disease is a hereditary disease that kills 1 in 360 000 individuals in the general population, but 1 in 4 800 among the Ashkenazi (Eastern European) Jews. The disease disrupts or halts proper formation of lysosomes and increases fat deposition around the nerve sheath. Individuals that are homozygous for the defective allele have Tay-Sachs disease and die at an early age. Studies suggest that heterozygous individuals have a higher survival rate against tuberculosis than the rest of the population. Biochemical tests can be done to determine if parents are carriers.

– from *Cummings*, 1994

Genetic screening can involve producing complimentary DNA probes of a gene's alleles and determining if these bind to an individual's DNA sample.

9. Genetic screening results show that an individual is a carrier of Tay-Sachs if the individual's DNA binds to

  A. none of the DNA probes

  B. two of the normal allele DNA probes

  C. two of the defective allele DNA probes

  D. one of the normal allele DNA probes and one of the defective allele DNA probes

  Source: January 2001

Use the following information to answer the next two questions.

Gene Loci for a Tomato Plant

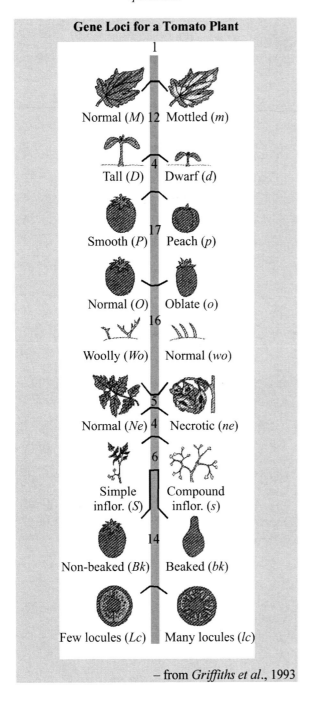

– from *Griffiths et al.*, 1993

10. During meiosis, which of the following pairs of genes given above has the greatest chance of being separated by crossing over?

    A. (*m*) and (*d*)   **B.** (*ne*) and (*p*)

    C. (*m*) and (*lc*)   **D.** (*p*) and (*o*)

    Source: January 2001

Use the following additional information to answer the next question.

Cross-over frequencies for some genes on a tomato plant:

Genes	Cross-Over Frequency
normal leaf (*M*) and tall plant (*D*)	12%
normal leaf (*M*) and normal tomato (*O*)	33%
normal leaf (*M*) and simple inflorescence (*S*)	64%
tall plant (*D*) and normal tomato (*O*)	21%
tall plant (*D*) and simple inflorescence (*S*)	52%

11. The cross-over frequency between genes *O* and *S* is

    A. 6%

    B. 29%

    C. 31%

    D. 97%

    Source: January 2001

Use the following information to answer the next three questions.

Researchers have found a gene known as *p*53. It codes for a protein that binds to specific areas of DNA and activates them. This causes the production of a set of proteins that halts cell division or, in some cells, activates the cell's suicide program (apoptosis). The *p*53 gene is activated when a cell is damaged and/or undergoes a DNA mutation.

– from *Seachrist*, 1996

12. The normal function of the *p*53 gene is likely to

    A. encourage a cell to undergo mitosis

    B. encourage a cell to undergo meiosis

    C. prevent an abnormal cell from reproducing

    D. prevent the transcription of a cell suicide gene

    Source: January 2001

Use the following additional information to answer the next two questions.

Research on the *p53* gene was initially done with cancer cells obtained from a laboratory animal. These cells were grown in a petri dish. A cell with two normal *p53* alleles was found to have normal cell division. Cells with one normal and one mutated *p53* allele were also found to have normal cell division. Cells that had mutations in both *p53* alleles were unable to control cell division and were associated with cancer.

13. The initial research findings described above

    A. demonstrate that the activated *p53* gene causes cancer in lab animals

    B. demonstrate that the *p53* protein causes the formation of cancer cells

    C. indicate that the normal *p53* gene is responsible for preventing cancer in all mammals

    D. indicate that the normal *p53* gene is responsible for preventing cancer under laboratory conditions

    Source: January 2001

14. Gene therapy that might stop uncontrolled cell division due to the mutant p53 allele would require

    A. one functional *p53* allele to be successfully inserted into cancer cells

    B. two functional *p53* alleles to be successfully inserted into cancer cells

    C. one functional *p53* allele to be successfully removed from cancer cells

    D. two functional *p53* alleles to be successfully removed from cancer cells

    Source: January 2001

Use the following information to answer the next three questions.

Chromosome Content of Human Cells During a Series of Events

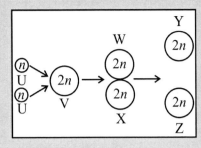

15. In humans, what process must occur before cell **V** forms cells **W** and **X**?

    A. Mitosis

    B. Meiosis

    C. Recombination

    D. Nondisjunction

    Source: January 2000

16. In humans, what process must have occurred to obtain the cells at **U**?

    A. Mitosis

    B. Meiosis

    C. Fertilization

    D. Differentiation

    Source: January 2000

17. In humans, cells **Y** and **Z** represent individual cells that

    A. are two eggs

    B. will no longer divide

    C. will become a $4n$ cell

    D. could develop into identical twins

    Source: January 2000

Use the following information to answer the next question.

Phases of Mitosis
1. Anaphase
2. Metaphase
3. Prophase
4. Telophase

Numerical Response

2. The phase of mitosis in the sequence in which they occur are _____, _____, _____, and _____

(Record your **four-digit** answer.)

Source: January 2000

Use the following information to answer the next question.

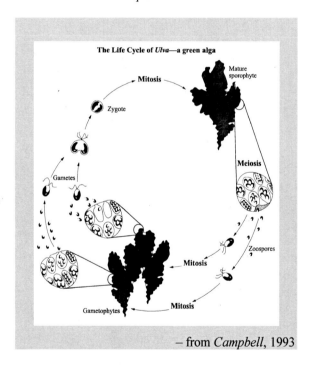

The Life Cycle of *Ulva*—a green alga

– from *Campbell*, 1993

18. Which structures in the life cycle of the *Ulva* are haploid (monoploid)?

A. Zoospores and the zygote

B. The sporophyte and the zygote

C. Zoospores and the gametophytes

D. The sporophyte and the gametophytes

Source: January 2000

Use the following information to answer the next three questions.

Investigators were interested in determining the role chromosomes play in the formation of the mitotic spindle. Using extracts of eggs from the African frog *Xenopus laevis*, they monitored spindle assembly in a test tube. The researchers replaced the chromosomes with beads coated with random sequences of DNA. The beads served as substitute genetic material, but centrosomes (centrioles) were absent. As well, a part of the centromere was missing.

Simplified Diagram of Normal Mitotic Cell

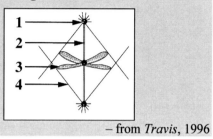

– from *Travis*, 1996

19. Which of the structures numbered above was replaced by the beads in the experimental setup?

A. 1

B. 2

C. 3

D. 4

Source: June 2000

Use the following information to answer the next question.

The investigators observed that the genetic material on the beads condensed and microtubules began to form. Within 90 minutes, the microtubules formed a spindle-like structure that lined up the beads along the centre of the cell.

–from *Travis*, 1996

20. Based on the results of this research, structures or molecules does **not** appear to be necessary for mitosis

A. DNA

B. Spindle

C. Centrosomes

D. Microtubules

Source: June 2000

Use the following information to answer the next question.

Other studies showed that the phase that involves pulling chromosomes to the two poles of mitotic cells can be delayed for up to 4.5 h by pulling a chromosome out of line from the centre of the cell.

–from *Travis*, 1996

21. The phase that is delayed and the phase in which the chromosomes line up at the equator are, respectively,

    A. telophase and anaphase

    B. metaphase and prophase

    C. interphase and telophase

    D. anaphase and metaphase

    Source: June 2000

Use the following information to answer the next question.

A five-month-old human female fetus produces approximately seven million developing ova (eggs) in her ovaries. Approximately 400 000 of these developing ova survive to puberty. Of these, approximately 400 will complete development and be released during a woman's lifetime.

22. This process is similar to spermatogenesis in males in that

    A. eggs and sperm are both diploid

    B. eggs and sperm are both haploid

    C. eggs and sperm are both produced before puberty

    D. an equal number of both eggs and sperm reach maturity

    Source: June 2000

Use the following information to answer the next two questions.

Amniocentesis is a common prenatal procedure used to obtain cells to test for genetic abnormalities that lead to disorders such as Down syndrome, cystic fibrosis, and hemophilia. The test is usually offered between the 15th and 18th weeks of pregnancy to women who have an increased risk of having children with genetic abnormalities.

23. Down syndrome is a trisomy disorder that can be caused by the presence of three copies of chromosome 21. Which of the following chromosome combinations identifies Down syndrome?

    A. 46 chromosomes consisting of 45 autosomes and 1 sex chromosome

    B. 46 chromosomes consisting of 44 autosomes and 2 sex chromosomes

    C. 47 chromosomes consisting of 45 autosomes and 2 sex chromosomes

    D. 47 chromosomes consisting of 44 autosomes and 3 sex chromosomes

    Source: June 2000

24. A genetic abnormality such as Down syndrome can be diagnosed by using the cells obtained during amniocentesis to create a

    A. karyotype

    B. therapeutic gene

    C. DNA fingerprint

    D. recombinant vector

    Source: June 2000

Use the following information to answer the next two questions.

Mature Human Oocyte   **Human Sperm**

– from *Nilsson*, 1990

25. The difference in size between the human oocyte and sperm is **mostly** due to the

   A. difference in magnification of the two photographs

   B. distance that the sperm must travel in order to reach the oocyte

   C. amount of cytoplasm present in the oocyte as compared with that in the sperm

   D. number of chromosomes in the nucleus of the oocyte as compared with the number in the sperm

Source: January 2001

26. The nucleus of a human oocyte would normally be

   A. diploid and contain 23 chromosomes

   B. diploid and contain 46 chromosomes

   C. haploid and contain 23 chromosomes

   D. haploid and contain 46 chromosomes

Source: January 2001

Use the following information to answer the next two questions.

Meiosis is a process that results in the reduction of the chromosome number from diploid to haploid. Sometimes chromosomes fail to separate, which results in an abnormal number of sex chromosomes.

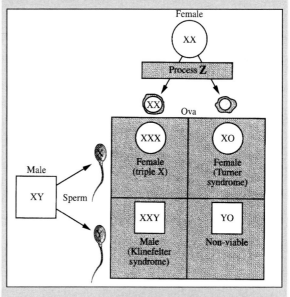

– from *Levine and Miller*, 1991

27. In the diagram above, process **Z** represents

   A. fertilization

   B. crossing-over

   C. nondisjunction

   D. spermatogenesis

Source: January 2001

Use the following additional information to answer the next question.

Partial Human Karyotype

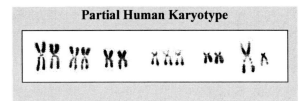

CHALLENGER QUESTION   53.6

28. This partial human karyotype represents the **last** six chromosome pairs, in numerical order. The karyotype presented is that of a

 A. male with trisomy 21

 B. female with trisomy 21

 C. male with Turner syndrome

 D. female with Turner syndrome

Source: January 2001

Use the following information to answer the next question.

Conifer Life Cycle

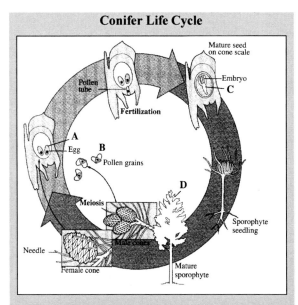

Major Stages in the Conifer Life Cycle

1. Haploid stage

2. Diploid stage

– from *Levine and Miller*, 1991

Numerical Response

3. Identify the stages in the conifer life cycle, as numbered above, that correspond with the letters that represent these stages on the diagram.

Stages: _____ _____ _____ _____

Diagram: A   B   C   D

Source: January 2001

Use the following information to answer the next four questions.

The flowering plant, *Mirabilis jalapa* (*M. jalapa*) may have branches with all white leaves, all green leaves, and all variegated leaves (leaves with green and white patches) on the same plant. Leaf colour is dependent on the colour of plastids present in cytoplasm. As in the case of other plants, pollen (containing sperm nuclei) contribute chromosomes but almost no cytoplasm to the zygote. The ovule contributes both chromosomes and cytoplasm to the zygote. The following data of offspring phenotypes were collected from crosses between flowers from various branches.

Source of pollen (male)	Source of ovule (female)	
	White branch	Green branch
White branch	White offspring	Green offspring
Green branch	White offspring	Green offspring
Variegated branch	White offspring	Green offspring

CHALLENGER QUESTION   50.8

29. These data indicate that, regardless of its branch source, pollen has no effect on the leaf colour of resulting offspring. A reasonable explanation for this observation is that

 A. leaf colour is a codominant trait

 B. leaf colour is a dominant-recessive trait

 C. cell organelles or cytoplasm are active only in pollen

 D. cell organelles or cytoplasm contain genetic information

Source: January 2000

Use the following additional information to answer the next question.

Several geneticists studied *M. jalapa* plants with deep crimson flowers and *M. jalapa* plants with yellow flowers. Cross-pollinating these plants produced plants with scarlet-red flowers (F_1 generation).

These F_1 plants were allowed to self-pollinate, and the resulting seeds produced *M. jalapa* plants with three different flower colours. Data similar to the following were collected for flower colour:
140 deep crimson
310 scarlet-red
160 yellow

–from *Engels*, 1975

30. With respect to the alleles for flower colour, these results indicate

A. X-linked inheritance

B. gene-linked inheritance

C. dominant-recessive inheritance

D. incomplete dominance inheritance

Use the following additional information to answer the next two questions.

A different variety of homozygous *M. jalapa* produces flowers that are light crimson. Pure breeding genotypes and phenotypes are:
$R^P R^P$ – deep crimson
RR – light crimson
rr – yellow
When two pure-breeding P_1 plants are cross-pollinated, only scarlet-red-flowered offspring ($R^P r$) are produced.
When another pair of pure-breeding P_1 plants are cross-pollinated, only orange-flowered offspring (Rr) are produced.

– from *Engels*, 1975

31. The likely genotypes of the P_1 plants for these two crosses is represented in row

Row	P_1 genotypes scarlet-red-flowered offspring	P_1 genotypes orange-flowered offspring
A.	$R^P R \times rr$	$RR \times rr$
B.	$R^P R^P \times rr$	$RR \times rr$
C.	$R^P r \times R^P r$	$Rr \times Rr$
D.	$R^P R^P \times RR$	$R^P R \times Rr$

32. Which of the following phenotypes is the predicted flower colour of *M. jalapa* with the genotype $R^P R$?

A. Yellow

B. Orange

C. Crimson

D. Scarlet-red

Use the following information to answer the next two questions.

Feather colour in parakeets is controlled by two genes. For one pigment gene, the *B* allele produces blue colour and the *b* allele does not produce any colour. For the other pigment gene, the *Y* allele produces yellow colour and the *y* allele does not produce any colour. Any genotype containing at least one *B* allele and one *Y* allele will produce a green parakeet.

33. Which of the following parental genotypes could produce offspring with the **four** different colour patterns?

A. $BBYy \times BbYy$

B. $BbYY \times Bbyy$

C. $bbYY \times bbyy$

D. $Bbyy \times bbYy$

CHALLENGER QUESTION	55.9

34. What is the probability of obtaining a blue parakeet when two green heterozygous parakeets are crossed?

A. 0

B. $\dfrac{3}{16}$

C. $\dfrac{1}{4}$

D. $\dfrac{9}{16}$

Use the following information to answer the next two questions.

A condition called "situs inversus" causes the internal organs of an animal to be reversed and end up on the wrong side of the body. Researchers have shown that insertion of a DNA fragment in one particular structural gene of mice may lead to this condition. Mice homozygous for this insertion are born with their organs reversed and die within a week of their birth. Mice heterozygous for this insertion are born with their organs in normal positions.

– from *Oliwenstein*, 1993

35. Which of the following statements is a **reasonable** conclusion based on this information?

 A. The gene with the inserted DNA fragment is recessive.

 B. The gene with the inserted DNA fragment is dominant.

 C. The affected gene produces a protein that influences embryonic development.

 D. The affected gene cannot be transcribed after foreign DNA has been inserted.

Source: January 2000

36. If two heterozygous mice were mated, what percentage of their offspring would be predicted to die from situs inversus?

 A. 0%

 B. 25%

 C. 50%

 D. 75%

Source: January 2000

Use the following information to answer the next question.

A rare defect inherited by 19 descendants of a Dominican man named Altagracia Carrasco caused genetically male children to be considered female until age 12. At this age, hormone levels increased dramatically and caused the testes to descend from the abdomen to the scrotum and male primary and secondary sexual characteristics to develop.
In their Dominican Republic village, these people were given the name "guevedoces," which means "penis at 12 years of age."

– from *Pringle*, 1992

37. The "guevedoces" were genetically programmed at conception by a sperm with

 A. a Y chromosome fertilizing an egg with a Y chromosome

 B. a Y chromosome fertilizing an egg with an X chromosome

 C. an X chromosome fertilizing an egg with a Y chromosome

 D. an X chromosome fertilizing an egg with an X chromosome

Source: June 2000

Use the following information to answer the next three questions.

A study published in the journal *Pediatrics* indicates that breast-fed infants have a substantially decreased risk of developing diarrhea compared with infants fed formula. Another study reported that although a majority of infants harbour populations of bacteria that would cause diarrhea in adults, breast-fed infants do not get sick. The bacterium *Clostridium difficile* produces a toxin that irritates the lining of the colon-causing diarrhea. Breast milk contains a protein called secretory component that binds to the toxin, thus causing the toxin to be ineffective.

– from *Science News*, 1997

The human milk protein, secretory component, can be manufactured by transgenic sheep. The following steps are necessary for producing transgenic sheep.

1. The gene for secretory component is isolated and cloned into a vector.

2. Vectors carrying the gene are microinjected into fertilized sheep eggs, which are then implanted into female sheep.

3. Heterozygous transgenic offspring are identified.

38. The heterozygous offspring described above are next mated to non-transgenic sheep. If the allele for human secretory protein is *s* and the absence of the human gene is *S*, the symbolic representation of the cross is

 A. *ss* × *ss*

 B. *Ss* × *ss*

 C. *Ss* × *SS*

 D. *SS* × *ss*

Source: June 2000

Numerical Response

4. The proportion of offspring from the mating of a heterozygous transgenic sheep and a non-transgenic sheep that are predicted to be heterozygotes is _____.
(Record your **answer as a value from 0 and 1, rounded to two decimal places.**)

Source: June 2000

CHALLENGER QUESTION   **46.1**

Numerical Response

5. The heterozygous offspring are then mated and their homozygous transgenic offspring are used for producing the milk product. Out of 220 offspring produced from these crosses, how many offspring are predicted to be transgenic homozygotes? _____
(Record your **answer as a whole number.**)

Source: June 2000

Use the following information to answer the next four questions.

Two different genes control the expression of kernel colour in Mexican black corn: black pigment gene B and dotted pigment gene D. Gene B influences the expression of gene D. The dotted phenotype appears only when gene B is in the homozygous recessive state. *A* colourless variation occurs when both genes are homozygous recessive.
After pure-breeding black-pigmented plants were crossed with colourless plants, all of the offspring were black-pigmented.

– from *Griffiths et al.*, 1993

39. The genotypes of the parents of these F_1 offspring could be

  A. $BBDD \times bbdd$

  B. $BbDD \times bbdd$

  C. $Bbdd \times bbDD$

  D. $bbDD \times Bbdd$

Source: June 2000

CHALLENGER QUESTION   **51.3**

40. Plants of the F_1 generation are suspected of being heterozygous for both genes. A test cross of colourless plants with the heterozygote plants should produce a phenotypic ratio in the offspring of

  A. 1:0

  B. 3:1

  C. 2:1:1

  D. 1:1:1:1

Source: June 2000

Numerical Response

6. What is the probability of dotted offspring being produced from the test cross described in Question 40 above? _____
(Record your **answer as a value from 0 and 1, rounded to two decimal places.**)

Source: June 2000

Numerical Response

7. If the total number of offspring produced in the test crosses was 1 024 plants, how many plants would you expect to be black-pigmented?

_____
(Record your answer as a whole number.)

Source: June 2000

Use the following information to answer the next question.

Amniocentesis is a common prenatal procedure used to obtain cells to test for genetic abnormalities that lead to disorders such as Down syndrome, cystic fibrosis, and hemophilia. The test is usually offered between the 15th and 18th weeks of pregnancy to women who have an increased risk of having children with genetic abnormalities.

Pedigree of a Family with Cystic Fibrosis

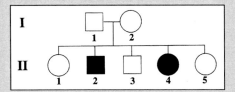

Note: Cystic fibrosis in the family is caused by a recessive allele that is found on chromosome 7.

41. Prior to performing amniocentesis, a genetic counsellor collected pedigree information regarding the incidence of cystic fibrosis within this family. The row that indicates the genotypes of individuals **I-1**, **I-2**, and **II-2** is

Row	I-1	I-2	II-2
A.	Aa	Aa	aa
B.	AA	aa	Aa
C.	$X^A Y$	$X^A X^A$	$X^a Y$
D.	$X^A Y$	$X^A X^a$	$X^A Y$

Source: June 2000

Use the following information to answer the next two questions.

In humans, the allele for normal blood clotting, *H*, is dominant to the allele for hemophilia, *h*. The trait is X-linked.

42. A female hemophiliac marries a man who is not a hemophiliac. The row that indicates the probability of this couple having a child that is a hemophiliac and the sex that the child would be is

Row	Probability	Sex of Affected Child
A.	0.25	male
B.	0.25	either female or male
C.	0.50	male
D.	0.50	either male or female

Source: June 2000

8. A woman who is not a hemophiliac has a father who is a hemophiliac. If this woman marries a man who is a hemophiliac, what is the probability of them having a hemophiliac son? _____ (Record your **answer as a value from 0 and 1, round to two decimal places.**)

Source: June 2000

Use the following information to answer the next two questions.

A high percentage of purebred dogs have genetic defects. Some examples of these defects follow.

1 Hip dysplasia, a defect in the hip joints that can cripple a dog, occurs in 60% of golden retrievers.
2 Hereditary deafness, due to a recessive autosomal disorder, occurs in 30% of Dalmatians.
3 Retinal disease, which may cause blindness, occurs in 70% of collies.
4 Hemophilia, an X-linked recessive disorder, is common in Labrador retrievers. Dwarfism is also common in this breed of dog.

– from *Lemonick*, 1994

43. Collies that are bred for long noses and closely set eyes are more likely to have retinal disease. The **best** explanation for this is that

A. closely spaced eyes cause retinal degeneration

B. breeders intentionally select for these three characteristics

C. genes for these three characteristics are on the same chromosome

D. the abnormal gene that causes retinal disease is on the X chromosome

Source: January 2001

Use the following additional information to answer the next question.

A healthy female Labrador retriever has won several ribbons for her appearance in dog shows. She was mated with two healthy male Labrador retrievers. In the two litters produced, some of the offspring had hemophilia and others were normal.

CHALLENGER QUESTION   **55.4**

44. If the female is bred to one of her male offspring that does not have hemophilia, then the probability of the female offspring of this cross having hemophilia is

     A.   0%

     B.   25%

     C.   75%

     D.   100%

Source: January 2001

Use the following information to answer the next question.

Meiosis is a process that results in the reduction of the chromosome number from diploid to haploid. Sometimes chromosomes fail to separate, which results in an abnormal number of sex chromosomes.

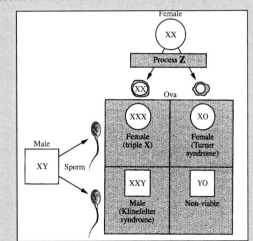

from *Levine and Miller*, 1991

Scientists studying Klinefelter and Turner syndromes wanted to determine which of several hypotheses about gender determination was most likely. These hypotheses were:

- presence of a Y chromosome causes maleness
- lack of a second X chromosome causes maleness
- the presence of two X chromosomes causes femaleness
- the Y chromosome is not involved in gender determination

Evidence noted by the scientists included the following points.

- Individuals with Klinefelter syndrome (XXY) have genitalia and internal ducts that are usually male, but their testes are underdeveloped.
- Individuals with Turner syndrome (XO) have female external genitalia and internal ducts; however, the ovaries are underdeveloped.

–from *Cummings and Klug*, 1997

45. This evidence **best** supports which of the scientists' hypotheses about gender determination?

     A.   The presence of a Y chromosome causes maleness.

     B.   The lack of a second X chromosome causes maleness.

     C.   The presence of two X chromosomes causes femaleness.

     D.   The Y chromosome is not involved in gender determination.

Source: January 2001

Use the following information to answer the next two questions.

Tay-Sachs disease is a hereditary disease that kills 1 in 360 000 individuals in the general population, but 1 in 4 800 among the Ashkenazi (Eastern European) Jews. The disease disrupts or halts proper formation of lysosomes and increases fat deposition around the nerve sheath. Individuals that are homozygous for the defective allele have Tay-Sachs disease and die at an early age. Studies suggest that heterozygous individuals have a higher survival rate against tuberculosis than the rest of the population. Biochemical tests can be done to determine if parents are carriers.

– from *Cummings*, 1994

46. What type of inheritance is demonstrated in Tay-Sachs disease?

A. Autosomal recessive

B. Autosomal dominant

C. Sex-linked recessive

D. Sex-linked dominant

Source: January 2001

Numerical Response

9. A young couple decided to have genetic screening done to determine if they were carriers of Tay-Sachs disease. If both individuals were carriers, what percentage of their offspring would be predicted to have protection from tuberculosis but not have Tay-Sachs disease?
Answer: _____% (Record your answer **as a whole number percentage.**)

Source: January 2001

Use the following information to answer the next two questions.

In tomato plants, purple stems (*P*) are dominant to green stems (*p*), and red tomatoes (*T*) are dominant to yellow tomatoes (*t*). The two genes are located on separate chromosomes.
A purple-stemmed, red-tomato plant is crossed with a purple-stemmed, yellow-tomato plant. They produce:
28 purple-stemmed, red-tomato plants
31 purple-stemmed, yellow-tomato plants
11 green-stemmed, red-tomato plants
9 green-stemmed, yellow-tomato plants

47. The genetic composition of the parents is

A. *PpTt* and *PPTT*

B. *PPTt* and *PpTT*

C. *PpTt* and *PpTt*

D. *PpTt* and *Pptt*

Source: January 2001

CHALLENGER QUESTION	59.3

48. One of the green-stemmed, red-tomato plants was crossed with another tomato plant. One of the offspring was a purple-stemmed, yellow-tomato plant. If this offspring were crossed with a green-stemmed, yellow-tomato plant, then the possible phenotype or phenotypes of the offspring would be

A. green-stemmed, yellow-tomato plants

B. green-stemmed, yellow-tomato plants and purple-stemmed, yellow-tomato plants

C. green-stemmed, yellow-tomato plants; purple-stemmed, yellow-tomato plants; and purple-stemmed, red-tomato plants

D. green-stemmed, yellow-tomato plants; purple-stemmed, yellow-tomato plants; purple-stemmed, red-tomato plants; and green-stemmed, red-tomato plants

Source: January 2001

Use the following information to answer the next three questions.

Punnett Square for a Dihybrid Cross to Investigate Coat Colour in Mice

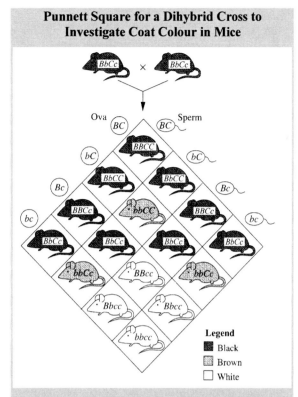

Coat colour in mice is controlled by the interaction of two genes. Three phenotypes result: black coat, brown coat, and white coat.

– from Campbell, 1993

49. In the dihybrid cross between the two black mice, the *C* allele codes for

A. black colour

B. brown colour

C. colour absent

D. colour present

Source: January 2001

Numerical Response

10. What is the expected phenotypic ratio that results from a cross between two black mice heterozygous for both genes?
Phenotypic Ratio: _____ : _____ : _____
Coat Colour: Black Brown White
(Record your answer to **three digits**.)

Source: January 2001

Numerical Response

11. What is the expected phenotypic ratio resulting from a cross between a *bbCc* female mouse and *BbCc* male mouse?
Phenotypic Ratio: _____ : _____ : _____
Coat Colour: Black   Brown   White

Source: January 2001

Use the following information to answer the next question.

Farmers who raise sheep for wool try not to produce offspring with black wool. Black wool is very brittle and difficult to dye; therefore, white wool is more desirable. If a farmer purchases a white ram, he will generally carry out a test cross to determine whether the ram is heterozygous or homozygous for white wool.
White wool (*W*) is dominant to black wool (*w*).

50. If the ram is heterozygous for white wool, the expected phenotypes of the offspring of the farmer's test cross would be

A. all black

B. all white

C. $\frac{1}{2}$ black and $\frac{1}{2}$ white

D. $\frac{3}{4}$ black and $\frac{1}{4}$ white

Source: January 2001

UNIT TEST 3 – CELL DIVISION, MENDELIAN GENETICS AND MOLECULAR GENETICS

1. As cells age, there is an increase in DNA damage and a decrease in DNA repair processes. The **initial** effect is

   A. a decrease in ATP synthesis

   B. an increase of cancerous cells

   C. the production of altered proteins

   D. the production of abnormal mRNA

Use the following information to answer the next question.

Portion of Insulin Protein

Phenylalanine–Valine–Asparagine–
Glutamine–Histidine

2. What is the strand of DNA that would code for this portion of insulin?

   A. AAG CAA TTA GTT GTA

   B. AAA CAA TTC CAC CTA

   C. CAC GAG AAC GTA TTC

   D. TTC GTA AAC GAG CAC

3. DNA is structurally different from RNA in that DNA

   A. contains uracil and is composed of double strands

   B. contains adenine and is composed of single strands

   C. contains guanine and is composed of single strands

   D. contains thymine and is composed of double strands

4. Analysis of a DNA sample showed that 15% of the nitrogen-base molecules present were adenine molecules. This sample would likely contain

   A. 15% thymine   B. 15% uracil

   C. 85% thymine   D. 85% uracil

Use the following information to answer the next two questions.

In DNA replication, the two strands of the double helix separate and a new strand forms along each old one. Each new DNA molecule has one old and one new strand.

5. Which of the following rows gives the name of the old DNA strand and the site of DNA replication?

Row	Name of Old Strand	Site
A.	a template	nucleus
B.	a template	cytoplasm
C.	haploid	nucleus
D.	haploid	cytoplasm

6. Which of the following rows identifies the backbone of a DNA molecule and the composition of A, C, T, and G?

Row	DNA Backbone	A, C, T, and G
A.	phosphate groups	deoxyribose sugars
B.	purines	deoxyribose sugars
C.	pyrimidines	nitrogen-containing bases
D.	sugars and phosphate groups	nitrogen-containing bases

Use the following information to answer the next question.

"It begins in your gut and quickly spreads to your heart and head. Your confidence is swept away with dark foreboding as your heart races and your stomach becomes nauseous."

This description was given by a person experiencing a "panic attack" induced by the injection of cholecystokinin (CCK). CCK is a molecule with different functions in different parts of the body. In the brain, it acts as a neurotransmitter that normally regulates memory and recall. It also arouses the emotional and motivational regions of the brain. A gene that encodes CCK has been located.

– from *Hall*, 1996

CHALLENGER QUESTION   **52.7**

7. After mRNA has been produced, the production of CCK is the result of

   A. translation

   B. replication

   C. transcription

   D. recombination

Use the following information to answer the next question.

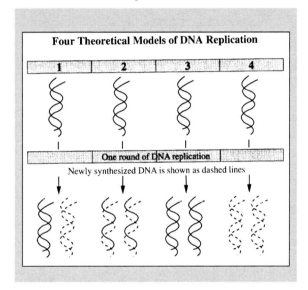

Four Theoretical Models of DNA Replication

One round of DNA replication

Newly synthesized DNA is shown as dashed lines

8. Which number above represents the model of DNA replication that occurs in human cells?

   A. 1

   B. 2

   C. 3

   D. 4

Use the following information to answer the next question.

The use of marker genes and the analysis of crossover frequencies of genes have enabled geneticists to map the location of many genes on human chromosomes. Blue colour vision and blue colourblindness (tritanopia) are controlled by a gene on chromosome 7. The gene for the production of trypsin (a digestive enzyme) and the gene responsible for cystic fibrosis are also found on chromosome 7. Some crossover frequencies of these genes are shown below.

Pair of Genes	Crossover Frequency
Marker gene–cystic fibrosis	18%
Marker gene–tritanopia	13%
Cystic fibrosis–trypsin	6%
Trypsin– tritanopia	1%

– from *Rimoin et al.,* 1996

9. Which of the following gene maps shows the correct sequence of these genes on chromosome 7?

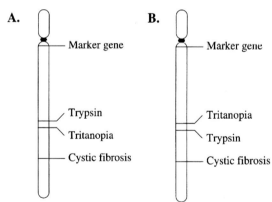

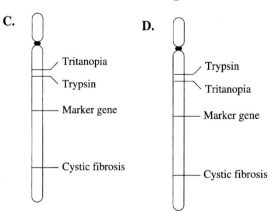

Use the following information to answer the next question.

A bacterium has been found that produces a form of plastic called polyhydroxybutyrate (PHB). Genes from this bacterium have been transferred into a weed called *Arabidopsis thaliana*. These weeds now produce a biodegradable plastic.

– from *Poirier, et al.*, 1997

10. The technology of transferring a gene from a bacterium into a green plant is based on the principle that

    A. all genes carry the same genetic information

    B. all genes have the same basic chemical components

    C. the genotypes of the bacterium and green plant are the same

    D. the phenotype of an organism is not altered when one gene is exchanged for another

Use the following information to answer the next two questions.

Biologists using light microscopes to study mitosis noticed that the nuclear membrane of a cell disappeared and then re-formed during the process. They could not explain this disappearance until they used electron microscopes to view mitotic cells. These observations revealed a large number of vesicles (small bubble-shaped structures bounded by membranes) that appeared in the cytoplasm during mitosis and then disappeared when mitosis was nearly complete. During mitosis, the nuclear membrane appeared to disintegrate and form these tiny vesicles. The vesicles disappeared when new nuclear membranes formed.

CHALLENGER QUESTION	59.9

11. The vesicles observed with the aid of an electron microscope appeared and disappeared, **respectively**, during

    A. prophase and anaphase

    B. prophase and telophase

    C. interphase and anaphase

    D. interphase and telophase

12. During mitosis, the chromosomes

    A. are located at the cell equator during prophase

    B. are located at the cell equator during telophase

    C. move toward the poles of the cell during anaphase

    D. move toward the poles of the cell during metaphase

13. One aspect of meiosis that is different from mitosis is that normally, by the end of meiosis, there are

    A. two diploid cells

    B. four diploid cells

    C. two haploid cells

    D. four haploid cells

14. In one type of cloning, the nucleus of a cell taken from the blastula stage of an embryo is inserted into an enucleated egg cell (an egg cell with its nucleus removed). The nucleus of a cell taken from a more mature embryo would be **less suitable** for this type of cloning because such a nucleus would

    A. be too large to fit inside an enucleated egg cell

    B. be specialized because differentiation would have begun

    C. lack some of the genes needed to develop into a total organism

    D. undergo only meiosis, whereas cells of early embryos would undergo only mitosis

Use the following information to answer the next question.

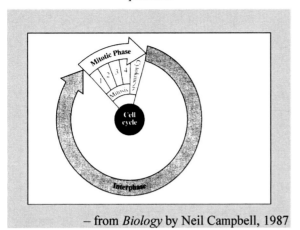

– from *Biology* by Neil Campbell, 1987

Numerical Response

1. Match the stages of the mitotic phase, as numbered above, with the appropriate stage of mitosis given below.
(Record your four-digit answer.)

Mitotic Phase:	_____	_____	_____	_____
Stage of Mitosis:	Anaphase	Metaphase	Prophase	Telophase

Use the following information to answer the next question.

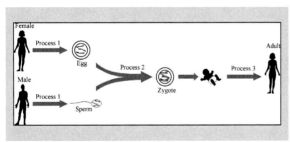

Numerical Response

2. Identify the processes, as labelled in the diagram above, that represent the activities given below.
(Record your three-digit answer.)

Process:	_____	_____	_____
Activity:	Division of diploid cells to produce diploid cells	Haploid cells combine to form a diploid cell	Division of diploid cells to produce haploid cells

Use the following information to answer the next question.

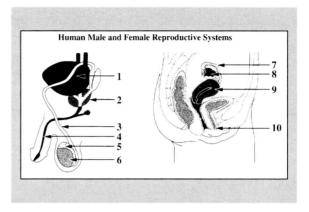

15. Meiosis occurs in which male and female structure numbered above?

A. 6 and 9, respectfully

B. 6 and 8, respectfully

C. 5 and 9, respectfully

D. 5 and 8, respectfully

16. Certain disorders result if an extra chromosome is present in all nucleated cells of the body (trisomy) or if a chromosome is missing from all nucleated cells of the body (monosomy). These disorders arise because of nondisjunction, a malfunction that occurs during

A. DNA replication

B. RNA transcription

C. telophase of mitosis

D. anaphase of meiosis

Use the following information to answer the next two questions.

Melanin pigments range in colour from yellow to reddish-brown to black. The amount and the colour of melanin in the skin account for differences in human skin coloration.

Albinism is a genetic disorder that results in unpigmented skin and other tissues. About one in 20 000 humans has albinism. In humans, it can be caused by an autosomal recessive allele (*a*). Its dominant allele (*A*) results in normal pigmentation.

17. In the type of albinism described above, because melanin production is controlled by an autosomal gene, it is expected that

    A. males will develop albinism as they mature

    B. males will inherit albinism from their mothers

    C. albinism will occur more frequently among males than females

    D. albinism will occur with equal frequencies among males and female

18. The fact that, for many humans, exposure to sunlight increases melanin production and produces a tan demonstrates that

    A. some people have mutations that prevent melanin production

    B. the expression of some genes is influenced by the environment

    C. the environment causes mutations that increase the chance of survival

    D. the environment causes mutations that have no effect on the chance of survival

Use the following information to answer the next question.

Cystic fibrosis is the most common genetic disorder among Caucasians, affecting one in 2 000 Caucasian children. The cystic fibrosis allele results in the production of sticky mucus in several structures, including the lungs and exocrine glands.
Two parents who are unaffected by the disorder can have a child with the disorder.

A girl and both her parents are unaffected by the disease. However, her sister is affected by cystic fibrosis.

19. The genotypes of the mother and father are

    A. both homozygous

    B. both heterozygous

    C. homozygous and heterozygous, respectively

    D. heterozygous and homozygous, respectively

Use the following information to answer the next question.

Marfan Syndrome is an autosomal-dominant disorder of humans. Affected individuals tend to be tall and thin. They have defects in the lens of the eye and weak connective tissue around the aorta.
Often, affected individuals excel in sports like volleyball or basketball but it is not uncommon for people with this syndrome to die suddenly.

20. Which of the following statements is a valid prediction about the frequency of this disorder in males and females?

    A. Males are affected more often than females.

    B. Females are affected more often than males.

    C. Males and females are affected with equal frequency.

    D. An accurate prediction cannot be made because the syndrome occurs randomly.

Use the following information to answer the next two questions.

In pea plants, tall (*T*) is dominant over short (*t*), and round seed (*R*) is dominant over wrinkled seed (*r*). The Punnett square below shows a cross between a heterozygous tall-heterozygous round-seed pea plant and a short-heterozygous round-seed pea plant. Different types of offspring are represented by numbers.

	TR	*Tr*	*tR*	*tr*
tR	1	2	3	4
tr	5	6	7	8

21. Which two types of offspring are pure breeders for both plant height and seed shape?

    A. 1 and 6

    B. 2 and 5

    C. 3 and 8

    D. 4 and 7

22. Which two types of offspring, when crossed, could be expected to produce a population in which 50% of their offspring would be tall and 100% would produce round seeds?

    A. 1 and 8

    B. 2 and 4

    C. 3 and 7

    D. 5 and 6

Use the following information to answer the next two questions.

A variation of leaf markings in white clover is controlled by an autosomal gene (locus). This locus may be occupied by one of several different alleles. The allele V^h produces white lines in long V-shapes on each leaf. The allele V^l produces white lines in short V-shapes, and the allele *v* produces unlined leaves when homozygous. The order of dominance is $V^h > V^l > v$, and it is assumed that dominance is complete.

A clover plant with long V-shaped lines on the leaves and a clover plant with short V-shaped lines on the leaves produced offspring. Some of the offspring had long V-shaped lines on the leaves, some had short V-shaped lines, and some had unlined leaves.

White Clover Line Patterns

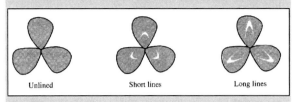

Unlined   Short lines   Long lines

– from *Griffiths, et al.*, 1993

23. The genotypes of the parent plant with long V-shaped lines and of the parent plant with short V-shaped lines are, **respectively**,

    A. $V^h V^l$ and *vv*

    B. $V^h v$ and $V^l v$

    C. $V^h V^l$ and $V^l v$

    D. $V^h v$ and $V^l V^l$

Numerical Response

3. What is the probability of these two parent plants producing offspring that have unlined leaves?

_____

(Record your **answer as a value from 0 to 1, rounded to two decimal places**.)

Use the following information to answer the next question.

F_1 **Blood Type Cross**	
$I^A I^B$	$I^A i$
$I^A I^B$	$I^A i$

24. The genotypes of the parents to whom this Punnett square applies are

    A. heterozygous B and homozygous A

    B. heterozygous O and homozygous A

    C. homozygous B and heterozygous A

    D. heterozygous B and heterozygous A

Use the following information to answer the next question.

There is some evidence that two genes, BRCA₁ and BARD₁, suppress certain types of cancer. If either of these genes is defective, ovarian and/or breast tumours may develop. The mutant form of BARD₁ is considered to be recessive.

Studies have shown that the proteins encoded by the BRCA₁ and BARD₁ genes differ from one another, but that they probably link up. In doing so, they somehow prevent tumour growth. The abnormal genes may result in the production of faulty proteins that will not link.

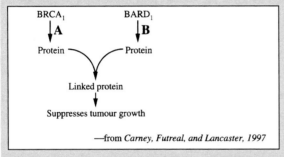

—from *Carney, Futreal, and Lancaster, 1997*

– from *Carney, Futreal, and Lancaster,* 1997

25. Four individuals undergo carrier screening for the two genes, and the following results are observed.

Which of the following individuals is most likely to develop ovarian and/or breast tumours?

Row		BRCA₁	BARD₁
A.	Individual 1	heterozygous	homozygous dominant
B.	Individual 2	heterozygous	heterozygous
C.	Individual 3	homozygous normal	homozygous normal
D.	Individual 4	heterozygous	homozygous recessive

Use the following information to answer the next question.

A, B, M, N, O, and Rh Blood Typing

The alleles for $A(I^A)$ and $B(I^B)$ are codominant, and both are dominant to $O(i)$.

The alleles for M and N are codominant.
The alleles for Rh^+ is dominant to the allel for Rh^-.

Blood groups can be used to determine relationships for a variety of legal and medical purposes.
The following is a list of phenotypes of four children.

Blood Types

Child 1	O	MN	Rh^+
Child 2	A	N	Rh^+
Child 3	A	MN	Rh^-
Child 4	AB	MN	Rh^-

26. Which children could belong to a couple in which the woman has blood type A, N, Rh^+ and the man has blood type O, M, Rh^+?

A. Children 1 and 3

B. Children 1 and 4

C. Children 2 and 3

D. Children 2 and 4

Use the following information to answer the next question.

The gene for a light-sensitive protein found in red cones and the gene for a light-sensitive protein found in green cones lie side by side on the X chromosome. A third gene for a light-sensitive protein found in blue cones was discovered on chromosome 7. Mutations to any of these genes result in the common forms of colourblindness. The mutant alleles for these disorders are recessive.

Pedigree of Red-Green Colourblindness in Humans

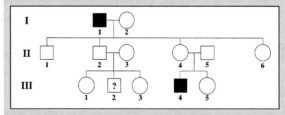

Note: Heterozygous individuals have not been identified. The Phenotype of III-2 is unknown.

CHALLENGER QUESTION   **58.6**

27. Which of the following statements provides a conclusion that can be drawn from this pedigree?

    A. The probability that individual II-4 is a carrier is 50%.

    B. It is impossible to determine whether individual II-6 is a carrier.

    C. If individual III-5 is a carrier, all of her female children will have red-green colourblindness.

    D. If individual II-3 is a carrier, there is a 50% chance that her male child will have red-green colourblindness.

CHALLENGER QUESTION   **53.1**

28. A valid assumption based on this information is that

    A. all types of colourblindness are sex-influenced

    B. males may be carriers for all types of colourblindness

    C. only females may be carriers for blue colourblindness

    D. blue colourblindness occurs in males and females with equal frequency

Use the following information to answer the next question.

Pedigree of Human ABO Blood Types

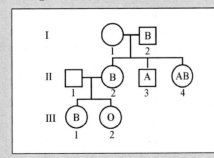

29. The genotype of individual **I-1** is

    A. *ii*   B. $I^A i$

    C. $I^B i$ D. $I^A I^A$

Use the following information to answer the next question.

Piebald spotting is a rare human disorder. Although this disorder occurs in all races, piebald spotting is most obvious in people with dark skin. A dominant allele appears to interfere with the migration of pigment-producing cells; thus, patches of skin and hair lack pigment, allowing "spots" to form.

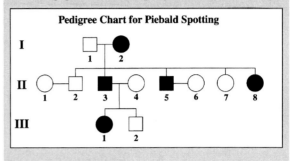

Numerical Response

4. What is the probability that any offspring produced by individuals II-5 and II-6 would have piebald spotting?
(Record your **answer as a value from 0 to 1 rounded to two decimal places.**)
Answer: _____

Use the following information to answer the next two questions.

Sickle cell anemia is caused by the sickle cell allele (*Hb^s*) of a gene that contributes to hemoglobin (*Hb*) production. The abnormal hemoglobin (hemoglobin-S) causes red blood cells to become deformed and block capillaries. Tissue damage results. Affected individuals homozygous for the sickle cell gene rarely survive to reproductive age. Heterozygous individuals produce both normal hemoglobin and a small percentage of hemoglobin-S. These individuals are more resistant to malaria than are individuals homozygous for the allele for normal hemoglobin (*Hb^A*). Their red blood cells are prone to sickling when there is a deficiency of oxygen.

A Pedigree That Illustrates the Inheritance of Sickle Cell Anemia

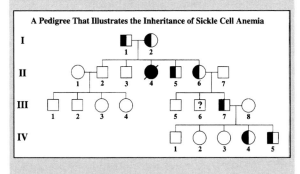

Numerical Response

5. The phenotype of III-6 is unknown. What is the probability this individual is a carrier of the sickle cell allele? (Record your **answer as a whole number percentage.**)
Answer: _____%

30. If a man and a woman who are both heterozygous for the alleles *Hb^A* and *Hb^s* have a child, the probability that the child would **not** be heterozygous is

A. 0.00

B. 0.25

C. 0.50

D. 0.75

Use the following information to answer the next two questions.

Cystic fibrosis is the most common genetic disorder among Caucasians, affecting one in 2 000 Caucasian children. The cystic fibrosis allele results in the production of sticky mucus in several structures, including the lungs and exocrine glands.
Two parents who are unaffected by the disorder can have a child with the disorder.
A girl and both her parents are unaffected by the disease. However, her sister is affected by cystic fibrosis.

Numerical Response

6. These parents, who are unaffected by cystic fibrosis, are planning to have another child. What is the percentage probability that their next child will be affected by cystic fibrosis?
_____%
(Record your **answer as a whole number percentage.**)

31. Which term **best** describes the allele for cystic fibrosis?

A. X-linked

B. Recessive

C. Dominant

D. Codominant

Use the following information to answer the next question.

Hypophosphatemia is one of the few genetic diseases caused by a dominant allele carried on the X chromosome. It causes a severe deficiency of phosphate ions in the blood.

– from *Rimoin, et al.,* 1996

CHALLENGER QUESTION   **57.0**

32. A female with hypophosphatemia whose father had a disease but whose mother did not will likely transmit the disorder to

   A. her sons only

   B. her sons and her daughters equally

   C. all of her daughters but none of her sons

   D. all of her daughters and 50% of her sons

Use the following information to answer the next question.

Marfan syndrome is an autosomal-dominant disorder of humans. Affected individuals tend to be tall and thin. They have defects in the lens of the eye and weak connective tissue around the aorta.
Often, affected individuals excel in sports like volleyball or basketball but it is not uncommon for people with this syndrome to die suddenly.

Numerical Response

7. A man, heterozygous for Marfan syndrome, and a homozygous recessive woman have a child. What is the probability that the child will be affected by Marfan syndrome? _____
(Record your **answer as a value from 0 to 1, rounded to two decimal places.**)

Use the following information to answer the next question.

In addition to the ABO system, human blood may be typed as Rh^+ or Rh^-. The blood types Rh^+ and Rh^- are controlled by the dominant allele R (Rhesus positive) and the recessive allele r (Rhesus negative).

Numerical Response

8. If a woman with the genotype $I^A I^B Rr$ and a man with the blood type O Rh^- have a child, what is the probability that the child will have blood type A Rh^-? _____
(Record your **answer as a value from 0 to 1, rounded to two decimal places.**)

Use the following information to answer the next question.

Scientists believe that a mutant form of an autosomal gene called $BRCA_1$ may be associated with 5% to 10% of all cases of breast cancer. About 80% of women who inherit the gene in its defective form are likely to develop a cancerous breast tumour.
Men who carry the faulty gene rarely develop breast cancer, but they may pass the gene to their offspring.

A couple have two children, a girl and a boy. The mother has a single mutant gene for breast cancer; the father is not a carrier of the mutant $BRCA_1$ gene.

– from *Richards,* 1996

CHALLENGER QUESTION   **57.0**

33. What is the probability that their daughter has inherited the mutant $BRCA_1$ gene?

   A. 75%

   B. 50%

   C. 25%

   D. 0%

Use the following information to answer the next question.

In garden peas, the allele for tall plant height (*T*) is dominant over the allele for short plant height (*t*), and the allele for axial flower position (*A*) is dominant over the allele for terminal flower position (*a*). The alleles for plant height and flower position assort independently.

34. A plant heterozygous for both traits was crossed with a plant homozygous recessive for both traits. What percentage of the offspring produced would be expected to display at least one of the dominant traits?

    A. 25%

    B. 50%

    C. 75%

    D. 100%

Use the following information to answer the next question.

"Alligator men" or "fish women" were exhibited for their physical abnormalities in fairs or circuses earlier this century. These people probably suffered from X-linked ichthyosis, which produces symmetric dark scales on the body. The disease occurs in 1 in 6 000 males and much more rarely in females. Ichthyosis is likely a recessive disorder.

– from *Cummings*, 1994

Numerical Response

9. If an "alligator man" were to marry a woman homozygous for the normal condition, what is the **percentage** probability that their children would have ichthyosis?
(Record your **answer as a whole number percentage.**)
Answer: _____ %

POPULATION GENETICS AND INTERACTION

Table of Correlations		
General Outcome	**Specific Outcome**	**Related Questions**
	Students are expected to:	
define populations in terms of their gene pools, by extending from Biology 20, Unit 3, the nature of variation and adaptation in populations, and by:	4.1.1.1 describing the Hardy-Weinberg principle and explaining its importance to population gene pool stability and the significance of nonequilibrium values; e.g., evolution of a population	4
	4.1.1.2 describing the conditions that cause the gene pool diversity to change; e.g., random genetic drift, gene migration, differential reproduction	1, 2, 3, 5, 6, NR3
	4.1.1.3 applying, quantitatively, the Hardy-Weinberg principle to observed and published data	NR1, NR2
	4.1.1.4 describing the molecular basis and significance of gene pool change over time; i.e., mutations	
demonstrate an understanding that interactions occur among members of the same population of a species as well as among members of populations of different species, by:	4.2.1.1 describing the basis of symbiotic relationships, i.e., commensalism, mutualism, parasitism, and interspecific and intraspecific competition, and their influences on population changes	7, 8, 13, 15, 23, 28
	4.2.1.2 describing the relationships between predator and prey species and their influence on population changes and by explaining the role of defence mechanisms in predation; e.g., mimicry, protective colouration	9
	4.2.1.3 explaining how mixtures of populations that define communities may change over time or remain as a climax community; e.g., primary succession, secondary succession	NR4, 17, 22
demonstrate an understanding that populations grow in characteristic ways and that the changes in population growth can be quantified, by extending from Biology 20, Unit 3, variations within populations, and by:	4.3.1.1 describing and explaining, quantitatively, factors that influence population growth; i.e., mortality, natality, immigration, emigration	10, 14, 16, 21, 27
	4.3.1.2 describing the growth of populations in terms of the mathematical relationship among carrying capacity, biotic potential, and the number of individuals in the population	11, 12, 24, 25
	4.3.1.3 explaining, quantitatively, the behaviour of populations, using different growth patterns; i.e., *r*- and *K*-strategies, J and S curves	
	4.3.1.4 describing the implications of the chaos theory for the study of biological systems, especially as they relate to population growth patterns	NR5, NR6, 18, 19, 20, 26

POPULATION GENETICS AND INTERACTION

4.1.1.1 describing the Hardy-Weinberg principle and explaining its importance to population gene pool stability and the significance of nonequilibrium values; e.g., evolution of a population

4.1.1.2 describing the conditions that cause the gene pool diversity to change; e.g., random genetic drift, gene migration, differential reproduction

4.1.1.3 applying, quantitatively, the Hardy-Weinberg principle to observed and published data

4.1.1.4 describing the molecular basis and significance of gene pool change over time; i.e., mutations

Early in the 1900s, Hardy and Weinberg determined that the frequency of an allele in a population would not change from generation to generation. This is referred to as the Hardy-Weinberg equilibrium, which can be altered if

- there is migration of a gene into or out of the population (immigration or emigration), or
- there is non-random mating with certain genotypes more likely to leave offspring, or
- the population is very small such that, by chance, a gene disappears or increases in frequency (genetic drift), or
- a mutation adds a new gene to the population, or
- natural selection favours certain genes for survival

When the frequency of the alleles that make up the gene pool of a population changes over time, the population is evolving.

The two Hardy-Weinberg equations are as follows: $p + q = 1.0$, in which p = all the dominant alleles, 1.0 = all the alleles for this trait in the gene pool, and q = all the recessive alleles, and $p^2 + 2pq + q^2 = 1.0$, in which p^2 = all homozygous dominant (e.g. *BB*) individuals

$2pq$ = all heterozygous (e.g. *Bb*) individuals
q^2 = all homozygous recessive (*bb*) individuals
1.0 = all of the individuals of the population

Related Questions: 1, 2, 3, 4, 5, 6, NR3, NR1, NR2

4.2.1.1 describing the basis of symbiotic relationships, i.e., commensalism, mutualism, parasitism, and interspecific and intraspecific competition, and their influences on population changes

4.2.1.2 describing the relationships between predator and prey species and their influence on population changes and by explaining the role of defence mechanisms in predation; e.g., mimicry, protective colouration

4.2.1.3 explaining how mixtures of populations that define communities may change over time or remain as a climax community; e.g., primary succession, secondary succession

4.3.1.1 describing and explaining, quantitatively, factors that influence population growth; i.e., mortality, natality, immigration, emigration

4.3.1.2 describing the growth of populations in terms of the mathematical relationship among carrying capacity, biotic potential, and the number of individuals in the population

4.3.1.3 explaining, quantitatively, the behaviour of populations, using different growth patterns; i.e., r-and K-strategies, J and S curves

4.3.1.4 describing the implications of the chaos theory for the study of biological systems, especially as they relate to population growth patterns

The size of a population is increasing if its natality and immigration exceeds its mortality and emigration. Interspecific competition refers to competition between one population and the population of a different species (e.g., moose and elk). Intraspecific competition involves competition between members of the same species.

Organisms have relationships with organisms of other species. Mutualism, is a relationship in which both organisms benefit. Commensalism is a relationship in which one organism benefits, and the other is unaffected. Parasitism is a relationship in which one organism benefits and the other is harmed.

In predator-prey relationships, the size of both populations fluctuates together. When there are more prey animals, the number of predators can increase. The predators keep the prey population from getting too large, and keep the prey population healthy by feeding on the old weak and sick.

The biotic potential (r) is the maximum rate at which a population can increase its size. All the limiting factors that keep a population from growing at its biotic potential are referred to as environmental resistance. Limiting factors can be density-dependent if the limiting factor has a greater impact when population density is greater. Density-dependent limiting factors tend to be biotic, such as food supply, predators, or disease. Density-independent limiting factors have the same effect on population regardless of the density of the population. These factors tend to be abiotic, such as climate or natural disasters.

The carrying capacity (K) refers to the maximum number of individuals that an environment can support. An r-selected population is one that relies on its high biotic potential. These are typically small, quick-growing organisms that produce large numbers of offspring, provide little parental care, and therefore have a very low survival rate. Their population size can increase rapidly, but will fluctuate wildly and can crash as quickly as it rises.

If released into a new area, an r-selected population will increase rapidly, exceed the carrying capacity, and then crash; as plotted on a graph. This exemplifies a J-shaped curve. A K-selected population relies on a high survival rate to maintain a population size that stays close to the environment's carrying capacity. These are usually large, slow-growing organisms that produce few offspring; and provide more parental care. Their population numbers increase slowly but remain more stable. If released into a new area, a K-selected population will increase slowly to the carrying capacity and level off; as plotted on a graph. This exemplifies an S-shaped curve.

Change in a community over time is called succession. If the community begins on bare rock with a pioneer species such as lichen or moss, and eventually becomes a climax community dominated by one species, this type of sucession is primary succession. If an established community is disrupted by fire or disease and then renews the march toward a climax community, the type of succession is secondary succession. The chaos theory states that it is impossible to take into account all the variables that affect a system as complex as an ecosystem. There will always be a certain amount of randomness that cannot be foreseen.

Related Questions: 7, 8, 13, 15, 23, 28, 9, NR4, 17, 22, 10, 14, 16, 21, 28, 11, 12, 24, 25, NR5, NR6, 18, 19, 20, 26

Use the following information to answer the next question.

The Amish are a group of people who rarely marry outside of their community. In one group of Amish in Ohio, the incidence of cystic fibrosis was 19 in 10 816 live births. A second group of Amish in Ohio had no affected individuals in 4 448 live births. No members of either group are related. These data illustrate what population geneticists refer to as the "founder effect."

from Klinger, 1983

CHALLENGER QUESTION   58.7

1. The "founder effect" seems to occur when

   A. the environment favours one population over another population

   B. a non-representative subpopulation forms the basis for an isolated population

   C. individuals from one population move into and become part of a second population

   D. two similar populations exist in the same community without being reduced in number

Source: January 2000

Use the following information to answer the next question.

The fathead minnow, a small fish common in Alberta waters, is used as a food source by many different predators. When injured, some minnows secrete a chemical (called *schreckstoff*) that both attracts predators and causes other minnows to huddle in large groups. Approaching predators tend to be distracted by the mass of minnows and by each other. Often, the injured minnow can escape.

— from *Gonick*, 1996

CHALLENGER QUESTION   56.5

2. In the future the frequency of the gene that controls the production of *schreckstoff* by minnows will likely

   A. increase in the gene pool of the population

   B. decrease in the gene pool of the population

   C. stay the same in the gene pool of the population because natural selection is occurring

   D. stay the same in the gene pool of the population because natural selection is not occurring

   Source: January 2000

Use the following information to answer the next question.

Many elk live in and around an 80 km^2 area that includes the Jasper town site.

3. If a disease were to kill 90% of these elk (an epidemic), what would be the likely consequence?

   A. The genetic variability in the population would decrease.

   B. The population's resistance to all diseases would increase.

   C. The mutation rate in genes for disease resistance would increase.

   D. The population's gene frequencies would return to pre-epidemic values through genetic drift.

   Source: January 2000

Use the following information to answer the next question.

A community of Pima Indians in the American Southwest has a very high rate of diabetes in their adult population. Of the population of adults over the age of 35, 42% to 66% develop diabetes.
The recessive trait that causes diabetes in this population is a distinct disadvantage to individuals whose diets are rich in carbohydrates.

— from *Cummings*, 1993

CHALLENGER QUESTION   35.5

Numerical Response

1. If 42% of the population has diabetes, then the percentage of the population who are carriers is calculated to be _____ %
(Record your **answer as a whole number.**)

Source: January 2000

Use the following information to answer the next two questions.

A high percentage of purebred dogs have genetic defects. Some examples of these defects follow.

1. Hip dysplasia, a defect in the hip joints that can cripple a dog, occurs in 60% of golden retrievers.
2. Hereditary deafness, due to a recessive autosomal disorder, occurs in 30% of Dalmatians.
3. Retinal disease, which may cause blindness, occurs in 70% of collies.
4. Hemophilia, an X-linked recessive disorder, is common in Labrador retrievers. Dwarfism is also common in this breed of dog.

— from *Lemonick*, 1994

CHALLENGER QUESTION   36.3

Numerical Response

2. What is the frequency of the abnormal allele that causes hearing defects in Dalmatians?
Answer: _____. (Record your **answer as a value from 0 to 1, rounded to two decimal places.**)

Source: January 2001

---

4. The breeding of purebred dogs for certain characteristics related to appearance is blamed for the disturbing number of genetic defects in these animals. These defects are **most likely** the result of

   A. natural selection

   B. non-random mating

   C. geographic isolation

   D. high rates of mutation

   Source: January 2001

Use the following information to answer the next question.

Tay-Sachs disease is a hereditary disease that kills 1 in 360 000 individuals in the general population, but 1 in 4 800 among the Ashkenazi (Eastern European) Jews. The disease disrupts or halts proper formation of lysosomes and increases fat deposition around the nerve sheath. Individuals that are homozygous for the defective allele have Tay-Sachs disease and die at an early age. Studies suggest that heterozygous individuals have a higher survival rate against tuberculosis than the rest of the population. Biochemical tests can be done to determine if parents are carriers.

– from Cummings, 1994

5. If tuberculosis regained its former role as one of the world's deadliest diseases, then the frequency of the Tay-Sachs allele over time would

   A. decrease because of a decreased selective advantage

   B. increase because of an increased selective advantage

   C. decrease because of an increased selective advantage

   D. remain the same as a result of Hardy–Weinberg equilibrium

   Source: January 2001

6. The flowers of the organ pipe cactus open during the night and close during the day to avoid dehydration during the heat of the day. This adaptation of the cacti to the desert climate **most likely** occurred as a result of

   A. increased mutation rates in flowers stimulated by high temperatures

   B. increased reproductive success of cacti with flowers that opened at night

   C. the intense heat of the desert, which destroyed all flowers that opened during the day and caused the cacti to open its flowers at night

   D. the reaction of the cacti to the extreme heat, which caused it to close its flowers during the day and to gradually develop the behaviour of opening its flowers at night

   Source: January 2001

Use the following information to answer the next question.

Terms and Description Related to Populations		
Term	**Effect of Small Population**	**Result of Rebuilt Population**
1 Carrying capacity	4 Increased mutation rate	7 Hardy-Weinberg equilibrium
2 Chaos theory	5 Chance loss of genes	8 Secondary succession to a different climax community
3 Genetic drift	6 Increased intraspecific competition	9 Reduced genetic variability

CHALLENGER QUESTION 39.9

Numerical Response

3. Drastic reduction of a population raises the concern that a rebuilt population may show significant differences from the original population. Identify the term, effect, and result, as numbered above, that describe this concern.

Answer: _____ _____ _____

        Term   **Effect**   **Result**

Source: January 2001

Use the following information to answer the next question.

The spermicide nonoxynol-9, which is applied to contraceptive devices such as diaphragms and condoms, has been linked to increased urinary tract infections in women. Although nonoxynol-9 is helpful in fighting the herpes virus and HIV, it also destroys beneficial bacteria (lactobacilli) that moderate the acidity of a woman's vagina.

As a woman's vagina and external genitalia become more acidic, another bacterium, *Escherichia coli* (*E. coli*), increases in number and invades her urethra. This overpopulation of *E. coli* causes a bladder infection.

– from *Vergano*, 1996

7. Which of the following rows identifies the relationships described above between the human female, lactobacilli, and *E. coli*?

Row	Human female/ lactobacilli	Human female/ E.coli	Lactobacilli/ E.coli
A.	parasitic	mutualistic	interspecific competition
B.	mutualistic	mutualistic	interspecific competition
C.	mutualistic	parasitic	interspecific competition
D.	parasitic	parasitic	interspecific competition

Source: January 2000

Use the following information to answer the next question.

In winter, snowshoe hares found in Jasper National Park create pathways in the snow between feeding and resting sites. These travel lanes are then used by porcupines, making the porcupines' movement through deep snow easier.

8. What relationship exists between the snowshoe hare and the porcupine?

   A. Mutualism

   B. Predator-prey

   C. Commensalism

   D. Intraspecific competition

Source: January 2000

Use the following information to answer the next question.

In areas where moose and caribou share habitat, they are both preyed upon by wolves. The population cycle of the moose is affected by the presence of a second prey species, the caribou.

– from *Mech*, 1996

9. A reasonable prediction based on these predator-prey relationships is that

   A. predator species would not show population changes caused by density-dependent factors

   B. low numbers of caribou would cause wolf starvation if the moose population was also low

   C. wolf and prey populations would decline as the same diseases spread through the three populations

   D. an area would have the same carrying capacity for moose as it has for caribou, even though each species has different food preferences

Source: January 2000

Use the following information to answer the next question.

A Possible location	B Community present	C Number of species
1 in an area clear cut by logging	1 pioneer	1 increase
2 on land bared by a forest fire	2 climax	2 decrease
3 on land released from a retreating glacier		

The following table describes characteristics of communities.

Numerical Response

4. Use the numbered phrases or words from columns, *A*, *B*, and *C* above to complete the statements below. Primary succession would occur __A__ , where the first organisms present are called a __B__ community. During the first 20 years in the development of a community, the number of species would be expected to __C__ .
Answer: ___ ___ ___
Letter: *A* *B* *C*

Source: January 2000

Use the following information to answer the next four questions.

A group of ecologists have studied the Jasper National Park animal populations and gathered data related to the growth of these populations.

J- and S-shaped Growth Curves of Theoretical Populations

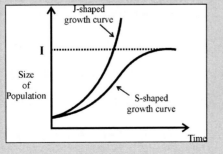

10. Ecological data gathered over a 20-year period indicate that the elk population fluctuates around the level marked **I** on the graph. The biotic factors that keep this population stabilized are

A. density dependent

B. density independent

C. independent of natality and mortality

D. independent of emigration and immigration

Source: January 2000

11. The level marked **I** on the graph represents the effect of factors such as climate, nutrients, soils, and water on the size of the elk population. A term to describe this section of the growth curve is

A. lag phase

B. biotic potential

C. carrying capacity

D. climax community

Source: January 2000

Use the following information to answer the next question.

Many elk live in and around an 80 km^2 area that includes the Jasper town site.

12. The elk population of this area at the beginning of a study year was 500. If there were 35 births and 5 deaths throughout the year, what was the per capita growth rate for the elk population during that year?

A. 0.03

B. 0.06

C. 6

D. 30

Source: January 2000

Use the following additional information to answer the next question.

Data generated by ecologists working in Jasper National Park are used by park planners. Identifying a population as *r*-selected or *K*-selected may aid in wildlife management. Populations of caribou, elk, and wolves have been studied extensively.

Population Characteristic	Population Descriptors
Offspring Number	1 Few offspring 2 Large numbers of offspring
Body Size	3 Small in size 4 Large in size
Reproductive Maturity	5 Early reproductive 6 Delayed reproductive maturity
Lifespan	7 Long lifespan 8 Short lifespan

Numerical Response

5. Identify the population descriptor, as numbered above, that **best** matches each of the population characteristics below for a *K*-selected population such as the caribou or elk.

Population Descriptor:	____	____	____	____
Population Characteristics:	Offspring Number	Body Size	Reproductive Maturity	Lifespan

Source: January 2000

Use the following information to answer the next question.

A Predator-Prey Relationship				
Location	Animal 1	Animal 2	Density of Predators (Number per 100 km²)	Number of Prey
Northwest Territories	Wolf	Caribou	0.3	500 000

CHALLENGER QUESTION   **48.1**

Numerical Response

6. The size of the wolf population in an area of $6\ 000\ km^2$ of the Northwest Territories is calculated to be _____ wolves.
(Record your **answer as a whole number.**)

Source: January 2000

Use the following information to answer the next question.

Some members of a porpoise population living off the northeast coast of Scotland have been found dead washed up on shore, the victims of violent, high-energy impacts. Zoologists have identified scratches on the dead porpoises that match the teeth of an unlikely killer, the bottle-nosed dolphin, long assumed to be playful and gentle. These two cetaceans (aquatic mammals), which share the same range and food supply, were thought to coexist peacefully.

– from *Discover*, 1996

13. What type of relationship do the bottle-nosed dolphin and the harbour porpoise exhibit?

    A. Symbiotic

    B. Predator-prey

    C. Intraspecific competition

    D. Interspecific competition

Source: June 2000

Use the following information to answer the next three questions.

Pacific herring play a key role in the marine food web of Canada's West Coast. They are prey fish and comprise 30% to 70% of the summer diets of Chinook salmon, Pacific cod, lingcod, and harbour seals in the coastal waters of southern British Columbia. The eggs of Pacific herring are important to the diets of migrating sea birds, gray whales, and some invertebrates. Pacific herring are not mature enough to spawn until age three. Spawning takes place in coastal areas where algae beds are abundant and the water is uncontaminated.

CHALLENGER QUESTION   42.7

14. Which of the following factors is an example of a density-independent factor that influences Pacific herring survival and growth?

    A. Algae populations

    B. Ocean temperatures

    C. Population of grey whales

    D. Imposition of fishing quotas

Source: June 2000

CHALLENGER QUESTION   45.6

15. In the mid-1960s, a combination of intense fishing harvests and unfavourable ocean conditions caused the Pacific herring population to decline drastically. Which of the following rows shows the changes in relationships, after this decline, that were probably exhibited among organisms that prey on the Pacific herring?

Row	Interspecific Competition	Intraspecific Competition
A.	decrease	decrease
B.	decrease	increase
C.	increase	decrease
D.	increase	increase

Source: June 2000

CHALLENGER QUESTION   34.5

16. Salmon fishing is an important industry on the West Coast of Canada. If the salmon population were to decrease because of overfishing, the Pacific herring population would probably remain relatively stable if other predators showed which of the following changes?

    A. Increased mortality and decreased emigration

    B. Decreased mortality and increased emigration

    C. Increased mortality and decreased immigration

    D. Decreased mortality and increased immigration

Source: June 2000

Use the following information to answer the next question.

Composition of a Forest Undisturbed for 67 Years

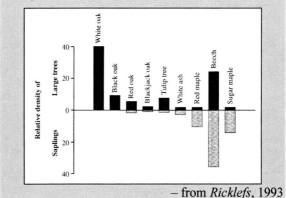

– from *Ricklefs*, 1993

CHALLENGER QUESTION   58.0

17. In which of the following ways would you expect this forest to change in the next 50 years?

    A. The relative density of all trees will increase.

    B. There will be an emergence of coniferous trees such as spruce or pine.

    C. There will be an increase in the relative density of beech and a decrease in the relative density of white oak.

    D. The relative density of blackjack oak, white ash, red maple, and sugar maple will decrease as a result of competition from the larger trees.

Source: June 2000

Use the following information to answer the next question.

Cystic fibrosis is a recessive Mendelian trait in the human population. A symptom of cystic fibrosis is the production of large amounts of mucin protein. New studies indicate that although the cystic fibrosis condition is present at birth, increased mucin production is preceded by an infection with the bacterium *Pseudomonas aeruginosa*. Individuals who are not affected by cystic fibrosis produce a natural antibiotic, defensin, that kills the *Pseudomonas aeruginosa* and eliminates the stimulus for increased mucin production. Defensin is destroyed by a high chloride content in the tissues of individuals with cystic fibrosis as a result of faulty chloride-channel proteins.

– from *Sternberg*, 1997

CHALLENGER QUESTION   **45.8**

18. In a normal individual, the population of *Pseudomonas aeruginosa* exhibits which of the following population growth curves following initial infection of the individual?

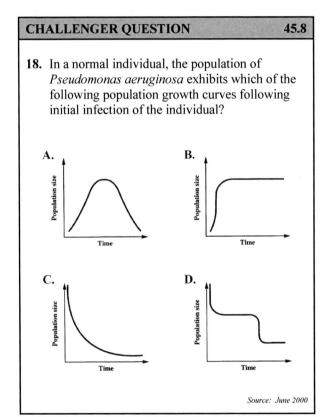

Source: June 2000

Use the following information to answer the next two questions.

The 42 000 wild horses and donkeys that live in the American West are reproducing at such a high rate that they could severely damage range lands in the future. In an effort to prevent overpopulation, some mares (females) are rounded up and injected with porcine zona pellucida (PZP), a long-lasting contraceptive. U.S. Food and Drug Administration guidelines prohibit the use of PZP until after a wild mare has had at least one successful pregnancy.

– from *McInnis*, 1996

19. Wild horses are considered to be a relatively *K*-selected species; however, one characteristic exhibited by these wild horses that is similar to an *r*-selected species is

 A. their large size

 B. their relatively long lifespan

 C. their relatively high reproductive potential

 D. the large amount of parental care devoted to their offspring

Source: June 2000

20. Assuming that the contraceptive program manages the wild horse population successfully, which of the following graphs would **best** represent the wild horse population growth curve over time?

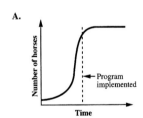
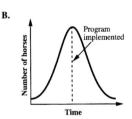
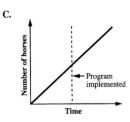
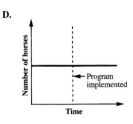

Source: June 2000

Use the following information to answer the next two questions.

The location of the Sonoran Desert results in unique climatic conditions. It has a warmer average temperature, less frequent frosts, and more rainfall than other deserts. This unique climate results in more diversity in the organisms that occupy this particular desert.

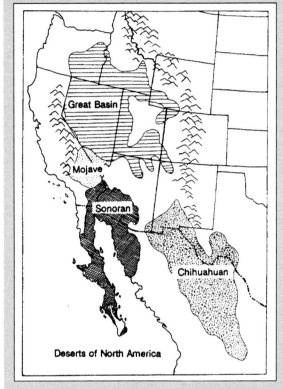

Deserts of North America

– from *Naylor*, 1995

21. The factors that contribute most to the relatively great diversity of organisms in the Sonoran Desert as compared with that in other deserts are

A. biotic factors that increase the biotic potential

B. abiotic factors that reduce reproductive isolation

C. abiotic factors that reduce environmental resistance

D. biotic factors that increase the carrying capacity of the area

Source: January 2001

22. In the Sonoran Desert, all the populations of all the organisms occupying that desert represent

A. a habitat

B. a community

C. a geographic range

D. an ecological niche

Source: January 2001

Use the following information to answer the next question.

Organ Pipe Cactus

The organ pipe cactus has flowers that open at night. Bats and insects pollinate these flowers. The fruit of the cactus is eaten by birds and small mammals. Birds and small mammals scatter and distribute the fruit seeds. The coyote, in turn, feeds on the birds and small mammals.

– from *Naylor*, 1995

23. The relationships described above between the organ pipe cactus and insects, and between the organ pipe cactus and small mammals are identified in row

Row	Cactus and Insects	Cactus and Small Mammals
A.	predator-prey	predator-prey
B.	predator-prey	mutualism
C.	mutualism	mutualism
D.	mutualism	predator-prey

Source: January 2001

Use the following information to answer the next three questions.

In Canada, to manage the harvest of fish, government departments issue quotas based on population estimates. Problems in salmon and cod fisheries have drawn attention to problems in the calculation of the estimates. Quotas based on these estimates have led to overharvesting and have driven the cod fishery into disaster.

CHALLENGER QUESTION	43.1

24. The carrying capacity for northern cod in Canada's Atlantic region may be described as the

    A. harvest quota that permits sustainable yield

    B. harvest quota that matches the natural mortality of the cod

    C. decline on a growth curve that shows the population size dropping

    D. plateau on a growth curve that shows the population size has reached a limit

Source: January 2001

25. The Atlantic cod moratorium was a government-enforced period of no fishing. The original two-year moratorium was extended. Which of the following measures would be **most useful** when predicting the size of the cod population two years in the future?

    A. Cod lifespan and natality rate

    B. Cod biotic potential and future fishing quotas

    C. Migration patterns and predator population size

    D. Present population size and present population growth rate

Source: January 2001

26. When fisheries' quotas were set too high, it may have been because assumptions were made by government regulators that led them to expect cod stocks to grow rapidly after harvest. One such assumption could have been that cod

    A. have low fecundity and high mortality

    B. are relatively *r*-selected with a high biotic potential

    C. have high competition and density independent natality

    D. are relatively *K*-selected in regions of high environmental resistance

Source: January 2001

Use the following information to answer the next two questions.

The red-winged blackbird's adaptability has allowed it to become one of the most abundant birds in North America.

A Study of a Red–Winged Blackbird Nesting Site

The initial population of red-winged blackbirds was 208.

	End of Year 1	End of Year 2
Births	22	43
Deaths	4	7
Birds entering area	0	2
Birds leaving area	2	5

27. A conclusion about this nesting site study is that the red-winged blackbird population increased because

    A. natality plus immigration exceeded mortality plus emigration

    B. mortality plus emigration exceeded natality plus immigration

    C. natality plus emigration exceeded mortality plus immigration

    D. mortality plus immigration exceeded natality plus emigration

Source: January 2001

28. Gause's principle states that when two different populations occupy the same ecological niche, one of the populations will be eliminated. Both the mallard duck and the red-winged blackbird occupy wetland areas. The duck and the red-winged blackbird can live in the same habitat because there is

    A. little intraspecific competition for food and breeding areas

    B. little interspecific competition for food and breeding areas

    C. significant intraspecific competition for food and breeding areas

    D. significant interspecific competition for food and breeding areas

Source: January 2001

UNIT TEST 4 – POPULATION GENETICS AND INTERACTION

Use the following information to answer the next two questions.

Sickle cell anemia is caused by the sickle cell allele (Hb^s) of a gene that contributes to hemoglobin (Hb) production. The abnormal hemoglobin (hemoglobin-S) produced causes red blood cells to become deformed and block capillaries. Tissue damage results. Affected individuals homozygous for the sickle cell gene rarely survive to reproductive age. Heterozygous individuals produce both normal hemoglobin and a small percentage of hemoglobin-S. These individuals are more resistant to malaria than individuals who are homozygous for the allele for normal hemoglobin (Hb^A). Their red blood cells are prone to sickling when there is a deficiency of oxygen.

The malaria-causing microorganism *Plasmodium falciparum* is injected by mosquitoes into the bloodstream of humans. Historically, the frequency of the Hb^s allele in Africa relates directly to the presence of malaria-causing organisms. In western Africa, the frequency of the Hb^s allele in the gene pool is 0.15. In central Africa, the frequency is 0.10, and in southern Africa, the frequency is 0.05.

1. Which of the following conclusions can be drawn from all the information provided on sickle cell anemia?

   A. The sickle cell gene will eventually disappear because of its interaction with malaria.

   B. Malaria causes heterozygous individuals to be less fertile than homozygous individuals.

   C. In Africa, sickle cell anemia will disappear since it is lethal in the homozygous condition.

   D. In Africa, carriers for sickle cell anemia have an advantage over homozygous individuals.

2. What is the frequency of the Hb^A allele in the human gene pool in western Africa?

   A. 0.72   B. 0.85

   C. 0.90   D. 0.95

Use the following information to answer the next question.

Weeds, insect pests, and disease result in a loss of about 45% of the world's food supply annually. The use of insecticides and herbicides reduces the loss of food supply.

3. The most serious drawback of using chemicals to control pests is that most pest populations, especially insects, develop genetic resistance to chemicals. How do insect populations develop this resistance and pass it to offspring?

   A. Mutations and natural selection give some insects an advantage, and eventually gene frequencies change until most have the trait.

   B. Through use of restriction enzymes and ligases, new sequences of DNA are created and passed to offspring.

   C. The pesticides cause the synthesis of new proteins with altered amino acid sequences.

   D. The offspring of insects that learned to avoid the spray also learn to avoid the spray.

Use the following information to answer the next question.

A program to detect carriers of ß-thalassemia (a mild blood disorder) found the incidence of the disease to be 4% in a particular population. A recessive allele found on an autosomal chromosome causes ß-thalassemia.

CHALLENGER QUESTION   **44.4**

Numerical Response

1. What is the frequency of the recessive ß-thalassemia allele in the gene pool of this population?
(Record your **answer as a value from 0 to 1, rounded to one decimal place.**)

Answer: _____

Use the following information to answer the next five questions.

From 1968 to 1990, the population of snow geese nesting near Churchill, Manitoba, increased from about 2 000 pairs (4 000 individuals) to about 22 500 pairs (45 000 individuals) with a nesting density of around 1 000 nests per square mile. Snow geese winter along the coasts of Texas and Louisiana. Prior to 1960, marshes along these coasts provided the main food sources (reeds, roots, and tubers) for the geese. Destruction of these marshes and increased crop production of rice, corn, and soybeans has occurred since that time. The stubble from these crops and spilled grains are easily obtained food sources for the snow geese. Reduction in hunting and greatly increased food supplies from cultivation near their wintering ground has cut mortality rates of snow geese in half over this period.

The high nesting density of the snow geese has left little foraging or nesting space for other species of birds, and a decline in several duck species and shore birds has been observed. Simultaneously, intensive foraging by the snow geese erodes and dries out patches of Arctic soil, reduces regrowth of grasses and sedges, and greatly increases soil salinity.

— from *Brodie*, 1997

CHALLENGER QUESTION   58.4

4. Given a further increase in the snow goose population, in the Churchill, Manitoba, nesting area

    A. interspecific competition will increase because of decreased species diversity

    B. interspecific competition will increase and intraspecific competition will decrease

    C. intraspecific competition will increase because available food supplies are decreasing

    D. intraspecific competition will decrease because fewer snow geese will be able to find nesting sites

5. Prior to 1960, the winter food sources in the marshes controlled the growth of the snow goose population. The available supply of reeds, roots, and tubers in the marshes was

    A. an example of a community of climax species

    B. an example of a community of pioneer species

    C. a density-dependent limiting factor for snow geese

    D. a density-independent limiting factor for snow geese

CHALLENGER QUESTION   19.2

Numerical Response

2. Based on the information provided, what is the per capital growth rate of the snow goose population between 1968 and 1990? _____
(Record your **answer rounded to one decimal place.**)

CHALLENGER QUESTION   49.5

6. To preserve the diversity of this ecosystem, the first logical human intervention would be to

    A. extend the hunting season and increase collection of snow goose eggs

    B. replant or reseed grasses and sedges depleted by snow goose foraging

    C. reintroduce the duck species and shore bird species that have disappeared from the coastal marshes

    D. prevent soil erosion by introducing plant species adapted to high salinity in order to anchor the top soil

CHALLENGER QUESTION   **45.1**

7. Based on the information provided, it would be reasonable to conclude that the snow goose population

     A. has increased its biotic potential

     B. has a higher mortality than natality rate

     C. is in a growth phase and environmental resistance is increasing

     D. has reached the carrying capacity of the ecosystem and environmental resistance is decreasing

Use the following information to answer the next question.

Examples of Ecological Relationships

1 Tropical acacia trees are hosts to a particular species of ants. The ants are provided with shelter and nutrients from the trees. The trees are protected from other predatory insects by the ants.

2 The protozoan *Opalina ranarum* lives in the digestive tract of some frogs and obtains nutrients in this way without harming the frog.

3 The protozoan *Plasmodium* is the cause of malaria. *Plasmodium* lives in the bloodstream of humans and reproduces inside red blood cells causing the red blood cells to burst.

Numerical Response

3. Match the ecological relationships, as numbered above, with the types of symbiosis given below. (Record your answer to **three-digits**.)

Type of Symbiosis: Ecological Relationship:

Commensalism   _____

Mutualism   _____

Parasitism   _____

Use the following information to answer the next three questions.

People living in certain tropical countries are at risk of becoming infected by guinea worms. An adult female worm lives under the skin in the human body where it grows up to 90 cm in length. An infected person shows no symptoms until the worm comes to the surface to release its larvae. When it emerges, the worm releases a toxin that causes a painful, burning blister that is relieved by immersion in cool water. When the blister is submerged, the worm releases its young. Over several weeks, the adult worm works its way out of the body.

During that time, infected people suffer and cannot work or go to school. People can be infected by drinking water that is contaminated by water fleas, the small aquatic animals in which the worm completes other parts of its life cycle.

Eradication Success in an African Village

The African village of Katri has a population of about 3 000 people. At the end of 1981, the village began a health education program about guinea worms. In 1984, new water wells were dug in the village. The chart below shows the number of people infected with guinea worms from 1981 to 1990.

Year	Number of Cases of Infection
1981	928
1982	535
1983	263
1984	125
1985	7
1986	2
1987	5
1988	0
1989	0
1990	0

–adapted from *Nuttall*, 1995

8. Which of the following rows best illustrates the relationship of guinea worms to both humans and water fleas?

Row	Guinea worm	Human	Water flea
A.	parasite	host	host
B.	parasite	host	prey
C.	predator	prey	prey
D.	predator	prey	host

9. Total elimination of the water fleas in places where guinea worms are a problem would result in

A. more infected people since the larvae would now infect people directly

B. fewer infected people since the guinea worm's life cycle would be broken

C. more infected people because the guinea worm's life cycle would be shorter

D. fewer infected people because there would be no way for the larvae to enter the water

---

CHALLENGER QUESTION   **38.6**

10. A correct interpretation of the data collected in Katri is that the problem of guinea worm infection

A. has been eliminated in African countries either through public education programs or by providing clean well-water

B. has been eliminated in African countries by providing educational programs and supplies of clean drinking water

C. could be eliminated either through public education programs or by providing clean well-water

D. could be eliminated by providing educational programs and sources of clean drinking water

---

11. Which of the following relationships would be considered to be a mutualistic relationship?

A. The myxoma virus was introduced to control the rabbit population in Australia.

B. The abandoned burrows of woodpeckers often become nesting sites for bluebirds.

C. Blowfly eggs, laid on the skin of sheep, develop into larvae that feed on sheep tissues.

D. The stomachs of cattle contain large populations of bacteria that aid in the digestion of cellulose.

12. When limited food supplies have threatened to check human population growth, people have used technology and social organization to clear forests, plow grasslands, grow crops, and harness science to agriculture. This indicates that food is

A. a biotic factor that humans can manipulate

B. an abiotic factor that humans can manipulate

C. a biotic factor that humans cannot manipulate

D. an abiotic factor that humans cannot manipulate

Use the following information to answer the next question.

At the global level, the human population growth rate has been changing at a rapid speed.

Estimates of World Population Growth Rates

1750	Population doubling every 100 years
1970	Population doubling every 34 years
1990	Population doubling every 40 years

– from *Luttwak*, 1996

CHALLENGER QUESTION   **51.7**

13. The change in world human population growth rate from 1970 to 1990 was probably **most influenced** by

A. food supplies

B. carrying capacity

C. population density

D. birth control measures

---

14. The rapidly growing human population is endangering populations of *K*-strategists while favouring *r*-strategists. Examples of *K*-strategists and *r*-strategists are, respectively,

A. whales and houseflies

B. elephants and spruce trees

C. cockroaches and dandelions

D. mosquitoes and woodpeckers

Use the following graph to answer the next question.

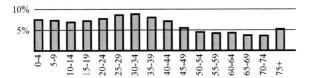

Population of Country X by age – 1990

15. According to the data above, in which of the following decades would the cost of health care for seniors (age 65 and over) create the greatest governmental concern?

   A. 1990 – 2000

   B. 2000 – 2010

   C. 2020 – 2030

   D. 2040 – 2050

Use the following information to answer the next question.

A swimming pool 50 m long and 20 m wide is filled with water to a depth of 3 m. The population density of bacteria in the water is 2.5×10^6 bacteria/m^3.

16. Approximately how many bacteria are there in the swimming pool?

   A. 2.5×10^9

   B. 7.5×10^9

   C. 2.5×10^{12}

   D. 7.5×10^{12}

WRITTEN RESPONSE

Use the following information to answer the next question.

Sperm count is measured in millions of sperm per millilitre of semen. The normal amount of ejaculate is 3 mL, and 30 to 100 million sperm/mL is considered within the normal range. A generation ago, 100 million sperm/mL was considered normal. A male whose sperm concentration falls below 20 million sperm/mL is likely infertile.

While working at the National University Hospital in Copenhagen, Denmark, Niels Skakkebaek prepared a report that combined the results of 61 separate studies of sperm count and quality over the last 50 years. His report was based on data involving a total of 14 947 men from 21 countries, including the United States, Europe, Asia, and Africa. His results showed that the average sperm count had fallen from 113 million sperm/mL in 1940 to 66 million sperm/mL in 1990. French research also showed a decline, on average, from 89 million sperm/mL in 1973 to 60 million sperm/mL in 1992. A Scottish study of 600 men showed a 2% decrease in the average sperm count each year for the past two decades. Skakkebaek also reported that the lowest sperm counts are in younger men and that the proportion of their deformed sperm is steadily rising.

Research on conditions during pregnancy or immediately after birth that could reduce the number of certain cells within the testes, called Sertoli cells, may help explain the reported decline in sperm counts. The number of Sertoli cells that a male possesses establishes an upper limit on sperm production, as these cells nourish immature sperm. The number of Sertoli cells is fixed in the fetal or newborn stage of human development, when the multiplication of these cells is catalysed by FSH. Dr. Richard Sharpe, of the Medical Research Council's Reproductive Biology Unit in Edinburgh, is investigating whether low sperm counts may be related to a reduction in the number of Sertoli cells in males

Estrogen-mimicking compounds found in the environment inhibit FSH production. People worldwide are exposed to thousands of chemicals, some of which mimic the effects of naturally produced estrogen. These chemicals include aromatic hydrocarbons produced by combustion, PCBs, and DDT.

– from *Nichols*, 1996,
Moomaw, 1996, *Stainsby*, 1996,
Raloff, 1994, *Lambton*, 1993

1. a) Write a hypothesis that relates sperm count to estrogen-mimicking compounds in the environment. **(2 marks)**

b) i) Draw and label a flow chart that illustrates the production of FSH and its effect on Sertoli cell development in male babies. Include all relevant organs and hormones. **(2 marks)**

ii) On the flow chart you have drawn, indicate the proposed effect of estrogen-mimicking compounds on FSH production and Sertoli cell development. **(1 mark)**

c) At low levels, estrogen-mimicking compounds in the environment appear to be harmful to fetuses but not to adults. Describe a possible reason for the greater sensitivity of fetuses to these compounds. **(1 mark)**

d) i) Using the data from the French research, calculate the percentage decrease in sperm count from the original value in 1973 to the value in 1992. (Show all calculations.) **(1 mark)**

ii) Predict a possible effect on French society or the French population if this trend continues. **(1 mark)**

e) Given that only one sperm fertilizes an egg, describe two reasons why a man with a sperm count of less than 20 million sperm/mL is likely infertile. **(2 marks)**

f) The effects of estrogen-mimicking compounds on sperm counts are not well established by scientists.

i) What is one possible question you would need answered before you could decide if there is a cause-and-effect relationship between environmental estrogen-mimicking compounds and lowered sperm counts? **(1 mark)**

ii) How would an answer to this question help you evaluate whether this is a cause-and-effect relationship? **(1 mark)**

Source: January 1999

Use the following information to answer the next question.

Ataxia telangiectasia (AT) is an autosomal recessive disorder occurring with an estimated frequency of 1 in 40 000 births. The first symptoms of the disease occur around two years of age and are progressive; they consist of a lack of balance and slurred speech. Soon after, tiny red (spider) veins appear in the corners of the eyes (telangiectasis). Older children with AT lose their ability to write, and reading becomes impossible as eye movements become difficult to control. Individuals are eventually confined to a wheelchair. Immune system disorders are common. Intelligence is normal in these individuals. Most individuals with AT die as children; however, some live up to 50 years.

Patients with AT develop blood system cancers 1 000 times more frequently than the general population. Treatment of cancer with conventional dosages of radiation can be fatal to AT patients because they are especially sensitive to radiation, which causes breakage of DNA. Even carriers have a higher incidence of cancer than does the general population.

The defect causing AT has been traced to a mutation on chromosome 11. The protein product of this gene is not expressed appropriately. The exact role of the gene remains a mystery. Normal cells respond to DNA damage by interrupting the cell cycle in interphase before DNA synthesis occurs. This allows for repair of the DNA. Scientists are investigating a link between the AT mutation and this cell repair process.

There is presently no cure for AT, but treatments to alleviate symptoms are currently being developed.

– from *NCBI*, 1997
A-T Children's Project,1997

2. Write a unified response addressing the following aspects of ataxia telangiectasia (AT).

- **Sketch** a diagram of the human brain and **label** four parts. **Identify** the area of the brain most affected by AT. **Identify** the symptoms of AT that relate to degeneration of this area of the brain, and **explain** how these symptoms indicate that this area of the brain has degenerated.

- **Identify** several environmental causes of DNA damage. **Explain** how interruption of the repair process in AT might lead to cancer.
- **Calculate** the frequency of the AT allele **and** the percentage of the population that are carriers. (Show your work.) **Identify** and **explain** how two societal factors and/or technologies could decrease the incidence of the AT disorder in the population of future generations or alleviate the symptoms of AT in individuals.

Source: January 1999

Use the following information to answer the next question.

On April 26, 1986, one of the worst technological, industrial, and environmental disasters known to humankind occurred. A nuclear reactor in Chernobyl exploded and showered radioactive debris over much of Eastern Europe. The extent of the environmental and health effects of the nuclear legacy of the Chernobyl disaster are still unknown.

Although the exact causes of many illnesses are not understood, there is little doubt that the enormous burst of radiation released from the reactor has had devastating effects on thousands of children. One of the most dangerous radioactive products released was iodine-131. It was inhaled by many children, exposing them to high levels of radiation. Iodine-131 was absorbed by the children's thyroid glands, causing inflammation of the gland and an increased incidence of thyroid cancer. Normally, iodine is absorbed from the blood by the thyroid gland in its synthesis of thyroxine.

The effects of this radiation over a long period of time were also studied. Researchers looked at DNA gene sequences five to 45 bases long from blood samples taken from parents and their children born in 1994 or later. They looked for any sequence in the child's DNA that did not occur in the blood cells of either parent. The children born near Chernobyl had twice as many of these mutations in their DNA as had the control group, which consisted of families in England whose children were also born in or after 1994.

– from *Monmaney*, 1996; *Shcherbak*, 1996

3. **a)** Explain one function of thyroxine.

(1 mark)

b) Draw a feedback loop that illustrates the regulation of the release of thyroxine. Include relevant glands and hormones.

(3 marks)

c) Thyroid cancer in infants can be treated by surgical removal of the thyroid gland. Identify two signs and/or symptoms that would indicate or would be caused by the absence of thyroxine in such an infant.

(2 marks)

d) The children exposed to radioactive iodine because of the nuclear accident were treated with high levels of non-radioactive iodine. Explain why this treatment was used.

(1 mark)

e) Describe and sketch one type of error at the molecular level of DNA that results in a mutation. (Create a hypothetical strand of DNA bases, then show the strand again, illustrating and clearly marking the change causing the error.)

(3 marks)

f) The evidence presented in the last paragraph of the reading suggests that mutations occurred in one of the parents' germ-line cells (precursor cells to oocytes or sperm cells). Describe how the germ-line cell mutations appeared in the children's white blood cells.

(2 marks)

Source: June 1999

Use the following information to answer the next question.

There is a worldwide shortage of organs for transplanting into humans. Some researchers are concentrating on xenotransplantation – using organs from other species – as a solution.

The pig is considered by researchers as the most suitable donor of transplant organs for humans, even though pigs are not as closely related genetically to humans as higher primates are. Pigs can be bred easily and up to three times a year. Sows have short pregnancies (about 115 days) and give birth to large litters. The offspring grow quickly to reach a large size.

Transplanted organs from ordinary pigs are quickly rejected by the human immune system. Researchers have isolated a human gene, called HDAF, that codes for a cell membrane protein known as RCA. The human HDAF gene can be inserted into pig DNA so the human RCA protein will be present on the surface of pig cells. Human RCA protein on cell membranes of pig cells is expected to inhibit the rejection of pig organs when they are transplanted into humans. A pig that has the human gene in all of its cells is referred to as a transgenic pig.

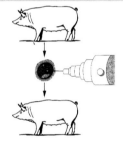

Fertilized eggs are harvested from a sow

Injection of HDAF gene into the nuclei of the fertilized eggs

Identification of heterozygote transgenic offspring (shaded grey) expressing RCA protein their organs

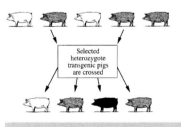

Selected heterozygote transgenic pigs are crossed

Identification of homozygote transgenic offspring (shaded dark grey) expressing RCA protein in their organs

* Approximately 60% of these offspring were transgenic heterozygotes

– from *Lanza, Cooper and Chick*, 1997; *Cozzi and White Hunter*, 1996

4. Write a unified response that addresses the following aspects of the use of pigs as a source of organs for transplantation.

Compare the biotic potential of pig populations with that of other mammals, such as primates or humans. **Explain** how two traits of pigs would have influenced researchers to choose pigs as the most suitable animals for xenotransplantation.

Describe one technology that researchers would have used to obtain the HDAF gene. **Explain**, in detail, what happens after the HDAF gene is injected into fertilized eggs to produce heterozygote transgenic offspring and normal offspring.

Explain why researchers performed crosses of heterozygote offspring and **explain** the observed outcome of these crosses using a Punnett Square to clarify your explanation.

Source: June 1999

Use the following information to answer the next question.

Scientists are working hard to learn about causes of cancers. It is known that in general terms cancer-causing agents produce mutations in a variety of genes that control cell reproduction.

Cancer can be caused by organisms. For example, when some viruses infect a human cell, the viral DNA may insert itself randomly into the DNA of human cells.

Of all the cancer-causing agents to which humans are commonly exposed, tobacco smoke appears to have caused the greatest harm. It is directly responsible for 30% of all cancer deaths in North America. Heavy smoking increases the likelihood of getting lung cancer by 2 000%. Passive (secondhand) smoke is less likely to cause cancer. It is about as harmful as all other forms of air pollution.

– from *Trichopoulos, Li, and Hunter*, 1996

5. **a)** A reasonable question for a researcher to ask would be "What percentage of smokers will die from cancer caused by tobacco smoke?" Assume that in a study to answer this question, you gather two groups of subjects and observe them over a long period of time.

i) Identify the manipulated variable and the responding variable for your study.

(2 marks)

ii) Identify two variables that you would be unable to control, and explain why these variables would influence the conclusions of your study.

(3 marks)

b) Hypothesize how viral infection of human cells may lead to cancer.

(2 marks)

Use the following additional information to answer the next part of the question.

Four percent of all cancer deaths can be linked to the reproductive history of a woman. Researchers have discovered that if a woman begins to menstruate at an early age and experiences late menopause, she is more likely to develop cancer in her reproductive organs. If a woman has several children and gave birth to them at a younger age, she is less likely to develop cancer of the ovary, breast, or endometrium.

– from *Trichopoulos, Li, and Hunter*, 1996

c) **i)** Identify a social or economic change in Canadian society over the past few decades that could have had an impact on the rate of cancer in women's reproductive systems. **(1 mark)**

ii) Describe how this change could affect the frequency of cancer in the reproductive systems of women in the Canadian population. **(1 mark)**

Use the following additional information to answer the next three parts of the question.

Scientists have been learning about a mechanism called the "cell cycle clock" that collects information from outside the cell. This information influences the activities of molecules within the cell that determine whether or not a cell will undergo mitosis.

Some molecules take the form of "go" signals, stimulating a cell to go through mitosis.

Other molecules take the form of "stop" signals to ensure that the cell does not start cell division.

For example, some cyclins and CDKs are molecules that act as "go" signals. If these are present in appropriate amounts, DNA replication will occur.

– from *Trichopoulos, Li, and Hunter*, 1996

d) At which phase of the cell cycle do these cyclins and CDKs appear to operate?

(1 mark)

e) Drug companies are working on developing a drug that blocks the activities of these cyclins and CDKs. Predict how such a drug could act at the molecular level to prevent cancer.

(1 mark)

f) A mutation could disrupt the production or activation of molecules that act as "stop" or "go" signals. Describe how such a disruption could lead to cancer.

(1 mark)

Source: January 2000

Use the following information to answer the next question.

Adrenoleukodystrophy (ALD) is a rare disease of the central nervous system. ALD is characterized by the accumulation of very-long-chain fatty acids in the white matter of the brain and in the adrenal glands. These fatty acids cause the myelin sheath on nerve fibres within white matter of the central nervous system to degenerate. Symptoms of this degeneration become more severe as more and more fatty acids accumulate. Symptoms start with tantrums and other behavioural problems; then motor function, speech, and hearing are impaired; and finally blindness, mental deterioration, and death occur. ALD also affects the endocrine system by causing adrenal gland degeneration. ALD can be partially diagnosed by abnormally high ACTH levels in the blood.

Hereditary diseases have diverse causes.

For example, the disease mutation may be dominant or recessive, or the mutated gene may be present on the X chromosome or on an autosome.

In some cases, similar diseases are caused by mutations in two different genes. One such case is ALD, where one gene is autosomal and the other is X-linked. In both forms of inheritance, the disease mutation is recessive. Scientists continue to research the causes of ALD.

The X-linked recessive form of ALD can be diagnosed prenatally.

ALD has not been treated successfully; however, bone marrow transplants and a diet restricted in very-long-chain fatty acids have shown promise.

One dietary substance, oleic acid (Lorenzo's oil), has been successful in normalizing levels of very-long-chain fatty acids in blood plasma. However, the results of clinical trials on ALD patients showed little improvement in symptoms, particularly in brain degeneration. Lorenzo's oil did produce positive clinical results when the treatment of patients began before neurologic symptoms were present.

– from *McKusick, et al*, 1997

6. Write a unified response that addresses the following aspects of adrenoleukodystrophy.

- **Explain** how the degeneration of the myelin sheaths on cells in the white matter of the central nervous system could result in any of the impaired brain functions of ALD patients. **Identify** one hormone secreted by the adrenal gland, and **describe** how a decrease in secretion of this hormone would affect the body.

- **Describe** one piece of evidence obtained from the analysis of a pedigree chart that could be used to determine whether the mode of inheritance of a human genetic disorder is X-linked or autosomal **and** one piece of evidence that could be used to determine whether it is recessive or dominant. **Construct** a pedigree of four generations that clearly illustrates **one** of the two types of inheritance of ALD. Clearly **label** where your pedigree shows evidence of X-linked recessive or autosomal recessive inheritance.

- **Describe** one procedure that could be used to collect fetal cells for genetic screening. **Describe** a benefit and a risk to the individual and/or to society of early diagnosis of disorders like ALD.

Source: January 2000

Use the following information to answer the next question.

Acquired immune deficiency syndrome (AIDS) research has centred on developing drug treatments and an AIDS vaccine. AIDS is caused by human immunodeficiency virus (HIV). The drug AZT can greatly reduce the chance of transmission of HIV from an infected woman to her unborn child.

The current AZT treatment is very costly. To make the treatment more affordable, African researchers have conducted a number of studies in which one group of HIV infected women was given a shorter than normal course of AZT treatments and another group of HIV infected women received a placebo (pill without medication).

A vaccine made from only the outer coating of the HIV is attached to a harmless virus. The vaccine is being tested on healthy human volunteers to see whether they develop antibodies that would help them produce a natural defence against AIDS. This type of vaccine has not yet been sufficiently effective to induce the desired immunity.

A similar AIDS vaccine tested in Canada did not work any better than a placebo.

Future treatments for AIDS may be based on newly acquired knowledge of how AIDS infection occurs and why some individuals are more resistant to infection. When body cells are damaged, they produce a protein (chemokine) to attract the body's immune cells (macrophages). The macrophages have receptors on their cell membranes that attach to the chemokine and rid the body of the damaged cells. The HIV attaches to one kind of chemokine receptor (CCR5) on the macrophage and enters the macrophage, but the HIV does not destroy it. Ultimately, the virus also infects T-cells and takes over their DNA replicating mechanisms. The macrophage infection may be necessary to activate the replicating mechanisms of T-cells.

It has been discovered that some people have inherited a resistance to HIV because the gene that makes the CCR5 receptor is mutated (missing 32 nucleotides). This CCR5 mutation results in a shorter receptor, thereby preventing the HIV from attaching to macrophages. Individuals in a study group who were homozygous for the mutant allele resisted infection despite many exposures to HIV. Individuals in the study group with one copy of the mutant allele had the onset of AIDS postponed for two to three years when compared with those in the study group that had no copies of the mutant allele. The mutated allele is most common in Caucasians.

– from Day, 1997; O'Brien and Dean, 1997

7. a) i) Using your knowledge of how experiments should be designed, explain why some African woman were given a placebo instead of the AZT drug. **(1 mark)**

ii) Why could it be considered ethically wrong to give one group of African women a placebo in place of the real AZT treatments? **(1 mark)**

b) Describe how it is physically possible for a pregnant woman with AIDS to pass the virus to her fetus. **(1 mark)**

c) Describe briefly the cellular mechanisms of transcription, translation, and protein synthesis that are involved in the production of the CCR5 receptor molecule. **(3 marks)**

Use the following information to answer the next three parts of the question.

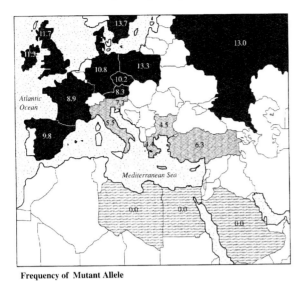

Frequency of Mutant Allele

■ 8.0 percent or higher   ▨ 0.1 to 7.9 percent   ▤ 0.0 percent   ☐ Data unavailable

d) Hypothesize why the northern European population has a much higher frequency of the CCRS mutant allele than the African population. **(2 marks)**

Use the following information to answer the next part of the question.

Frequency of the Mutated CCR5 Allele in Various Populations

Population	Frequency of Mutant Allele
Caucasian-European	0.100
Caucasian-American	0.111
African-American	0.017
Native American, African, East Asian	0.000

e) What percentage of the Caucasian-American population would be heterozygous for the mutated CCR5 allele? Show all work and formulas. **(2 marks)**

f) The discovery of how the mutant CCR5 allele works to make a person resistant to HIV infection has led scientists to work on new ways to treat or prevent AIDS. Describe a scientific technology that could be used to treat or prevent AIDS that utilizes this new knowledge. **(2 marks)**

Source: June 2000

Use the following information to answer the next question.

Human growth hormone (HGH) stimulates the growth of bones and muscles and also has insulin-like properties that result in the deposition of fat in body tissues. Sometimes, for medical purposes, an individual is prescribed a supplement of HGH. Unfortunately, at high levels, HGH has some unpleasant side effects. At a high dosage, HGH can cause insensitivity to insulin. In extreme cases, permanent diabetes mellitus can result.

Dr. J.F. Mueller made an interesting discovery. He observed that mice infected with the plerocercoid larvae of the tapeworm *Spirometra mansonoides* showed accelerated growth. Careful analysis revealed that the larvae produced plerocercoid growth factor (PGF) that is remarkably similar to HGH in structure and function. Further study showed PGF to be molecularly similar to HGH, but it had no anti-insulin effect.

How is it that a tapeworm larva produces a substance so similar to HGH? Even closely related animals have quite different hormones, so it is not likely that this is a chance occurrence. One hypothesis that has been suggested involves viral transduction of the HGH gene. When a virus infects a host cell, the viral DNA becomes incorporated into the host DNA. Later, the host cell is tricked into assembling new viruses. The viral DNA is replicated and placed in the new viruses. Sometimes a section of host DNA is added along with the viral DNA. If the new virus infects a second host, the second host receives the DNA from the first host. This host-to-host transfer of DNA is called viral transduction.

The life cycle of the tapeworm allows it to easily infect not only humans but several other vertebrates. Almost all tapeworms are hermaphrodites (contain both male and female sex organs). Multiple testes and ovaries found in segments on a single tapeworm produce gametes that come together and result in the production of fertilized eggs (either by self-fertilization or cross-fertilization). The fertilized eggs are released into the intestine of the final host and leave the host through the feces. The host's fecal matter enters the water system where the eggs hatch into ciliated coracidia (hair-covered circular organisms). The coracidia are eaten by small crustaceans called copepods. Copepods are ingested by fish, mice, cats, humans, and other organisms that drink the contaminated water. Once inside the new host, each coracidium may develop into a pleurocercoid larva that forms a cyst in the muscle.

When this host is eaten by another animal, the pleuroceroid larva attaches to the small intestine wall and develops the reproductive segments of the adult tapeworm.

– from *Barnard and Behnke*, 1990; *Phares*, 1987

8. Write a unified response that addresses the discovery of the PGF protein in tapeworms and its potential use in science and medicine.

Draw a diagram of the tapeworm life cycle, indicating the timing of important cell divisions such as mitosis and meiosis. **Explain** the value of these two types of cell divisions as they apply to the tapeworms.

Describe the series of steps that would have to occur in order for the gene for HGH to end up in tapeworm DNA as hypothesized.

Describe the disorder that results from not having enough HGH during childhood development. Treatment could involve the use of PGF instead of HGH. Identify specific effects that make it advantageous to use PGF instead of HGH.

Source: June 2000

Use the following information to answer the next question.

Insulin-dependent diabetes mellitus (IDDM), also known as Type I diabetes or juvenile diabetes is a disorder of glucose homeostasis in which the body's ability to produce insulin is impaired. People suffering from IDDM experience high blood sugar levels, increased thirst, frequent urination, extreme tiredness, and weight loss (despite an increased appetite). These symptoms can result in long-term complications that affect the eyes, kidneys, nerves, and blood vessels.

– from *OMIM*

9. **a)** Explain why people with untreated IDDM often suffer from extreme tiredness and why they experience weight loss even though their blood sugar levels are higher than normal.
(2 marks)

b) Diabetes insipidus is a disorder that results from underproduction of ADH. Both diabetes mellitus and diabetes insipidus result in a large increase of urine output. Explain how a urine sample produced by a patient with diabetes mellitus and a urine sample produced by a patient with diabetes insipidus are different.
(1 mark)

c) About one in seven IDDM diabetics also suffer from "polyglandular autoimmune syndrome." In addition to their diabetic symptoms, these individuals have thyroid disease and poorly functioning adrenal glands.

i) Identify a hormone that is produced in either the thyroid gland or the adrenal gland that affects blood sugar levels.

(1 mark)

ii) State the normal effect this hormone has on blood sugar levels when its secretion increases. Explain what causes the change in blood sugar levels.

(2 marks)

Use the following information additional information to answer the next part of the question.

Of individuals with IDDM, 50% also suffer from diabetic neuropathy. Nerves are progressively destroyed, possibly due to blockage of the tiny blood vessels that supply blood to the nerves.

– from *National Eye Institute*

d) One patient with diabetic neuropathy walked on a broken ankle for two weeks without knowing it. Others, unknowingly, have foot ulcers (bleeding sores) on the soles of their feet. Based on this information, predict the type of neuron you suspect is damaged in these patients. Explain how the symptoms of diabetic walked on a broken ankle for two weeks without knowing it. Others, unknowingly, have foot ulcers (bleeding sores) on the soles of their feet. Based on this information, predict the types of neuron you suspect is damaged in these patients. Explain how the symptoms of diabetic neuropathy support your prediction.

(2 marks)

Use the following additional information to answer the next part of the question.

The most common eye disease in individuals with IDDM is "diabetic retinopathy." This disease is characterized by changes in the blood vessels of the retina. In some people, the blood vessels may swell and leak fluid, and in other people, abnormal blood vessels grow on the surface of the retina.

– from *National Eye Institute*

e) Explain why diabetic retinopathy may result in some vision loss or blindness. In your answer, refer to the eye structure and the pathway of impulses to the brain.

(2 marks)

f) Insulin is a protein hormone. It has been hypothesized that a change in the 57th amino acid of this hormone from asparagine to another amino acid will result in an increased risk for developing IDDM.

i) Write a DNA triplet that codes for asparagine.

(1 mark)

ii) Show how a single base change in this DNA triplet would code for an amino acid other than asparagine. Identify the amino acid coded for by the mutated DNA triplet.

(1 mark)

Use the following information to answer the next question.

Larry and Danny Gomez, two boys known as "Wolf Boys," have made the circus their adoptive family. Both boys perform as trampoline acrobats, and Danny also does motorcycle stunts. The boys have a condition called congenital hypertrichosis (CH), which is a very rare X-linked dominant inherited condition. CH is characterized by the growth of dark hair over the body, particularly on the face and upper torso in males. The palms of the hands, soles of the feet, and mucus membranes are not affected by this condition.

A press release about the circus stated that Larry and Danny have travelled to many countries in search of a cure. When asked about the search for a cure in an interview by David Staples of *The Edmonton Journal* (May 14, 1997), Larry said, "I'd never take it off. I'm very proud to be who I am." Outside the circus, the boys enjoy activities typical of most boys their age. Danny likes to play video and board games, and Larry is interested in science and is taking astronomy by correspondence.

Researchers continue to investigate the process of hair growth and the causes of hair distribution at the molecular level. The relevant molecules are expected to act on hair follicles. Hair follicle distribution in humans is primarily a hormone-dependent secondary sex characteristic. In addition to searching for a cure for CH, research in this area may also have significant applications in the treatment of acquired or inherited baldness.

The incidence of CH is very rare: only about 50 affected individuals have been reported since the Middle Ages. The incidence of this condition is considerably higher in a small Mexican village than it is in the rest of the human population. In 1984, researcher Macias-Flores studied CH in a large, five-generation Mexican family and found 19 individuals with CH.

A partial pedigree showing the sampled individuals from the Macias-Flores study is shown below.

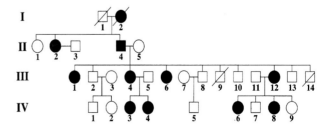

– from *Staples*, 1997, and *Figuera et al.*, 1995

10. Write a unified response on the following aspects of CH.

- **Identify** the hormone responsible for secondary sex characteristics in males **or** females, and **describe** the secondary sex characteristics, including hair follicle distribution patterns, resulting from this hormone's stimulation.

- **Identify** the genotypes for individuals II-4, II-5, III-11, III-12, IV-6, IV-7, IV-8, and IV-9 in one of the lines of inheritance on the pedigree. (Provide a key for the allele symbols you use.) **Construct** a Punnett square to predict the probability of individuals III-11 and III-12's next child being a male with CH. **Explain** why more females than males inherited CH in generation III.

- **State** a possible experimental problem that could be investigated to find out more about CH or hair follicle distribution. **Evaluate** whether conducting research would be useful for affected individuals **or** for society. (An evaluation includes at least one advantage and one disadvantage.)

Source: January 2001

ANSWERS AND SOLUTIONS
NERVOUS AND ENDOCRINE SYSTEMS – UNIT REVIEW

1. A	8. D	14. B	21. D	NR2. 2, 5, 1, 4
2. A	9. B	15. A	22. B	28. C
3. C	NR1. 2, 1, 5, 4	16. C	23. A	29. D
4 B	10. A	17. B	24. C	30. D
5. C	11. D	18. D	25. C	31. C
6. A	12. A	19. A	26 C	32. D
7. D	13. A	20. C	27. A	33. A
				34. B

1. A

When the nerve fibre is at rest, it is said to be polarized because inside the fibre is about –70mV relative to the outside. That is, the inside is a negative pole and the outside is a positive pole. Upon stimulation, ion channels open and flows into the fibre, making it more + inside. We say that the fibre has been depolarized. This depolarization flows as a wave along the membrane of the neuron fibre.

B A negative feedback loop typically refers to the control of the level of hormones in blood.
C Summation refers to the overall effect of excitory and inhibitory neurotransmitters simultaneously stimulating a neuron.
D Ions can be moved across a membrane by active transport, but not by an electrical potential.

2. A

Syphilis damages neurons of the central nervous system. Interneurons are the neurons of the central nervous system. Sensory neurons, somatic motor neurons, and autonomic motor neurons all exist in peripheral nerves outside of the CNS.

3. C

The neurilemma is a membrane that allows nerve fibres to regrow following damage. Axons and dendrites are the fibres themselves, and the node of Ranvier is the space between the Schwann cells of the myelin.

4. B

II – By preventing serotonin from binding to post-synaptic membranes, this drug is a competitive inhibitor.

I – By causing serotonin to remain in the brain for longer periods of time, these drugs slow down the removal of serotonin.

5. C

Clozapine prevents serotonin from binding on the post-synaptic membranes. Therefore, Clozapine will reduce the effect of serotonin. Since a shortage of serotonin has been linked to depression, it would not make sense to use this drug on a person suffering from depression.

6. A

A neurotransmitter such as serotonin is stored in a vesicle. The W indicates a vesicle of neurotransmitter being released into the synapse. Vesicles of neurotransmitter are released from the ends of axons.

7. D

The diagram shows a typical motor neuron. It would carry an action potential from the CNS at the left, toward a muscle at the right. Acetylcholine is a neurotransmitter. Neurotransmitters are released from the ends of the axons into a synapse to stimulate a dendrite or cell body. Label 4 is pointing to the end of the axon, 1 points to a dendrite, 2 points to myelin sheath, and 3 points to nodes of Ranvier.

8. D

Acetylcholine stimulates an action potential on the postsynaptic membrane of the next neuron. The stimulation depolarizes the postsynaptic membrane. Cholinesterase is an enzyme that breaks down acetylcholine to stop the stimulation of the next neuron. If acetylcholine is released but no cholinesterase is present, the stimulation of the next neuron does not stop. As a result, the postsynaptic neuron is in a constant state of depolarization.

9. B

Because cocaine binds to the dopamine transporters, the dopamine transporters are not able to return the dopamine to the cell that created it. As a result, the dopamine remains in the synapse in a higher concentration and for a longer time than it otherwise would. Therefore, good feelings are enhanced.

NR 1. 2 1 5 4

2, a sensory nerve fibre transmits information to the spinal cord
1, a sensory receptor in the skin detects touch
5, is a muscle that has been stimulated to contract by
4, a motor nerve fibre from the spinal cord

10. A

The cerebrum is responsible for conscious thought. This includes perception of vision and other sensory information, coordination of language activities, personality traits, as well as storage of information into memory and the recall of memorized information.

B The cerebellum coordinates muscular contractions.

C The pituitary produces hormones and regulates some of the endocrine glands.

D The medulla oblongata controls a variety of unconscious activities, such as breathing and heart rate.

11. D

The medulla oblongata controls a variety of unconscious activities, such as breathing and heart rate, swallowing, vomiting, and digestion.

A The cerebrum is responsible for conscious thought including perception of sensory information, coordination of language activities, personality traits, and memory.

B The cerebellum coordinates muscular contractions.

C The pituitary produces hormones and regulates some of the endocrine glands.

12. A

The sympathetic system prepares the body for physical activity by increasing blood flow to the brain, heart, and skeletal muscles.
The sympathetic system also causes the heart rate and stroke volume to increase.
These are changes that would be required for physical activities such as jogging.
The parasympathetic system normalizes metabolic activities, diverting more blood to the digestive and other internal organs. Impulses of the parasympathetic system would be decreased during physical activity.

13. A

If the man could not move his wrist, then a signal was not able to get through Point 2, the motor nerve. If the man could not feel sensations in his hand, then a signal was not able to get through Point 1, the sensory nerve.

B cannot be correct because if there were damage to Point 4, the cerebellum, the man would not be able to move his wrist normally.

C is not a good answer, because if Point 3, the spinal cord, were damaged, it is quite likely that the man would not be able to feel sensations from his hand.

D is incorrect because if Point 2, the motor nerve, were damaged, the man would not be able to move his wrist normally.

14. B

The cerebrum is responsible for personality. The medulla takes care of basic unconscious functions relating to internal systems such as circulation digestion. The cerebellum is responsible for coordinating motor activities. The hypothalamus controls the endocrine system.

15. A

The sympathetic system diverts blood to the skeletal muscles, brain, and heart from the skin and internal organs. The hormone epinephrine has similar effects. These are appropriate physiological responses to a stressful situation.

16. C

The sequence, or order, of events involves pulling your hand away, and then being aware of the pain later. Pulling away the hand is a reflex response. During this reflex response, a sensory neuron carries the pain signal to the CNS, where the signal is interpreted by interneurons, and a response is sent through motor neurons to muscles that pull the hand away. At the same time, a signal is sent up through the spinal cord to the brain, which only then becomes aware of the original stimulus.

17. B

The sympathetic nervous system prepares the body for action. In this case, the individual is in imminent, or immediate, danger. The question asks the student to select the response that would not be appropriate to deal with the danger. Constriction of the bronchioles of the lungs will decrease the air flow in and out of the lungs. That does not help to deal with danger.
The other three answers are correct responses of the sympathetic system. Dilation of the pupils allows more light in for clearer vision, constriction of the arterioles of the intestines and dilation of the arterioles of the skeletal muscles diverts blood to where it is most needed.

18. D

The information tells us that at high doses, morphine suppresses heart contraction and breathing. We have to select the part of the brain that regulates heart contraction and breathing, and that part is the medulla oblongata.
The pituitary influences the endocrine system, the cerebrum takes care of higher thought and that which makes us individual humans, and the cerebellum coordinates fine muscle movements.

19. A

Movement of hair cells of the organ of Corti inside the fluid of the cochlea stimulates fibres of the auditory nerve. Therefore, it is the cochlea that is directly responsible for stimulating nerve endings.

B The eardrum transmits sound energy from the outer ear to the middle ear.

C The Eustachian tube allows air pressure to be equalized between the outer ear and the middle ear.

D The semicircular canal transmits balance information to the brain.

20. C

The occipital lobe, at the back of the cerebrum, receives and coordinates visual information.

A The frontal lobe is associated with personality.

B and **D**. The parietal and temporal lobes are involved with hearing and language.

21. D

Accommodation refers to changing of focus to see near or far objects clearly. This requires changing the shape of the lens, which is pulled into a round or flat shape by contraction or relaxation of the ciliary muscles.

A Blind spots exist at the spots in the eyeball where fibres of the optic nerve gather to exit the eye.

Rods (**B**) are light receptors that detect light (not colour), and cones (**C**) are light receptors that perceive colour.

22. B

Structure 2 labels the semicircular canals, which detect motion. When a person moves, the semicircular canals move, but the fluid inside the canals does not move because of inertia. This is like a person standing on a bus when it starts out. The movement causes the cilia of hair cells inside the semicircular canals to bend, which stimulates the auditory nerve. When a person feels dizzy after movement stops. It is because the fluid inside the semicircular canals is now moving (like a person standing on the bus when it comes to a sudden halt).

23. A

6 – the eardrum (tympanic membrane) vibrates in response to sound waves. The vibration of the eardrum causes movements in the three tiny middle ear bones, which are labelled 1. They are designed like a lever, so that a small vibration in the eardrum results in a larger vibration through the middle ear bones.

24. C

3 is pointing to the retina of the eye. The retina contains the rods and cones, receptors that stimulate action potentials in the optic nerve.

25. C

Since the defect that causes blindness in the dogs is called retinal disease, we can assume the problem is with the retina. Arrow 3 points to the retina, which is the light- receptive structure. Here, the rods and cones absorb light energy and convert it to action potentials in the optic nerve. The rods cannot detect colour but they can operate in low light conditions. The cones require bright light, but they can detect red, green, and blue light.

26. C

ADH stimulates the kidney tubules to be more porous, allowing more water to diffuse from the kidney tubules back to the blood. Oxytocin causes uterine muscles to contract during labour. Oxytocin also causes the mammary glands to secrete milk.

27. A

A releasing factor is a hormone from the hypothalamus that stimulates the pituitary to release a hormone. A gonadotropin is a hormone that stimulates release of a hormone in a gonad, or sex organ (testes and ovaries). So, GnRF causes the pituitary to release LH (leutenizing hormone), which causes ovulation and progesterone secretion from the ovary and the release of testosterone from the testes. GnRF also causes the pituitary to release FSH, which in turn causes the ovaries to produce eggs and the testes to produce sperm.

NR 2. 2 5 1 4

2, STH (HGH) (growth hormone) causes bones and muscles to grow in size.

5, LH (lutenizing horomore) causes ovulation – the egg bursts out of the mature follicle in which it was produced and out of the ovary itself. Then, the LH causes the remains of the mature follicle to reform itself into the corpus luteum.

1, TSH (thyroid-stimulating hormone) stimulates the thyroid gland to secrete thyroxine.

4, FSH (follicle-stimulating hormone) causes egg follicles to be made in ovaries and sperm to be made in the testes.

28. C

The hormone aldosterone is released from the adrenal cortex when the level of water and salt in body fluid is too low. Aldosterone causes cells lining the kidney tubules to move more water and salt back into the blood, therefore less water and salt is lost with the urine.

29. D

ACTH is secreted by the anterior pituitary, labelled 2. ACTH stands for adrenocorticotrophic hormone. It stimulates the cortex of the adrenal gland, labelled 5.

30. D

The control group has not been given an experimental treatment and, therefore, serves as a comparison for the groups that have been given an experimental treatment. In this case, the experimental treatments involve increasing metabolic rate (by increasing thyroxine) or decreasing metabolic rate (by decreasing thyroxine). Group IV remained about the same weight and consumed a moderate amount of oxygen. These are indications that the metabolic rate was neither increased nor decreased.

31. C

These are the most likely diets for the groups of rats:

Group	Weight change	Oxygen consumption	Metabolic rate must be	Diet
I	Increase	Low	Low	Z – the lack of iodine reduced thyroxine production
II	Decrease	High	High	Y – the diet contained thyroxine which would increase metabolism.
III	Increase	Low	Low	X – the chemical in the diet counteracted the effects of thyroxine.
V	Same	Moderate	Moderate	W – a diet that would neither increase nor decrease the effects of thyroxine.

32. D

Gonadotropins are hormones secreted by the anterior pituitary that stimulate the gonads or sex organs. The hypothalamus produces gonadotropin-releasing hormones that stimulate the anterior pituitary to secrete gonadotropins. During the early winter, when there is decreased light, there would be an increase in melatonin. If this stimulated the hypothalamus to not release gonadotropin-releasing hormones, the anterior pituitary would not release the gonadotropins FSH and LH. As a result, the ovaries would not make and release eggs, and fertility would be reduced.

33. A

In a cause-effect study, the manipulated variable is the cause and the responding variable is the effect. The amount of licking that a rat received from its mother (manipulated variable) was the cause of the amount of ACTH the rat secreted as an adult (responding variable).
Controlled or fixed variables are any variables that may have an effect on the responding variable other than the manipulated variable. It is possible that the size of the rats' cages may affect stress, so cage size must be kept the same for all the rats.

34. B

The medulla of the adrenal gland secretes epinephrine and norepinephrine that have effects on the body similar to that of the sympathetic system.

The thyroid gland (**A**) produces thyroxin, which regulates metabolic rate. The anterior pituitary (**C**) and posterior pituitary (**D**) glands store and produce a variety of hormones, none of which mimic the sympathetic nervous system.

ANSWERS AND SOLUTIONS
NERVOUS AND ENDOCRINE SYSTEMS – UNIT TEST 1

1. C	6. C	11. A	16. D	21. A
2. C	7. C	12. D	17. D	22. B
3. C	8. D	13. D	18. D	23. B
4. C	9. C	14. C	19. B	24. C
5. D	10. A	15. C	20. D	25. D

1. C

Recall that an axon is part of a neuron (nerve cell) that transmits nerve impulses. A nerve impulse is a wave of depolarization of the nerve cell membrane that travels along the neuron (in the direction of dendrites → axon). In the diagram given, the dotted line marks the threshold for excitation – the membrane potential required for the wave of membrane depolarization (nerve impulse) to occur. According to the table, only 2 out of 4 (50%) of the impulses resulted in a membrane potential above the threshold (therefore **A** is incorrect). **C** is the best answer because the two stimuli that produced a nerve impulse are the two strongest stimuli. A stimulus must be strong enough to cause the voltage-gated sodium channels in the nerve cell membrane to open, thereby causing depolarization. Notice that the strongest two stimuli resulted in nerve impulses of the same strength (about +30mV). **B** and **D** are therefore incorrect. In fact, a nerve impulse (action potential) is always about the same within a species. For example, in humans, any nerve impulse has a magnitude of about +50mV.

2. C

The structure labelled Q represents the Schwann cells that make up the myelin sheath surrounding a nerve cell. The purpose of the myelin sheath is to insulate the axon, preventing the parts of the membrane that are covered in the sheath to be depolarized. Depolarization can only happen at the non-insulated parts (called the nodes of Ranvier).

Because depolarization can only happen at the non-insulated nodes along the axon, the action potential "jumps" from node to node (called saltatorial conduction), resulting in increased speed of conduction. In the absence of the myelin sheath, the nerve impulse could only travel by sequential depolarization of the entire membrane of the nerve cell. (**B** is therefore incorrect.) The speed of impulse transmission would therefore be slower. **C** is therefore correct. Acetylcholine is a neurotransmitter (a molecule that carries a nerve impulse across the synapse, from the axon terminus of one neuron to the dendrites of the next neuron). Cholinesterase is an enzyme that degrades acetylcholine, preventing a nerve impulse from being transmitted indefinitely.
Neither cholinesterase nor acetylcholine would be affected by absence of the Schwann cells, so **A** and **D** are incorrect.

3. C

Recall that in the transmission of a nerve impulse across a synapse:

- the nerve impulse reaches the tip of the axon which causes small vesicles full of the neurotransmitter acetylcholine to be released into the space surrounding the axon terminus
- some acetylcholine molecules travel across the synapse and reach the dendrites of a nearby neuron (or the muscle cells if the synapse is a neuromuscular junction), and bind to its membrane, thereby starting a new wave of depolarization in that neuron (or stimulating muscular contraction).
- to prevent the nerve impulse from being sent indefinitely, an enzyme (cholinesterase) is released shortly after the acetylcholine is released. Cholinesterase degrades acetylcholine, thereby preventing the nerve impulse from reaching the adjacent neuron or muscle cell

In the preamble, we learn that neostigmine is an anticholinesterase drug (meaning that it inhibits the activity of cholinesterase, so **D** is incorrect). Inhibition of cholinesterase would result in the presence of excess amounts of active acetylcholine in the synapse. **C** is therefore correct. The excess acetylcholine results from the failure of its degradation by cholinesterase, not by increased production of acetylcholine, so **B** is incorrect. Neostigmine restores some normal muscular activity in people with myasthenia because the drug results in an increase in the amount of acetylcholine. The increased acetylcholine provides a stronger and longer-lasting stimulus for the less-sensitive muscle fibers of a person with this disease.

4.   **C**

Since transmission of a nerve impulse across a synapse is dependent on neurotransmitters (such as acetylcholine), a limited amount of neurotransmitter present in an axon terminal would also limit the number and duration of nerve impulses. Such a situation would occur, for example, if many nerve impulses are sent across a particular synapse in a short time. **C** is correct. When the axon terminal is "empty" of neurotransmitter, the nerve impulse can no longer be sent across the synapse. This is called "fatigue of synaptic transmission."

5.   **D**

By process of elimination, **C** can be disregarded because CCK inhibitors would suppress a "panic attack." Choices **A** and **B** are the same. In both cases, low levels or impaired production of CCK would result in suppressed emotional response. Administration of CCK by injection would normalize the response. If a person has an excess of CCK receptors, then the natural response to CCK whether self-generated or injected – will be the same: an over-reaction or "panic attack."

6.   **C**

Recall the responses controlled by the sympathetic nervous system associated with the flight-or-fight response. These responses occur when impulses are carried to target organs by motor neurons. For example, imagine such an impulse going to your adrenal glands. Interneurons (**A**) transmits signals within the CNS. Sensory neurons (**B**) travel toward the CNS, which is the wrong direction. Stimulation of parasympathetic neurons (**D**) would have the opposite effect.

7.   **C**

Recall the direction of transmission. The neurotransmitter is released by vesicles in the axon terminal that crosses the synaptic gap and is received by the dendrite of the next neuron. Cell bodies (**A**) is not specific enough. Dendrites and Schwann cells (**B**) can be eliminated because the dendrites are not releasing sites for acetylcholine and the Schwann cells have a different function. The same applies to **D**.

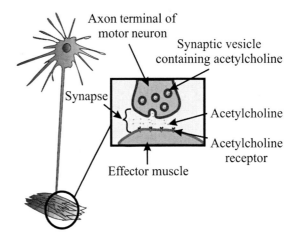

8.   **D**

This is a polarization question. Think about depolarization caused by a neurotransmitter. Picture a synapse. **A** refers to a presynaptic membrane that should be releasing the neurotransmitter. **B** is a good choice but not when it refers to a presynaptic membrane. **C** would result in hyperpolarization.

9. C

In the preceding paragraph NGF is said to promote axon regeneration. As choice **C** indicates, the nucleus controls protein synthesis. In other words, the nucleus is necessary to guide regeneration. NGF only promotes it.

All complete cells need a nucleus to function, so **A** is incorrect. While it is true that red blood cells in mammals are anucleate and still function, they are considered sub-cellular and cannot regenerate themselves. Organelles other than the nucleus do cause cell growth, which makes **B** a close second choice. However, these organelles still require the nucleus for direction and control. **D** is also a good second choice because essentially it is true. Without a nucleus, a cell will die. However, **D** can be rejected because ion transport is not part of the discussion.

10. A

The association here is amongst acetylcholine, cholinesterase, and transmission. Acetylcholine is important in synaptic transmission, cholinesterase destroys acetylcholine.

So how would a drug that inhibits cholinesterase affect acetylcholine? Choice **B** can be rejected because inhibiting cholinesterase should initially increase transmission. **C** can be rejected because axon terminals do not release sodium ions.

D is incorrect because huperzine A directly affects cholinesterase not acetylcholine. Notice the phrase "strong inhibitor of cholinesterase" in the information.

11. A

From the diagram, both neurons 2 and 3 possess Schwann cells surrounding the axon, so **C** and **D** are incorrect. (Recall that myelination refers to the presence of the myelin sheath, which is composed of the Schwann cells.) A reflex arc is used for reflex responses (such as touching a hot object and then jerking the hand away), which involve nerve impulses that travel directly to and from the spinal cord without reaching the brain. A reflex is therefore unconscious.

In the diagram, neuron 2 appears to be connected to epithelial cells (eg., skin cells) by long spindles that could represent the dendrites. (Recall that a nerve impulse travels in the direction of dendrites/cell body → axon.) Therefore, 2 is the sensory neuron.

The nerve impulse travels from the sensory neuron to the interneuron, and then along the motor neuron (3) that ends in muscle fibers. **A** is correct.

12. D

Even though she is burned, a mother does not drop a pot of boiling water when her child is standing by her side. Dropping the pot would be a good example of a reflex action. Not dropping the pot would require conscious effort.

A, **B**, and **C** describe reflex actions that are not being consciously controlled.

13. D

The parasympathetic system is responsible for returning the body systems to normal following, for example, a stressful situation. **D** is correct. See also the solution to question 19.

The sympathetic system (**C**) is responsible for the stress response. The central nervous system (**A**) includes the nerves of the brain and spinal cord. The somatic nervous system (**B**) includes the nerves that control skeletal muscles, bones and skin.

14. C

The word *respectively* is important to indicate the order of the answers. Reject **A** because the medulla is not an area controlling muscle coordination. Reject **B** because the order is incorrect. Reject **D** because the hypothalamus is not directly involved in controlling memory or muscle coordination.

15. C

Arrow 3 in the diagram points to the fovea centralis—the most sensitive portion of the retina for light perception. The fovea centralis receives most of the light that enters the eye, and although it has no rod cells, it contains a high concentration of cones. Arrow 4 points to the entry location of the optic nerve from the brain. The entry point of the optic nerve is called the "blind spot" because there are no light-sensitive cells (rods or cones) at this location in the retina. Therefore, the correct response is **C**. Arrow 1 points to the cornea, the outer transparent layer of the eye. Arrow 2 points to the lens, which focuses incoming light on the retina.

16. D

Motion, changes in body position, and balance are sensed by the vestibule and the semicircular canals, both present in the inner ear. Movement of fluid according to the body position is sensed by the nerve cells within these two structures and sent to the brain. Motion sickness, caused by irregular movements, can therefore be alleviated by inhibiting the transmission of nerve signals from the vestibule and semicircular canals to the brain. **D** is correct. The cochlea, organ of Corti, and basilar membrane are all structures that function in hearing, and therefore do not have a role in motion sickness.

17. D

According to the data, as age increases, the eye can no longer focus on objects as near as it could before. The eye loses its ability to focus on nearby objects and only focuses on objects an increasing distance away. **A**, **B**, and **C** are all basically the same answer. They are all positive. Notice that in the data box, Near Point Accommodation is explained as the shortest distance at which focus is achieved. Since this distance increases as a person ages, the eye is losing its former ability.

18. D

Temperature sensations are determined by the number of impulses per second and the specific type of receptors. This is exactly what the graph is illustrating. **A** is incorrect because 5°C is shown to be more painful than 50°C.
Choice **B** can be rejected because coolness seems to be a single receptor (X) sensation. Reject **C** because no threshold levels are shown.

19. B

In an emergency situation, the adrenal gland (more specifically, the adrenal medulla) releases two hormones: adrenaline/epinephrine, and Noradrenaline/norepinephrine. These hormones cause:

(i) blood sugar to rise (so **B** is correct) by converting glycogen to glucose (so **D** is incorrect) to increase the amount of readily available energy for use by muscles,

(ii) an increased heart rate,

(iii) an increased breathing rate,

(iv) a dilation of blood vessels to increase blood flow to tissues,

(v) dilation of the iris to increase the light entering the eye.

All of these responses are characteristic of stimulation of the sympathetic nervous system, so **C** is incorrect. The parasympathetic nervous system can be thought of as stimulating the return of the body's systems to the normal state. Thus, the parasympathetic system would return the body back to its normal state following a stressful situation. **A** is incorrect because insulin is responsible for conversion of glucose to the storage form of sugar called glycogen. Increased insulin levels would be a response to activation of the parasympathetic system.

20. D

Observation 6 is the key observation. When the chemical mixture derived from the removed organ was injected into normal female rats, the rats changed in two ways: they had accelerated body growth and they produced increased amounts of estrogen. Recall that the function of estrogen, which is released by the ovary, is to stimulate the growth of the endometrium (uterus lining) and regulate the development of female secondary sex characteristics. Estrogen does not regulate overall body growth. Growth is regulated by growth hormone/somatotropin, which is released by the anterior pituitary.
How can increased amounts of estrogen and increased growth be caused by the chemicals removed from only one "suspected" endocrine gland? Recall that the pituitary is also called the "master gland" because it has numerous regulatory functions. In fact, the pituitary also releases a hormone, FSH, that stimulates follicle growth. The follicles within the ovary secrete the estrogen. Therefore, the "suspected" endocrine organ is most likely the pituitary, and **D** is correct.

21. A

Epinephrine and norepinephrine are stimulators of the sympathetic nervous system. Refer to the solution for question 19 for the effects of epinephrine and norepinephrine on various body systems. **A** is the correct response.

22. B

Recall the functions of the hormones provided in the choices:

Hormone	Target organ	Primary function
aldosterone	Kidneys (distal tubule and collecting duct)	Increase Na^+ absorption from urine, thereby increasing water absorption from urine indirectly
insulin	Body cells	Causes body cells to become permeable to glucose; liver cells convert internalized glucose into glycogen
glucagon	Liver	Stimulates liver cells to convert stored glycogen into glucose, which is released into blood
epinephrine	Multiple targets	Stimulates increase in blood sugar level, increases heart and breathing rate, pupils dilate, blood vessels dilate
antidiuretic hormone (ADH)	Kidney (upper distal tubule and collecting duct)	Increases the permeability of the tubules to water to increase water absorption from urine

Although both **B** and **D** present the hormones in the correct order relative to their target organs and function, aldosterone functions by increasing the absorption of sodium ions, whereas ADH works by directly increasing tubule permeability to water. Therefore, **B** is correct.

23. B

The thyroid releases two hormones: thyroxine and triiodothyronine. The chemical structure of both hormones includes the element iodine. Intuitively you might think that a diet deficient in iodine would cause shrinkage of the thyroid gland because the thyroid gland would be unable to synthesize its hormones. However, recall that thyroid hormone synthesis is regulated by negative feedback:

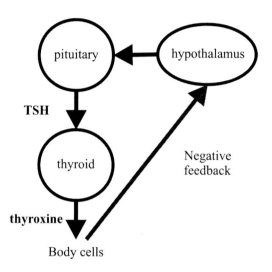

Thyroid stimulating hormone (TSH) stimulates the cells of the thyroid to enlarge and develop so that they can produce hormone. In the absence of the component iodine required for thyroid hormone synthesis, body cells fail to receive thyroid stimuli. The hypothalamus senses the absence and sends a signal to the pituitary to release more TSH. More TSH stimulates the thyroid cells to enlarge and develop even more, thus causing goiter/enlargement of the thyroid gland. **B** is correct.

24. C

Focus on the connection between the pituitary gland and some hormone that is associated with urination. Look for word associations like this in most questions. Choices **A**, **B**, and **D** can be rejected because although these hormones do come from the pituitary, they are not part of the control of urination.

25. D

Note the association between nervous and endocrine system in the information. Imagine a sympathetic motor nerve impulse going to the adrenal glands during a stressful experience. What will be secreted? Adrenaline.... or "epinephrine." HGH (**A**) can be rejected as not directly associated with stress.
Thyroxine (**B**) can be rejected because thyroxine secretion is controlled by secretion of TSH, (a hormone-to-hormone association).
The question is calling for a nerve-to-hormone connection. Aldosterone (**C**) can be rejected as it is not strongly related to stress.

26. A

"Respectively" means that the order of hormones is important. Do not confuse glucagon with glycogen. In **B**, the order is wrong.
Reject **C** and **D** because glycogen is included, which is incorrect.

27. D

In question 26, we determined that hormone X is insulin and hormone Y is glucagon. Since the question does not specify an increase or decrease in blood glucose, either hormone could be needed. The pancreas will stimulate the appropriate hormones, so **D** is the best choice. You can reject **A** because if blood glucose levels change the body will need to secrete hormones to maintain homeostasis. **B** is incorrect because hormones do not have more (or less) active forms. Reject **C** because it does not make sense that "other" endocrine glands would be involved and because the "other" glands are not specified.

ANSWERS AND SOLUTIONS
REPRODUCTIVE SYSTEMS, HORMONES, DIFFERENTIATION, AND DEVELOPMENT –UNIT REVIEW

1. B	9. C	17. A	23. C	NR4. 3, 1, 2, 4
2. B	10. C	NR1. 3, 8, 5, 1 or	NR2. 1, 5, 4, 3	NR5. 3, 4, 2, 1
3. D	11. A	5, 1, 3, 8	24. B	29. A
4. B	12. C	18. A	25. C	30. A
5. D	13. A	19. A	26. C	31. D
6. D	14. B	20. D	27. D	32. C
7. A	15. D	21. A	28. D	
8. D	16. A	22. C	NR3. 4, 3, 2, 1	

1. B

Sperm production occurs inside of seminiferous tubules, which are inside the testes. The testes also produce testosterone. The prostate gland produces an alkaline secretion that is added to the semen. The seminal vesicles add a sugar solution to the semen.

2. B

Following a vasectomy, sperm cannot make their way through the vas deferens to the penis; however, testosterone is produced by endocrine tissue in the testes and continues to be released into the blood. As a result, after a vasectomy, testosterone continues to reach all body tissues.

3. D

By failing to descend, the testes will be trapped within the body cavity, hence they will be kept at normal body temperature. Sperm production is most effective a few degrees lower than normal body temperature, which is why the testes are kept in the scrotum outside of the body cavity. Fewer sperm would be produced at body temperature, and many of these would be deformed. Sterility would be the result.

4. B

We don't know for sure that syphilis mutated from yaws, but it may have. It appears that yaws and bejel existed before syphilis, and they are similar disease organisms, all being members of the same genus.

A Because persons in Florida had syphilis 800 to 1 600 years ago doesn't mean that it was easy to contract it in a warm climate.

C Since syphilis (sexually transmitted) appears later, it is not logical to suggest that the earlier forms, yaws and bejel (non-sexually transmitted), came from the sexually transmitted disease.

D The age of the sufferers is not given in the information.

5. D

Semen is composed of sperm and fluids secreted by three sets of male reproductive glands. These glands are the Cowper's glands, prostate gland, and seminal vesicles.

6. D

The guevedoces might have reduced fertility. The reason a man's testes descend into the scrotum is that sperm production is more effective a few degrees below body temperature. The sperm develop in the seminiferous tubules inside the testes, so the late descent of the testes may cause problems in these tubules.

7. A

In males, FSH stimulates sperm formation inside the seminiferous tubules. In females, FHS stimulates egg production inside the ovaries. During the process of meiosis, four sperm are produced and one egg is produced, as shown in the following diagram.

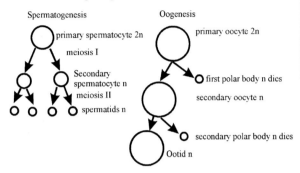

8. D

Semen is composed of sperm and the seminal fluid that they are found in. The seminal fluid is produced by the three sets of a man's reproductive glands—the seminal vesicles, the prostate gland, and the Cowper's glands. These glands produce a variety of substances that are needed in the seminal fluid. Two important substances are fructose, a sugar that nourishes the sperm, and the alkaline buffer that protects the sperm from the acid environment of the woman's vagina. FSH and testosterone are hormones produced in a man's body that affect sexual functioning, but they are not found in his semen.

9. C

FSH stimulates the development of an egg, and LH stimulates ovulation so that the egg is released into the Fallopian tube. The birth control pill contains hormones that have a negative feedback effect on the pituitary so that FSH and LH are not released. Hormones that inhibit egg production by acting upon the pituitary are estrogen and progesterone. Therefore, birth control pills contain hormones that act in a similar fashion to estrogen and progesterone.

10. C

It is the increase of testosterone production at about age 12 that stimulates the changes we associate with puberty. It is testosterone that would cause the guevedoces to acquire their male characteristics. One of the male characteristics associated with puberty is an increased larynx or voice box.

11. A

The flow chart shows that it is high estrogen levels that stimulate the hypothalamus to stimulate the pituitary to produce the hormone that stimulates the breast tissue to make milk. If the estrogen level is low, dopamine inhibits breast milk production.

12. C

Hormone X would appear to be either estrogen or prolactin, because both are involved in milk production, and estrogen levels and breast feeding influence the production of both of them. However, it must be prolactin, because the diagram shows hormone X being produced by the anterior pituitary. Prolactin is produced by the anterior pituitary, (Oxytocin is produced by the hypothalamus/posterior pituitary).

13. A

Increased FSH would cause a woman to produce more eggs. LH causes ovulation, so it is reasonable to assume that increased LH would cause more eggs to be released. Increased estrogen and progesterone would have a negative feedback effect, inhibiting egg production and release. Decreased estrogen and progesterone would probably have no effect on egg production and release in the short term although may inhibit them in the long term.

14. B

The structure labelled 2 is the ovary which produces eggs in response to FSH. The ovary releases the eggs in response to LH. The Fallopian tube (1) and the uterus (3 and 4) do not produce eggs.

15. D

Progesterone is needed to maintain the endometrium or uterine lining. Structure 2 is the corpus luteum, what remains of the mature follicle after ovulation. It is the corpus luteum that produces progesterone.

16. A

FSH causes a follicle (containing an egg) to develop; this then produces estrogen. When the hypothalamus detects a high level of estrogen in the blood, it instructs the anterior pituitary to shut down production of FSH. If lomiphene citrate decreases the estrogen level, then the hypothalamus will not instruct the anterior pituitary to stop producing FSH. The very high level of FSH will provide a much stronger stimulus to the ovary to produce follicles (eggs).

17. A

LH, or lutenizing hormone, is produced by the anterior pituitary about halfway through a woman's monthly cycle. It stimulates ovulation and the subsequent formation of the corpus luteum. The corpus luteum produces progesterone. As the progesterone level rises in the woman's body, it has a negative feedback effect on the hypothalamus that causes the anterior pituitary to shut down production of LH. The production of LH will rise again midway through the next cycle.

NR 1.   3 8 5 1 or 5 1 3 8

FSH, or follicle stimulating hormone directly stimulates the production of sperm in males and eggs in females. FSH is produced by the anterior **pituitary gland**. The hormone **testosterone** stimulates the development and maintenance of the male reproductive system, so it is also involved in sperm production, although indirectly. Testosterone is produced by the **testis**.

18. A

Typically, eggs are released from the ovaries into the Fallopian tubes (oviducts) where they can be met by sperm making their way up from the vagina. Fertilization normally will occur here.

19. A

The diagram shows that the hypothalamus stimulates the adrenal gland of the lamb to secrete cortisol. The cortisol causes progesterone, which normally inhibits uterine contraction, to be converted to estrogen that stimulates uterine contractions in the pregnant sheep.

20. D

The (–) sign on the diagram indicates that the progesterone from the placenta is inhibiting uterine contraction. This inhibition allows gestation to continue until cortisol from the fetus stimulates the progesterone to be converted to estrogen, which causes the uterine contractions of birth to begin.

21. A

It is the activity of the hypothalamus and adrenal gland of the fetal lamb that causes the increase in estrogen necessary for the birth process. The production of fetal cortisol initiates, not delays, birth. Fetal hormones must be passing into the mother, because it is the fetal cortisol that is causing the changes in the mother's hormones.

22. C

By inhibiting the fetal hypothalamus or adrenal gland, the chemical in skunk cabbage could prevent the uterine contractions that cause the birth. If the chemical increases uterine sensitivity to estrogen, decreases placental production of progesterone, or increases the conversion of progesterone to estrogen, birth might come earlier.

23. C

Fertilization involves the fusion of two gametes; in the case of humans, the gametes are sperm and egg. The gametes are n and the fertilized egg is $2n$. Mitosis produces 2 genetically identical daughter cells from one parent cell. Meiosis (sperm and egg formation) produces n cells from a $2n$ cell. Differentiation results in specialized tissue cells that are genetically identical to the parent cell.

NR 2.   1 5 4 3

The numbered structures and processes are the oocyte or egg (1), the sperm (2), fertilization (3) to form a zygote, which then immediately begins mitosis (4), and after a few days arrives at the uterus as a hollow blastocyst (5)

24. B

The acrosome is a storage structure at the head of a sperm. It contains hydrolytic enzymes. Hydrolytic enzymes are enzymes that break down complex molecules. For example, digestive enzymes are hydrolytic enzymes. The hydrolytic enzymes in the acrosome of the sperm are released when the sperm meets the egg. These enzymes break down the membrane of the egg, allowing the sperm to enter.

25. C

For the first few days, the developing embryo is moving down the Fallopian tube. At that point, it is just a cluster of cells, not attached to anything. It relies on the large amount of cytoplasm that was in the original egg as a source of nourishment. There won't be any amniotic fluid for a month, HCG is a hormone, and the mitochondria are not a source of energy at any time.

26. C

The hormone that indicates that pregnancy has occurred is HCG. HCG, or human chorionic gonadotroin, is a hormone produced by the outer layer of the embryo, or chorion. It stimulates the ovary to continue to produce progesterone. If a woman has HCG in her urine, she can be sure that there is an embryo in her body. The term gonadotropin refers to the fact that the hormone affects the gonads (ovaries) and is a tropin – a hormone that stimulates the release of other hormones. Normally, the progesterone level will drop, and the endometrium is shed during menstruation. With HCG, the endometrium remains intact and able to support the embryo.

27. D

The males seemed to copulate normally and there was no alcohol in the females' blood. There is no reason to assume that alcohol in the male would increase pituitary secretions. It is possible that alcohol in the semen may make a poisonous environment for fertilization.

28. D

Although the male rats that were supplied with alcohol copulated normally, they were less likely to fertilize the females. Reducing the rate of meiosis, preventing maturation of sperm, and depressing motility of sperm would all reduce male fertility. The only answer that would not reduce male fertility is **D**, stimulating sperm motility.

NR 3.   4 3 2 1

In the first week after fertilization, mitosis (4) occurs, rapidly resulting in a hollow sphere of cells called a blastocyst, no larger than the original egg. After several days, the blastocyst (3) has arrived at the uterus and implants into the endometrium. Development is rapid and by the third week, the embryo is a hollow tube differentiated (2) into three germ layers: the ectoderm, mesoderm, and endoderm. Starting about the fourth week, the embryo's heart, which is only a hollow tube, begins to beat (1).

NR 4.   3 1 2 4

Label 3 is pointing to the umbilical cord, which transports (A) nutrients from mother to embryo and wastes from embryo to mother. Label 1 is the amnion filled with amniotic fluid. It protects the embryo (B). Being in a sac of fluid prevents the embryo from being bumped or squeezed. Label 2 is the placenta. The placenta forms from the chorion of the embryo. Its many folds, called chorionic villi, contain numerous capillaries filled with embryonic blood. On the mother's side, blood pools around the villi and materials are exchanged (C) across the chorion. Label 4 is pointing to the yolk. While mammal embryos have a yolk, it has no real function and shrinks away early on during gestation. In birds and reptiles, the yolk, being a source of pure fat, provides energy for the developing embryo (D). Mammals get the energy from the mother.

NR 5.   3 4 2 1

The pressure of the baby's head prompts sensory receptors that stimulate a nerve signal that travels to the brain, and ultimately, the hypothalmus (3). The hypothalamus then causes the posterior pituitary to release the hormone oxytocin (4). This hormone travels through the blood (2), as all hormones do, eventually making its way to muscles surrounding the uterus. The oxytocin causes the muscles of the uterus to contract (1). This muscular contraction we refer to as labour, and is the force that pushes the baby out.

29. A

The normal gestation period for a human baby is about 40 weeks. Prior to 24 weeks, the organs are generally formed but they are not yet ready to function outside of the uterus and on their own. Cell specialization began after only a few weeks to form ectoderm, mesoderm, and endoderm, and soon after, a variety of tissues. The amniotic fluid is not a source of oxygen or nutrients. These come from the mother across the placenta and through the umbilical cord.

30. A

A birth control pill contains the female hormones estrogen and progesterone. These have a negative feedback effect on the hypothalamus so that FSH and LH are not produced. As a result, an egg is not produced in the ovary and released into the Fallopian tube.

31. D

If more than one sperm were injected into the egg, the resulting zygote would not have the normal (for a human) 46 chromosomes. It would not be $2n$. It might be $3n$ or $4n$ or $5n$, depending on how many sperm were injected. Down Syndrome results when there is a single extra chromosome, and in this case, the results would be much more severe. It is quite likely that the zygote would not even begin to develop.

32. C

Clomiphene citrate causes a higher level of FSH to be in a woman's blood. FSH causes the development of a number of follicles in the ovaries. Normally only one follicle matures and is released during ovulation. It is likely that with clomiphene citrate, the level of FSH is so high that more than one follicle reaches maturity and is released. Fraternal twins or triplets can be the result.

ANSWERS AND SOLUTIONS
REPRODUCTIVE SYSTEMS, HORMONES, DIFFERENTIATION, AND DEVELOPMENT – UNIT TEST 2

NR1. 2, 3, 6	4. C	9. A	NR3. 2, 4, 1, 3	NR4. 1, 3, 4, 2
1. B	5. C	10. B	14. D	18. D
NR2. 1, 4, 3, 2	6. B	11. D	15. C	19. A
2. C	7. A	12. A	16. D	
3. C	8. C	13. C	17. B	

NR 1.   2 3 6

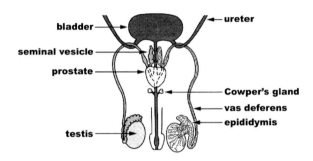

Refer to the labelled diagram above. Sperm are produced in the testes (within the seminiferous tubules) and are stored within the epididymis. During ejaculation, sperm are released into the vas deferens, a tube that connects the testis to the urethra leading out of the body through the penis. As the sperm travel along the vas deferens and urethra, fluid is sequentially added from three glands.

First, the seminal vesicles (**3**) add fluid containing fructose sugar (to provide energy for sperm) and prostaglandins (to promote rhythmic contractions of the female reproductive tract that push sperm toward the Fallopian tubes).

Second, the prostate gland (**2**) adds alkaline fluid (to neutralize any acid within the urethra and vagina).

Third, the Cowper's glands (**6**) add a milky fluid rich in mucus. Semen is therefore composed of sperm plus fluid from all three of these glands.

1.   B

The scrotum is the sac that encloses the testis in the male. The temperature within the scrotum is normally a few degrees below normal body temperature (normal temperature is 37°. In fact, the testes hang away from the body in order to maintain a lower temperature. The correct response is, therefore, **B**. Sperm cannot survive at normal body temperature. In fact, some males with a disorder that prevents the testicles from descending into the scrotum during development are sterile (cannot have children) because they cannot release live sperm.

NR 2.   1 4 3 2

Recall the functions of the four hormones given as choices:

Hormone	Primary function
FSH (follicle-stimulating hormone)	Stimulates follicle (egg) development in the ovary (1)
LH (luteinizing hormone	Stimulates development of and maintains the corpus luteum; stimulates ovulation (4)
Estrogen	Responsible for development of secondary sex characteristics; promotes thickening of the endometrium (3)
Progesterone	Stimulates growth and maintenance of the endometrium; inhibits uterine contraction; inhibits ovulation (2)

2. C

The vas deferens (3) carries sperm. The Fallopian tubes (7) carry ova. Both carry gametes. Choice **D**, 4 and 10, can be rejected because although the urethra in males and females has the same function, it is not a reproductive structure in females. Choice **B**, 2 and 8, can be rejected because the prostate gland in males and ovary in females are unrelated. Reject **A**, 1 and 9, for the same reason: the bladder in males and the uterus in females are not related.

3. C

Choice **C** is the only one that makes sense here. The glands produce fluids that contain a combination of vitamins, nutrients, and buffers. Testosterone is produced by the testis, reject **A**. Spermatogenesis is stimulated by FSH from the pituitary: reject **B**. The hypothalamus stimulates the pituitary, so reject **D**.

4. C

The genital ridge produces estrogen in a potential female embryo. This may be new information for you, but it is an easy question. Reject **A** and **B** because chromosomes do not secrete hormones. Reject **D** because testosterone is incorrectly associated with a potential female embryo. Notice how important it is to look for correct associations.

5. C

This is an association question. Notice the incorrect association between LH and estrogen in **A**. The association between LH and progesterone is correct in **B** but is not the primary controller of secondary characteristics. Choice **D** would be appropriate after puberty.

6. B

In both males and females, FSH stimulates gametogenisis, the production of sperm or ova. Recall the hypothalamus-pituitary-sex organ complex. Recall the diagrams of hormones, secretions, and target organs in your text. LH (**A**) can be rejected as stimulating testosterone or progesterone secretion. Testosterone (**C**) is only applicable to males. Progesterone (**D**) is only applicable to females.

7. A

The hormone in question here is LH. It is transported from the pituitary to the interstitial cells by the blood. LH is sometimes referred to as ICSH, interstitial cell stimulating hormone. Reject **B** because the vas deferens carry sperm. Reject **C** because the tubules are the location of sperm formation. **D** is an interesting choice but, if true, would require that each hormone producing gland have a duct going to the target organ. The body uses the bloodstream instead.

8. C

Recall the association between FSH and estrogen and between LH and progesterone. Each is controlled by negative feedback. As estrogen rises, feedback suppresses FSH. Likewise, as progesterone rises, secretion of LH is suppressed. In this way, you can accurately predict that if a woman is given estrogen and progesterone therapy, her FSH and LH secretion will be inhibited. Choice **A** can be rejected because the ovaries respond to FSH not estrogen. Choice **B** is possible but remember this woman is menopausal – follicles are depleted. Choice **D** is wrong because estrogen and progesterone suppress the production of FSH and LH, not stimulate it.

9. A

The preamble describes a method by which HCG (human chorionic gonadotropin) is inhibited from performing its normal function. Recall that HCG is produced by the outer layer of cells of an implanted blastocyst. HCG functions to maintain the corpus luteum within the ovary. The corpus luteum produces both estrogen and progesterone, both of which are required to maintain the endometrium (uterine lining) during pregnancy. A blastocyst can only implant permanently in a thick, vascularized endometrium. Although both **A** and **B** are indirect consequences of inhibiting HCG function and both lead to prevention of pregnancy, **A** is the better response because loss of the endometrium would lead directly to loss of the blastocyst; i.e., the end result of low progesterone levels following implantation would be loss of the endometrium. **C** is incorrect because development of new follicles in the ovary is regulated by FSH, which itself is not regulated by HCG. **D** is also incorrect because hormones do not control cilia movement in the Fallopian tubes.

10. B

See also the solution to question 9. HCG functions to maintain the corpus luteum (derived from the follicle after ovulation), which in turn secretes estrogen and progesterone that stimulate development and maintenance of the endometrium. Because the pregnant woman in this case is postmenopausal (and therefore could neither ovulate nor produce a corpus luteum for HCG to act upon), **B** is correct. In fact, this woman must receive hormone supplements to ensure that the endometrium is maintained for an implanted embryo for the first three months of pregnancy. (See also the solution to questions 15 and 16.)

11. D

Recall that the chorion (a layer in the developing embryo) does not form until after implantation in the endometrium. Therefore, **A**, **B**, and **C** are incorrect. The correct order of events following contact of the egg and sperm in the Fallopian tubes is as follows:

Fertilization - producing a diploid zygote;

Cleavage/mitosis - producing more diploid cells derived from the zygote parent cell; and giving rise to the multicellular blastocyst;

Implantation - the blastocyst attaches to the uterine wall/ endometrium;

Development of the blastula which possesses a hollow centre and the gastrula (which possesses the three germ layers: ectoderm, endoderm and mesoderm) is followed by development of the chorion and then by **organogenesis** (development of organs). **D** is correct.

12. A

The hypothalamus releases GnRH, which goes to the pituitary and stimulates the release of FSH and LH. Reject **B** because it would mean that the pituitary stimulates itself. Reject **C** and **D** as not part of the endocrine system.

13. C

Prolactin stimulates lactation (milk production). Oxytocin causes contraction of smooth muscles and the subsequent ejection of milk along milk ducts. You need to know your hormones and their effects. Reject **A** and **B** because relaxin functions to relax pelvic ligaments during birth. Reject **D** because the respective sequence is incorrect.

NR 3. 2 4 1 3

2 (ovulation), 4 (fertilization), 1 (release of HCG), and 3 (implantation). That ovulation occurs prior to fertilization is obvious. Recall that HCG is produced by the blastocyst while it still travelling down the Fallopian tube. The HCG replaces failing LH levels and maintains the corpus luteum. This maintains the endometrium and makes implantation possible.

14. D

During pregnancy, both estrogen and progesterone levels must remain high in order to maintain a thick vascularized endometrium and to prevent premature uterine contractions. Although both estrogen and progesterone levels drop sharply after childbirth, the drop in progesterone level is thought to be responsible for the onset of labour. **D** is therefore correct. LH functions to stimulate ovulation and maintains the corpus luteum, so **A** is incorrect. FSH functions to stimulate development of the follicle prior to ovulation, so **B** is also incorrect.

15. C

For the first three months of pregnancy, HCG released from the embryo signals the corpus luteum to continue producing both estrogen and progesterone, which in turn maintain the endometrium (uterine lining). Around the fourth month of pregnancy, the placenta (not the pituitary, so **D** is wrong) starts producing its own estrogen and progesterone. Therefore, **C** is correct. Both **A** and **B** are incorrect because oxytocin promotes uterine contraction during childbirth.

16. D

A post-menopausal woman's ovaries are non-functional– no more eggs are released. For this reason, eggs must be obtained from a donor female (meaning that the follicle is not required in the postmenopausal woman, so **A** and **C** are incorrect) and be fertilized *in vitro* (in a culture dish). The fertilized egg then is inserted directly into the uterus of the postmenopausal woman. Recall that any fertilized egg (blastocyst) requires a thick, vascularized endometrium to implant, and that the endometrium in order to implant and that the endometrium must be maintained until childbirth. Both estrogen and progesterone are responsible for promoting thickening of the endometrium, and then for maintaining it. Therefore, **D** is correct. FSH and LH promote the development of the follicle, so **B** is an incorrect statement.

17. B

Notice the effect of mercury poisoning described in the information preceding the question: deterioration of short-term memory and inaability to coordinatoe muscle movements. The relationship to the neural tube should be clear. Reject **A** because there is no relevant connection here between mercury and the amniotic fluid. Reject **C** because the ovaries are not directly implicated. No mention is made of any ovarian hormones. Reject **D** for the same reason. Be reminded that answers should be chosen first on the basis of information or evidence given in the question.

NR 4.   1 3 4 2

1 (ovulation), 3 (fertilization), 4 (implantation), 2 (placenta forms). That ovulation occurs before fertilization is obvious. The occurrence of implantation prior to the formation of the placenta is correct because implantation occurs in the endometrium, and then the placenta begins to development.

18. D

LH therapy (**A**) would affect testosterone production but would have no effect on the vas deferens. Reject **B** for the same reason. Extraction of sperm from the male's urethra (**C**), is questionable at best and not feasible here because without vas deferens, the sperm cannot travel to the urethra.

19. A

The genital tract here refers to the vagina. As the child finally passes through the vagina at birth, it may be exposed to a variety of infectious organisms. The zygote (**B**) has not yet passed through the genital tract. Nothing in the information provided indicates that the infections are related to amniotic fluid (**C**). As well, amniotic fluid is generated by the developing fetus. Choice **D** can be rejected on the basis that the blood from the uterine veins does not enter the fetus.

ANSWERS AND SOLUTIONS
CELL DIVISION, MENDELIAN GENETICS AND
MOLECULAR GENETICS – UNIT REVIEW

1. C	12. C	23. C	34. B	42. C
2. B	13. D	24. A	35. A	NR8. 0.25
NR1. 4, 2, 3, 1	14. A	25. C	36. B	43. C
3. B	15. A	26. C	37. B	44. A
4. A	16. B	27. C	38. C	45. A
5. C	17. D	28. A	NR4. 0.50	46. A
6. A	NR2. 3, 2, 1, 4	NR3. 1, 1, 2, 2	NR5. 55	NR9. 50
7. D	18. C	29. D	39. A	47. D
8. C	19. C	30. D	40. C	48. B
9. D	20. C	31. B	NR6. 0.25	49. D
10. C	21. D	32. C	NR7. 512	NR10. 9:3:4
11. C	22. B	33. D	41. A	NR11. 3:3:2 or 6:6:4
				50. C

1. C

There must be the same amount of adenine in DNA as thymine because adenine and thymine are complementary base pairs. Wherever there is thymine on one side of a DNA strand, there must be adenine on the other side. Therefore, the amount of adenine and thymine are always equal.

2. B

The sequence of nucleotides in one gene determines the order of amino acids that makes up a protein, for example an enzyme.
A is incorrect because a gene doesn't actually do anything, other than to serve as a code for how to make something.
C is incorrect because one gene codes for just one protein.
D is incorrect because the sequence of amino acids in an enzyme is determined by the nucleotide sequence in the gene.

NR 1.   4 2 3 1

4–The DNA of a gene transcribes a strand of mRNA, which is moved from the nucleus to the ribosomes.

2–The ribosome reads the mRNA and causes the correct sequence of tRNAs to bind with the mRNA. Amino acids are attached to the tRNAs, so the amino acids are being transported to the ribosomes.

3–The polypeptide is the sequence of amino acids. As it is formed, it folds itself into a specific shape that will make it a functional enzyme.

1–When the polypeptide is a functional enzyme, it is released from the ribosome.

3. B

During genetic engineering, a section of bacterial DNA is opened using a restriction enzyme.

Restriction enzymes can be thought of as being like scissors. The same restriction enzyme is used to cut out a gene that will be inserted into the bacterial DNA.

Ligase enzymes are then used to fasten the pieces of DNA together. Ligase acts like a molecular glue.

4. A

The function of insulin is to lower the blood sugar level. It does this by stimulating the liver and skeletal muscles to absorb glucose from the blood and store it as glycogen. Insulin is most important after a meal when a large amount of sugar passes from the small intestine into the blood. Without properly functioning insulin, an individual would experience a chronic increase in blood sugar after meals.

5. C

When a protein is made, mRNA is translated by the ribosomes into a chain of amino acid called a polypeptide. When the polypeptide coils, it becomes a functional protein, such as secretory component. DNA is replicated every time a cell undergoes mitosis, but this has nothing to do with the production of a protein.

6. A

It seems that the faulty chloride-channel proteins result in a high level of chloride ions. These ions destroy the natural antibiotic defensin, which allows the bacteria to increase in number. This increase results in excessive mucin production. So, the original problem is that a faulty amino acid sequence is unable to correctly form the chloride-channel proteins.

7. D

The following diagram shows the structure of DNA and the molecules that make it up.

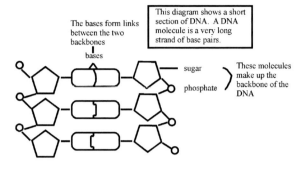

8. C

mRNA codes like this:

DNA base	Corresponding mRNA base
Adenine	Uracil
Thymine	Adenine
Cytosine	Guanine
Guanine	Cytosine

It is important to remember that in RNA, uracil, not thymine, is opposite to adenine.

For this question:

DNA template	mRNA nucleotides produced
Adenine 20%	Uracil 20%
Thymine 30%	Adenine 30%
Cytosine 10 %	Guanine 10%
Guanine 40%	Cytosine 40%

9. D

A carrier has one normal allele and one defective allele. If an individual is a carrier, one of the normal DNA probes will bind to his or her normal allele, and one of the defective allele DNA probes will bind to his or her defective allele.

10. C

Crossing over occurs during prophase I of meiosis. At that time, sections of homologous chromosomes are exchanged. Genes that are close together on a chromosome are likely to be exchanged together or remain together. Genes that are far apart are more likely to become separated during crossing over, with one gene being exchanged and the other being left behind. So, in this question, we are selecting the genes that are farthest apart. The genes *m* and *lc* are separated by 78 map units, so they have the greatest chance of being separated by crossing over.

11. C

The easiest way to determine the cross-over frequency between *O* and *S* is to construct a gene map. Cross-over frequency is an indication of the distance between genes.

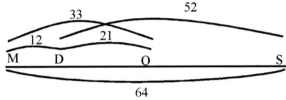

The cross-over frequency between *O* and *S* can be calculated by subtraction.
64 – 21 – 12 = 31. The cross-over frequency between *O* and *S* is 31%.

12. C

The information tells us that *p53* is active when a cell is damaged or mutant. The *p53* gene then causes the cell to halt cell division or undergo suicide. As a result, *p53* ensures that a damaged or mutant cell does not reproduce. If *p53* works properly, cancer should never occur, which suggests that whenever a person gets cancer, the *p53* gene is one part of the DNA that is damaged.

13. D

When the *p53* gene was normal, the cells in the petri dish divided normally. That means the cells were not cancerous, so **A** and **B** are not correct answers. This study was done with the cells from one kind of laboratory animal. *p53* did seem to prevent cancer under those conditions. However, to conclude that *p53* prevents cancer in all mammals is not shown by this evidence, so **C** is incorrect.

14. A

p53 stops cancer, so we would not want to remove the *p53* from cells, so **C** and **D** are not correct answers. From the information it appears that only one normal *p53* allele is needed to control cell division, so **A** is the correct answer.

15. A

Mitosis is the cellular process in which the 2*n* nuclear material of one cell divides to make the 2*n* nuclear material for two cells.

B Meiosis results in *n* cells.

C Recombination usually refers to the process (during prophase I of meiosis) in which crossing over occurs to produce genetically unique cells.

D Nondisjunction refers to an error in cell division in which daughter cells end up containing only one chromosome of a pair (monosomy) or three of a pair (trisomy). There is no reason to assume that nondisjunction has occurred between V and W and X.

16. B

The cells at U are *n*, or haploid, so they must have resulted from meiosis. Human cells that form during mitosis (**A**) are always diploid or 2*n*. Fertilization (**C**), the fusion of two gametes, produces a 2*n* cell, and differentiation (**D**) results in specialized 2*n* cells.

17. D

These cells were joined and were on their way to being part of an embryo, but they have separated. They can both develop into a complete individual, each genetically identical to the other. This is how genetically identical twins form.

NR 2.   3 2 1 4

3– Prophase is the first phase in which chromosomes are visible. The nuclear membrane disappears as does the nucleolus. The two centrioles begin to form asters and migrate to the poles.

2– During metaphase, the spindle forms from the asters and the chromosomes line up on the cell equator.

1– During anaphase, chromatids are pulled by spindle fibres to the poles.

4– During telophase, chromosomes unwind to become chromatin, and the nuclear membrane and nucleolus reform.

18. C

Haploid cells containing unpaired chromosomes result from meiosis. Examples in humans are sperm and eggs. In the life cycle of *Ulva*, zoospores result from meiosis, so it can be concluded that zoospores are haploid.
The gametophyte develops from the zoospore through a mitosis, which involves production of genetically identical cells, so the gametophyte must also be haploid.

19. C

Label 3 refers to the chromosome in the diagram and the text states that the beads coated with DNA replaced the chromosomes.

20. C

It appears from the description that centrosomes (centrioles) were not part of the experiment and mitosis can progress normally. The genetic material containing DNA (**A**) formed the microtubules (**D**) that became the spindle (**B**). All of these were needed.

21. D

Prophase and metaphase have been completed if the chromosomes are at the centre of the cell. According to the studies referred to, if a chromosome is pulled out of line, the phase where chormosomes move to the poles will be delayed. The phases that are delayed are the phases that follow metaphase. Anaphase is the phase that involves pulling the chromosomes to the poles. Following anaphase is telophase, which cannot occur until anaphase has been completed.

22. B

Eggs and sperm are both haploid or 1*n*. They contain 23 unpaired chromosomes and are both produced by meiosis. They are produced after puberty, and there are many more sperm produced than eggs.

23. C

Normally a person has 46 chromosomes, made up of 22 pairs of autosomes and one pair of sex chromosomes. Down syndrome is caused by trisomy 21. Autosome pair 21 has three copies rather than the normal two. In Down Syndrome, the one pair of sex chromosomes is normal.

24. A

During amniocentesis, amniotic fluid is withdrawn. Inside the amniotic fluid are cells from the fetus. The cells can be grown in a petri dish. As one of the cells undergoes mitosis, a photograph can be taken of its chromosomes and the chromosomes can be lined up to form a karyotype. This will reveal chromosomal abnormalities such as trisomy 21.

25. C

The sperm is a means of delivering the genetic material to the oocyte. It has very little of what we know as cytoplasm. The oocyte on the other hand contains the same amount of nuclear DNA as the sperm, but also contains a large amount of cytoplasm. The large amount of cytoplasm is needed because the fertilized egg must have enough energy and cell organelles to survive through many cell divisions before it can start to gain energy from the mother's endometrium.

26. C

A mature human oocyte would be a secondary oocyte. A secondary oocyte has already completed meiosis I. During meiosis I, the oocyte lost half of its chromosomes (one of each homologous pair) to the polar body.
This reduces the chromosome number from 46 to 23 and changes it from diploid to haploid.

27. C

Process Z shows that when the two X chromosomes were supposed to separate into two different eggs during meiosis, they did not. One egg received both Xs and the other none. This failure of the chromosomes to separate properly is called nondisjunction.

28. A

The last pair of chromosomes (23rd pair) are the sex chromosomes. In this case, there is one X chromosome and a smaller Y chromosome. That makes the individual a male so the answer is **A** or **C**. The third-last pair (21st pair) is actually three chromosomes. Having three instead of two is called trisomy. This individual has trisomy 21, so **A** is the correct answer. Trisomy 21 is the chromosomal abnormality that causes Down Syndrome.

NR 3. 1 1 2 2

Haploid refers to cells that are *n*. In *n* cells the chromosomes are not paired. A human haploid cell, a sperm or an egg, has 23 unpaired chromosomes. A diploid cell has paired chromosomes. Human diploid cells have 46 chromosomes in 23 pairs. The egg (**A**) is haploid because it was formed by meiosis. Meiosis forms haploid cells. The pollen grain (**B**) is also haploid. The pollen grain is the plant equivalent of a sperm and is also formed by meiosis. The cells of the embryo (**C**) are diploid, since the embryo is the result of fertilization in which the two haploid cells, the egg and the pollen, fuse. The mature sporophyte (**D**) is diploid. It is a multicellular structure that grew from the embryo by mitosis.

29. D

The female gamete (ovule) contributes all the cytoplasm, including the plastids to the zygote. It would appear that the colour of the plastid is not dependent on genes from the pollen or ovule nucleus. We have to conclude that the plastids (cell organelles of the cytoplasm) contain their own genetic information.

30. D

With incomplete dominance, both alleles are expressed, which result in an intermediate form of the trait. In this case: *RR* deep crimson, *Rr* scarlet-red, and *rr* yellow.

Crossing two scarlet-red plants would result in 1 deep crimson:2 scarlet-red:1 yellow. This is illustrated in the following Punnett square.

	R	r
R	RR	Rr
r	Rr	rr

The results of the F_1 cross show this 1:2:1 ratio.

31. B

The crosses are illustrated below. Note that the P_1 plants are pure-breeding, or homozygous. These are the only P_1 combinations that will result in the offspring observed.

$R^P R^P \times rr$

	R^P	R^P
r	$R^P r$	$R^P r$
r	$R^P r$	$R^P r$

offspring – only scarlet-red

$RR \times rr$

	r	r
R	Rr	Rr
R	Rr	Rr

offspring – only orange flowered

32. C

The genotype $R^P R$ should produce a phenotype that is an intermediate form between $R^P R^P$ (deep crimson) and RR (light crimson). Yellow and orange can be eliminated right away because both require *r*, and from question 30, we know that scarlet-red is an intermediate form between deep crimson and yellow. As a result, crimson is the most reasonable choice.

33. D

The following shows how to get four different phenotypes:
B_yy–blue
*bbY_*–yellow
*B_Y_*–green
bbyy–no colour
A blank space (_) could be either a dominant (capital) or a recessive (lower case) allele.
To have an offspring with no colour (*bbyy*), each parent must have at least one *b* and one *y*.

This eliminates answers **A**, **B**, and **C**.
The cross below shows that *Bbyy* × *bbYy* can produce offspring with four different colour patterns.

Bbyy × bbYy

	By	*by*
bY	*BbYy* green	*bbYy* yellow
by	*Bbyy* blue	*bbyy* no colour

34. B

Green heterozygous parakeets are dihybrids–*BbYy*. Crossing two dihybrids results in a 9:3:3:1 ratio. In this case, 3/16 will be blue, as shown in the Punnett square below.

	BY	*By*	*bY*	*by*
BY	*BBYY*	*BBYy*	*BbYY*	*BbYy*
By	*BBYy*	*BByy*	*BbYy*	*Bbyy*
bY	*BbYY*	*BbYy*	*bbYY*	*bbYy*
by	*BbYy*	*Bbyy*	*bbYy*	*bbyy*

☐ indicates a blue parakeet

35. A

The gene with the inserted DNA has no effect on the phenotype of the mouse when it is in the heterozygous condition, so it would appear to be recessive

B This cannot be correct because if the gene with the inserted DNA was dominant, a heterozygous mouse would have its organs reversed.

C The affected gene may produce a protein that influences embryonic development, but we cannot be sure from the information we are given.

D This is incorrect because we cannot tell whether the gene can be transcribed from the information given.

36. B

If two heterozygous mice were mated, 25% of the offspring would be homozygous recessive. This cross is illustrated in the Punnett square below.

Rr × Rr

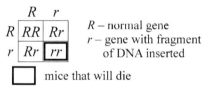

	R	*r*
R	*RR*	*Rr*
r	*Rr*	*rr*

R – normal gene
r – gene with fragment of DNA inserted

☐ mice that will die

These would have their organs reversed and die a short time after birth.

37. B

Since the guevedoces are genetically male, they have one Y chromosome and at least one X chromosome. To make a genetically male child, the sperm contains the Y (since a female does not have a Y chromosome), and the egg contains the X.

38. C

Ss × *SS* The heterozygous offspring is *Ss*. The *S* is for the normal, non-transgenic gene, and the *s* is for the inserted allele for secretory component. The non-transgenic sheep do not contain the allele for secretory component, so they are *SS*.

NR 4. 0.50

The symbolic representation of the cross is $Ss \times SS$. The $Ss \times SS$ cross results in a 50% chance of Ss, or 0.50 rounded to two decimal places.

NR 5. 55

Crossing $Ss \times Ss$ results in 25% ss. 25% of 220 is 55.

39. A

The colourless plant must be $bbdd$. Since the black pigmented plants are pure breeding, they are homozygous, BB. This is confirmed by the fact that all of the offspring were black. The offspring could all be Bb and appear black only if the black parent always gave a B. Hence, the black parent must have been BB. The dotted phenotype only appears if the individual is bb, so there will be no dotted offspring if the parents are $BBDD$ and $bbdd$.

40. C

2 black, 1 dotted, 1 colourless, as shown below. The colourless individual ($bbdd$) can only produce the gamete bd. The heterozygote ($BbDd$) can produce the gametes BD, Bd, bD, and bd.

	BD	Bd	bD	bd
bd	$BbDd$	$Bbdd$	$bbDd$	$bbdd$
	black	black	dotted	colourless

NR 6   0.25

From the Punnett square for question 40, we can see that dotted offspring occur 1 out of 4 times.

NR 7   5 1 2

If the test cross is between a heterozygote ($BbDd$) and a colourless plant ($bbdd$), 50% of the offspring will be black. See the Punnett square for question 40. 50% of 1 024 is 512.

41. A

Since individual II-2 has cystic fibrosis, he must be homozygous recessive, aa. His parents, I-1 and I-2, do not have cystic fibrosis, but they each gave him a recessive allele so they are both heterozygous, Aa.

42. C

Hemophilia is a sex-linked disorder in which the affected allele is on the X chromosome. If the woman has hemophilia, her genotype is $X^h X^h$. Since the man does not have hemophilia, his genotype is $X^H Y$. For all female children, his sperm contains the chromosome $X^H X^H$. Therefore, none of his female children will have hemophilia, although they will all be carriers. For male children, his sperm contains the Y chromosome. Since the woman always provides an egg with the affected allele, all of the male children will have hemophilia.

NR 8. 0.25

The symbolic representation of the woman is $X^H X^h$ while the man she marries is $X^H Y$. If you cross them together, it results in a 50% chance of having a hemophiliac child. The chances of having a hemophiliac son are $0.50 \times 0.50 = 0.25$.

43. C

Genes that are on the same chromosomes are called linked genes. During gamete formation, segregation (in which pairs of chromosomes separate) occurs so that a gamete gets either one or the other of a pair of chromosomes. All the genes that are on one chromosome, therefore, go to a gamete as a set. If a breeder is selecting for one characteristic, he or she gets all other genes linked to the gene for the selected characteristic.

It appears that the genes for long nose and closely set eyes are on the same chromosome as the gene for retinal disease. Therefore, if you are breeding for one of these characteristics, you are likely to get all three.

44. A

A Punnett square shows this cross. She is healthy but has had offspring with hemophilia, so we know she is a carrier. Her genotype is $X^H X^h$. The genotype of the healthy male she is mated with has a genotype $X^H Y$.

	X^H	X^h
X^H	$X^H X^H$	$X^H X^h$
Y	$X^H Y$	$X^h Y$

None of the female offspring will have hemophilia. Half of the female offspring will be carriers, though.

45. A

The evidence supports the idea that the Y chromosome causes maleness. Individuals with Klinefelter syndrome who have a Y are male and individuals with Turner syndrome who don't have have a Y are female. Individuals with Turner syndrome have only one X and they are female, so **B** is incorrect. Individuals with Klinefelter syndrome (XXY individuals) have two X chromosomes but they are not female, so **C** is incorrect. Individuals who have a Y chromosome are all male and those without a Y chromosome are all female, so **D** is incorrect.

46. A

If the disease were sex-linked dominant or recessive, males could not be heterozygous, and if it were sex-linked recessive, it would be far more common in males. From what we are told, it appears to be autosomal. That means that the gene is located on one of the first 22 pairs of chromosomes, not on the sex chromosomes. Since individuals have to be homozygous for the defective allele to get Tay-Sachs and heterozygous individuals don't have the disease, the inheritance is autosomal recessive.

NR 9   50

This question is quite easily done using a Punnett square. Both parents are carriers. That means they are heterozygous for this autosomal recessive trait.
Let's give them the genotypes $Tt \times Tt$.

	T	t
T	TT	Tt
t	Tt	tt

The individuals with protection from tuberculosis are those that are heterozygous, 50% of the offspring.

47. D

Because these genes are located on different chromosomes, they are not linked.
During gamete formation, the alleles sort independently. We can work this out using two Punnett squares: 3/4 of the offspring have purple stems and 1/4 have green stems.
A cross of $Pp \times Pp$ will give us these results.

	P	p
P	PP	Pp
p	Pp	pp

Half of the offspring have red tomatoes and half have yellow tomatoes.
A cross of $Tt \times tt$ will give us these results.

	t	t
T	Tt	Tt
t	tt	tt

So, the genotypes of the parents are $PpTt$ and $Pptt$.

48. B

The logic required to answer this question is illustrated below. It is always best in this type of question to convert the described phenotype into a genotype that can be written down.

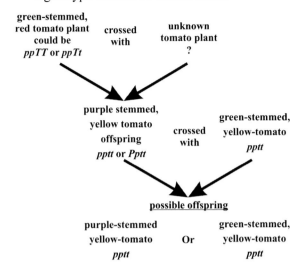

49. D

All of the offspring that have at least one uppercase *C* have coat color, either brown or black. If the offspring have two recessive lower case *c*'s, then the offspring has no coat color. A gene that controls the expression of another gene—whether or not the coat colour gene is expressed—is called an epistatic gene.

NR 10   9:3:4

To answer this question, we have to use the Punnett square that has been drawn for us. We can see that there are 9 black:3 brown:4 white.

NR 11.   3:3:2 OR 6:6:4

For this question, we can draw a Punnett square. *bbCc* × *BbCc*

	BC	*Bc*	*bC*	*bc*
bC	*BbCC*	*BbCc*	*bbCC*	*bbCc*
bc	*BbCc*	*Bbcc*	*bbCc*	*bbcc*
bC	*BbCC*	*BbCc*	*bbCC*	*bbCc*
bc	*BbCc*	*Bbcc*	*bbCc*	*bbcc*

Key: Dark grey box–black mouse
     Light grey box–brown mouse
     White box–white mouse

Phenotypic ratio: 6 black:6 brown:4 white or,
                  3 black:3 brown:2 white
Either answer is correct.

50. C

In a test cross, an organism of dominant phenotype (you don't know whether it is homozygous or heterozygous) is crossed with an organism of recessive phenotype. We always know that the recessive organism is homozygous.
In this case the test cross would be *WW* or *Ww* (ram) × *ww* (ewe). If the ram is heterozygous, one would expect half white offspring and half black offspring as shown in the Punnett square below.

	W	*w*
w	*Ww*	*ww*
w	*Ww*	*ww*

Key: White squares–white sheep
       Grey squares–black sheep

ANSWERS AND SOLUTIONS
CELL DIVISION, MENDELIAN GENETICS AND MOLECULAR GENETICS – UNIT TEST 3

1.	D	9.	A	15.	B	23.	B	NR4.	0.50
2.	A	10.	B	16.	D	NR3.	0.25	NR5.	50
3.	D	11.	B	17.	D	24.	A	30.	C
4.	A	12.	C	18.	B	25.	D	NR6.	25
5.	A	13.	D	19.	B	26.	A	31.	B
6.	D	14.	B	20.	C	27.	D	32.	B
7.	A	NR1.	3, 2, 1, 4	21.	C	28.	D	33.	B
8.	B	NR2.	3, 2, 1	22.	A	29.	B	34.	
								NR7.	0.50

1. D

Each of the four alternatives involves a different cellular process that could be a consequence of increased DNA damage/decreased DNA repair. Because the question is asking about the initial effect of increased DNA damage, the key to this question is understanding the flow of information from the nuclear DNA through to the synthesis of proteins.

Information is stored and inherited in the form of double-stranded DNA. Recall that DNA makes up chromosomes, and that information on chromosomes is divided into numerous individual messages called genes. To translate the code within each gene into a gene product (a protein), two processes must occur:

1. **Transcription**—RNA polymerase copies the information from one of the DNA strands of a gene into a single-stranded piece of RNA called a messenger RNA (or mRNA). The mRNA then leaves the nucleus and enters the cytoplasm.

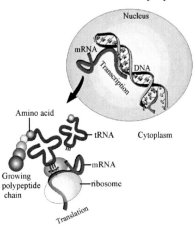

2. **Translation**—The mRNA attaches to the ribosome (the site of protein synthesis in the cell) where the message within the mRNA is translated into a string of amino acids (a polypeptide, or protein). Recall that the mRNA is read three base pairs at a time (one codon at a time), and that the appropriate amino acid is carried to the ribosome and added to the growing polypeptide chain by tRNAs, each of which carries only one amino acid.

D is the correct response because initially altered DNA would affect transcription, the first step in the transfer of information from the DNA to a final product. The altered mRNA possibly would then lead to the production of an abnormal protein. An abnormal protein in a cell could lead to production of a cancerous cell (for example, if the normal function of the protein was to regulate cell growth), or abnormal cell function such as a decrease in the cell's synthesis of ATP (for example, if the protein's normal function was to synthesize ATP).

2. A

First find the codons corresponding to the amino acids in the portion of the insulin protein. Then convert the RNA codon sequence into a DNA sequence. Recall that RNA contains the base uracil (U), which, in DNA, is the base thymine (T).

Amino acid	Phenylalanine	Valine	Asparagine	Glutamine	Histidine
RNA codon	UUU, UUC	GUU, GUC, GUA, GUG	AAU, AAC	CAG, CAA	CAU, CAC
DNA	AAA, AAG	CAA, CAG, CAT, CAC	TTA, TTC	GTC, GTT	GTA, GTG

In the table above, the DNA sequences given correlate the strand of DNA from which the RNA was transcribed. Therefore, the DNA sequences are complementary to the RNA sequences.

The only choice that provides the correct DNA sequences for all of the amino acids is **A**.

3. D

Recall that DNA is a double-stranded helix composed of a sugar-phosphate backbone and the four nitrogen bases A (adenine), T (thymine), G (guanine), and C (cytosine). RNA is single-stranded and is also made of a sugar-phosphate backbone and four nitrogen bases A, U (uracil), G, and C.

D is the correct response.

4. A

Recall that DNA contains two chains paired along their length according to **base-pairing rules**: the nitrogen bases **A** and **T** pair with each other, and the bases **G** and **C** pair with each other. Therefore, for every A in one chain, there must be a T in the opposite chain; likewise, for every G in one chain, a C must exist in the other chain. (See diagram of a random sequence below.)
A - C - G - A - T - T - A - C - C - G - T -T - ...
(3/12 are A)
T - G - C - T - A - A - T - G - G - C - A - A - ...
(3/12 are T)

Therefore, if 15% of the DNA sample in the question contains adenine molecules, then an equal proportion, 15%, should be thymine molecules. **A** is correct. This means that 30% of the DNA is composed of A-T base pairs.
Both **B and D** are incorrect because uracil (U) is found only in RNA.

5. A

In DNA replication, the old strand serves as the **template** for formation of the new strand. Nucleotides are added to the new strand based on the **base-pairing rules** such that the sequence of the old and new strands are exactly complementary. Also, recall that all DNA in the cell remains in the **nucleus**.
Therefore, replication also occurs in the nucleus, and **A** is correct. In contrast to DNA, RNA is present both in the nucleus and in the cytoplasm.

6. D

The backbone of DNA, analogous to the rails of a ladder, is composed of alternating molecules of deoxyribose sugar and phosphate groups.
The four bases (A, T, C, G) are analogous to the rungs of the ladder, and chemically, they are called nitrogen bases. **D** is therefore the correct response.

7. A

Recall protein synthesis. The sequence of production of CCK requires transcription of the appropriate DNA code into mRNA, then translation from mRNA to an amino acid sequence at the ribosomes. Replication (**B**) would refer to production of more DNA. Transcription (**C**) has to occur first. Recombination (**D**) has nothing to do with the process.

8. B

Model 2 shows a parent DNA strand replicating into two daughter strands. Each daughter strand contains one of the parental strands and a new strand. This is semi-conservation replication. Choice **A** can be rejected as both parent strands have stayed intact. Choice **C** can be rejected because there is no new DNA present. Choice **D** can be rejected as there is no old or parental DNA remaining.

9. A

Recall that crossover frequency is directly proportional to the map distances between genes on a linear chromosome. Using the frequencies provided in the preamble, the following map can be generated:

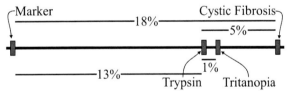

This order and arrangement of genes on the map corresponds to the chromosome shown in **A**.

10. B

As a chemical, DNA is essentially the same in all living organisms. There is also great similarity between the principle of DNA replication and protein synthesis. As the late Carl Sagan once said "Any oak tree could read my DNA." The similarity in the structure of DNA and of genes makes DNA quite transferable between organisms of different kinds. Choices **A**, **C**, and **D** can be rejected in this question because none of them are true. Genes do not all carry the same information, genotypes of bacteria and plants are not the same, and the phenotype of an organism may be altered if one gene is exchanged for another.

11. B

Recall the cell cycle:

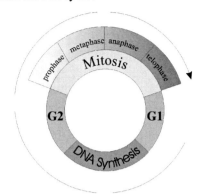

From the information, we know that the vesicles appeared during mitosis around the time that the nuclear membrane dissolved, and the vesicles later disappeared when the nuclear membrane re-formed.

During the normal cell cycle, the nuclear membrane dissolves during prophase at the start of mitosis, and then re-forms when the chromosomes have reached opposite poles at telophase. **B** is therefore the best response. At anaphase, the chromosomes are still moving from the metaphase plate (equator) toward opposite poles; if the nuclear membrane were to form during anaphase, the chromosomes would not necessarily end up within the nucleus. During interphase (comprised of the G1, DNA synthesis, and G2 phases), the nuclear membrane remains intact, enclosing the DNA in the nucleus. Both **C** and **D** are therefore incorrect.

12. C

During prophase, the chromosomes are located in the cell nucleus. The nucleus dissolves and the chromosomes begin to move to the cell equator (so **A** is incorrect). During metaphase, chromosomes line up along the cell equator (so **D** is incorrect). During anaphase, spindle fibres pull the chormosomes toward the poles of the cell (so **C** is the correct answer). During telophase, chromosomes reach the poles of the cell and a new nuclear membrane forms (so **B** is incorrect). **C** is the only correct statement.

13. D

Whereas the purpose of mitosis is to produce more cells identical to the parent cell (eg., diploid parent cell gives rise to diploid daughter cells), the purpose of meiosis is to create haploid cells (gametes) from a normal diploid cell. **A** and **B** are therefore incorrect. Meiosis occurs in two stages (two divisions: meiosis I and II) that result in a final product of four haploid cells, so **D** is correct.

14. B

The blastula is the product of numerous mitoses of the fertilized egg cell. At the blastula stage, all cells are essentially the same. Each cell can adopt any fate, so these cells are called pleuripotent.

(Fates include any cell type in the body. For example: liver, nerve, blood, skin, muscle, etc., are all different cell types that have unique phenotypes and functions that are determined by (i) the expression of a unique set of genes, (ii) the pattern of development and (iii) the location of the cell in the body.) After the blastula implants in the endometrium and develops further, individual cells begin to lose their pleuripotency and become restricted as to the type of cell that they can become. This restriction of cell fate is called differentiation.

B is the correct response. For cloning to work, the cell from which the nucleus is derived must be pleuripotent, and not differentiated, otherwise the resulting developing embryo would be missing some cell types. **A** is incorrect because the size of the nucleus in a living cell normally does not change during development. **C** is incorrect because genes are not removed or added from a cell during development. All cells have the same genes. What makes one cell different from another is the number and combination of genes that are **expressed** or **silent**. **D** is incorrect because cells in the early embryo undergo only mitosis, not meiosis. (Recall that meiosis is used for the production of gametes).

NR 1.   3, 2, 1, 4

Anaphase (3), Metaphase (2), Prophase (1), Telophase (4). Be very careful here. First recall the order of the phases: prophase, metaphase, anaphase, telophase. Next, arrange the numbers to match the names of the stages. If you look at the question carefully, you do not need the diagram.

NR 2.   3, 2, 1

The division of diploid cells to produce more diploid cells is growth, process 3. When haploid cells or sperm and eggs combine to form a diploid cell, this is fertilization, process 2. In process 1, the male and female are producing gametes. The male and female consist of diploid cells. Their gametes are haploid. So the process is formation of gametes, fertilization, and growth, and the correct answer is 3, 2, 1.

15. B

Meiosis occurs in the testis in males and ovaries in females. Actually, meiosis II occurs after ovulation in the Fallopian tubes in females but this is not relevant in this question.
Reject **A** because number 9 indicates the uterus.
Reject **C** because of the epididymis, where sperm mature, and the uterus.
Reject **D** because number 5 indicates the epididymis. This is a question where you need to know the structure and function of the male and female reproductive organs.

16. D

Nondisjunction describes an event that happens during an abnormal meiosis. Recall that during metaphase I of meiosis, homologous chromosomes line up at the metaphase plate/equator. At this time, recombination occurs, resulting in the exchange of information from one set of homologous chromosomes with the other. Anaphase follows, during which the homologous chromosomes separate from each other, migrate to opposite poles, and then eventually end up in separate cells.
Each of the cells at the end of meiosis I is haploid (having only one set of each chromosome). Nondisjunction describes the failure of homologous chromosomes to segregate to opposite poles during anaphase I.
D is therefore correct. **A** and **B** are not correct because an error in either DNA replication or RNA transcription would probably, at most, alter one gene or gene product, not an entire chromosome. **C** is not correct because a mistake during mitosis would not result in nondisjunction. Probably, a mistake at telophase of mitosis would result in loss of one or both of the daughter cells following mitosis.

17. D

Autosomal inheritance is equal among males and females; which is different than X-linked inheritance. Reject **A** because nothing in the information indicates that albinism is related to maturity. Reject **B** and **C** because they each imply that albinism is X-linked.

18. B

Sunlight increases melanin production. The amount of production is genetically controlled. This, then, is a genetic condition that depends on an environmental factor for expression. Choice **A** is a true statement but does not demonstrate what happens in people who are able to produce melanin.
Choices **C** and **D** are irrelevant to the information given in the question, survival is not discussed.

19. B

Refer also to the solution for question 34. In the cross shown in the solution 34, both parents are carriers and therefore heterozygous for the cystic fibrosis allele. Note that the chance of two heterozygous parents having a child with cystic fibrosis is 1/4, or 25%, and the corresponding chance for them to have a normal child is 3/4, or 75%. The correct response is **B**.

20. C

From the preamble, we learn that Marfan syndrome is an autosomal disorder. This means that the gene for Marfan syndrome is located on an autosomal chromosome (chromosomes 1 to 22) not a sex chromosome (X or Y).
Therefore, males and females (who possess equal numbers of autosomal chromosomes) are affected equally.

C is therefore the correct response.
If the gene for Marfan syndrome were on the X chromosome, females would be more likely to have the syndrome (because the syndrome is dominant, and females who have two X chromosomes, giving them a greater chance of inheriting the X chromosome with the Marfan allele). **D** is incorrect because whether the disease occurs randomly has no affect on the frequency of affected females versus the frequency of affected males.

21. C

	TR	*Tr*	*tR*	*tr*
tR	TtRR **1**	TtRr **2**	ttRR **3**	ttRr **4**
tr	TtRr **5**	Ttrr **6**	ttRr **7**	ttrr **8**

Pure breeders are homozygous for the respective gene. Therefore, in order for a plant to be a pure breeder for both plant height and seed shape, the plant must be homozygous for both the height and shape alleles. Only individuals 3 and 8 are homozygous at both genes, so **C** is correct. Homozygous individuals are called "pure-breeding" because they can donate only one kind of allele of the relevant gene to the offspring.

22. A

Determine the genotypes required in the parents separately for each allele. First, for 100% of the offspring to have round seeds, one parent must have two R alleles, and the other parent must have a least one R allele.
(**i.e. RR × RR or Rr**) Therefore, **B** and **D** can be ruled out because the alleles of the parents in these choices are not correct for the round alleles. Test the remaining choices for the tall phenotype:

$A – Tt × tt →$ progeny: ½ *Tt* and ½ *tt*
(tall)   (short)

A is therefore correct. In **C**, the cross would be as follows:

$tt × tt →$ progeny: all *tt* (short)

C is therefore incorrect.

23. B

From the information we learn that three alleles control the pattern on the clover leaf, and that they have an order of dominance:

V^h – long V-shaped lines > V^l – short V-shaped lines > *v* – no lines

The information states that "A clover plant with long V-shaped lines ... and a clover plant with short V-shaped lines... produced offspring." The offspring included all types of phenotypes, including plants with unlined leaves. Recall that the plants with unlined leaves must be homozygous recessive (*vv*). This means that both parents must be heterozygous for the leaf marking gene. The breeding diagram for the cross is shown below:

long lines × short lines
$V^h v$ $V^l v$
↓

	V^h	*v*
V^l	$V^h V^l$ long lines	$V^l v$ short lines
v	$V^h v$ long lines	*vv* no lines

B is therefore the correct response.

NR 3.   0.25

Refer to the Punnett square provided in the previous solution (MC 23). The chance that the offspring will have unlined leaves is 1/4, or 25%, or 0.25.

24. A

There are numerous ways to solve this question. If you cross $AA × Bi$, you will get the right answer. Notice that the heterozygous *B* appears before the homozygous *A*. Choice **B** contains heterozygous *O*, which does not exist. If you try homozygous *B* crossed with heterozygous *A* you will produce *AB/Bi* offspring. So reject **C**. If you cross heterozygous *B* with heterozygous *A*, you will produce *AB, Ai, Bi, ii* offspring. So reject **D**.

25. D

Let *A* represent the BRCA allele and *B* represent the BARD allele. What you are looking for here is the occurrence of any recessive genes. Individual 4 is heterozygous for BRCA (*Aa*) and homozygous recessive for BARD (*bb*). This individual has three out of four recessive genes and so is most likely to develop tumours. Individual 1 has only one recessive gene, *Aa, BB*. Individual 2 has two recessive genes, *Aa, Bb*. Individual 3 has none, *AA BB*.

26. A

The solution to this question is simplified by eliminating choices **B** and **D**. If a woman has blood type A and a man has blood type O, they cannot produce a child with blood type AB such as child 4. So reject **B** and **D**.
Now check child 1 blood type O, MN, Rh⁺.
A woman type A, N, Rh⁺ and a man type O, M, Rh⁺ could produce this child in a Ai, N, Rh⁺ × ii, M, Rh⁺ cross.
Now check the possible parents of child 2 with type A, N, Rh⁺ blood. Since alleles M and N are codominant, a child with only N could not be produced by these parents. Reject child 2 and choice **C**. You are now left with **A**. Just to be sure, check child 3, blood type A, MN, Rh⁺. Parents A, N, Rh⁺ and O, M, Rh⁺ could produce this child.

27. D

Each of the choices should be evaluated separately. Recall the basics of pedigrees:

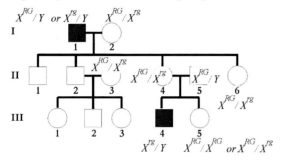

- males are represented as squares
- females are represented as circles
- affected individuals (in this case, individuals with colourblindness) are filled symbols
- unaffected (normal) individuals are unfilled symbols

Refer to the pedigree for the genotypes of the individuals relevant to the question:
(Recall from the information that red-green colourblindness is X-linked.)

A can be rejected because the chance that II-4 is a carrier is 100%, not 50%.
B can be ruled-out because II-6 is definitely a carrier.
C is an incorrect statement because if III-5 is a carrier (she has a 50% chance of being a carrier), then only the children who inherit both their mother's rg allele (and in the case of daughters, also their father's rg allele) will be colourblind. Of her sons, 50% have the chance to inherit the recessive rg allele and therefore will be colourblind.
D is correct because it II-3 is a carrier (she has a 50% chance of being a carrier), then half of her sons will inherit X^{RG} and not be colourblind and half will inherit X^{rg} and be colourblind.

28. D

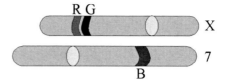

According to the preamble, the gene controlling red colourblindness (R) and the gene controlling green colourblindness (G) are both on the X chromosome. The gene for blue (B) colourblindness is on chromosome 7. Moreover, the mutant forms of the genes responsible for causing colourblindness are recessive.
Recall also that males and females are both diploid (possess two of each chromosome) for all of the autosomal chromosomes (chromosomes 1–22), but differ in their sex chromosomes – males are XY (possess one X and one Y chromosome) and females are XX (possess two X chromosomes).

D is the correct response. Because the B gene is on chromosome 7, an autosome for which both males and females are diploid, both males and females should have an equal opportunity to have the bb genotype that causes blue colourblindness.
A is incorrect because blue colourblindness is not influenced by sex. (See above.)
B is incorrect because males cannot be carriers for the sex-linked forms of colourblindness (red and green; see table below). If males have the recessive form of r or g, they will be colourblind (thus not carriers).
C is incorrect because both males and females can be carriers (heterozygous) for blue colourblindness (see table below).

Cone colour	Gene alleles	Male (XY)		Females (XX)	
		Normal	Colour-blind	Normal	Color-blind
Red	R-normal	$X^R Y$	$X^r Y$	$X^R X^r$, $X^R X^R$	$X^r X^r$
	r-mutant				
Green	G-normal	$X^G Y$	$X^g Y$	$X^G X^g$, $X^G X^G$	$X^g X^g$
	g-mutant				
Blue	B-normal	BB, Bb	bb	BB, Bb	bb
	b-mutant				

29. B

Recall the possible genotypes of the different blood types:

	A	**B**	**AB**	**O**
genotype:	I^A/I^A or I^A/i	I^B/I^B or I^B/i	I^A/I^B	ii

Therefore, individual I-2 can be only I^B/I^B or I^B/i, and the blood type of individual I-1 must therefore be A. For the A blood type, the genotype can be either heterozygous or homozygous. Because this couple has a child with blood type B (who has no I^A alleles), and a child with blood type A (who has no I^B alleles), both parents must be heterozygous.
That is, I-1 genotype is I^A/i and II-2 is I^B/i.
B is correct.

NR 4.   0.50

Note that piebald spotting is caused by a dominant allele (P), so individual II-6 is homozygous recessive (pp). The question is what is the genotype of individual II-5. Look at the parents I-1 and I-2. Parent I-1 is obviously pp. Parent I-2 carries at least one dominant allele: PP or Pp. Both II-2 or II-7 are pp, so they must have received a recessive allele from each parent; therefore parent I-2 must be heterozygous (Pp). This means, therefore, individual II-5 is also heterozygous (Pp).

Now, set up a Punnett square to find the possible offspring of II-5 (Pp) and II-6 (pp). You will see that a dominant allele will be found in half of their offspring or 50%. The probability is 0.50.

NR 5.   50

Start this solution by finding the genotypes of parents II-6 and II-7. Parent II-6 is a carrier, Nn. Parent II-7 is homozygous normal, NN. Cross these parents on a Punnett square. You will see that half the offspring are NN and half are Nn. So the probability of producing a carrier is 50%.

30. C

If you set up a Punnett square and cross $Hb^A Hb^s \times Hb^A Hb^s$, the following offspring will be produced: $Hb^A Hb^A$, $Hb^A Hb^s$, $Hb^s Hb^s$ in a ratio 1:2:1. Half of the offspring are heterozygous, half are not. The probability of a child not being heterozygous is 0.50.

NR 6.   25

Because neither parent is affected, they could each be NN or Nn. Since one of their children is affected (nn), both parents must be heterozygous (Nn). Two heterozygous parents have a 25% probability of producing a non-carrier child (NN), a 50% probability of producing a carrier (Nn), and a 25% probability of producing an affected child (nn). Therefore, 25% is correct.

31. B

If two normal parents can have a child affected with cystic fibrosis, then both parents must be carriers of the alleles that causes cystic fibrosis.

If CF = normal, and cf = cystic fibrosis allele:

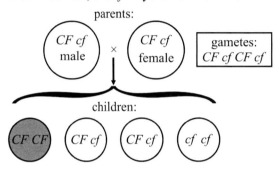

If both parents can be carriers of the cystic fibrosis allele but not have the disease themselves, then the disease allele must be recessive. **B** is correct. **A** is incorrect because if the disease were X-linked (meaning the gene for cystic fibrosis is on the X chromosome), the father would have been affected by the disease, whether the allele was recessive or dominant. That is, knowing that males have only one X chromosome, the father's genotype would have been XcfY, and he would have had the disease. Both **C** and **D** are incorrect because both parents as carriers would also have been affected with the disease if the allele were either dominant or codominant. Recall that codominant means that both alleles are expressed. For example, roan cattle have both red and white hairs (giving them the "roan" color) due to expression of the allele coding for red hair as well as expression of the allele coding for white hair.

32. B

A breeding diagram is constructed below using the information provided in the information and question.

X^H – hypophosphatemia allele
X^h – normal allele

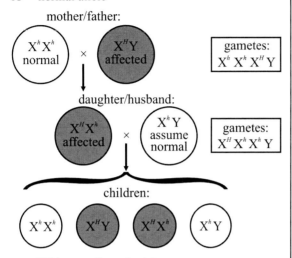

— **50% are affected with hypophosphatemia, 50% are normal**

— **50% of her sons and 50% of her daughters are expected to have the disease.**

B is the correct response.

NR 7.   0.50

From the information, we learn that Marfan syndrome is an autosomal dominant disorder. Therefore:

M–Marfan syndrome allele
m–normal allele

The heterozygous man, who must have Marfan syndrome, and homozygous recessive woman therefore have the genotypes *Mm* and *mm*, respectively. This couple have a child:

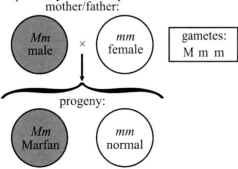

The probability that the child will have Marfan syndrome is therefore 50%, or 0.50.

NR 8.   0.25

Create a Punnett square for the couple:
The female's genotype is given and the male must be homozygous recessive (*ii rr*) because he has the O Rh⁻ phenotype. Rh⁺ is controlled by a dominant allele (*R*) and Rh⁻ is controlled by the recessive allele (*r*).

	female			
	$I^A R$	$I^A r$	$I^B R$	$I^B r$
male *i r*		$I^A i\ rr$		

The chance that the child will be have the blood type A Rh– is 1/4, or 25%, or 0.25.

33. B

Since the condition is autosomal, there is no difference in inheritance by males or females. As well, the inheritance in question is of just one gene. If the mother has a single mutant gene, she is a carrier. The father is not a carrier, so he is homozygous dominant. If you set up a basic Punnett square, you will see that 50% of the offspring have a recessive gene and 50% are homozygous dominant.

34. C

A homozygous recessive plant can only produce the gamete *ta*. When crossed with a heterozygous plant, as shown in the Punnett square below, 50% of the offspring will display the tall trait, and 50% will show the axial flower trait. 75% show **at least one** of those two traits.

	TA	*Ta*	*tA*	*ta*
ta	*TtAa*	*Ttaa*	*ttAa*	*ttaa*
	tall	**tall**	short	short
	axial	terminal	**axial**	terminal

NR 9.   0

Ichthyosis is a recessive disorder that is X-linked. Label the normal allele *N* and the recessive allele *n*. An "alligator man" would carry a single recessive allele, *n*.
The homozygous normal woman would carry two normal alleles, *NN*. If you set up a Punnett square, you will see that all male offspring will carry a single *N* allele from the woman and all female offspring will be heterozygous, *Nn*. Therefore, none of the children would have ichthyosis.

ANSWERS AND SOLUTIONS
POPULATION GENETICS AND INTERACTION
– UNIT REVIEW

1. B	6 B	11. C	16. D	23. C
2. A	NR3. 3, 5, 9	12. B	17. C	24. D
3. A	7. C	NR5. 1, 4, 6, 7	18. A	25. D
NR1. 46	8. C	NR6. 18	19. C	26. B
NR2. 0.55	9. B	13. D	20. A	27. A
4. B	NR4. 3, 1, 1	14. B	21. C	28. B
5. B	10. A	15. D	22. B	

1. B

The two populations of Amish are genetically different, since one population contains the cystic fibrosis gene and the other does not. As a result, at least one of the populations is non-representative of all Amish. It is an isolated population, since none of its members are related to the other population. The founder effect involves a small number of individuals beginning a new population. Their small gene pool may be different from the gene pool of the larger population that the founding individuals came from.

2. A

Since only some of the minnows secrete *schreckstoff*, and *schreckstoff* appears to provide the minnow that secretes it a survival advantage, the frequency of the gene that codes for it is probably increasing in the gene pool. That is because minnows that have the gene are more likely to survive and have offspring. Individuals that do not have the gene are not as likely to survive.

3. A

With a large population becoming quite a small population, the number of genes in the gene pool is bound to decrease. As a result, we can conclude the genetic variety of the population will decrease.

NR 1. 46

Because this is a recessive trait, carriers must be heterozygous. To calculate the percentage that is heterozygous, use the Hardy-Weinberg formula

$p^2 + 2pq + q^2 = 1.0$.

42% of the population have the recessive condition diabetes. Therefore,

$q^2 = 0.42$ (recessive condition)

$q = 0.65$ (recessive allele)

$p = 1 - q = 1 - 0.65 = 0.35$ (dominant allele)

$2pq = 2 \times 0.35 \times 0.65 = \textbf{0.46}$ (heterozygous condition)

NR 2. 0.55

This question requires the use of the Hardy-Weinberg equations.

$p^2 + 2pq + q^2 = 1.0$
$p + q = 1.0$

We are told that 30% of Dalmatians have this autosomal recessive disorder, $q^2 = 30\%$, which equals 0.3. We are asked for the frequency of the abnormal allele: q.

$q^2 = 0.3$
$q = \sqrt{0.3}$
$q \approx 0.55$

4. B

The breeding of dogs involves non-random mating. That is, the breeder selects dogs with certain desired characteristics to breed. This is a form of inbreeding that reduces genetic variety and increases the frequency of genetic defects. It is not natural selection, (**A**) because nature is not selecting which animals will reproduce, humans are. Geographic isolation (**C**) refers to a population being separated from other populations of the same species by a physical barrier such as a mountain range or a river. Geographic isolation by itself won't affect the frequency of genetic defects. Mutations (**D**) can happen spontaneously or can be caused by something in the environment. There is no reason to assume that mutation rates will be higher in purebred dogs than in crosses or wild animals.

5. B

If tuberculosis regains its former role as a deadly disease, that means people will die from it.
It appears from the reading that individuals that are heterozygous for Tay-Sachs are less likely to die from tuberculosis, so heterozygous individuals are more likely to survive tuberculosis and pass their genes on to the next generation. Therefore, the frequency of the Tay-Sachs allele, if it becomes advantageous, would be likely to increase.

6. B

Perhaps at one time, the cactus flowers were open throughout the day and night. Water loss from the flowers during the day was a problem in the desert climate and reduced the survival rate of the cacti. Because there is variation in all organisms, there may have been some cacti that opened their flowers during the night and closed them during the day. Those cacti lost less water, and therefore had a greater chance of survival to reproduce. They produce offspring that would also open their flowers only during the night. Since the cacti that opened their flowers only during the night had a higher survival rate, eventually all the cacti opened their flowers only at night.

NR 3. 3 5 9

Normally, the variations in a population remain roughly the same from generation to generation. However, if a population is very small, random fluctuations can create significant differences from one generation to the next.
When randomness is caused by a small population size is called **genetic drift** (3). When the population shrinks, there will be less genetic variety simply because there are fewer organisms. When there is a small number of organisms, the gene pool is smaller.
This effect can be described as the **chance loss of genes** (5). Even when the number of individuals in the population increases to a reasonable size, the individuals will still have only the gene pool of the few organisms they descended from. As a result, this rebuilt population has **reduced genetic variability** (9).

7. C

A mutualistic relationship is one in which both organisms are helped. The human female is protected from *E. coli*, and the lactobaccili are provided with the habitat they require.
A parasitic relationship is one in which one organism benefits and the other is harmed. *E. coli* gains that habitat it needs, but the human female gets an infection. Interspecific competition involves competition between organisms of different species. In this case, both lactobaccili and *E. coli* are competing for the same habitat.

8. C

A commensalistic relationship is one in which one organism benefits and the other is unaffected. The porcupines appear to be helped by the hares, but the hares do not appear to be helped or harmed by the porcupines.

A This would only be correct if both the hares and the porcupines benefited from each other.

B This would only be correct if either the hare or the porcupine was eating the other.

D Intraspecific competition is competition that occurs between members of the same species.

9. B

This is the most reasonable answer. If both caribou and moose populations were low, the wolves would probably face a shortage of food.

A This is not correct because all populations change as a result of density-dependent factors.

C This is not correct because wolves, moose, and caribou are quite different animals and it is unlikely that there are many diseases that they all share.

D This is not correct. Since moose and caribou do not share the same niche (that is, they have different specific requirements), the area's carrying capacity for the two animals would differ.

NR 4. 3 1 1

3—Primary succession refers to the changes in a community of organisms that begins on a site where there is no community at all. The land released from a retreating glacier would qualify.

1—A pioneer community is one that first invades the area.

1—Since the community begins with the first species to invade an area, after 20 years the number of species is sure to have increased.

10. A

Some of the biotic factors that keep the population stabilized are food supply, predators, diseases, competition between the elk, and competition between elk and other species. These are all density-dependent factors. That is, the larger the elk population is, the more these biotic factors limit the elk population.

11. C

Carrying capacity refers to the number of organisms that the area can support.

A Lag phase refers to the time just prior to a rapid increase in population size.

B Biotic potential means the maximum rate at which the population can increase if environmental conditions are perfect.

D A climax community is a community in which successional changes are no longer occurring. This community is dominated by one species.

12. B

Per capita growth rate is determined by dividing the change is number of organisms (+30) by the original number of organisms (500).

NR 5. 1 4 6 7

K-selected populations are ones that try to keep their populations stable at K, the carrying capacity. As a result, they try to resist explosive increases or decreases in population size. They have few offspring and provide a lot of parental care to maximize survival of the offspring. They do not begin to reproduce until they are larger and older, so that they will be physically mature and experienced enough to be good parents. They tend to be large animals with a long life-span, such as caribou and elk.

NR 6. 18

The wolves are predators and there are 0.3 wolves per 100 km^2 in the Northwest Territories. In 6 000 km^2, one would expect 18 wolves. The calculations are shown below.

$$\frac{0.3}{x} = \frac{100 \text{ km}^2}{6\,000 \text{ km}^2}$$
$$100x = 0.3 \times 6\,000$$
$$x = 18$$

13. D

Since these two species of animals share the same range and food supply, they are competitors. Competition between organisms of different species is called interspecific.

14. B

Algae populations, populations of grey whales, and the imposition of fishing quotas all will have a different impact on the Pacific herring depending on their density. If the ocean temperature has a direct effect on the Pacific herring population, however, it will not matter whether the herring are densely populated or not. Ocean temperature is a density-independent factor.

15. D

With such an important food supply less plentiful, the various predators of herring would all find it much more difficult to find food. As a result, both intraspecific competition (between members of the same species) and intraspecific competition (between members of different species) would increase.

16. D

If the salmon population declines, the herring population should increase. If the herring population does not increase, there must be an increase in some other predator.
That increase could be a result of decreased mortality, or increased immigration, or both.

17. C

There are a lot of large white oak trees but no saplings. Therefore, as the older white oak die, there are no young ones to take their place, so the density of white oak should decline.
However, there are many beech saplings.
As they get bigger, the density of beech should increase.

18. A

In a normal individual, the infection would be introduced, so it would begin at a low level, eliminating **C** and **D**. The bacteria population density would increase rapidly, but in a normal person, production of the natural antibiotic defensin would cause the bacteria population to drop rapidly.

19. C

K-selected species tend to be large, have a long life span, and devote a large amount of parental care for their offspring. It is r-selected species that tend to have a high reproductive potential.

20. A

We know that the population of horses has been increasing, so **D** is not correct. If all of the mares were injected with the contraceptive, and therefore only were allowed to have one offspring, the population would decline.

However, since only some of the mares were being injected, some mares would continue to have more than one offspring. It is reasonable to assume that the wildlife management officers would want to keep the population at a stable number, so **A** is the best answer.

21. C

A greater diversity of organisms suggests that this is a favourable environment for many organisms. A very harsh environment such as Antarctica could be expected to have little diversity of organisms. Abiotic factors are non-living-factors such as temperature, rainfall, sunlight, and wind speed. If abiotic factors are harsh, many species of organisms could not survive in the habitat. It seems that in the Sonoran Desert, abiotic factors are favourable. The environmental resistance is the sum of all the factors that restrict a population from thriving. The environmental resistance must be reduced in the Sonoran Desert if so many types of organisms can live there.

22. B

A population is all the organisms of one species that live and interact in one area. A community is defined as all the populations of organisms that live and interact in a particular area.
An ecosystem is a community as well as its physical environment.

23. C

Mutualism refers to a relationship between two types of organisms in which both benefit. In this case, the flowers of the organ pipe cactus provide the bats and insects with food and the bats and insects spread pollen for the organ pipe cactus. Both benefit. Later, birds and small mammals eat the cactus fruit. They then scatter and distribute the seeds for the cactus. Again, both benefit.

24. D

Carrying capacity is the maximum population size that a habitat can support. If you made a graph of population growth, carrying capacity would be the part of the graph that levelled off, or plateaued. This is the limit of the population size. Although the reading is about harvest quotas, they are not directly related to carrying capacity.

25. D

Natality (birth) rate and biotic potential (maximum reproductive rate) are important to population size but only when compared with mortality (death) rate, along with immigration and emigration. To predict the size of the population in the future, it is most useful to know the size of the population now, and how fast the population is growing. Population growth rate is a sum of natality rate, mortality rate, immigration, and emigration.

26. B

An *r*-selected population depends on *r*, the biotic potential. Mosquitoes are an example of an *r*-selected population. Such a population has a large number of offspring, and although they provide little parental care and the offspring have a low survival rate, these populations tend to grow quickly. Government regulators may have felt that the cod population would have rebounded rapidly like mosquitoes during a mosquito outbreak.

27. A

A population grows if the total of the natality (birth rate) plus the immigration exceeds the total of the mortality (death rate) and emigration. In this case, the natality for the two years was $22 + 43 = 65$ and the immigration was $0 + 2 = 2$, for a total of 67. The mortality was $4 + 7 = 11$ and the emigration was $2 + 5 = 7$, for a total of 18. As a result, the population increased by $67 - 18 = 49$ birds.

28. B

Gause's principle states that two populations cannot both occupy the same niche and both survive there. The niche is more than just where the animals live. It includes what they eat, who their predators are, what kind of diseases affect them, and their nesting sites. It appears that although the blackbirds and mallards both live in wetlands, they don't occupy *exactly* the same niche. There is little competition between them for such things as food and breeding areas. Intraspecific competition means competition between members of the same species and interspecific competition is between members of different species, such as between blackbirds and mallards.

ANSWERS AND SOLUTIONS
POPULATION GENETICS AND INTERACTION – UNIT TEST 4

1. D	4. C	7. C	10. D	14. A
2. B	5. C	NR3. 2, 1, 3	11. D	15. C
3. A	NR2. 10.3	8. A	12. A	16. B
NR1. 0.2	6. A	9. B	13. D	

1. D

In Africa, carriers for sickle cell anemia have an advantage over homozygous individuals. Carriers are more resistant to malaria than are individuals homozygous normal. Note that individuals homozygous for sickle cell anemia die young. So the heterozygous individuals have an advantage over both homozygous normal and homozygous recessive individuals.
Reject **A** because no evidence indicates the gene will disappear. Reject **B** because no evidence implicates fertility. Choice **C** is not likely because the gene will be maintained by carriers who survive and pass it on to their offspring.

2. B

Use the Hardy-Weinberg Principle to find this solution. Recall that $p + q = 1$. If p equals 0.15 then q will equal $1 - p$ or $1 - 0.15$.
Therefore, $1 - 0.15 = 0.85$

3. A

Mutations and natural selection give some insects an advantage, and eventually gene frequencies change until most have the trait. Random mutations occasionally give insects a survival advantage when environmental factors change. One such change could be the use of insecticides. If some insects with a chance mutation survive, they will produce offspring with the survival mutation. Eventually most insects will carry the mutation and be resistant to the insecticide. Insects do not purposefully use restriction enzymes and ligases to alter their DNA, so reject **B**. Choice **C** is not supported by the information. Choice **D** is nonsense unless the avoidance is a behaviour caused by a mutation.

NR 1. 0.2

Use the Hardy-Weinberg equation $p^2 + 2pq + q^2 = 1$ to find this answer. You need to determine the value of q. If q^2 is 4% or 0.04, then q will be the square root of 0.04: that is 0.2.

4. C

*Inter*specific competition refers to the competition between organism of *different* species, for example between the snow geese and other shore birds and duck species. *Intra*specific competition refers to the competition within the snow goose species. In the Churchill, Manitoba area, the increase in the snow goose population has already led to the decrease of other bird populations. A further increase in the goose population will therefore likely lead to an increase in competition among the snow geese for nesting grounds and food. That is, increasing numbers of snow geese will decrease the food supply until the snow geese compete amongst themselves (intraspecific competition) for the food. **C** is the best response, and **D** is incorrect. Both **A** and **B** are incorrect because the interspecific competition can increase only if species diversity increases. In this example, the species diversity is decreasing.

5.   C

Before 1960, reeds, roots, and tubers were the food supply for the snow geese in the wintering grounds. Recall that food supply is a **density-dependent factor** because a higher density of snow geese leads to a lower food supply.
As a result of the limiting food supply when the population of geese was too high, the reeds, roots, and tubers acted as a factor that controlled the population size of the geese. **C** is correct and **D** is incorrect. The definitions of climax and pioneer species are provided below:

Community of climax species—final and relatively stable community of organisms developed following numerous stages of succession (rise and fall of different communities of various numbers and types of organisms)

Pioneer species—the first species to inhabit an area in the stages of succession

NR 2.   10.3

The formula for per capita growth rate is

$$cgr = \frac{\Delta N}{N}$$

ΔN = (population in 1990) – (population in 1968)

N = population in 1968

So $cgr = \dfrac{45\,000 - 4\,000}{4\,000} = \dfrac{41\,000}{4\,000} = 10.25$

Rounded to one decimal place, 10.25 = 10.3

6.   A

In order to preserve the diversity (numbers of different species in the area), it would be logical to first attempt to decrease the number of snow geese in the area. **A** is a good response because increasing the amount of geese that are hunted and collection of eggs would lead to a decrease in the goose population. Once the goose population is lowered, the other species (plants and other birds) may return on their own when the resources for their survival are once more available.

B and **D** are not good choices because replanting of food sources for the geese would only lead to a further increase in the goose population and a further decrease in species diversity. **C** is also not a good choice because without first making available more nesting grounds and food supplies, the reintroduced shore birds and duck species would face strong competition and would likely perish or move away.

7.   C

The snow goose population size is increasing, so it is reasonable to assume that the population is in a growth phase (making B incorrect; because mortality is the death rate and natality is the birth rate). As the population grows, nesting space and food supplies will become more limited. Both nesting space and food are environmental factors that will limit the growth of the goose population. Therefore, the environmental resistance is increasing as the number of snow geese increases. **C** is correct. **A** is incorrect because the biotic potential (defined as the maximum number of offspring that can be produced by a species under **ideal** environmental conditions) cannot be altered. **D** is incorrect because the snow goose population is still growing and therefore cannot have reached the carrying capacity. Carrying capacity is the point at which the population size no longer increases because of the lack of resources.

NR 3.   2 1 3

Recall the definitions of the various relationships:

Commensalism—One organism within the relationship benefits while the other is unaffected. This is described in the relationship between the protozoan and the frog (2).

Mutualism—Both organisms in a relationship benefit, as described in the relationship between the acacia tree and the ants (1).

Parasitism—This describes a relationship in which one organism benefits at the expense or harm to the other. For example, Plasmodium infects humans, causing malaria, a potentially fatal disease (3).

8. A

The guinea worm is a parasite. Humans and water fleas are hosts. Reject **B** because water fleas are not a natural prey for humans or guinea worms. Actually, water fleas ingest guinea worm larvae but the larvae enters the water flea body cavity before digestion.

Reject **C** and **D** because the guinea worm is not a predator. It lives in a symbiotic relationship with its two hosts.

9. B

The guinea worm, *Dracunculus*, requires two hosts to complete a life cycle. Humans are the primary host carrying the adult worms. Water fleas, *Cyclops*, are the intermediate host supporting the larvae. The guinea worm cannot successfully reproduce where only one host is present. Choice **A** is false because the guinea worm needs water fleas. Choice **C** is unlikely for the same reason. Choice **D** is nearly possible. Larvae would still be released into the water but would not find any water fleas in which to continue the life cycle.

Elimination of an intermediate host is a fairly common way of controlling a parasite.

10. D

The data refers to a study in the village of Katri and implicates the use of education programs and clean water supplies together. You can reject **A** and **B** because you cannot assume that the problem of guinea worm infection has been eliminated in all African countries just because it has been eliminated in this village. You can reject choice **C** because nothing in the information indicates that one change alone would work. Both an education program and clean water supplies are needed.

11. D

The stomachs of cattle contain large populations of bacteria that aid in the digestion of cellulose. Cattle depend on the bacteria to begin cellulose digestion. The bacteria depend on cattle to provide the ingested cellulose and to provide an environment in which to live. Cattle and gut bacteria are mutually dependent. The myxoma virus is a parasite in rabbits, so reject **A**. You can reject **B** because the woodpeckers do not benefit from bluebird activity. This is a one-way relationship called commensalism. Blowfly larvae are parasitic on sheep, so reject **C**.

12. A

Food is a common biotic factor influencing the size of populations. Humans control food by growing more. Reject **B** because food is biotic not abiotic. Reject **C** because humans can and do manipulate food supplies. Reject **D** for both these reasons.

13. D

According to the information, the population growth rate appears to have decreased between 1970 (population doubling every 34 years) and 1990 (population doubling every 40 years). Although all the choices are valid factors that would lead to a decrease in the growth rate of a population, the most influential factor for the human population would most likely be the introduction and use of birth control measures. So far, with regard to human populations in most of the world, food shortages, population density and other factors related to the carrying capacity (the ability of the environment to sustain a certain population size) have not led to an overall decrease in population growth rate.

14. A

Recall the characteristics of both *K*-selected and *r*-selected populations.

K–selected	*r*-selected
• relatively stable environment	• fluctuating environmental conditions
• large size	• small size
• young are slow-growing; dependent on parents	• young are fast-growing; little or no dependence on parents
• long lifespan eg., bears, dolphins	• short lifespan eg., insects, bacteria

The best examples of *K*- and *r*-selected populations in the choices are given in **A**. Whales are large, few in number, have few offspring (1 or 2) and require parental help for growth and development.

Houseflies are a good example of an *r*-selected population because they produce many offspring, are small in size, and have young that develop independently of their parents. **C** and **D** are definitely incorrect. **B** is not the best choice because although elephants are a good example of a *K*-selected population, spruce trees are not a good example of an *r*-selected population. Although trees have a large number of offspring that are independent of their parents, they grow slowly and have a long lifespan.

15. C

The population histogram was made in 1990. The largest proportion was 30 to 34 years of age. This group will reach 65 years of age in 31 to 35 years (from 1990), or between 2020 and 2025.

16. B

First, find the volume of the swimming pool in cubic metres. Then, multiple by the number of bacteria per cubic metre.

Volume $= 50 \text{ m} \times 20 \text{ m} \times 3 \text{ m}$

$\qquad = 3\ 000 \text{ m}^3$

Density $= 2.5 \times 10^6 \text{ bacteria/m}^3$

Total number of bacteria $= 3\ 000 \times 2.5 \times 10^6$

$\qquad\qquad\qquad\qquad = 7.5 \times 10^9$

ANSWERS AND SOLUTIONS
WRITTEN-RESPONSE

1. **a)** *An increase in estrogen-mimicking compounds in the environment decreases sperm count.* **(1 mark)**

   - *Estrogen-mimicking compounds inhibit FSH production in male fetuses or newborns thereby decreasing multiplication of Sertoli cells and subsequently lowering sperm counts later in life.* **(2 marks)**

   - *If the level of estrogen-mimicking compounds is increased, then sperm count will decrease because estrogen-mimicking compounds inhibit FSH and thereby decrease Sertoli cell production.* **(2 marks)**

   b) **i)**   **ii)**

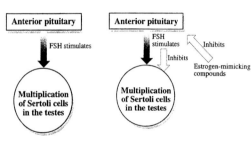

   - pituitary and indication of FSH production **(1 mark)**

   - A broken line should be drawn that leads to the anterior pituitary or FSH **(1 mark)**

   - stimulatory effect of FSH on Sertoli cell numbers **(1 mark)**

   c) *The number of Sertoli cells becomes fixed during the fetal or newborn stage of human development. As an adult, the number of Sertoli cells is established and therefore environmental levels of estrogen-mimicking compounds have little or no effect.*

   or

   - *Fetal cells are rapidly dividing cells so environmental compounds can have a greater effect on them than on adult cells.*

   or

   - *Estrogen-mimicking compounds activate or deactivate certain genes in the developing fetus with greater consequences than in the adult.*

   d) **i)** *% decrease in sperm count*

   $$= \frac{89 - 60}{89} \times 100$$
   $$= 33\% \ (a\ decrease\ of\ 33\%)$$

   ii) *Family size could be decreased on average.*

   or

   - *The population structure could change, resulting in a decreased proportion of young individuals and an increased proportion of older individuals.*

   or

   - *Total population size could start to decrease.*

   or

   - *French couples could increase their use of sperm banks.*

   or

   - *Adoption from other countries could increase in the society.*

   or

   - *Any other reasonable answer.*

   e) *Any two of the following for one mark each:*

   - *Some sperm die as a result of the acidity of female reproductive tract.*

   - *Some sperm die as a result of the immune system of the female.*

   - *Some sperm may miss the path to the Fallopian tube.*

   - *Some sperm may go up the Fallopian tube that does not contain the oocyte.*

   - *Many sperm are required for effective swimming or for protection.*

   - *Some sperm are abnormal.*

   - *Enzymes of approximately 500 sperm are required for a single sperm to penetrate the oocyte.*

f) **i)** *Any one of the following:*

- *Have there been changes in the amounts of estrogen-mimicking compounds in the environment, and do these changes correlate to changes in sperm count?*

- *Are the amounts of estrogen-mimicking compounds in the environment sufficient to inhibit FSH production in humans?*

- *Were the semen samples from the different time periods collected from men of the same age, health, etc.?*

- *Are there individual differences in exposure to estrogen-mimicking compounds, and do these differences correlate with lower sperm counts?*

- *Is there any evidence that the average number of Sertoli cells per male has declined since 1940?*

- *Does a reduction in the number of Sertoli cells decrease sperm count?*

- *Are there geographic regions in which estrogen-mimicking compounds are not present and, if so, is the average sperm count in these regions higher than elsewhere?*

- *Have other environmental chemicals increased since 1940 that might affect sperm count?*

- *Have other scientists provided evidence to support the hypothesis that reduced Sertoli cells produce a reduction in sperm count?*

- *Were the studies described in the article published in journals with high standards, were they conducted by credible researchers, and are the conclusions generally accepted in the research community?*

- *Or another question that deals **with evidence, methods, cause-effect, or credibility.***

ii) *The student responses will vary with the answers given in part **f) i)**. The student should link his/her answer to his/her question to the decision he/she would make about the effect of these compounds on sperm counts.*

2.

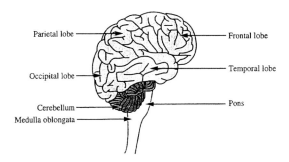

The sketch should include any four of the following labels: cerebrum, cerebellum, hypothalamus, pituitary gland, medulla oblongata, frontal lobe, parietal lobe, temporal lobe, occipital lobe, or any others.

Brain Area and Symptoms

The area of the brain affected by ataxia telangiectasia (AT) is the cerebellum or the motor cortex of the cerebrum (frontal lobe). This is shown by the decrease in motor coordination as the disease progresses. Related symptoms are lack of balance, slurred speech, loss of writing ability, difficulty controlling eye movements, and eventual use of a wheelchair (problems walking).

- **Environment Causes of DNA Damage/Repair Process**
  Possible causes of DNA damage are UV light, pesticides, X-rays, natural high-energy radiation, tobacco smoke, aromatic hydrocarbons (e.g. benzene), etc.

- **Cancer Link**
  Disruption of the repair process could lead to cancer because mutations are not corrected. Mutations can lead to cancer if the mutation affects the control of cell division.

  or

  The normal protein may be involved in arresting the cell cycle. The abnormal AT protein may therefore lead to increased cell division (cancer).

Calculation of AT Allele Frequency

The frequency of the homozygous recessive individuals in the population is q^2.

$$q^2 = \frac{1}{40\ 000} \quad q = 0.005$$

∴ The frequency of the AT allele is 0.005.

$$p = 1 - q$$
$$p - 0.995$$
$$2pq = 2(0.995)(0.005)$$
$$= 0.009\ 95$$

∴ This shows that approximately 1.0% or 0.995% of the population are carriers of the AT allele.

Two Societal Factors and/or Technologies

(Any two of the following)

Factors that could decrease the frequency of AT in the population

- Society could increase funding for genetic counselling. If this information were used to decrease the number of children produced by couples at risk, there would be a decrease in the frequency of the allele in the population.

or

- In vitro fertilization could be combined with pre-implantation screening to select embryos without the disorder for implantation. (In cases where there is a high risk of inheriting the AT disorder).

or

- A genetic screening test could be used to identify fetuses with AT. If this screening is followed by abortion, there would be a decrease in the frequency of the allele in the population.

Factors that could alleviate the symptoms of AT

- Gene therapy could be used to insert the normal gene from chromosome 11 into a bacterium. The bacterium could be cloned and then used to mass produce the protein coded for by the gene. This protein product could be used in treatment of AT to alleviate symptoms.

or

- Use an alternative treatment for cancer (e.g. chemotherapy) that does not use radiation for individuals with AT. This would prevent further chromosome damage.

or

- Electronic technology could be used to compensate for the lack of coordination displayed by individuals with AT (e.g., wheelchair).

or

- Laser surgery could be used to improve the appearance of the spider veins in the eye.

or

- Society could reduce the mutagens in the environment, which would reduce the incidence of cancer in AT patients.

or

- Physiotherapy could be used to improve the overall health and muscle coordination of the AT patient.

or

- Any other reasonable societal factor or technology.

3. a) Any one of the following:

- stimulates/regulates metabolic processes (metabolism)
- stimulates regulates cellular respiration (energy release, ATP production)
- stimulates/regulates heat production
- regulates body temperature

b)

Alternative 1:

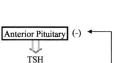

Alternative 2:

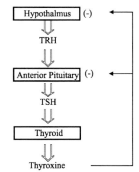

For scoring:

- pituitary and TSH **(1 mark)**
- thyroid gland and thyroxine **(1 mark)**
- appropriate stimulation and inhibition is indicated **(1 mark)**

c) Any two of the following:

- low energy (lethargy) (fatigue) (sleepiness)
- low metabolic rate (low BMR)
- blood test (low thyroxine, high TSH)

- *stunted growth and development (failure to thrive)*
- *slowed mental development (cretinism)*
- *obesity*
- *low body temperature*
- *thick tongue, thick neck*
- *slowed heart rate*
- *constipation*
- *dry skin*
- *puffiness in the face*
- *increased blood cholesterol*
- *decreased breathing rate*

Note: If more than two are given, mark the first two only.

d) *Any one of the following:*

- *High levels of non-radioactive iodine will be absorbed in greater amounts than the radioactive iodine, thereby reducing the effects of the radioactive iodine.*
- *The non-radioactive iodine will decrease the inflammation of the thyroid gland or decrease the incidence of thyroid cancer.*
- *Since part of the thyroid gland is destroyed, provision of non-radioactive iodine maximizes the production of thyroxine in the remaining functional portion of the thyroid gland.*

e) Any one of these sketches of the mutation is acceptable.

	Deletion	Insertion	Substitution	Or Any Pairing Error
was	T	T	T	
	G	G	G	
	C	C	C	A – T
	A	A	A	T – C
	T	T	T	T – A
	T	→T	T	
	↓	↓	↓	
become	T	T	T	
	G	G	G	
	C	C	C	
	T	A	T	
	→T	T	T	
		A	T	
		T		

For scoring:

- *sketch of a DNA strand before and after mutation* **(1 mark)**
- *Change in the DNA clearly indicated* **(1 mark)**
- *The description of the mutation must match the student's sketch of the mutation. If the mutation sketched is correctly named, then this can be considered to be a sufficient description. The mutation does not need to be named.* **(1 mark)**

f) *Germ cells (with mutations) combined in fertilization to form a zygote (fertilized egg)* **(1 mark)**. *The zygote divided by mitosis to form all the cells of the new individual; therefore all cells, including white blood cells, contain the mutation(s).* **(1 mark)**

4. **Biotic Potential Comparison**

Pigs have a higher biotic potential than many other mammals of their size, e.g. humans or other primates because:

- *pigs reach maturity at a younger age than primates and can therefore begin to produce offspring earlier*
- *pigs can be bred more than once per year (3 times), whereas primates can be bred only once a year*
- *pigs have many offspring per pregnancy as contrasted to primates, which usually have only one offspring per pregnancy*
- *pigs have shorter gestation periods (115 days) than primates, which allows pigs to have more litters per year*

Researchers likely chose pigs for the following traits:

Any two of the following:

- *the short pregnancy term, many offspring per litter, 3 litters per year possible, reach sexual maturity earlier than primates; yields many organs for transplants or further research*
- *organs of adequate size are produced*
- *pigs have a similar physiology to humans*
- *other animals, such as primates, have more complex social interactions and researchers may have felt that using these animals as donors would have been ethically unacceptable*

- *pigs are used as a source of food already, therefore more acceptable than using primate mammals*
- *relatively low cost because there is high output*
- *pigs are quite different genetically from humans and therefore the transmission of disease from pigs to humans is less likely than if primates were used*
- *Or any other acceptable considerations.*

Technology

The student describes one of the following technologies that could have been used to obtain the HDAF gene.

- *Restriction enzymes would have been used to cut out the HDAF gene from the human chromosome. These enzymes cut only specific sequences of DNA.*
- *Gel electrophoresis could be used to separate human DNA for analysis and help to locate the HDAF gene.*
- *Tissue sampling (such as blood sampling) would provide a source of human DNA from which to search for the gene or to detect expression of the RCA protein.*
- *Chromosome mapping (gene mapping) can be used to identify the position of genes on a chromosome. This can then be used to identify a candidate for the HDAF gene.*
- *Cloning of DNA would produce many copies of the desired gene to work with. Cloning can be achieved using recombinant bacteria or newer techniques such as PCR.*

or

- *Any other acceptable technology.*

Outcome of HDAF Injection

*After the HDAF gene is injected into a fertilized egg, the **fertilized egg's DNA may recombine** with the HDAF gene. If this occurs, every cell in the pig that arises from that fertilized egg will contain the HDAF gene. This produces the **heterozygote transgenic** offspring. **Normal** (non-transgenic) offspring arise when the fertilized egg's DNA **does not recombine with** the HDAF gene.*

Crosses of Heterozygote Offspring

Crosses of heterozygote transgenic offspring were performed in order to produce offspring that were homozygous for the HDAF gene. The homozygous offspring could then be used for breeding stock to produce more homozygous transgenic pigs. These pigs would have organs that displayed more of the human RCA protein than the heterozygotes.

Researchers would want to use these organs in transplant trials since they would be less likely to be rejected by the recipient than the organs from heterozygote pigs or non-transgenic pigs.

Punnett Square:

HDAF⁺ HDAF⁻ × HDAF⁺ HDAF⁻

	HDAF⁺	HDAF⁻
HDAF⁺	HDAF⁺ HDAF⁺	HDAF⁺ HDAF⁻
HDAF⁻	HDAF⁺ HDAF⁻	HDAF⁻ HDAF⁻

The offspring of a cross between two heterozygous pigs would produce: homozygous transgenic pigs (HDAF⁺ HDAF⁺) expressing the RCA protein in their organs (1/4), heterozygous transgenic pigs (HDAF⁺ HDAF⁻) (1/2), homozygous non-transgenic pigs (HDAF⁻ HDAF⁻) (1/4)

5. a) i)

- *mv—whether or not smokers die of cancer caused by smoking*
- *rv—percentage of smokers dying of cancer caused by smoking*

or

- *mv—whether or not a subject smokes*
- *rv—death rate due to cancer*

ii)

- *not able to control diet, type of tobacco, exposure to radiation, environmental chemicals, and secondhand smoke, genetic predisposition to cancer, or other aspects of lifestyle*
  (any 2 variables—2 marks)
- *other factors may influence the incidence of cancer, so conclusions about smoking may only be partly valid*
  (1 mark)

b) *If the viral DNA is inserted into a gene* **(1 mark),** *it could lead to uncontrolled cell division (mitosis).* **(1 mark)**

or

The virus attacks cells in the immune system **(1 mark)** *and therefore the immune system is ineffective in destroying cancerous cells.* **(1 mark)**

c) i) *Any one of the following:*

- *women are living longer*
- *women are having fewer children*
- *women are having children later*
- *birth control pills are widely used*
- *nutrition has improved*
- *health care has improved*
- *environmental estrogens have increased*

or

- *any other acceptable social or economic changes*

ii) *Any one of the following linked to the corresponding change above.*

- *if women live longer, the chances are greater that they will develop cancer*
- *having fewer children is linked to a higher rate of cancer in reproductive organs*
- *having children later is linked to a higher rate of cancer in reproductive organs*
- *birth control pills allow women to reduce number of offspring and to have their children later, and they affect hormone levels. These could all lead to higher cancer rates in reproductive organs*
- *better nutrition has resulted in earlier sexual maturity which is linked to a higher rate of cancer in reproductive organs **or** better nutrition has reduced exposure to carcinogens, which leads to a lower rate of cancer in reproductive organs*
- *exposure environmental estrogens are linked to a higher rate of cancer in reproductive organs*

- *better health care increases longevity, which leads to a higher rate of cancer in reproductive organs or better health care has decreased the rate of cancer in reproductive organs (e.g., Pap smears)*

d) *The phase in the cell cycle likely affected by cyclins and CDKs is interphase (G_1, S-phase, G_2)*

e) *If the drug blocked the CDKs or cyclin molecules then DNA replication would not occur and the cell would not divide.*

or

The drug could block receptor sites within the cell (act as a competitive inhibitor) for CDKs or cyclins so that cell division is decreased (normal).

or

The drug could prevent the production of CDKs or cyclin molecules so that cell division is decreased (normal).

or

The drug could destroy the CDKs or cyclin molecules so that cell division is decreased (normal).

f) *Too many "go" signals or not enough "stop" signals could lead to increased cell division and thus cancer.*

6. *Myelin Sheath Function*

The myelin sheath surrounds the axons of neurons in the white matter of the central nervous system. It increases the speed of transmission of an action potential along the axon. Damage to the myelin sheath would slow down nervous response time or result in uneven nerve impulse transmission (if the myelin sheath were partially damaged). This would lead to the symptoms of motor function inhibition, impaired hearing, impaired speech, blindness, and mental deterioration.

Adrenal Gland Hormone

Damage to the adrenal cortex is indicated by high levels of ACTH in the blood.

Aldosterone *is secreted by the adrenal cortex. It controls sodium ion concentration in the blood and helps regulate blood volume and pressure. With a decrease in aldosterone secretion, sodium ion concentration in the blood would decrease, blood volume would decrease, and blood pressure would decrease. Since sodium ions are not reabsorbed in the kidney nephrons, sodium ions in the urine and urine volume would both increase.*

or

Cortisol *is secreted by the adrenal cortex. It stimulates the liver to increase secretion of glucose into the blood. It does this by converting amino acids and glycerol into glucose. Cortisol also plays a role in stress control and in immune responses. It increases free amino acids in the blood. These can be used by cells for protein synthesis to repair damaged cells. A decrease in cortisol would lead to decreased use of amino acids and fats in metabolism. It would also decrease amino acids available to cells. This would cause fatigue and weakness. It could also result in failure to cope with physical or mental stress.*

or

Adrenal androgens *are produced by the adrenal cortex. These have the same effects as male testosterone but are secreted in much smaller amounts. A decrease in secretion has little if any noticeable effects since other sex hormone secretions are responsible for primary and secondary sexual characteristics.*

or

Adrenal medulla hormones, e.g., epinephrine, could be described although it is the adrenal cortex that is affected. ***Example:*** *Epinephrine (norepinephrine) is released in response to stress (real or imagined). It increases the conversion of fuels to glucose, increases heart rate and breathing rate, increases blood flow to skeletal muscles and to the heart and reduces blood flow to other areas of the body, and dilates the pupils. A decreased secretion of epinephrine would reduce the response to stress.*

Determining Form of Inheritance

Evidence of X-linked Inheritance/Evidence of Autosomal Inheritance

- *A greater number of males than females have the disorder/the number of males and females with the disorder is roughly equal.*
- *The disorder appears to be inherited from the maternal side of the family/the disorder appears to be inherited from either parent equally.*

Evidence of Recessive Inheritance/Evidence of Dominant Inheritance

- *Two parents without the disorder have a child with the disorder/two parents with the disorder have a child without the disorder.*
- *The disorder skips generations/the disorder is present in each generation or disappears completely from successive generations.*

Sample Pedigree for an Autosomal Recessive Disorder

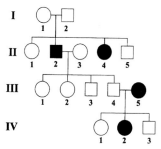

Labelling of this pedigree should indicate the following evidence:
This pedigree does not show any evidence that males or females inherit the disease more often, so there is no evidence that it is sex-linked. The first generation (parents) do not have the disorder, but two of their children have the disorder. This indicates that it is a recessive disorder that is not expressed in the parents, who are carriers of the disease allele.

Sample Pedigree for a Sex-linked Recessive Disorder

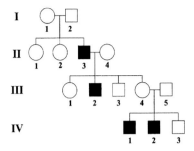

Labelling of the pedigree should indicate the following evidence:

This pedigree shows evidence that males inherit the disorder more often than females. This is consistent with a disease allele that is carried on the X chromosome. It is recessive: II-3 does not pass on the disease to any of his daughters, even though they would have a copy of his X chromosome with the disease allele.

Collection of Fetal Cells

***Chorionic villus sampling** (CVS) can be used to obtain fetal cells. In this procedure, a catheter is inserted through the cervix to the chorion and a sample of the chorionic villi is obtained. These cells are fetal cells.*

or

***Amniocentesis** can be used to obtain fetal cells. In this procedure, a hollow needle is inserted through the abdominal wall into the amniotic cavity. Amniotic fluid and some sloughed off fetal cells are withdrawn.*

Risks/Benefits of Early Diagnosis
 (One risk and one benefit from the list below.)

Benefits

The individual who has a disorder like ALD diagnosed early can use any treatments or lifestyle modifications sooner to alleviate the disease symptoms or progression.

or

Early fetal diagnosis could lead to abortion of an affected fetus with a disorder. This would decrease the cost to the society of treating a medical disorder.

or

Any other reasonable benefit to society or the individual.

Risks

An individual who has a disorder like ALD diagnosed early will have to live with the knowledge of his/her inheritance of a progressively degenerative disease before the onset of any symptoms. This could cause increased stress.

or

Early diagnosis of disorders like ALD may be used inappropriately by outside sources if the diagnosis is not kept in confidence. This would harm society if it led to discrimination against these individuals, and therefore threatened the common good.

or

Any other reasonable risk to society or the individual.

Science

Score	Scoring Criteria
	The student…
5 **Excellent**	• clearly explains the effect of myelin degeneration on the CNS that results in ALD symptoms related to impaired brain function • identifies an adrenal hormone and clearly describes the symptoms resulting from a decreased secretion of this hormone • clearly describes two pieces of evidence used to determine the mode of inheritance illustrated by a pedigree • draws an accurate four-generation pedigree chart that clearly illustrates the mode of inheritance selected, and labels the evidence
4 **Proficient**	• explains the effect of myelin degeneration on the CNS • identifies an adrenal hormone and describes some of the symptoms resulting from a decreased secretion of this hormone • clearly describes one piece of evidence and suggests one piece of evidence used to determine the mode of inheritance illustrated by a pedigree • draws a four-generation pedigree chart that could illustrate the mode of inheritance selected

Score	Scoring Criteria
3 Satisfactory	• partially explains the effect of myelin degeneration • identifies an adrenal hormone and describes one of the symptoms resulting from a decreased secretion of this hormone • describes one piece of evidence used to determine the mode of inheritance illustrated by a pedigree **or** suggests two pieces of evidence • draws a partially correct pedigree chart that could illustrate either autosomal recessive or X-linked inheritance
2 Limited	• describes the function of the neuron or a part of the neuron • identifies an adrenal gland hormone **or** describes the function of this hormone **or** describes one symptom of decreased secretion of an adrenal hormone • partially describes one piece of evidence used to determine the mode of inheritance illustrated by a pedigree • draws a partial pedigree chart
1 Poor	• addresses only one of the four scoring bullets at 2, 3, or 4 level

INSUFFICIENT is a special category. It is not an indication of quality. It should be assigned to papers that do not contain a discernible attempt to address the questions presented in the assignment or that are too brief to assess in this or any other scoring category.

Technology and Society

Score	Scoring Criteria
	The student…
5 Excellent	• identifies either amniocentesis or CVS **and** clearly describes the technology • clearly describes a risk **and** a benefit of early diagnosis of ALD to an individual and/or to society
4 Proficient	• identifies either amniocentesis or CVS **and** partially describes the technology • clearly describes a risk or a benefit **and** partially describes another risk or benefit of early diagnosis of ALD
3 Satisfactory	• identifies either amniocentesis **or** CVS or partially describes one of the two technologies • clearly describes either a risk or a benefit of early diagnosis of ALD **or** partially describes both a risk and a benefit
2 Limited	• identifies **or** describes a technology that may have been used in genetic screening or ALD research • partially describes a risk or a benefit of early diagnosis of ALD **or** describes a risk or a benefit of the ALD disorder or of research into the ALD disorder
1 Poor	• addresses one of the two scoring bullets at a 2 level

INSUFFICIENT is a special category. It is not an indication of quality. It should be assigned to papers that do not contain a discernible attempt to address the questions presented in the assignment or that are too brief to assess in this or any other scoring category.

7. a) i) *The women taking the placebo are the control group (used as a comparison with the women taking AZT).*

   or

   A placebo is used to determine if the psychological effects of treatment (taking a pill) are causing any observed changes.

   ii) *Doctors should do everything in their power to help people with known diseases, especially if there is a chance of transmission to others.*

   b) *Viruses are small enough to pass through the placental membranes from maternal blood to the fetal blood.* **(1 mark)**

   or

   HIV can directly infect the baby at birth since there is a possibility of maternal/fetal blood contact. **(1 mark)**

c) *The mutated DNA gene is transcribed into an mRNA molecule. The mRNA molecule leaves the nucleus and attaches to a ribosome in the cytoplasm. The mRNA is translated into a sequence of amino acids based on the three base codons of the mRNA molecule. Amino acids are brought to the ribosome by tRNA molecules, which have anti-codons to complement the mRNA codons. Amino acids join together to form the protein (CCR5 receptor molecule).*

d) *There may have been a epidemic of a infection similar to the HIV in northern Europe generations ago. Without treatment, many people would have died. People with a mutant CCR5 allele would have a selective advantage over people without the allele, thereby increasing its frequency.*

or

The mutated CCR5 allele occurred in an European individual originally.
The geographic isolation or reproductive isolation of the European people maintained the allele in Europe until recent times. (Founder effect) (Bottleneck effect)

e) $p + q = 1$
$q = 0.111$
$p = 0.889$
$2pq = 0.197$

so 19.7% or 20%

Marks:
1 mark: correct work shown
1 mark: correct answer calculated

f) *Possible technologies are:*

- *Use genetic engineering to introduce the CCR5 mutant allele into the macrophages, thereby preventing the HIV from attaching to them*

- *Drugs or chemicals that would plug the CCR5 receptors and prevent the HIV from binding onto these sites*

- *A vaccine made of fragments of CCR5 receptors that could induce the recipient's immune system to produce its own CCR5 binding antibodies*

- *Or, any other reasonable answer.*

8. *Meiosis in a tapeworm results in haploid sperm and egg cells. This is necessary before a sperm and egg can recombine to form a diploid cell. Meiosis makes fertilization, which recombines genetic information to produce variation in a population, possible. Variations allow individuals in the population to survive under varying conditions.*

Life Cycle

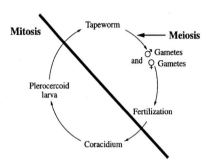

Mitosis allows for growth of the tapeworm and repair of tissues in a tapeworm. It maintains all the instructions in the original cell since the cells produced are identical. The tapeworm also changes forms in various hosts to exploit various environments. Mitosis makes these changes possible.

Incorporation of HGH Gene Into Tapeworm

A virus entered a human body cell and its DNA became incorporated into the human DNA. By chance, the viral DNA became incorporated close to the human gene for HGH. When the human DNA began replicating viral DNA, the HGH was replicated as well and became a part of the viral genome.

The virus mutated in such a way as to allow it to enter the reproductive cells of a tapeworm gamete. Once inside a tapeworm cell, the viral genetic information became incorporated into the tapeworm DNA. The gene for HGH then became part of that tapeworm's DNA. Since it was a gamete, this altered gene would be passed on to subsequent generations of tapeworms.

Dwarfism and Treatment

Lack of HGH during childhood development results in the disorder known as dwarfism. Children with dwarfism develop at a greatly reduced rate, however body proportions are relatively normal. At puberty, children who lack HGH have long bones that are greatly reduced in length, and hence they are dwarfs as adults.

Advantages of using PGF instead of human HGH:

- *produces growth in a similar way to HGH*
- *does not cause insensitivity to insulin*
- *no risk in leading to diabetes*
- *blood glucose would not elevate; other diabetic symptoms would not occur*

or

any other reasonable response

Science

Score	Scoring Criteria
	The student…
5 **Excellent**	• draws an accurate tapeworm life cycle diagram that includes most of the following: gametes, fertilized egg, coracidium, plerocercoid, and adult tapeworm. Mitosis and meiosis are clearly and correctly indicated on the diagram • clearly describes the value of mitosis and meiosis to a tapeworm • clearly describes the three necessary steps in the transfer of the human growth hormone gene to a tapeworm
4 **Proficient**	• draws a tapeworm life cycle diagram that is fairly complete and correctly indicates mitosis and meiosis on the diagram or draws an accurate tapeworm lifecycle with mitosis or meiosis indicated on the diagram • clearly describes the value of either mitosis or meiosis **and** partially describes the value of either mitosis or meiosis • clearly describes two of the three steps in the transfer of the HGH gene to a tapeworm or partially describes all three steps
3 **Satisfactory**	• draws a tapeworm life cycle diagram that is partially complete and correctly indicates mitosis or meiosis on it **or** clearly draws an accurate tapeworm life cycle diagram • clearly describes the value of either mitosis or meiosis **or** partially describes the value of both mitosis and meiosis • clearly describes one of the three steps in the transfer of the HGH gene to a tapeworm **or** partially describes two steps

2 **Limited**	• attempts a tapeworm life cycle diagram **or** describes when mitosis or meiosis occurs • partially describes the value of either mitosis or meiosis • partially describes one of the steps in the transfer of a human gene to another organism
1 **Poor**	• addresses only one of the three bullets at a 3 or 2 level

INSUFFICIENT is a special category. It is not an indication of quality. It should be assigned to papers that do not contain a discernible attempt to address the questions presented in the assignment or that are too brief to assess in this or any other scoring category.

Technology and Society

Score	Scoring Criteria
	The student…
5 **Excellent**	• clearly describes dwarfism **and** identifies two advantageous effects of using PGF in its treatment
4 **Proficient**	• describes dwarfism and identifies one advantageous effect of using PGF and suggests one advantageous effect **or** partially describes dwarfism and identifies two advantageous effects of using PGF in its treatment
3 **Satisfactory**	• partially describes dwarfism and identifies one advantageous effect of using PGF or identifies two advantageous effects of using PGF in treatment of low HGH **or** clearly describes dwarfism
2 **Limited**	• identifies or partially describes dwarfism and suggests one advantageous effect of using PGF in its treatment **or** identifies one advantageous effect of using PGF to treat low HGH
1 **Poor**	• identifies or partially describes dwarfism **or** suggests one advantageous effect of using PGF to treat low HGH

INSUFFICIENT is a special category. It is not an indication of quality. It should be assigned to papers that do not contain a discernible attempt to address the questions presented in the assignment or that are too brief to assess in this or any other scoring category.

9. **a)** *Although there is a high level of glucose in the blood, in the absence of insulin, body cells are impermeable to glucose; therefore, glucose is not available as an energy source and fatigue results. Since glucose cannot be used as an energy source, fat or protein stores are metabolized which results in weight loss. Also, glucose is not stored, therefore weight gain is not possible.*

b) *Glucose would be found in the urine of the patient with diabetes mellitus.*

or

The urine produced by a patient with diabetes insipidus would be insipid (tasteless). (The urine produced by a patient with diabetes mellitus would be sweet).

or

The urine of the patient with diabetes mellitus could also have ketones present and could be slightly acidic.

c) **i)** *Thyroid gland → thyroxine*
Adrenal gland → cortisol, epinephrine

ii) *Thyroxine would decrease blood glucose level by increasing cellular metabolism rates. Cortisol would increase blood sugar level by converting amino acids (or fatty acids or glycerol or fats or proteins) to glucose. Epinephrine stimulates the conversion of glycogen to glucose by liver and muscle tissue, thereby increasing blood sugar levels.*

d) *Sensory neurons were damaged because the patients could not feel the pain caused by the broken ankle or lesions but could still move their limbs, (i.e., motor skill intact).*

e) *Damage to or irregular functioning of blood vessels of the retina may result in permanent damage to the cells making up the retina (i.e., lack of O_2/nutrients). If the rods or cones are damaged, then there will be reduced sensory reception and reduced impulses in neurons to the occipital lobe. This would result in some vision loss or even blindness.*

or

If the optic nerve is damaged by decreased blood flow, the sensory information is not passed to the occipital lobe of the brain. This would result in vision loss or blindness.

or

The increase in blood vessels may obstruct the light reception by retina cells, resulting in vision loss or blindness. Reduced sensory stimulation would occur, so the neurons would send reduced impulses to the occipital lobe of the cerebrum.

f) **i)** *DNA: TTA or DNA: TTG*

ii) *Must show a point mutation (e.g., TTC codes for a.a. lysine).*

10. **Male secondary sex characteristics**

Hormone: Testosterone
- *Growth of facial, axillary, and pubic hair*
- *Receding hairline*
- *Growth of the larynx, which causes lowering of the voice*
- *Strengthening of the muscles*
- *Increased secretion of body oils (acne)*
- *Thickening of the skin*
- *Increased red blood cell count*
- *Growth of long bones (and final fusing of epiphyses)*
- *Increased basal metabolic rate*

or

Female secondary sex characteristics

Hormone: Estrogen
- *Growth of axillary and pubic hair*
- *Maintains low blood cholesterol levels*
- *Growth of the breasts*
- *Increased deposits of subcutaneous fat, especially in hips and breasts (female fat distribution)*
- *Widening (and lightening) of the pelvis*
- *Increased basal metabolic rate*
- *Facilitates calcium uptake*
- *Increased water content of skin*

- *Growth of long bones (and final fusing of epiphyses)*
- *Increased secretion of body oils (acne)*
- **Alleles:** X^C – *CH*; X^c – *normal*
  Genotypes:

  II-4: $X^C Y$ IV-6: $X^C X^c$
  II-5: $X^c X^c$ IV-7: $X^c Y$
  III-11: $X^c Y$ IV-8: $X^C X^c$
  III-12: $X^C X^c$ IV-9: $X^c X^c$

Punnett Square:

	X^C	X^c
X^c	$X^C X^c$	$X^c X^c$
Y	$X^C Y$	$X^c Y$

- *Probability of III-11 and III-12's child being male with CH*

  (male with CH) $X^C Y = \dfrac{1}{4}$ *or 25%*

- *More females than males inherit CH in generation III because individual II-4, a male, has CH, and because CH is X-linked dominant, the father's will be passed on to all his female children in generation III (but not to his sons, who received the father's Y chromosome).*

State a possible experimental problem

- *What effect does increasing (or decreasing) testosterone (or estrogen) have an hair follicle distribution?*
- *What gene(s) on the X chromosome code(s) for hair follicle distribution?*
- *What effect would increasing (decreasing) testosterone (estrogen) levels have on CH individuals?*
- *What protein molecule is produced in CH individuals that differs from individuals with normal hair follicle distribution?*
- *Or any other reasonable experimental problem that could be investigated.*

Evaluate whether conducting research would be useful for affected individuals

Possible Advantages

- *An advantage of CH research for individuals is that the research might ultimately lead to a cure for CH.*

- *An advantage of CH research for individuals is that the research might lead to treatment for individuals with acquired or inherited baldness.*
- *An advantage of CH research for individuals is that the information gained about the nature of CH could be used in counselling individuals who have CH and are planning on having children.*
- *An advantage of CH research to society is that is may lead to a better understanding of the actions of testosterone and estrogen. This increased knowledge could benefit society as a whole, potentially leading to health benefits for society.*
- *An advantage of CH research to society is that is may provide a better understanding of other X-linked traits. This increased knowledge could benefit society as a whole, potentially leading to health benefits for society.*
- *Other responses may be appropriate.*

Possible Disadvantages

- *A disadvantage to society of research to find a cure for CH is that it is very costly and may not be warranted for such a small population of affected individuals.*
- *A disadvantage to society of research to find a cure for CH is that is sends the message to society that if an individual does not appear normal, a cure must be found to rid society of a particular phenotype. Finding a cure does not promote the notion that society is at its best when made up of a mosaic of individuals.*
- *Other responses may be appropriate.*

Science

Score	Scoring Criteria
	The student…
5 **Excellent**	• identifies testosterone or estrogen and describes three secondary sex characteristics (one of which is hair follicle distribution) resulting from stimulation by the identified hormone • correctly identifies all the individuals' genotypes, using sex-linked notation, and provides a clear legend for the symbols • communicates, using a Punnett square, the probability of a CH male clearly explains why more females than males inherit CH in generation III

4 **Proficient**	• identifies testosterone or estrogen and describes 2 secondary sex characteristics resulting from stimulation by the identified hormone **or** describes 3 secondary sex characteristics • correctly identifies most of the individuals' genotypes, using sex-linked notation • communicates, using a Punnett square, the probability of a CH male, and partially explains why more females than males inherit CH in generation III, **or** partially communicates the probability of a CH male and explains why more females than males inherit CH in generation III
3 **Satisfactory**	• identifies testosterone or estrogen and describes 1 secondary sex characteristic resulting from stimulation by the identified hormone **or** describes 2 secondary sex characteristics • correctly identifies some of the individuals' genotypes, using sex-linked notation • communicates, using a Punnett square, the probability of a CH male **or** explains why more females than males inherit CH in generation III **or** partially communicates the probability of a CH male and partially explains why more females than males inherit CH in generation III
2 **Limited**	• identifies testosterone or estrogen or describes one secondary sex characteristic resulting from stimulation by the identified hormone • identifies some of the individuals' genotypes as if autosomal dominant inheritance, autosomal recessive inheritance, or sex-linked recessive inheritance occurred • constructs a Punnett square, **or** communicates the probability of a CH male, **or** partially explains why more females than males inherit CH in generation III
1 **Poor**	• One of the bullets is addressed at a 2 or 3 level

Technology and Society

Score	Scoring Criteria
	The student…
5 **Excellent**	• clearly states a possible experimental problem that could be investigated to find out more about CH or hair follicle distribution • evaluates whether conducting this research would be useful by describing one advantage and one disadvantage of CH research to the individual and/or society
4 **Proficient**	• states a possible experimental problem that could be investigated to find out more about CH or hair follicle distribution, but either the manipulated variable or responding variable is not clearly identified in the problem statement • evaluates whether conducting this research would be useful by describing one advantage and partially describing one disadvantage **or** by partially describing an advantage and describing one disadvantage of CH research to the individual and/or society
3 **Satisfactory**	• suggests an experimental problem, or identifies an area of research that could be investigated to find out more about CH or hair follicle distribution • evaluates whether conducting this research would be useful by describing one advantage or one disadvantage **or** partially describing one advantage and partially describing one disadvantage of CH research to the individual and/or society
2 **Limited**	• suggests one area of research that could be investigated to find out more about CH or hair follicle distribution • evaluates whether conducting this research would be useful by partially describing one advantage **or** one disadvantage of CH research
1 **Poor**	• One of the bullets is addressed at a 2 level

Science

Score	Scoring Criteria
	The student…
5 **Excellent**	• sketches the fetal environment accurately and correctly labels four parts • clearly describes in detail how the fetal environment supports the fetus at three months of development • clearly describes the pathway for sensory interpretation in a fetus or newborn from a specific stimulus
4 **Proficient**	• sketches the fetal environment accurately and correctly labels three parts • describes how the fetal environment supports the fetus • describes the pathway for sensory interpretation from a specific stimulus
3 **Satisfactory**	• sketches the fetal environment and correctly labels two parts • partially describes how the fetal environment supports the fetus • partially describes a pathway for sensory interpretation
2 **Limited**	• attempts a sketch of the fetal environment and correctly labels one part **or** draws an accurate sketch • describes at least one supporting structure in the fetal environment • identifies one step in a pathway for sensory interpretation
1 **Poor**	• only one of the bullets is addressed at a 2 or 3 level

INSUFFICIENT is a special category. It is not an indication of quality. It should be assigned to papers that do not contain a discernible attempt to address the questions presented in the assignment or that are too brief to assess in this or any other scoring category.

Technology and Society

Score	Scoring Criteria
	The student…
5 **Excellent**	• identifies and describes two relevant technologies or government polices that would stimulate neural development • clearly explains how each technology or government policy would affect neural development
4 **Proficient**	• identifies two relevant technologies or government polices and describes one **or** identifies and partially describes two relevant technologies or government policies • explains how one technology or government policy would affect neural development and partially explains the other
3 **Satisfactory**	• identifies one relevant technology or government policy and partially describes the other **or** identifies or partially describes two • explains how one technology or government policy would affect neural development **or** partially explains both
2 **Limited**	• identifies one relevant technology or government policy or partially describes one • partially explains how one technology or government policy would affect neural development
1 **Poor**	• addresses one of the two scoring bullets at a 2 level

INSUFFICIENT is a special category. It is not an indication of quality. It should he assigned to papers that do not contain a discernible attempt to address the questions presented in the assignment or that are too brief to assess in this or any other scoring category.

KEY STRATEGIES

FOR

SUCCESS ON EXAMS

NOTES

KEY STRATEGIES FOR SUCCESS ON EXAMS

There are many different ways to assess your knowledge and understanding of course concepts. Depending on the subject, your knowledge and skills are most often assessed through a combination of methods which may include performances, demonstrations, projects, products, and oral and written tests. Written exams are one of the most common methods currently used in schools. Just as there are some study strategies that help you to improve your academic performance, there are also some test writing strategies that may help you to do better on unit test and year-end exams. To do your best on any test, you need to be well prepared. You must know the course content and be as familiar as possible with the manner in which it is usually tested. Applying test writing strategies may help you to become more successful on exams, improve your grades, and achieve your potential.

📖 STUDY OPTIONS FOR EXAM PREPARATION

Studying and preparing for exams requires a strong sense of self-discipline. Sometimes having a study buddy or joining a study group

- helps you to stick to your study schedule
- ensures you have others with whom you can practice making and answering sample questions
- clarifies information and provides peer support

It may be helpful to use a combination of individual study, working with a study buddy, or joining a study group to prepare for your unit test or year-end exam. Be sure that the study buddy or group you choose to work with is positive, knowledgeable, motivated, and supportive. Working with a study buddy or a study group usually means you have to begin your exam preparation earlier than you would if you are studying independently.

Tutorial classes are often helpful in preparing for exams. You can ask a knowledgeable student to tutor you or you can hire a private tutor. Sometimes school jurisdictions or individual schools may offer tutorials and study sessions to assist students in preparing for exams. Tutorial services are also offered by companies that specialize in preparing students for exams. Information regarding tutorial services is usually available from school counsellors, local telephone directories, and on-line search engines.

📖 EXAM QUESTION FORMATS

There is no substitute for knowing the course content. To do well in your course you need to combine your subject knowledge and understanding with effective test writing skills. Being familiar with question formats may help you in preparing for quizzes, unit tests or year-end exams. The most typical question formats include multiple choice, numerical response, written response, and essay. The following provides a brief description of each format and suggestions for how you might consider responding to each of the formats.

MULTIPLE CHOICE

A multiple choice question provides some information for you to consider and then requires you to select a response from four choices, often referred to as distracters. The distracters may complete a statement, be a logical extension or application of the information. In preparing for multiple choice questions you may wish to focus on:

- studying concepts, theories, groups of facts or ideas that are similar in meaning; **compare and contrast their similarities and differences**; ask yourself "How do the concepts differ?", "Why is the difference important?", "What does each fact or concept mean or include?" "What are the exceptions?"
- **identifying main ideas, key information**, formulas, concepts, and theories, where they apply and what the **exceptions** are
- memorizing important definitions, examples, and applications of key concepts
- learning to **recognize** *distractors* that may lead you to apply plausible but incorrect solutions, and *three and one splits* where one answer is obviously incorrect and the others are very similar in meaning or wording
- **using active reading techniques** such as underlining, highlighting, numbering, and circling important facts, dates, basic points
- making up your own multiple choice questions for practice

NUMERICAL RESPONSE

A numerical response question provides information and requires you to use a calculation to arrive at the response. In preparing for numerical response questions you may wish to focus on:

- memorizing formulas and their applications
- completing chapter questions or making up your own for practice
- making a habit of **estimating the answer** prior to completing the calculation
- paying special **attention to accuracy** in computing and the use of significant digits where applicable

WRITTEN RESPONSE

A written response question requires you to respond to a question or directive such as "explain", "compare", contrast". In preparing for written response questions you may wish to focus on:

- ensuring your response **answers the question**

- recognizing **directing words** such as "list", "explain", "define"

- providing **concise answers** within the time limit you are devoting to the written response section of the exam

- identifying subject content that lends itself to short answer questions

ESSAY

An essay is a lengthier written response requiring you to identify your position on an issue and provide logical thinking or evidence that supports the basis of your argument. In preparing for an essay you may wish to focus on:

- examining **issues** that are relevant or related to the subject area or **application of the concept**

- comparing and contrasting two points of view, articles, or theories

- considering the merits of the opposite point of view

- identifying **key concepts**, principles or ideas

- providing **evidence**, examples, and **supporting information** for your viewpoint

- preparing two or three essays on probable topics

- **writing an outline** and essay within the defined period of time you will have for the exam

- understanding the "marker's expectations"

KEY TIPS FOR ANSWERING COMMON EXAM QUESTION FORMATS

Most exams use a variety of question formats to test your understanding. You must provide responses to questions ranging from lower level, information recall types to higher level, critical thinking types. The following information provides you with some suggestions on how to prepare for answering multiple choice, written response and essay questions.

MULTIPLE CHOICE

Multiple choice questions often require you to make fine distinctions between correct and nearly correct answers so it is imperative that you:

- begin by answering only the questions for which you are certain of the correct answer
- read the question stem and formulate your own response before you read the choices available
- read the directions carefully paying close attention to words such as "mark **all** correct", "choose the **most** correct" and "choose the **one best** answer"
- use active reading techniques such as underlining, circling, or highlighting critical words and phrases
- watch for superlatives such as "all", "every", "none", "always" which indicate that the correct response must be an undisputed fact
- watch for negatives such as "none", "never", "neither", "not" which indicate that the correct response must be an undisputed fact
- examine all of the alternatives in questions which include "all of the above" or "none of the above" as responses to ensure that "all" or "none" of the statements apply *totally*
- be aware of distracters that may lead you to apply plausible but incorrect solutions, and 'three and one splits' where one answer is obviously incorrect and the others are very similar in meaning or wording
- use information from other questions to help you
- eliminate the responses you know are wrong and then assess the remaining alternatives and choose the best one
- guess if you are not certain

WRITTEN RESPONSE

Written response questions usually require a very specific answer. In answering these questions you should:

- underline key words or phrases that indicate what is required in your answer such as "three reasons", "list", or "give an example"
- write down rough, point-form notes regarding the information you want to include in your answer
- be brief and only answer what is asked
- reread your response to ensure you have answered the question
- use the appropriate subject vocabulary and terminology in your response
- use point form to complete as many questions as possible if you are running out of time

ESSAY

Essay questions often give you the opportunity to demonstrate the breadth and depth of your learning regarding a given topic. In responding to these questions it may be helpful to:

- read the question carefully and underline key words and phrases
- make a brief outline to organize the flow of the information and ideas you want to include in your response
- ensure you have an introduction, body, and conclusion
- begin with a clear statement of your view, position, or interpretation of the question
- address only one main point or key idea in each paragraph and include relevant supporting information and examples
- assume the reader has no prior knowledge of your topic
- conclude with a strong summary statement
- use appropriate subject vocabulary and terminology when and where it is applicable
- review your essay for clarity of thought, logic, grammar, punctuation, and spelling
- write as legibly as you can
- double space your work in case you need to edit it when you proof read your essay
- complete the essay in point form if you run short of time

📖 *KEY* TIPS FOR RESPONDING TO COMMON 'DIRECTING' WORDS

There are some commonly used words in exam questions that require you to respond in a predetermined or expected manner. The following provides you with a brief summary of how you may wish to plan your response to exam questions that contain these words.

- ◆ **EVALUATE** (to assess the worth of something)
  - ▸ Determine the use, goal, or ideal from which you can judge something's worth
  - ▸ Make a value judgment or judgments on something
  - ▸ Make a list of reasons for the judgment
  - ▸ Develop examples, evidence, contrasts, and details to support your judgments and clarify your reasoning

- ◆ **DISCUSS** (usually to give pros and cons regarding an assertion, quotation, or policy)
  - ▸ Make a list of bases for comparing and contrasting
  - ▸ Develop details and examples to support or clarify each pro and con
  - ▸ On the basis of your lists, conclude your response by stating the extent to which you agree or disagree with what is asserted

- ◆ **COMPARE AND CONTRAST** (to give similarities and differences of two or more objects, beliefs, or positions)
  - ▸ Make a list of bases for comparing and contrasting
  - ▸ For each basis, judge similarities and differences
  - ▸ Supply details, evidence, and examples that support and clarify your judgment
  - ▸ Assess the overall similarity or difference
  - ▸ Determine the significance of similarity or difference in connection with the purpose of the comparison

- ◆ **ANALYZE** (to break into parts)
  - ▸ Break the topic, process, procedure, or object of the essay into its major parts
  - ▸ Connect and write about the parts according to the direction of the question: describe, explain, criticize

- ◆ **CRITICIZE** (to judge strong and weak points of something)
  - ▸ Make a list of the strong points and weak points

Develop details, examples, and contrasts to support judgments

Make an overall judgment of quality

♦ **EXPLAIN** (to show causes of or reasons for something)

In Science, usually show the process that occurs in moving from one state or phase in a process to the next, thoroughly presenting details of each step

In Humanities and often in Social Sciences, make a list of factors that influence something, developing evidence for each factor's potential influence

♦ **DESCRIBE** (to give major features of something)

Pick out highlights or major aspects of something

Develop details and illustrations to give a clear picture

♦ **ARGUE** (to give reasons for one position and against another)

Make a list of reasons for the position

Make a list of reasons against the position

Refute objections to your reasons for and defend against objections to your reasons opposing the position

Fill out reasons, objections, and replies with details, examples, consequences, and logical connections

♦ **COMMENT** (to make statements about something)

Calls for a position, discussion, explanation, judgment, or evaluation regarding a subject, idea, or situation

Is strengthened by providing supporting evidence, information, and examples

♦ **DEMONSTRATE** (to show something)

Depending upon the nature of the subject matter, provide evidence, clarify the logical basis of something, appeal to principles or laws as in an explanation, supply a range of opinion and examples

♦ **SYNTHESIZE** (to invent a new or different version)

Construct your own meaning based upon your knowledge and experiences

Support your assertion with examples, references to literature and research studies

(Source: http://www.counc.ivic.ca/learn/program/hndouts/simple.html)

📖 TEST ANXIETY

Do you get test anxiety? Most students feel some level of stress, worry, or anxiety before an exam. Feeling a little tension or anxiety before or during an exam is normal for most students. A little stress or tension may help you rise to the challenge but too much stress or anxiety interferes with your ability to do well on the exam. Test anxiety may cause you to experience some of the following in a mild or more severe form:

• "butterflies" in your stomach, sweating, shortness of breath, or a quickened pulse

• disturbed sleep or eating patterns

• increased nervousness, fear, or irritability

• sense of hopelessness or panic

• drawing a "blank" during the exam

If you experience extreme forms of test anxiety you need to consult your family physician. For milder forms of anxiety you may find some of the following strategies effective in helping you to remain calm and focused during your unit tests or year-end exams.

• Acknowledge that you are feeling some stress or test anxiety and that this is normal

• Focus upon your breathing, taking several deep breaths

• Concentrate upon a single object for a few moments

• Tense and relax the muscles in areas of your body where you feel tension

• Break your exam into smaller, manageable, achievable parts

• Use positive self-talk to calm and motivate yourself. Tell yourself, "I can do this if I read carefully/start with the easy questions/focus on what I know/stick with it/. . ." instead of saying, "This is too hard."

• Visualize your successful completion of your review or the exam

• Recall a time in the past when you felt calm, relaxed, and content. Replay this experience in your mind experiencing it as fully as possible.

📖 *KEY* STRATEGIES FOR SUCCESS BEFORE AN EXAM – A CHECKLIST

Review, review, review. That's a huge part of your exam preparation. Here's a quick review checklist for you to see how many strategies for success you are using as you prepare to write your unit tests and year-end exams.

KEY Strategies for Success Before an Exam	*Yes*	*No*
Have you been attending classes?		
Have you determined your learning style?		
Have you organized a quiet study area for yourself?		
Have you developed a long-term study schedule?		
Have you developed a short-term study schedule?		
Are you working with a study buddy or study group?		
Is your study buddy/group positive, knowledgeable, motivated and supportive?		
Have you registered in tutorial classes?		
Have you developed your exam study notes?		
Have you reviewed previously administered exams?		
Have you practiced answering multiple choice, numerical response, written response, and essay questions?		
Have you analyzed the most common errors students make on each subject exam?		
Have you practiced strategies for controlling your exam anxiety?		
Have you maintained a healthy diet and sleep routine?		
Have you participated in regular physical activity?		

📖 *KEY* STRATEGIES FOR SUCCESS DURING AN EXAM

Doing well on any exam requires that you prepare in advance by reviewing your subject material and then using your knowledge to respond effectively to the exam questions during the test session. Combining subject knowledge with effective test writing skills gives you the best opportunity for success. The following are some strategies you may find useful in writing your exam.

- ◆ Managing Test Anxiety

  - ▸ Be as prepared as possible to increase your self-confidence.
  - ▸ Arrive at the exam on time and bring whatever materials you need to complete the exam such as pens, pencils, erasers, and calculators if they are allowed.
  - ▸ Drink enough water before you begin the exam so you are hydrated.
  - ▸ Associate with positive, calm individuals until you enter the exam room.
  - ▸ Use positive self-talk to calm yourself.
  - ▸ Remind yourself that it is normal to feel anxious about the exam.
  - ▸ Visualize your successful completion of the exam.
  - ▸ Breathe deeply several times.
  - ▸ Rotate your head, shrug your shoulders, and change positions to relax.

- ◆ While the information from your crib notes is still fresh in your memory, write down the key words, concepts, definitions, theories or formulas on the back of the test paper before you look at the exam questions.

  - ▸ Review the entire exam.
  - ▸ Budget your time.
  - ▸ Begin with the easiest question or the question that you know you can answer correctly rather than following the numerical question order of the exam.
  - ▸ Be aware of linked questions and use the clues to help you with other questions or in other parts of the exam.

If you "blank" on the exam, try repeating the deep breathing and physical relaxation activities first. Then move to visualization and positive self-talk to get you going. You can also try to open the 'information flow' by writing down anything that you remember about the subject on the reverse side of your exam paper. This activity sometimes helps you to remind yourself that you do know something and you are capable of writing the exam.

📖 GETTING STARTED

MANAGING YOUR TIME

- Plan on staying in the exam room for the full time that is available to you.

- Review the entire exam and calculate how much time you can spend on each section. Write your time schedule on the top of your paper and stick as closely as possible to the time you have allotted for each section of the exam.

- Be strategic and use your time where you will get the most marks. Avoid spending too much time on challenging questions that are not worth more marks than other questions that may be easier and are worth the same number of marks.

- If you are running short of time, switch to point form and write as much as you can for written response and essay questions so you have a chance of receiving partial marks.

- Leave time to review your paper asking yourself, "Did I do all of the questions I was supposed to do?", "Can I answer any questions now that I skipped over before?", "Are there any questions that I misinterpreted or misread?"

USING THE FIVE PASS METHOD

- **BROWSING STAGE** – Scan the entire exam noting the format, the specific instructions and marks allotted for each section, which questions you will complete and which ones you will omit if there is a choice.

- **THE FIRST ANSWERING PASS** – To gain confidence and momentum, answer only the questions you are confident you can answer correctly and quickly. These questions are most often found in the multiple choice or numerical response sections of the exam. Maintain a brisk pace; if a question is taking too long to answer, leave it for the Second or Third Pass.

- **THE SECOND ANSWERING PASS** – This Pass addresses questions which require more effort per mark. Answer as many of the remaining questions as possible while maintaining steady progress toward a solution. As soon as it becomes evident the question is too difficult or is tasking an inordinate amount of time, leave it for the Third Answering Pass.

- **THE THIRD ANSWERING PASS** – During the Third Answering Pass you should complete all partial solutions from the first two Passes. Marks are produced at a slower rate during this stage. At the end of this stage, all questions should have full or partial answers. Guess at any multiple choice questions that you have not yet answered.

- **THE FINAL REVIEW STAGE** – Use the remaining time to review the entire exam, making sure that no questions have been overlooked. Check answers and calculations as time permits.

USING THE THREE PASS METHOD

- **OVERVIEW** – Begin with an overview of the exam to see what it contains. Look for 'easy' questions and questions on topics that you know thoroughly.

- **SECOND PASS** – Answer all the questions that you can complete without too much trouble. These questions help to build your confidence and establish a positive start.

- **LAST PASS** – Now go through and answer the questions that are left. This is when you begin to try solving the questions you find particularly challenging.

📖 *KEY* EXAM TIPS FOR SELECTED SUBJECT AREAS

The following are a few additional suggestions you may wish to consider when writing exams in any of the selected subject areas.

ENGLISH LANGUAGE ARTS

Exams in English Language Arts usually have two components, writing and reading. Sometimes students are allowed to bring approved reference books such as a dictionary, thesaurus and writing handbook into the exam. If you have not used these references on a regular basis, you may find them more of a hindrance than a help in an exam situation. In completing the written section of an English Language Arts exam:

- plan your essay
- focus on the issue presented
- establish a clear position using a thesis statement to direct and unify your writing
- organize your writing in a manner that logically presents your views
- support your viewpoint with specific examples
- edit and proof read your writing

In completing the reading section of an English Language Arts exam:

- read the entire selection before responding
- use titles, dates, footnotes, pictures, introductions, and notes on the author to assist you in developing an understanding of the piece presented
- when using line references, read a few lines before and after the identified section

MATHEMATICS

In some instances, the use of calculators is permitted (or required) to complete complex calculations, modeling, simulations, or to demonstrate your use of technology. It is imperative that you are familiar with the approved calculator and the modes you may be using during your exam. In writing exams in mathematics:

- use appropriate mathematical notation and symbols
- clearly show or explain all the steps involved in solving the problem
- check to be sure you have included the correct units of measurement and have rounded to the appropriate significant digit
- use appropriate labelling and equal increments on graphs

SCIENCES

In the Sciences written response and open-ended questions usually require a clear, organized, and detailed explanation of the science involved in the question. You may find it helpful to use the acronym **STEEPLES** to organize your response to these types of questions. STEEPLES stands for **S**cience, **T**echnological, **E**cological, **E**thical, **P**olitical, **L**egal, **E**conomical, and **S**ocial aspects of the issue presented. In writing exams in the sciences:

- use scientific vocabulary to clearly explain your understanding of the processes or issues
- state your position in an objective manner
- demonstrate your understanding of both sides of the issue
- clearly label graphs, diagrams, tables, and charts using accepted conventions
- provide all formulas and equations

SOCIAL STUDIES, HISTORY, GEOGRAPHY

Exams in these courses of study often require you to take a position on an issue and defend your point of view. Your response should demonstrate your understanding of both the positive and negative aspects of the issue and be supported by well-considered arguments and evidence. In writing exams in Social Studies, History or Geography, the following acronyms may be helpful to you in organizing your approach.

- **SEE** – stands for **S**tatement, **E**xplanation, **E**xample. This acronym reminds you to couple your statement regarding your position with an explanation and then an example.
- **PERMS** – stands for **P**olitical, **E**conomic, **R**eligious or moral, **M**ilitary, and **S**ocietal values. Your position statement may be derived from or based upon any of these points of view. Your argument is more credible if you can show that recognized authorities such as leaders, theorists, writers or scientists back your position.

📖 SUMMARY

Writing exams involves a certain amount of stress and anxiety. If you want to do your best on the exam, *there is no substitute for being well prepared.* Being well prepared helps you to feel more confident about your ability to succeed and less anxious about writing tests. In preparing for unit or year-end exams remember to:

- use as many senses as possible in preparing for exams
- start as early as possible set realistic goals and targets
- take advantage of study buddies, study groups, and tutorials
- review previously used exams
- study with positive, knowledgeable, motivated, and supportive individuals
- practice the material in the format in which you are to be tested
- try to simulate the test situation as much as possible
- keep a positive attitude
- end your study time with a quick review and then do something different before you try to go to sleep on the night before the exam
- drink a sufficient amount of water prior to an exam
- stay in the exam room for the full amount of time available
- try to relax by focusing on your breathing

If you combine your best study habits with some of the strategies presented here, you may increase your chances of writing a strong exam and maximizing your potential to do well.

DIPLOMA EXAMINATIONS

A Guide to Writing The Diploma Examination

The *Diploma Examination* section contains all of the questions from the June 2001 and January 2002 diploma examinations. The questions presented here are distinct from those in the Unit Review section. It is recommended that students work carefully through these exams as they are reflective of the format and difficulty **level of the final exam that students are likely to encounter**.

THE KEY contains detailed answers that illustrate the problem-solving process for every question in this section.

When writing practice exams, students are encouraged to simulate actual Diploma Exam conditions. This will help students become:

- *aware of the mental and physical stamina required to sit through an entire exam*
- *familiar with the exam format and how the course content is tested*
- *aware of any units or concepts that are troublesome or require additional study*
- *more successful in managing their review effectively*

To simulate the exam conditions, students should:

- *use an alarm clock or other timer to monitor the time allowed for the exam*
- *select a quiet writing spot away from all distractions*
- *place their picture ID on the desk or table where the exam is being written*
- *assemble the appropriate materials that are allowed for writing the exam such as pens, HB pencils, calculator, dictionary*
- *use "test wiseness" skills*
- *complete as much of the exam as possible within the allowable time*

In writing the practice exam, students should:

- *read instructions, directions, and questions carefully*
- *organize writing time according to the exam emphasis on each section*
- *highlight key words*
- *think about what is being asked*
- *plan their writing; once complete, proof for errors in content, spelling, grammar*
- *watch for bolded words such as most, least, best*
- *in multiple-choice questions, cross out any choices students know are incorrect*
- *if possible, review all responses upon completion of the exam*

JUNE 2001 DIPLOMA EXAMINATION

Use the following information to answer the first two questions.

Between seven and 12 months of age, infants begin to display a marked fear of strangers. Infants also begin to socially reference their responses during the same period. Some research indicates that extremely fearful children often have very anxious parents.

1. The division of the nervous system that is directly responsible for physiological responses to fear is the

   A. sensory nervous system

   B. somatic nervous system

   C. sympathetic nervous system

   D. parasympathetic nervous system

Use the following additional information to answer the next question.

Biofeedback consists of conscious efforts to control body responses that are normally involuntary. This technique can be used to control abnormal fear.

2. Conscious efforts to control body responses through biofeedback originate in the

   A. medulla

   B. cerebrum

   C. cerebellum

   D. hypothalamus

Use the following information to answer the next four questions.

Parkinson's disease is a degenerative brain disorder. Symptoms of the disease include tremors, rigid muscles, and problems with coordinated movements such as walking and talking. Researchers have discovered that in people with Parkinson's disease, the neurons that produce dopamine, a neurotransmitter in the brain, have died. Based on this research, a number of potential treatments for the disease are being tested. Three of these treatments are explained as follows.

1. In one treatment, fetal pig brain cells that produce dopamine were used. After cloning these cells, the cloned cells were injected into 11 people with Parkinson's disease. Most of the people showed some improvement in their symptoms during the following year.

2. Levadopa is a drug that replaces missing dopamine. Unfortunately, in large doses, it has severe side effects, including nausea and heart problems.

3. A new drug called seligiline acts as an inhibitor of the enzyme monoamine oxidase B, which breaks down dopamine.

—from *Henahan*, 1998

3. *During the cloning of a fetal pig's brain cells, the cells underwent the process of __i__, which increased their numbers, and after injection into people with Parkinson's disease, the cells produced dopamine when the __ii__ code for it was translated.*

   The row that completes the statement above is row

Row	*i*	*ii*
A.	meiosis	DNA
B.	meiosis	mRNA
C.	mitosis	DNA
D.	mitosis	mRNA

4. The drugs levadopa and seligiline are similar in that they both

   A. require cloning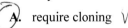

   B. act as inhibitors

   C. prevent the death of neurons

   D. increase neurotransmission in the brain

Use the following additional information to answer the next question.

Schematic Diagram of the Actions of Levadopa, Dopamine, Seligiline, and Monoamine Oxidase B in a Neural Synapse

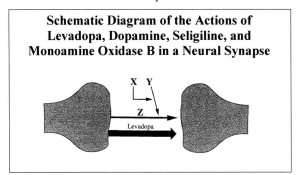

5. Which of the following rows correctly identifies the substances that correspond to X, Y, and Z in the diagram above?

Row	Dopamine	Seligiline	Monoamine Oxidase B
A.	X	Y	Z
B.	Z	X	Y
C.	Z	Y	X
D.	X	Z	Y

Use the following additional information to answer the next question.

People affected by Parkinson's disease have unusually low levels of the neurotransmitter dopamine. Studies have shown that the risk of developing Parkinson's disease is about double for non-smokers than for smokers. Brain scans of smokers and non-smokers reveal that levels of the enzyme monoamine oxidase B (MAOB) are about 40% lower in smokers than in non-smokers. MAOB is one of the enzymes involved in breaking down dopamine.

6. A possible reason for the link between smoking and a reduced risk of developing Parkinson's disease is that smoking

   A. reduces the level of dopamine and of MAOB

   B. increases the level of dopamine and of MAOB

   C. reduces the level of dopamine by increasing the level of MAOB

   D. increases the level of dopamine by decreasing the level of MAOB

Use the following information to answer the next question.

Individuals know that touching a hot stove can be painful. When an individual accidentally touches a hot stove, a reflex arc is initiated, which causes the person to withdraw his or her hand before he or she senses the pain.

7. Which of the following lists identifies the neural pathway in a reflex arc?

   A. Receptor, sensory neuron, effector, motor neuron

   B. Motor neuron, interneuron, sensory neuron, effector

   C. Sensory neuron, receptor, interneuron, motor neuron

   D. Receptor, sensory neuron, interneuron, motor neuron

Use the following information to answer the next question.

Alternative medicine, such as aromatherapy, is becoming increasingly popular in western society. Aromatherapy uses natural oils and plant extracts. The scents of the oils and extracts are inhaled or the fragrant oils are massaged into the skin. Proponents of aromatherapy hypothesize that odours affect the brain and its release of neurochemicals. These neurochemicals may then relieve pain.

Hypothesized Steps in Aromatherapy Action

1 Olfactory neurons depolarize.
2 Olfactory receptors are stimulated.
3 Neurochemicals affect pain interpretation.
4 Neurochemicals are released from axon terminals.

Numerical Response

1. If it is assumed that the hypothesis is correct, the order in which the steps above would occur to result in pain relief in a person having just inhaled the scent from an aromatherapy oil or extract is __2__ , __1__ , __4__ , and __3__ .

Use the following diagram to answer the next question.

The Human Brain

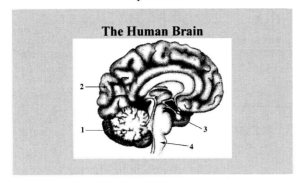

8. The area of the brain that controls the sympathetic and parasympathetic nervous systems is labelled

   A. 1

   B. 2

   C. 3

   D. 4

Use the following information to answer the next four questions.

Erectile dysfunction is defined as the inability to maintain an erection adequate enough to achieve a satisfactory sexual experience. When erectile dysfunction is related to inadequate blood flow to the penis, the medication Viagra can be prescribed.

A side effect of Viagra is that it sometimes results in temporary difficulties in distinguishing between the colours of blue and green. For this reason, pilots have been banned from using the drug within six hours of a flight.

The Human Eye

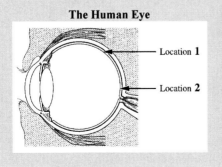

9. The cells in the eye that are affected by Viagra and the primary location of these cells, as labelled above, are, respectively,

   A. rod cells and location 1

   B. rod cells and location 2

   C. cone cells and location 1

   D. cone cells and location 2

Use the following additional information to answer the next question.

A chemical in the body known as cyclic GMP initiates the muscular and vascular changes that lead to an erection. Receptors for cyclic GMP are found in erectile tissue. Normally, the enzyme PDE5 breaks down cyclic GMP. Viagra blocks the action of this enzyme.

10. Viagra could be prescribed to treat impotence in males with

   A. normal levels of GMP but low levels of PDE5

   B. low levels of GMP but normal levels of PDE5

   C. high levels of GMP but normal levels of GMP receptors

   D. normal levels of GMP but high levels of GMP receptors

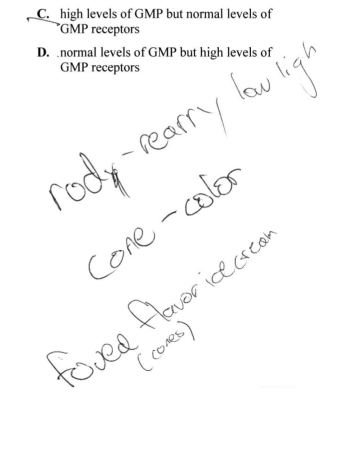

Use the following additional information to answer the next two questions.

Erectile dysfunction can result in the inability of a couple to conceive. However, infertility is more commonly associated with insufficient sperm production. The feedback loop below illustrates the hormonal control of sperm production.

Hormonal Regulation of Sperm Production

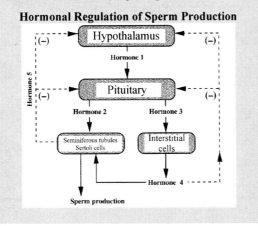

11. In the diagram above, the hormones FSH, LH, and testosterone are labelled, respectively,

A. 2, 3, 4 ✓

B. 2, 3, 5 ✓

C. 3, 2, 4

D. 3, 2, 5

12. If infertility were due to decreased production of hormone 1 by the hypothalamus, then fewer sperm would be produced because there would be

A. low levels of hormone 2

B. high levels of hormone 3

C. high levels of hormone 4

D. low levels of hormone 5

Use the following information to answer the next four questions.

Sex-based differences in mental ability are controversial subjects of research. An article by Doreen Kimura in *Scientific American* summarized some of the studies conducted in this area.
One study was carried out to compare males' and females' performance on a variety of mental tasks. The males and females in the study had either relatively low testosterone or relatively high testosterone levels. (Females produce small amounts of testosterone in the adrenal cortex.) Results for the spatial skills component of the study are provided below.

Spatial Skills Performance

—Graph and excerpt adapted from *Sex Differences in the Brain* by Doreen Kimura. Copyright © 1992 by Scientific American Inc. All rights reserved.

13. Two manipulated variables in this study are

A. sex and spatial skills

B. test scores and spatial skills

C. sex and testosterone levels

D. test scores and testosterone levels

14. Based on the results shown in the graph above, the effect that administering extra testosterone to females and males will have on their respective spatial skills is shown in row

Row	Females	Males
A.	improved	improved
B.	weakened	improved
C.	improved	weakened
D.	weakened	weakened

15. The cells that produce testosterone in females and in males are given in row

Row	Females	Males
A.	follicle cells	interstitial cells
B.	adrenal cortex cells	interstitial cells
C.	follicle cells	seminiferous tubule cells
D.	adrenal cortex cells	seminiferous tubule cells

Use the following additional information to answer the next question.

Researchers have found evidence that during the part of the menstrual cycle in which a woman's estrogen level is highest, her spatial skills are weakest while her motor skills and articulation skills are enhanced. Another study summarized by Kimura measured testosterone levels in saliva. The study found that relatively low testosterone levels in males enhanced their mathematical reasoning, but there was no correlation between testosterone levels and a woman's mathematical reasoning ability.

—from *Kimura,* 1992

Statements Related to Womens' Hormonal Levels and Skill Levels

1 Increased testosterone and increased estrogen increase a woman's spatial skills.
2 Increased testosterone and decreased estrogen increase a woman's spatial skills.
3 During pregnancy, a woman's spatial skills are enhanced.
4 During pregnancy, a woman's motor skills are enhanced.
5 During pregnancy, a woman's articulation skills are reduced.
6 A woman's spatial skills are enhanced around day 1 of her menstrual cycle.
7 A woman's motor skills are enhanced around day 14 of her menstrual cycle.
8 A woman's mathematical skills are enhanced around day 14 of her menstrual cycle.

Numerical Response

2. This research supports the **four** statements numbered ___2___, ___4___, ___5___, and ___1___.

(Record your four-digit answer in lowest-to-highest numerical order.)

Use the following information to answer the next question.

Research performed on *Drosophila* has revealed the presence of genes that code for products that influence learning. Researchers have isolated a *dunce* gene known to code for an enzyme involved with learning. Flies with a mutated form of the gene cannot learn to associate between a specific odour and an electric shock. Flies with normal genes can learn the association. Although the enzyme is prevalent throughout the nervous system, it is concentrated in structures in the brain that are involved in learning and memory.

—from *Levine and Suzuki,* 1993

16. The concept that is **most strongly** supported by this discovery is that

A. genes are involved in enzyme production that influences learning

B. genes are involved in enzyme production that controls stimuli creation

C. learning is a wholly inherited trait and is not influenced by the environment

D. learning is not an inherited trait and is wholly influenced by the environment

Use the following information to answer the next two questions.

Alpha reductase type II is an enzyme that converts the hormone testosterone into dihydroxytestosterone (DHT). A variation in the allele that codes for the enzyme results in a single amino acid change: a valine replaces a leucine. The enzyme that contains valine instead of leucine is more efficient and results in the production of more DHT. DHT may increase the susceptibility of prostate cells to cancer.

—from *Travis,* 1996

17. The incidence of prostate cancer is likely highest in men who are

A. homozygous for the normal allele

B. homozygous for the allele variation

C. heterozygous, because these men produce both versions of the enzyme

D. heterozygous, because these men produce neither version of the enzyme

18. Possible DNA triplets for valine and leucine are identified in row

Row	Valine	Leucine
A.	CAT	GTG
B.	CAA	GAA
C.	GTT	CTT
D.	GUU	CUC

Use the following information to answer the next two questions.

One cause of reduced fertility in males may be related to azoospermia. Males with this condition are not completely sterile but produce low numbers of sperm, which results in reduced fertility.
The gene *DAZ* located on the Y chromosome may be vital to spermatogenesis. Deletion of this gene by mutation may lead to infertility, even if the rest of the Y chromosome is intact. In a particular study, tissue samples from a male with azoospermia revealed the lack of the *DAZ* gene in blood cells and in sperm.
—from *Travis, 1996*

19. Which of the following pieces of evidence would indicate that the male examined in this study did not experience a genetic mutation in his gonadal cells but **more likely** inherited the condition?

    A. Azoospermia is found in 3% to 4% of males.

    B. The *DAZ* gene once deleted can never be regained.

    C. Deletion of the *DAZ* gene occurs more commonly during meiosis.

    D. Both blood cells and sperm of the subject were lacking the *DAZ* gene.

20. If a male with azoospermia were to father sons through *in vitro* fertilization, what percentage of his sons would be expected to have azoospermia?

    A. 0%

    B. 25%

    C. 50%

    D. 100%

Use the following information to answer the next three questions.

Ideas concerning the nature of inheritance have very early origins, but the conceptual breakthrough that established modern genetics as a science was made less than 150 years ago by an Austrian monk, Gregor Mendel.

21. Alternate forms of the same gene are known as

    A. alleles

    B. gametes

    C. genotypes

    D. heterozygotes

22. Mendel's principle of segregation states that alternate forms of a gene separate during

    A. fertilization

    B. seed dispersal

    C. cross-pollination

    D. gamete formation

23. An organism is heterozygous for two pairs of genes. The number of different combinations of alleles that can form for these two genes in the organism's gametes is

    A. 1

    B. 2

    C. 4

    D. 8

Use the following information to answer the next three questions.

Deaf-mutism is an autosomal recessive trait that is caused by two genes. Individuals who are homozygous recessive for either gene will have deaf-mutism. The two genes are designated as *D* and *E* in the diagram below.

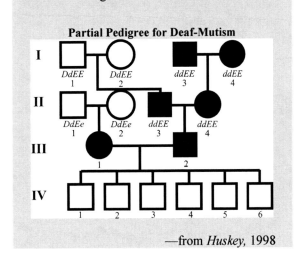

Partial Pedigree for Deaf-Mutism

—from *Huskey*, 1998

24. A possible genotype of individual IV-3 is

   A. *ddEE*

   B. *ddEe*

   C. *DDee*

   D. *DdEe*

25. Individuals **III-1** and **III-2** are expecting their seventh child. What is the probability of this child having deaf-mutism?

   A. 0.00

   B. 0.25

   C. 0.50

   D. 0.75

Numerical Response

3. What is the probability of a couple that are heterozygous for both genes having a child with deaf-mutism?

   Answer: _____ (Record your answer as a value from 0 to 1, rounded to two decimal places.)

Use the following information to answer the next three questions.

In the hypothetical pedigree below, shaded individuals have sickle cell anemia and are homozygous for the defective allele Hb^S. The normal allele is Hb^A. Carriers of the Hb^S allele are not identified in the pedigree.

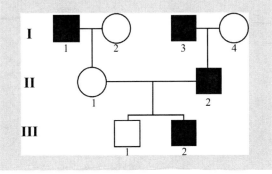

26. Individual **III-1** has blood type A. His genotype could be

   A. $I^A i \ Hb^A Hb^S$

   B. $I^A I^A \ Hb^S Hb^S$

   C. $I^A I^B \ Hb^A Hb^S$

   D. $I^A I^B \ Hb^A Hb^A$

27. If individual **II-1** has blood type A and individual **II-2** has blood type B, which of the following genotypes would be possible for their third child, if they had one?

   A. $I^A i \ Hb^A Hb^S$

   B. $I^A I^A \ Hb^S Hb^S$

   C. $I^A I^B \ Hb^A Hb^S$

   D. $I^A I^A \ Hb^A Hb^A$

28. Which of the following rows indicates the relationship between the I^A and I^B alleles and the relationship between the I^A and i alleles for the blood type gene?

Row	Relationship between I^A and I^B	Relationship between I^A and i
A.	codominant	codominant
B.	codominant	dominant-recessive
C.	dominant-recessive	codominant
D.	dominant-recessive	dominant-recessive

Use the following information to answer the next three questions.

A dominant allele, X^E, carried on the X chromosome causes the formation of faulty tooth enamel and causes either very thin or very hard enamel.

Hypothetical Pedigree Showing the Incidence of Faulty Tooth Enamel

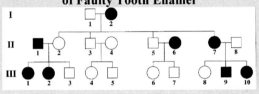

29. The genotypes of individuals **II-6** and **III-7** are identified in row

Row	II-6	III-7
A.	$X^E X^E$	$X^E Y$
B.	$X^E X^e$	$X^e Y$
C.	$X^e X^e$	$X^E Y$
D.	$X^E X^E$	$X^e Y$

4. A woman heterozygous for faulty tooth enamel marries a man with normal tooth enamel. What is the probability that their first child will be a boy with normal tooth enamel?

Answer: _____ (Record your answer as a value from 0 to 1, rounded to two decimal places.)

30. The faulty tooth enamel trait will appear in all of the daughters but none of the sons if the children have a father with

A. normal tooth enamel and a mother with normal tooth enamel

B. normal tooth enamel and mother with faulty tooth enamel

C. faulty tooth enamel and a mother with normal tooth enamel

D. faulty tooth enamel and a mother with faulty tooth enamel

Use the following information to answer the next two questions.

Cross-over Frequencies of Some Genes on Human Chromosome 6

Genes	Approximate Cross-over Frequencies
Diabetes mellitus (1) and ovarian cancer (2)	21%
Diabetes mellitus (1) and Rhesus blood group (3)	12%
Ragweed sensitivity (4) and Rhesus blood group (3)	10.5%
Rhesus blood group (3) and ovarian cancer (2)	9%
Ragweed sensitivity (4) and ovarian cancer (2)	19.5%

5. On human chromosome 6, the order of the genes numbered above is

_____, _____, _____, and _____.

31. What is the approximate cross-over frequency between the diabetes mellitus gene and the ragweed sensitivity gene?

    A. 1.5%

    B. 10.5%

    C. 15.0%

    D. 22.5%

Use the following information to answer the next three questions.

Desert-grassland whiptail lizards are all female, so they must reproduce by parthenogenesis. This is a type of reproduction in which females produce offspring from unfertilized eggs that have undergone chromosome doubling after meiosis. Although all whiptail lizards are females, they undergo courtship patterns similar to other types of lizards that have both sexes.

Sexual Behaviour in Parthenogenetic Lizards

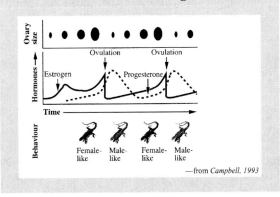

—from *Campbell, 1993*

32. A correlation that can be made based on the data above is that

    A. male-like behaviour is correlated with relatively large ovaries

    B. female-like behaviour is correlated with relatively small ovaries

    C. male-like behaviour is correlated with high blood levels of estrogen

    D. female-like behaviour is correlated with high blood levels of estrogen

33. A similarity between lizard reproductive hormones and human reproductive hormones is that

    A. after ovulation, ovaries decrease in size

    B. before ovulation, ovaries increase in size

    C. before ovulation, estrogen is secreted in decreasing amounts

    D. after ovulation, progesterone is secreted in increasing amounts

34. According to the information on parthenogenetic lizards, the somatic cells of offspring produced from the whiptail lizard's unfertilized eggs would have a chromosome number of

    A. *n*

    B. *2n*

    C. *4n*

    D. *n + 2*

Use the following information to answer the next four questions.

Elephants communicate mainly by means of infrasonic sound. This means that the sound is below the frequency of sound that a human can hear. Elephants also emit a few higher-frequency trumpeting sounds that are audible to humans.

The infrasonic calls of elephants travel great distances. Researchers are now beginning to understand elephant behaviour based on this communication method. Certain calls are crucial in reproductive behaviour. The females use a distinctive infrasonic call when they are sexually receptive, which occurs for only four days every four years.

—from *The Edmonton Journal*, 1997

35. In the human ear, audible trumpeting sounds would be translated into nerve impulses in the

    A. ossicles

    B. oval window

    C. organ of Corti

    D. semicircular canals

36. In comparison with humans, elephants would be considered

    A. *r*-selected, and they have a lower biotic potential than humans

    B. *r*-selected, and they have a higher biotic potential than humans

    C. *K*-selected, and they have a lower biotic potential than humans

    D. *K*-selected, and they have a higher biotic potential than humans

37. Reproductive hormones function in a similar manner in elephants and in humans.
    The hormone change that stimulates ovulation every four years in female elephants is

    A. an increase in LH levels

    B. a decrease in FSH levels

    C. a decrease in estrogen levels

    D. an increase in progesterone levels

Use the following additional information to answer the next question.

Some female mammals, such as humans and elephants, exhibit a variety of differences in their reproductive cycles.

Characteristics of Female Mammalian Reproductive Cycles

1 The cycle is called an estrous cycle.
2 The cycle is called a menstrual cycle.
3 The endometrium is shed if no pregnancy occurs.
4 The endometrium is absorbed if no pregnancy occurs.
5 There are pronounced behavioural changes around ovulation.
6 There are some behavioural changes throughout the cycle.

Numerical Response

6. The three characteristics of most female elephants' reproductive cycles but not of most female humans' reproductive cycles are _____, _____, and _____.
(Record your three-digit answer in lowest to highest numerical order.)

Use the following information to answer the next two questions.

Fertilization occurs when a sperm fuses with an egg to form a zygote. In this diagram of a zygote, the sperm and egg nuclei are just fusing. (One polar body is also visible).

Fertilization

38. The event depicted above normally occurs in the

    A. ovary

    B. uterus

    C. vagina

    D. Fallopian tube

39. The zygote shown above is composed of

    A. one diploid cell

    B. two diploid cells

    C. one monoploid (haploid) cell

    D. one monoploid (haploid) and one diploid cell

Use the following information to answer the next two questions.

Fertilized Human Eggs (Two Zygotes)   **Eight-Cell Human Embryo**

---

40. Which of the following statements **best** describes one of the diagrams above?

    A. The two zygotes will form identical twins.

    B. The two zygotes are about to undergo meiosis.

    C. The cells of the eight-cell human embryo have differentiated.

    D. The cells of the eight-cell human embryo contain identical DNA.

41. The process that occurs to form an eight-cell embryo stage from a zygote is

    A. mitosis of diploid cells

    B. mitosis of haploid cells

    C. meiosis of diploid cells

    D. meiosis of haploid cells

Use the following information to answer the next two questions.

Sam Wasser, a biologist, trains drug-sniffing dogs to locate feces of owls, wolves, and bears. The feces contain DNA that can be extracted and analyzed.

Researchers have used feces located by the dogs to obtain evidence to evaluate a wildlife management strategy that was being used by timber companies. The timber companies were feeding bears to discourage them from tearing bark off trees. Genetic analysis of their fecal matter indicated that the male bears were eating the food supplied and the female bears were eating bark from the trees.

—from *Simon*, 1997

42. One piece of evidence that the researchers used to determine that the timber companies' strategy was **not** working for all bears was that some of the feces contained

    A. bark chips and cells with two X chromosomes

    B. bark chips and cells with one Y chromosome

    C. food particles consistent with the food provided and cells with two X chromosomes

    D. food particles consistent with the food provided and cells with one Y chromosome

Use the following additional information to answer the next question.

Biologists have been able to map the large territory inhabited by the bear population by locating their feces. In order to use DNA found in feces to track bears, it is necessary to identify individual bears by the DNA found in their feces. One technique that is used to do this is DNA fingerprinting.

43. In DNA fingerprinting, gel electrophoresis is used to

    A. cut DNA into fragments

    B. separate fragments of DNA

    C. match a gene with its function

    D. pair homologous chromosomes

Use the following information to answer the next two questions.

Researchers analyzing spotted owl pellets found high levels of stress hormones in owls whose nests are within a quarter mile of logging areas. This information could be used to determine how large of a buffer zone is needed between the birds and the logging areas.

Animal Stress Response Flowchart

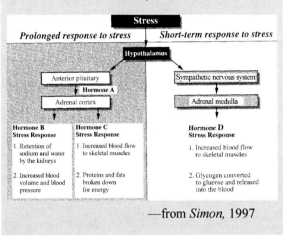

—from *Simon,* 1997

Use the following additional information to answer the next question.

Hormones Involved in an Owl's Stress Response That Could be Measured by Scientists

1 Cortisol
2 Aldosterone
3 ACTH
4 Epinephrine

Numerical Response

7. Match the hormones, as numbered above, to the letters A, B, C, and D in the flowchart above.

Hormone Number: _____ _____ _____ _____

Flowchart Letter: **A** **B** **C** **D**

44. In the owls, short-term response to stress occurs faster than prolonged response to stress because the

  A. blood from the adrenal medulla travels faster than does the blood from the adrenal cortex

  B. adrenal medulla responds to nervous stimulation, which is faster than hormonal stimulation

  C. adrenal medulla is controlled by the hypothalamus whereas the adrenal cortex is controlled by the pituitary

  D. hormone from the adrenal medulla acts on cells more quickly than the hormones from the adrenal cortex

Use the following information to answer the next three questions.

The burrowing owl is an endangered species in Canada's western provinces. Research data collected in Saskatchewan's Burrowing Owl Recovery Project indicate that the population has declined by 20% per year over the past five years. In 1996, a population estimate showed that the number of burrowing owls had declined to 800 breeding pairs.

To obtain this population data, researchers reached into the burrows to collect and count baby owls. When they did this, the researchers heard a hiss like a rattlesnake coming from the baby owls in the burrow. The owls were attempting to scare off the intruders.

—from *The Globe and Mail,* 1997

45. The hissing behaviour of the baby owls is an example of

  A. mimicry

  B. mutualism

  C. camouflage

  D. commensalism

Numerical Response

8. If the decline of the burrowing owl population continued at the same rate, how many breeding pairs would there have been in 1998?

Answer: _____ breeding pairs
(Record your answer as a whole number.)

Use the following additional information to answer the next question.

The burrowing owl habitat is open prairie grass. The owls live in ground squirrel holes that have been enlarged by badgers. The young owls are cared for by both parents who feed them a diet consisting of mice, moles, and insects.
Other prairie predators such as the rattlesnake and kestrel (sparrow hawk) also rely upon these same food sources.

46. The relationship between the kestrel and the burrowing owl and the relationship between the burrowing owl and badger are given in row

Row	Kestrel/ Burrowing Owl	Burrowing Owl/Badger
A.	predator–prey	mutualism
B.	predator–prey	commensalism
C.	interspecific competition	mutualism
D.	interspecific competition	commensalism

Use the following information to answer the next question.

The population of a colony of honey bees (*Apis mellifera*) in Alberta varies seasonally as illustrated in the following graph.

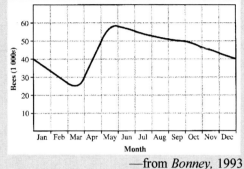

—from *Bonney*, 1993

47. The portion of the graph for April **most likely** indicates the effect of

A. an increase in parasitism

B. a decrease in competition

C. a decrease in limiting factors

D. an increase in environmental resistance

Use the following information to answer the next question.

Mites (*Acaropis woodii*) can live in the trachea of a bee. These mites obtain nutrients from bee tissue. Beekeepers worry when mite populations reach numbers that have the potential to destroy the bee colony.
—from *Bonney*, 1993

48. The relationship between bees and mites is called

A. parasitism

B. commensalism

C. interspecific competition

D. intraspecific competition

Written Response—15%

Use the following information to answer the next question.

Although doctors were astonished, relatives were not surprised when Benjy Stacy was born with skin the colour of a bruised plum. Two days of medical tests to rule out possible heart and lung disease revealed no cause for the newborn's dark blue skin. Not until Benjy's grandmother asked the puzzled doctors if they had ever heard of the blue Fugates of Troublesome Creek was the mystery solved. When baby Benjy inherited his mother's red hair and his father's lankiness, he also received his great-great-great-grandfather Martin Fugate's blue skin.

In 1820, a French orphan named Martin Fugate settled on the banks of Troublesome Creek. He and his red-headed American bride Elizabeth had seven children, four of which were reported to be blue-skinned. Isolated in the hills of eastern Kentucky, the family multiplied. Intermarriages between "blue Fugates" were common. Over time, the inherited blue trait began to disappear as the arrival of railways and roads allowed family members to marry outside their communities. Six generations after Martin Fugate first settled in Troublesome Creek, baby Benjy was born.

Based on Benjy's grandmother's account and further testing, doctors concluded that the newborn carried one copy of a mutated gene for methemoglobinemia. Hereditary methemoglobinemia is a rare autosomal recessive blood disorder. Blue people have an absence of the enzyme diaphorase in their red blood cells. In a normal individual, hemoglobin, the blood's red, oxygen-carrying molecule, is slowly converted to a non-functional blue form called methemoglobin. Diaphorase then converts methemoglobin back to hemoglobin. The absence of diaphorase in affected individuals is caused by a mutation in the enzyme's structural gene. This causes the accumulation of blue methemoglobin, which replaces the red hemoglobin responsible for pink skin in most Caucasians.

—from *Trost*, 1982

1. a) Explain how a gene mutation could alter the diaphorase enzyme's amino acid sequence **(2 marks)**

Use the following additional information to answer the next three parts of the question.

In one account of the Fugate family's pedigree from 1750 to 1889, six of the 55 individuals expressed the blue phenotype as adults.

b) Determine the frequency of the recessive allele for the Fugate family during this time. Show your work. **(2 marks)**

c) Predict the theoretical percentage of individuals in the Fugate family that were heterozygotes during this time. Show your work. **(2 marks)**

d) Explain why the frequency of the blue skin phenotype was higher in the Fugate family than in the general American population. **(1 mark)**

e) Identify two ways in which the population, which consisted of six generations of the Fugate family, did not meet the conditions for Hardy–Weinberg equilibrium. **(2 marks)**

Use the following additional information to answer the next part of the question.

RBC NADH Diaphorase Activity

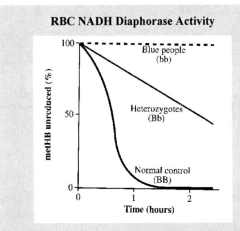

The data above were obtained by extracting red blood cells from three different groups of individuals. The red blood cells were then evaluated for their ability to convert methemoglobin to hemoglobin.

—from *Huskey,* 1996

f) Although he was very blue at birth, within his first few weeks, Benjy's skin colour changed to normal with no treatment required. At the age of seven, other than purplish blue lips when he was cold or angry, Benjy's coloration was normal.

i) What is Benjy's genotype?

(1 mark)

ii) Give a possible explanation for the change in Benjy's phenotype over time.

(1 mark)

iii) Individuals with hereditary methemoglobinemia can be treated easily with methylene blue pills. Methylene blue acts as an "electron donor" converting methemoglobin to hemoglobin, which results in pink skin colouration. Explain why treated blue people can still produce offspring with hereditary methemoglobinemia.

(1 mark)

Written Response—15%

Use the following information to answer the next question.

Development of a fetus in the uterus is of interest to both scientists and expectant parents. An embryo develops a neural tube (a fluid-filled structure that will later develop into a brain and a spinal cord) at five weeks and tastebuds at 15 weeks. Fetuses have been known to show dream-like patterns through rapid eye movement (REM) at nine weeks. In the uterus, the fetus yawns and may experience taste and smell. The heart rate of a fetus decreases in response to its mother's voice. This suggests that the fetus somehow recognizes its mother's voice and is calmed by it. Even at birth, a baby already responds to and prefers its mother's voice. There is also evidence that stress in mothers increases cortisol levels and produces more active fetuses, and that more active fetuses are, in turn, more irritable infants. A baby's predisposition to certain tastes may be linked to what it was exposed to in the uterus. The amniotic fluid contains traces of chemicals from the foods the mother eats, and the fetus swallows amniotic fluids.

A study headed by pediatric neurologist Dr. Peter Hultenlocher has provided evidence that the majority of connections between neurons are made in the first three years of an child's life. The study indicates that a child's brain contains twice as many neurons and consumes twice as much energy as a normal adult brain. A study done at Baylor College of Medicine indicates that children who do not play or who are rarely touched by their mothers develop brains that are 20% to 30% smaller than normal for their age. Other studies show that in neural development from the fetal stage to ten years of age, connections between neurons develop as a result of the firing activity of neurons. Stimulation causes axons and dendrites to grow and produce synapses. If these connections are not reinforced by activity, they are eliminated from the brain's circuitry.

Studies of infants faced with emotional or physical trauma show that they also increase secretions of cortisol in response to stress. Cortisol has been shown to shrink regions of the brain involved in learning and memory. A newborn can also recognize and express emotion. Smiling mothers elicit a smiling, gurgling response in their babies. The infant's early response is linked to the social skill development needed for interpersonal relationships. The language spoken to a baby has been found to influence brain development. For example, babies spoken to in Japanese have different neural circuits than those spoken to in English.

Of the 100 000 human genes, 50 000 are dedicated to constructing and maintaining the nervous system. Some of these genes have been linked directly to learning. In fruit flies, a gene called CREB has been shown to increase its activity as a result of motor neuron stimulation. When this gene was inhibited in giant snails, their short-term memory developed but their long-term memory did not. The same gene is found in humans. Other genes may also be involved in learning.

—from *Newberger*, 1997
Nash, 1997
Hopson, 1998

2. Write a unified response addressing the following aspects of fetal development and development in early childhood.

- **Sketch** a diagram of the fetus and its environment at approximately three months development and **label** four structures that support the fetus in this environment. **Describe** how the environment in the uterus and structures associated with the fetus support the fetus during this stage of development.
- **Describe** the pathway for sensory interpretation in a fetus or newborn. Start from a **specific** stimulus to the part of the CNS that is stimulated in order for interpretation to occur.
- **Identify** and **describe** two technologies and/or government policies that might result in stimulation of appropriate neural development in children. **Explain** how each of these would affect neural development in early childhood.

JANUARY 2002 DIPLOMA EXAMINATION

Use the following information to answer the first three questions.

The thyroid gland secretes the hormones thyroxine and calcitonin. Embedded in the thyroid gland are the four parathyroid glands. The parathyroid glands secrete the parathyroid hormone (PTH).
Calcitonin and PTH work antagonistically to maintain homeostasis of calcium ion concentrations in the blood. High levels of calcium ions stimulate the secretion of calcitonin, which causes deposition of calcium in the bones.

1. Low levels of calcium ions in the blood cause

   A. decreased secretion of PTH and increased deposition of calcium in the bones

   B. decreased secretion of calcitonin and increased deposition of calcium in the bones

   C. increased secretion of PTH and movement of calcium from the bones to the blood

   D. increased secretion of calcitonin and movement of calcium from the bones to the blood

2. The release of thyroxine from the thyroid is directly regulated by

   A. TSH

   B. TRH

   C. iodine

   D. thyroxine

3. A characteristic symptom of hyperthyroidism, a disorder of the thyroid gland, is

   A. lethargy

   B. weight loss

   C. intolerance to cold

   D. slowed mental processes

4. Which of the following hormones plays a role in returning the salt concentration in the blood to homeostatic levels following heavy exercise?

   A. Cortisol

   B. Thyroxine

   C. Aldosterone

   D. Epinephrine

Use the following information to answer the next question.

Chemicals found in alcohol and tea have a diuretic effect. Diuretics cause the body to produce greater-than-normal volumes of urine.

5. Diuretic chemicals counteract the effect of the hormone

   A. ADH

   B. insulin

   C. cortisol

   D. prolactin

Use the following information to answer the next five questions.

Multiple sclerosis (MS), a disease of the nervous system, typically has symptoms of uncontrolled muscle responses, weakness, paralysis, and vision difficulties. Researchers believe that MS occurs as a result of the body's immune system destroying the myelin sheath that surrounds the axon of a nerve cell. The result is a scarring of brain tissue or of spinal cord tissue.

6. Damage to the myelin sheath of an optic neuron affects the speed of neural transmission to the visual centre, which is found in which lobe of the cerebrum?

   A. Frontal lobe

   B. Parietal lobe

   C. Occipital lobe

   D. Temporal lobe

Numerical Response

1. Another symptom of MS is an exaggerated pupillary light reflex. Some of the events that occur during this reflex are listed below.

1   Motor neuron depolarizes
2   Sensory neuron depolarizes
3   Interneuron depolarizes
4   Light receptors stimulated

The order in which the events listed above occur during a pupillary light reflex is _____, _____, _____, and _____.

Use the following additional information to answer the next three questions.

Stimulation of a sensory neuron produces an action potential. An abnormal pattern in this action potential can be used to detect MS in its early stages. The graph below illustrates the membrane potential of a normal neuron after stimulation.

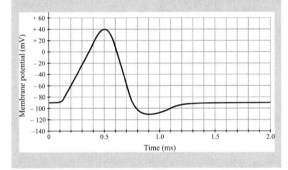

Numerical Response

2. What is the resting membrane potential for this neuron, expressed to two digits, **and** what is the maximum membrane potential during depolarization, expressed to two digits? (Record your answers as absolute values.)

Answer: _____ _____, _____ _____
Membrane   **Resting**   **Maximum During**
Potential: **Depolarization**

7. Which of the following types of ion movement across an axon membrane would cause the action potential to change during the interval from 0.2 ms to 0.4 ms?

A.   Sodium ions moving into the axon

B.   Sodium ions moving out of the axon

C.   Potassium ions moving into the axon

D.   Potassium ions moving out of the axon

8. On the graph, the period from 0.5 ms to 1.0 ms represents the neuron's

A.   refractory period, which is when repolarization occurs

B.   refractory period, which is when minimum depolarization occurs

C.   threshold period, which is when repolarization occurs

D.   threshold period, which is when minimum depolarization occurs

Use the following information to answer the next four questions.

Monoamine oxidase (MAO) is an enzyme that breaks down the neurotransmitters dopamine, serotonin, and norepinephrine. Individuals who are involved in extreme sports, such as rock climbing, generally have low levels of MAO and, therefore, higher-than-normal levels of these neurotransmitters.

Dopamine and serotonin are linked to pleasurable feelings. Norepinephrine is released in the fight-or-flight response. One hypothesis for why individuals participate in extreme sports is that in order for individuals with high resting levels of these neurotransmitters to achieve a pleasurable sensation, they require a greater surge of these chemicals than do other people.

—from *Zorpette*, 1999

9. The site in the neural pathway where MAO is active is the

A.   axon

B.   synaptic cleft

C.   cell body

D.   Schwann cell

10. The area of the brain that normally initiates the fight-or-flight response is the

   A. pons

   B. cerebrum

   C. cerebellum

   D. hypothalamus

Use the following additional information to answer the next two questions.

Serotonin stimulates the release of endorphins, and endorphins eventually cause the release of more dopamine. Studies of individuals involved in extreme sports have found that these people have lower-than-normal numbers of two of the five types of dopamine receptors.

—from *Zorpette,* 1999

11. The endorphin met-enkephalin is comprised of the amino acids methionine, phenylalanine, glycine, glycine, and tyrosine. Possible mRNA codons for the production of met-enkephalin are

   A. ATG TTT GGT GGT TAT

   B. ATG TTG GGC GGC TAT

   C. AUG UUC GGT GGT UAC

   D. AUG UUU GGC GGC UAC

12. When individuals participate in extreme sports, their neurons release more dopamine, which results in a pleasurable sensation because

   A. less serotonin is released from neurons

   B. more dopamine receptors are produced

   C. the fight-or-flight response is inhibited

   D. a neuron containing dopamine receptors reaches threshold depolarization

Use the following information to answer the next two questions.

New research has led to advances in the development of male contraceptives. One of the most promising contraceptive methods involves injecting androgens (testosterone or other male hormones) into a male's muscles. The androgens produce a negative feedback effect on the hypothalamus and pituitary gland. In trials involving a combination of androgens, sperm counts were reduced to zero in test subjects, but this method was effective for only three weeks.

Events in a Negative Feedback Loop Controlling Sperm Production

1 Production of sperm is inhibited
2 Hormone levels in the blood return to normal
3 Production of FSH and LH is inhibited
4 High levels of the injected androgens circulate in the blood

—from *Alexander,* 1999

Numerical Response

3. The order in which the events listed above would occur following the injection of androgens into a male's muscle is _____, _____, _____, and _____.

Use the following additional information to answer the next question.

Researchers developing male contraceptives have found other methods of interfering with various stages of sperm development and sperm release from the body. Some methods of contraception currently being investigated are given below.

1 Interfering with the process of meiosis by which sperm are produced
2 Blocking the release of hormones that stimulate the release of FSH and LH
3 Using removable polyurethane plugs to block the tubes that transport sperm
4 Administering a calcium-blocking drug that interferes with the final maturation of sperm

Numerical Response

4. Match each of the methods of contraception described above with the structure given below that is targeted by that method.

Structure:	Method of Contraception:
Seminiferous tubules	_____
Epididymis	_____
Vas deferens	_____
Hypothalamus	_____

Use the following information to answer the next three questions.

> Benign prostatic hyperplasia (BPH), an enlargement of the prostate gland, causes urination problems such as dribbling and pain. BPH is not a precursor to prostate cancer. Prostate cancer is linked to the absence of a protein coded for by the p27 gene. The absence of this protein leads to uncontrolled cell growth in prostate tissue.
>
> —from *Seppa*, 1998

13. The movement of which of the following substances could **not** be affected by BPH?

A. Urine

B. Sperm

C. Testosterone

D. Seminal vesicle secretions

Use the following additional information to answer the next question.

Some Male Reproductive Structures

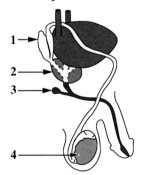

14. In the diagram above, the structure **most affected** by the absence of the protein coded for by the *p27* gene is numbered

A. 1

B. 2

C. 3

D. 4

15. In normally functioning cells, the protein coded for by the *p27* gene is produced continuously. The process by which the *p27* gene's code is read from the DNA and the name of the molecule formed in the process are identified in row

Row	Process	Molecule
A.	transcription	mRNA
B.	translation	mRNA
C.	transcription	tRNA
D.	translation	tRNA

Use the following information to answer the next two questions.

Human Spermatogenesis

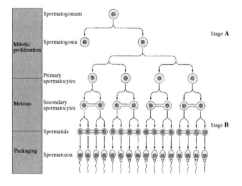

—from *Waller and Waller*, 1994

16. The mitotic proliferation stage of spermatogenesis occurs in the

A. epididymis

B. vas deferens

C. seminal vesicles

D. seminiferous tubules

17. The chromosome number at stage **A** and the chromosome number at stage **B** are, respectively,

   A. 46 and 46

   B. 46 and 23

   C. 23 and 46

   D. 23 and 23

Use the following information to answer the next question.

The birth of the Dionne Quintuplets on May 28, 1934, near Callander, Ontario, surprised the world. The quintuplets had a combined weight of 6 kg, and theirs was the first known case in which all members of a quintuplet set survived. The process by which the quintuplets were formed is thought to be as diagrammed below.

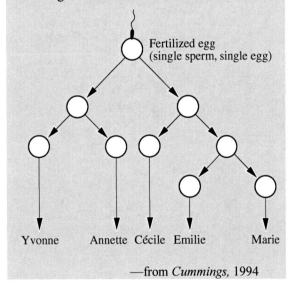

—from *Cummings, 1994*

18. The development of the Dionne Quintuplets was **most likely** the result of

   A. pre-embryo splitting, which resulted in fraternal quintuplets

   B. pre-embryo splitting, which resulted in identical quintuplets

   C. fertility drugs, which resulted in multiple ovulation and produced fraternal quintuplets

   D. fertility drugs, which resulted in multiple ovulation and produced identical quintuplets

Use the following information to answer the next three questions.

Most autosomal trisomies are lethal. The average survival age for infants with Patau syndrome (trisomy 13) is six months. Infants with Edward syndrome (trisomy 18) survive, on average, only two to four months. Individuals with Down syndrome (trisomy 21) can survive into adulthood. In order to identify autosomal trisomies, chorionic villus sampling (CVS) can be used to obtain cells that are then used to create a karyotype like the one shown below.

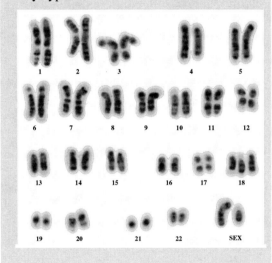

19. The sex and the condition of the individual whose karyotype is shown above are given in row

Row	Sex	Condition
A.	female	Patau syndrome
B.	female	Down syndrome
C.	male	Edward syndrome
D.	male	normal

20. The villus region sampled using CVS develops from the

   A. amnion

   B. chorion

   C. ectoderm

   D. endoderm

Use the following additional information to answer the next question.

A Developing Fetus and Associated Structures

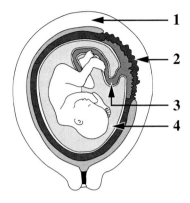

21. Progesterone and HCG, which are used to maintain the developing fetus, are both produced in the structure numbered

    A. 1

    B. 2

    C. 3

    D. 4

Use the following information to answer the next six questions.

Mutated mitochondrial DNA has been linked with many disorders. For example, mitochondrial DNA mutations are believed to cause approximately 1.5% of all cases of diabetes mellitus. Type I diabetes mellitus is characterized by low insulin levels. In addition to insulin, blood glucose can be affected by glucagon.

—from *Wallace*, 1997

22. Which of the following statements summarizes the effect of insulin and the effect of glucagon on blood glucose levels?

    A. Both insulin and glucagon tend to raise blood glucose levels.

    B. Both insulin and glucagon tend to lower blood glucose levels.

    C. Insulin tends to raise blood glucose levels; whereas, glucagon tends to lower blood glucose levels.

    D. Insulin tends to lower blood glucose levels; whereas, glucagon tends to raise blood glucose levels.

Use the following additional information to answer the next four questions.

A deletion mutation in mitochondrial DNA causes Kearns–Sayre syndrome (KSS). A large sample of different types of somatic cells was removed from a male with KSS, tested, and found to contain the deletion. The only type of mitochondrial DNA that was found in somatic cells from the man's mother was mitochondrial DNA that did not have the KSS deletion.

23. A reasonable hypothesis to explain these results is that the mutation in the mitochondrial DNA that caused KSS in the man first occurred in the

    A. mother's oocytes

    B. man's somatic cells

    C. man's spermatocytes

    D. mother's somatic cells

24. Both males and females can be affected by mitochondrial mutations, but only females can transmit genetic mutations to their offspring. For this inheritance pattern, which of the following rows gives the contributions to the zygote made by the sperm and by the egg?

Row	Sperm Contribution	Egg Contribution
A.	nuclear contents only	both nuclear and cytoplasmic contents
B.	both nuclear and cytoplasmic contents	nuclear contents only
C.	neither nuclear nor cytoplasmic contents	both nuclear and cytoplasmic contents
D.	both nuclear and cytoplasmic contents	neither nuclear nor cytoplasmic contents

25. Mitochondrial DNA and nuclear DNA both code for the formation of proteins. Which of the following statements about protein synthesis is true?

A. An mRNA anticodon binds with an amino acid codon, which results in the placement of a specific tRNA molecule in the polypeptide chain.

B. An mRNA anticodon binds with a tRNA codon, which results in the placement of a specific polypeptide molecule in the amino acid chain.

C. A tRNA anticodon binds with an mRNA codon, which results in the placement of a specific amino acid molecule in the polypeptide chain.

D. A tRNA anticodon binds with a polypeptide codon, which results in the placement of a specific mRNA molecule in the amino acid chain.

Use the following additional information to answer the next question.

In an individual with KSS, part of the coding strand of mitochondrial DNA that has been deleted has the following base sequence.

ACC TCC CTC ACC AAA

26. The third amino acid coded for by this segment of mitochondrial DNA is

A. lysine

B. threonine

C. glutamate

D. phenylalanine

Use the following additional information to answer the next question.

Over time, mitochondrial DNA accumulates non-lethal mutations at a constant rate. There is a higher degree of variation in mitochondrial DNA in earlier populations than in more recent populations. Scientists have taken samples of mitochondrial DNA from people living on different continents and compared the number of mitochondrial DNA mutations in these samples. They used these data as evidence to determine the order in which Earth's continents were populated.

27. In this study, the manipulated variable was the

A. amount of mitochondrial DNA tested

B. time of migration from one continent to another

C. amount of variation in mitochondrial DNA base sequences

D. geographic location of subjects whose sample of mitochondrial DNA was tested

Use the following information to answer the next three questions.

Descriptions and Symbols Used to Represent One Type of Coat Colour in Horses

1	2	3	4
DNA	*TT, Tt*	*T*	Tobiano (white spotting pattern)
sequence	*tt*	*t*	Not tobiano (no white for coat spotting pattern) colour

Numerical Response

5. Using the numbers above, match these descriptions and symbols with the term below to which they apply.

Description or Symbol

Number: _____ _____ _____ _____

Term: gene allele phenotype genotype

28. What are the genotypes for coat colour of two horses that are predicted to produce offspring in a 1:1 genotypic ratio?

    A. *Tt* and *tt*

    B. *Tt* and *Tt*

    C. Tobiano and tobiano

    D. Tobiano and not tobiano

Numerical Response

6. Given that the diploid number for horses is 64, what is the number of chromosomes found in a horse's somatic cell and what is the number of chromosomes found in a horse's gamete cell?

Number of
Chromosomes: _____ _____ , _____ _____
Cell Type: somatic cell   gamete cell

Use the following information to answer the next six questions.

Cat coat colour results from the interaction of three different genes. A gene for black-based colours is located on an autosomal chromosome. A gene for red-based colours is located on the X chromosome. A different gene located on a separate autosomal chromosome determines pigment density in cat hair.

The black-based gene has three possible alleles: *B*–black, *b*–chocolate, and *b^l*–cinnamon.
If pigmentation in cat hair is dense, the phenotypes listed below are possible.

Genotype	Phenotype
BB, Bb, Bb^l	black
bb, bb^l	chocolate
b^l b^l	cinnamon

29. According to the data above, the relationship among these alleles is such that the

    A. black allele is codominant with the chocolate and cinnamon alleles

    B. black allele is codominant with the chocolate allele, and the chocolate allele is codominant with the cinnamon allele

    C. black allele is dominant over the chocolate and cinnamon alleles, and the chocolate allele is dominant over the cinnamon allele

    D. black allele is dominant over the chocolate and cinnamon alleles, and the chocolate and cinnamon alleles are codominant

Use the following additional information to answer the next two questions.

There are two alleles for the pigment-density gene: dense pigment (*D*) and dilute pigment (*d*).
The chart below shows the interaction of two autosomal genes affecting coat colour—the black-based gene and the density gene.

Black-based pigment gene	Density gene	
	*D_*	*dd*
*B_*	*B_D_* black colour	*B_dd* blue colour
bb; bb^l	*bbD_; bb^lD_* chocolate colour	*bbdd; bb^ldd* lilac colour
b^l b^l	*b^l b^l D_* cinnamon colour	*b^l b^l dd* fawn colour

30. A blue-coloured female cat is bred with a cinnamon-coloured male cat. The offspring produced are black-coloured, blue-coloured, chocolate-coloured, and lilac-coloured.
The genotypes of the parental cats are indicated in row

Row	Female Cat	Male Cat
A.	*Bb^l dd*	*b^l b^l Dd*
B.	*Bb^l dd*	*b^l b^l DD*
C.	*Bbdd*	*b^l b^l Dd*
D.	*Bbdd*	*b^l b^l DD*

31. A black-coloured female cat with the genotype *BbDd* is bred with a fawn-coloured male cat. The percentage of their offspring predicted to be chocolate-coloured is

    A. 13%

    B. 19%

    C. 25%

    D. 50%

Use the following additional information to answer the next three questions.

In cats, red pigmentation is dominant to black pigmentation. The red pigment gene, which is located on the X chromosome, has two alleles: X^R and X^r. Cats with at least one X^R allele have some orange-coloured hair as a result of having the red-based pigment. Cats with only X^r alleles have no red-based pigment. Male cats with the X^R allele will be orange. However, female cats express the genes on only one X chromosome in each cell. This expression is random. Therefore, an orange-and-black (tortoiseshell) female cat is possible if it is $X^R X^r$. Some genotypes and their resulting phenotypes are shown below. In all cases, pigment density is high.

Genotype	Phenotype
$X^R Y B b$	Orange male cat
$X^r Y B b^l$	Black male cat
$X^R X^r B b$	Orange-and-black female cat (tortoiseshell)

32. The phenotype of a female cat with genotype $X^r X^r B b^l$ would be

   A. a black cat

   B. an orange cat

   C. an orange-and-black cat

   D. an orange, black, and cinnamon cat

33. A cinnamon-coloured male cat ($X^r Y b^l b^l$) is bred with an orange-coloured female cat ($X^R X^R B B$). What possible phenotypes could be produced in the offspring?

   A. Tortoiseshell-coloured female cats and orange-coloured male cats

   B. Tortoiseshell-coloured female cats, black-coloured female cats, and black-coloured male cats

   C. Cinnamon-coloured male cats, orange-coloured female cats, and tortoiseshell-coloured female cats

   D. Cinnamon-coloured male cats, black-coloured male cats, black-coloured female cats, orange-coloured female cats, and tortoiseshell-coloured female cats

Use the following additional information to answer the next question.

When the three genes that code for black-based colour, red-based colour, and density combine, they produce other coat colours in cats.

34. What is the predicted phenotype of a female cat with genotype $X^R X^R B b^l dd$?

   A. Black

   B. Orange

   C. Cinnamon

   D. Cream (light orange)

Use the following information to answer the next six questions.

Sickle cell anemia is an autosomal recessive genetic disorder. Because individuals affected by sickle cell anemia have defective hemoglobin proteins, their blood cannot transport oxygen properly. There appears to be a relationship between the incidence of malaria and sickle cell anemia. Individuals with sickle cell anemia and carriers of the sickle cell allele have some resistance to malaria. Malaria is caused by the parasite *Plasmodium* and is transmitted between humans by mosquitoes.

35. The probability of two carrier parents having a child with sickle cell anemia is

   A. 25%

   B. 50%

   C. 75%

   D. 100%

36. If scientists are successful in significantly reducing or eliminating malaria, the **best** prediction for what will happen to the allele for sickle cell anemia in the population is that it will

   A. not be affected by the elimination of malaria

   B. increase as its selective advantage is increased

   C. be reduced as its selective advantage is decreased

   D. quickly disappear as its selective advantage is increased

Use the following additional information to answer the next two questions.

Plasmodium Life Cycle

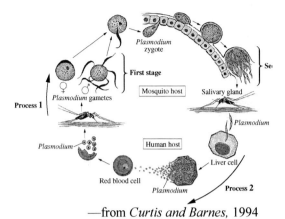

—from *Curtis and Barnes*, 1994

37. The row below that identifies process **1** and process **2** is

Row	Process 1	Process 2
A.	mitosis	meiosis
B.	mitosis	mitosis
C.	meiosis	mitosis
D.	meiosis	meiosis

38. The row below that identifies the chromosome number at the first stage and the chromosome number at the second stage is

Row	First Stage	Second Stage
A.	diploid	haploid
B.	diploid	diploid
C.	haploid	diploid
D.	haploid	haploid

Use the following additional information to answer the next two questions.

Insecticides have been used to control mosquito populations in order to prevent the spread of malaria, but mosquitoes in malaria-infested areas are developing resistance to these insecticides.
In addition, the antimalarial drug chloroquine, once very effective in protecting individuals against *Plasmodium,* has become ineffective, which has resulted in a resurgence of malaria. Scientists have identified a gene, called *cg2*, in *Plasmodium* that allows the *Plasmodium* to mount resistance to chloroquine. This research could be used by scientists to develop new versions of chloroquine that will sidestep the parasite's resistance and, therefore, effectively protect people against malaria.

—from *Travis*, 1997

39. Some investigators have suggested that some strains of *Plasmodium* have become chloroquine-resistant because these strains have an increased ability to pump chloroquine from their bodies. Other investigators suggest that the resistance stems from changes in some strains of *Plasmodium* that prevent chloroquine from entering the parasites in the first place.
These two suggestions can best be described as

A. theories

B. hypotheses

C. conclusions

D. observations

40. A possible reason that the *Plasmodium* parasite may have resistance to chloroquine is that the *cg2* gene codes for a protein that seems to play a role in membrane transport of the drug.
If this is true, researchers may want to develop compounds that specifically block this resistance mechanism by

A. preventing mutation of the *cg2* gene

B. stimulating translation of the *cg2* gene

C. preventing transcription of the *cg2* gene

D. stimulating DNA replication of the *cg2* gene

Use the following information to answer the next five questions.

Komodo Island National Park is one of the last refuges of the Komodo dragon lizard. It is estimated that there are 3 500 Komodo dragons living in the 520 km² park. The Komodo dragon can grow to over three metres in length, weigh up to 70 kg, and run up to 20 km/h. These lizards grow slowly and can live up to 30 years. Female Komodo dragons mate once a year. Females may lay on the nest to protect the eggs.
After the eggs hatch, young Komodo dragons live in trees until they are one year old to avoid being eaten by adult Komodo dragons and other predators.

—from *Ciofi*, 1999

Use the following additional information to answer the next question.

Characteristics of Komodo Dragons
1 Classified as reptiles
2 Can live up to 30 years
3 Females lay between 20 and 30 eggs per year
4 Sexually mature at about six years of age
5 Females mate once a year
6 Over three metres in length and weigh up to 70 kg
7 The young live in trees until they are one year old
8 Adult Komodo dragons will eat young Komodo dragons

Numerical Response

7. Four characteristics of Komodo dragons that allow scientists to classify them as relatively *K*-selected strategists are _____, _____, _____, and _____.
(Record your **four-digit** answer **in lowest-to-highest numerical order**.)

Numerical Response

8. What is the population density of Komodo dragons in Komodo Island National Park?
Answer: _____ dragons/km²
(Round and record your answer to **two decimal places**.)

41. Because the retina of the Komodo dragon consists of only cones, Komodo dragons have a limited ability to see

A. colour
B. fine detail
C. prey at a distance
D. prey in low-intensity light

42. Komodo dragons have a poor range of hearing, partially because they have only one ossicle— the stapes. In humans, three ossicles work together to increase vibrations of the

A. cochlea
B. oval window
C. eustachian tube
D. tympanic membrane

Use the following additional information to answer the next question.

Komodo dragons have up to 50 strains of bacteria living on the meat stuck between their teeth.
If a deer that has been bitten by a Komodo dragon manages to escape, it will die within a week as a result of bacterial infection. Komodo dragons can then feast on the dead deer. The Komodo dragons themselves are resistant to bacterial infection.

43. Which of the following rows identifies the relationship between the Komodo dragon and bacteria and the relationship between the deer and bacteria?

Row	Komodo Dragon and Bacteria	Deer and Bacteria
A.	mutualism	predator–prey
B.	parasitism	predator–prey
C.	mutualism	parasitism
D.	parasitism	parasitism

Use the following information to answer the next three questions.

In heavily populated regions of Canada, the landscape is now dominated by what scientists call "invasive" non-native species. Horticultural expert Bill Granger has described the Norway maple as a "tree on steroids" because of its dense rooting system. This tree reaches sexual maturity quickly and spreads many seeds over a wide area. Another invasive species, pampas grass, is described by Dr. Spencer Barrett as an "excellent opportunist." Pampas grass relies on allies such as humans to cut out vegetative competition before it proceeds to dominate the landscape.

—from *Cundiff,* 1996

44. By maintaining a stronghold on the environment and preventing further environmental changes, the Norway maple could be described as

    A. a climax species

    B. a pioneer species

    C. a seral stage species

    D. an intermediate species

45. The relationship exhibited between pampas grass and other native plants is

    A. parasitism

    B. commensalism

    C. interspecific competition

    D. intraspecific competition

46. Two strategies that give the Norway maple a high biotic potential are identified in row

Row	Strategy 1	Strategy 2
A.	is on steroids	reaches sexual maturity early
B.	reaches sexual maturity early	has large number of seeds
C.	spreads seeds over a large area	is on steroids
D.	spreads seeds over a large area	has strong root system

Use the following information to answer the next two questions.

Because insects are probably our main ecological competitors, scientists search for ways to get rid of them. Scientists have discovered that the hormone ecdysone, produced by the prothoracic gland of all insects, stimulates moulting and development into adult insects. The corpora allata gland secretes another hormone, juvenile hormone (JH), which inhibits the effect of ecdysone and maintains the insect juvenile state (pupa). Typically, insects winter as pupae and emerge as adults in spring.

—from *Wallace, Sanders, and Ferl,* 1996

47. An effective insecticide would be one that

    A. inhibits JH in the spring

    B. stimulates ecdysone in the spring

    C. maintains a high level of JH in the fall

    D. inhibits the release of ecdysone in the spring

48. Which of the following statements gives a valid prediction about the effect of the increased light in the spring on the hormones that control the emergence of an adult insect from its pupa case?

    A. The light stimulates the release of JH

    B. The light inhibits the release of ecdysone

    C. The light stimulates the release of ecdysone

    D. The light inhibits the release of both ecdysone and JH

Written Response—15%

Use the following information to answer the next question.

The Blood Reserve is Canada's largest First Nations reserve. Prior to 1700, the Blood Tribe migrated within the area surrounding what is now Red Deer. By 1750, their migration area had changed to include more of southern Alberta and part of what is now Montana. During the 1800s, two smallpox epidemics killed almost the entire Blood population. These epidemics may have influenced the decision of the Blood Tribe to sign a treaty that led to the creation of the Blood Reserve in southern Alberta. After settling on the reserve, an influenza epidemic in 1918 further reduced the population to about 1 100. The present population is about 7 000 people.

Population of the Blood Tribe

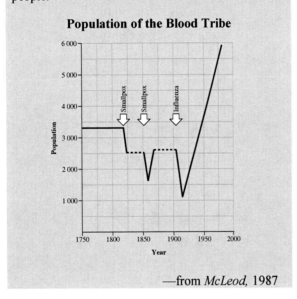

—from *McLeod*, 1987

Blood Tribe Migration Patterns (Shaded areas)

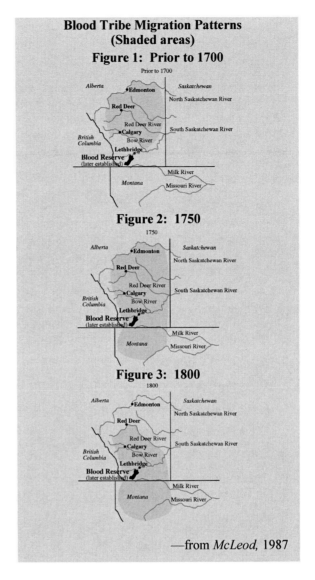

—from *McLeod*, 1987

1. **a)** Examine the migration pattern maps for the Blood Tribe from prior to 1700 (Figure 1) and in 1750 (Figure 2). **Describe** a possible explanation for the change in migration pattern of the tribe over this period of time.

(1 mark)

b) The graph shows that from 1750 to 1817, the population of the Blood Tribe was stable. **Describe** two factors that might have contributed to this stability. **(2 marks)**

c) **Describe** two possible explanations for the population change from 1920 to the present.

(2 marks)

Use the following additional information to answer the next three parts of the question.

Ornithine transcarbamylase (OTC) deficiency has been studied in a large Blood Tribe family that lived in an isolated area on the Blood Reserve.
This X-linked recessive disorder has not been identified in any members of the Blackfoot and Peigan Tribes that, together with the Blood Tribe, make up the Blackfoot Nation.

The disorder is the result of an incorrectly formed or absent OTC enzyme. The normal OTC enzyme is part of a pathway that converts ammonia (from excess protein in the diet) into urea in liver cells. When the OTC enzyme is defective, ammonia accumulates in the blood. Ammonia is toxic to the central nervous system. Untreated OTC deficiency produces symptoms of lethargy, coma, and eventual death in early infancy.

The error in the OTC gene is usually a point mutation. Treatment is successful in prolonging life. However, in the Blood Tribe family studied, the mutation is a result of a large deletion of a portion of the gene. This results in more severe symptoms of the deficiency. Of males with this mutation, 100% die in early infancy.

Partial Pedigree of Ornithine Transcarbamylase Deficiency in a Blood Tribe Family

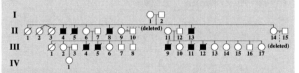

Note: Some of the pedigree was deleted for ease in interpretation. Some of the deceased males are assumed to be OTC deficient, although diagnosis did not occur before death.
—from *McLeod,* 1987

—Adapted from *Emery and Rimoin's Principles and Practice of Medical Genetics 3/e,* volume 1, edited by Alan E.H. Emery, David L. Rimoin, J. Michael Connor, and Reed E. Pyeritz, pages 620–622, 1888, © 1997, by permission of the publisher Churchill Livingstone and by permission of Dr. David L. Rimoin.

d) Explain how it is possible that a male fetus with OTC deficiency could develop and the infant be born alive, yet become ill and die shortly after birth. **(2 marks)**

e) Assume that individuals **III-2** and **III-3** are expecting another child. **Construct two** Punnett squares to illustrate the two possible crosses, based on the mother's (**III-2**) two possible genotypes. **Calculate** the probability of this child being a son with OTC deficiency. (Provide a legend to identify the symbols used for the two alleles.) **(4 marks)**

Use the following additional information to answer the next part of the question.

A new therapy for OTC deficiency is being researched. In this therapy, viruses containing the normal OTC gene are injected into the bloodstream of an individual with OTC deficiency.
These viruses travel to the liver and "infect" liver cells. Currently, this method has been successful in correcting OTC deficiency in mice. Approval is pending for human trials.

—Adapted from *Emery and Rimoin's Principles and Practice of Medical Genetics 3/e,* volume 1, edited by Alan E.H. Emery, David L. Rimoin, J. Michael Connor, and Reed E. Pyeritz, pages 620–622, 1888, © 1997, by permission of the publisher Churchill Livingstone and by permission of Dr. David L. Rimoin.

f) **Explain** how this viral therapy could be used to treat OTC deficiency in a patient. **(1 mark)**

Use the following information to answer the next question.

Herbal medications have recently been gaining popularity in Canada and the rest of the western world. Most of these medications have been used for thousands of years in Native and Asian medicine. Many people assume that "natural" herbal medications are "safer" than western-style medicines produced in chemistry laboratories. However, like other medicines, herbal remedies contain chemicals that interact with other medications. As well, many natural plants such as hemlock (which was used by Socrates to commit suicide) and milkweed contain toxins that can cause serious damage to the body or be fatal.

The Canadian Health Regulatory Board classifies edible substances as either food or drugs. Most herbs have not been tested by pharmaceutical companies because companies cannot patent a naturally growing plant. For herbs to be classified as drugs and for companies to make health claims about them, they must go through tests similar to other drugs. Current herbal therapy regulations classify herbs as food supplements and, therefore, they are not controlled in terms of purity, concentration, or testing for drug interactions. For example, because Ginkgo biloba inhibits platelet action, it should not be used in conjunction with Aspirin. Because herbal therapies are not classified as drugs, the cost to the consumer is not covered by most insurance companies or provincial health-care plans.

Consider the following sources.

Source 1: Wild Yam cream

In a report obtained from the Internet entitled "Everything your doctor hasn't shared with you about the causes of PMS and menopausal discomfort…and the revolutionary new natural solution," Beth Rosenthal describes her own personal experiences. She had very severe symptoms of premenstrual syndrome, which she attributed to supplements containing high levels of estrogen that her mother took during her pregnancy. (Symptoms of premenstrual syndrome include depression and premenstrual cramps.) Rosenthal began to use Wild Yam cream. She rubbed it into her skin three times a day for 21 of the 28 days of her menstrual cycle. She reported an increase in sex drive, a greater sense of well-being, and a dramatic decrease in the strength and pain of her menstrual cramps, all without side effects. She then began to advertise her story on the Internet so that she could sell the cream. She claims that the cream, which contains natural progesterone, overcomes "estrogen dominance," which is the cause of many women's menstrual cycle-related problems.

—from *Rosenthal*, 2000

Source 2: Ginkgo biloba

Ginkgo biloba has been used to treat nervous disorders such as mild Alzheimer's disease, short-term memory loss, lack of attention, and mild depression. Studies have shown that Ginkgo increases the flow of oxygenated blood to the brain. An abstract obtained from the Internet describes a year-long study conducted by Dr. Pierre LeBars to determine both the effectiveness and the safety of this herb. In the study, 202 people with mild-to-severe Alzheimer's disease were given three different tests of memory-related mental abilities, specifically designed to diagnose Alzheimer's disease.

Subjects were assigned to two parallel groups and were either administered Ginkgo extracts in a pill form or a placebo pill (containing no active ingredient).

The study was a double-blind study conducted from several different medical centres. (In a double-blind study, neither the participants in the study nor the researchers know which group is receiving the placebo.) The cognitive tests were then readministered. The people who were given Ginkgo achieved significantly higher scores on all three tests after the year-long study than did those who were given the placebo. For example, 27% of those receiving the Ginkgo extract pills showed a four-point improvement on a cognitive scale called the ADAS-Cog (which tests memory function) compared with 14% of those taking the placebo pills. There was not a significant difference in either the number or the severity of side effects that were described by either group.

The researchers concluded that Ginkgo was safe and resulted in modest but significant improvements in cognitive function in people with Alzheimer's disease.

The Journal of the American Medical Association

—from *Le Bars, Katz, Berman, Itil, Freedman*, and *Schatzberg*, 1997

Written Response—15%

2. Write a unified response that addresses the following aspects of the use of herbal remedies in modern medicine.

- **Compare** the scientific validity of the two sources given.

- **Describe** the normal roles of estrogen and progesterone in the human female reproductive system. **Hypothesize** how Wild Yam cream would have to interact with a woman's hormones if it were to produce the benefits attributed to it by the source 1 article.

- **Describe** one advantage and one disadvantage of the current regulation of herbal therapies. **State** a revised regulation for herbal therapies, and **explain how** this revision would address the disadvantage(s) of the current regulations.

ANSWERS AND SOLUTIONS
JUNE 2001 DIPLOMA EXAMINATION

1.	C	12.	A	23.	C	31.	A	42.	A
2.	B	13.	C	24.	D	32.	D	43.	B
3.	D	14.	C	25.	A	33.	D	NR7.	3, 2, 1, 4
4.	D	15.	B	NR3.	0.44	34.	B	44.	B
5.	B	NR2.	2, 4, 6, 7	26.	A	35.	C	45.	A
6.	D	16.	A	27.	A	36.	C	NR8.	5, 1, 2
7.	D	17.	B	28.	B	37.	A	46.	D
NR1.	2, 1, 4, 3	18.	B	29.	B	NR6.	1, 4, 5	47.	C
8.	D	19.	D	NR4.	0.25	38.	D	48.	A
9.	D	20.	D	30.	C	39.	A		
10.	B	21.	A	NR5.	1, 4, 3, 2 or 2, 3, 4, 1	40.	D		
11.	A	22.	D			41.	A		

1. C

The term sensory nervous system is not often used. When it is, it refers to the network of sensory nerves, such as the optic nerve, carries information from sense organs to the brain. The somatic nervous system refers to the nerves that carry signals from the central nervous system to muscles. The parasympathetic system normalizes the body after a stressful experience. The sympathetic system is responsible for physiological responses to fear. These responses include diversion of blood from the skin and internal organs to skeletal muscles, the heart, and the brain. As well, pupils dilate to allow more light into the eyes, and bronchioles dilate to allow more air into the lungs. The heart speeds up and more glucose is added to the blood. The responses of the sympathetic system are similar to those of the hormone epinephrine.

2. B

The medulla is responsible for such unconscious activities as swallowing, breathing, and altering heart rate. The cerebellum coordinates fine motor skills–essentially making the muscles work together to carry out movements.

The hypothalamus is the part of the brain that controls the body's endocrine system.
The cerebrum is the conscious part of the brain. It is the part where thoughts, feelings, and all decisions originate.

3. D

Meiosis is the type of cell division in which gametes (such as sperm and eggs) are formed. During meiosis a $2n$ cell divides to become n cells. The resulting n cells are not genetically identical to each other or to the $2n$ parent cell. In contrast, mitosis is a process in which the cells divide to increase in number, producing a large number of cells genetically identical to the parent cell. Copying the DNA code to make mRNA is called transcription, and reading the mRNA code to make an amino acid sequence is called translation.

4. D

Levadopa replaces dopamine in the brain. Since dopamine is a neurotransmitter that causes neurotransmission, levadopa increases neurotransmission. Seligiline inhibits monoamine oxidase B, which breaks down dopamine so seligiline results in more dopamine and, therefore, more neurotransmission.
Fetal pig brain cells were used in this experiment as a source of dopamine, not as a source of the drugs. Only seligiline acts as an inhibitor, levadopa does not. The two drugs do not prevent the death of cells–they ensure that neurotransmission lost when cells die is resumed.

5. B

Dopamine (Z) is a neurotransmitter that is released from the end of an axon and diffuses across a synapse to stimulate the post-synaptic membrane of a dendrite. Monoamine oxidase B is an enzyme that acts on dopamine, breaking it down. Y is shown as acting on Z. Seligiline is an inhibitor of monoamine oxidase B. X is shown as acting on Y.

6. D

Levels of monoamine oxidase B (MAOB) are lower in smokers than in non-smokers. MAOB breaks down dopamine, and low level of dopamine is linked to Parkinson's disease. It appears that there is something in smoking that reduces the level of MAOB so that the level of dopamine is increased.

7. D

A reflex is a response that is involuntary. That is why a person pulls his or her hand away before they sense pain. During a reflex, a receptor (in this case a pain receptor), stimulates a sensory neuron. The sensory neuron carries a signal to the CNS, generally the spinal cord. Neurons within the CNS are referred to as interneurons. The interneurons formulate a response. The response (in this case, the withdrawing of the hand), is directed to the muscles through the motor neurons.

NR1.   2, 1, 4, 3

Olfactory (smell) receptors are stimulated by the molecules of the aroma (**2**). They cause a depolarization (signal) in the sensory neurons of the olfactory nerve (**1**). The aroma signal is carried to the brain. By affecting the brain, the aroma signals are causing neural activity in the brain. During the neural activity, neurotransmitters, or neurochemicals, are released from the ends of axons (**4**), and, in some way, these neurochemicals have an effect on pain interpretation. (**3**).

8. D

The cerebellum (**1**) coordinates fine motor skills – essentially making the muscles work together to carry out movements. The cerebrum (**2**) is the conscious part of the brain. It is the part where thoughts, feelings, and all decisions originate. The pituitary (**3**) controls the endocrine system. The medulla (**4**) is responsible for such unconscious activities as swallowing, breathing, and heart rate.

9. D

Viagra sometimes interferes with the perception of colours, in which case, it is affecting the cones. The rods are receptors that perceive light only in black and white, and are responsible for vision in low light conditions. Location 2, straight back from the lens, is the fovea, a spot densely packed with cones, where we see with greatest detail. Location 1, off to the periphery, has fewer receptors, most of which are rods. At location 2, images are not seen with great clarity.

10. B

This question is asking the reader to identify the male that would experience impotence. Since GMP is necessary for an erection, a male with a low level of GMP would suffer from impotence, especially if he had a normal level of PDE5, the enzyme that breaks down GMP. All the other options describe males that would have no problem achieving erections because they have normal to high levels of GMP and they do not have an excess of PDE5 that breaks down the GMP.

11. A

FSH is 2, a hormone that is released from the anterior pituitary gland and that stimulates the Sertoli cells of the testes to produce sperm in the seminiferous tubules of the testes.
LH is 3, a hormone that is released from the anterior pituitary gland and that stimulates the interstitial cells of the testes to produce testosterone.
Testosterone is 4. It is produced by the testes, and as its level rises in the blood, it has a negative feedback effect on the hypothalamus and pituitary, causing a reduction in LH production. (In females, FSH causes egg and estrogen production in the ovary and LH causes ovulation, formation of the corpus luteum, and production of progesterone).

12. A

If there is a low level of hormone 2 (FSH), there will be fewer sperm produced in the seminiferous tubules of the testes. A high level of 3 (LH) or 4 (testosterone) will stimulate the seminiferous tubules to create more sperm.
A low level of 5 will result in no negative feedback effect on the hypothalamus and pituitary and, therefore, no restriction in sperm production.

13. C

A manipulated variable is one that the experimenter manipulates or controls. In this case, the experimenter divided the subjects into groups based on their sex and their testosterone level. Therefore, sex and testosterone level are the manipulated variables. The manipulated variables are different from the responding variable, which is what the experimenter observes and measures. In this case, the responding variable is the test score on the test of spatial skills, so **A**, **B**, and **D** are incorrect.

14. C

Spatial skills involve perceiving an overall sense of something and are necessary for artistic processes. We associate spatial skills with the right hemisphere of the brain. The graph indicates that when testosterone level is higher in a woman, her spatial skill improves. In a man, the opposite occurs: when his testosterone level increases, his spatial skill declines.

15. B

The reading indicates that in females, testosterone is produced in the cells of the adrenal cortex. In males, testosterone is produced by the interstitial cells, which are squeezed between the seminiferous tubules of the testes. In a female, follicle cells stimulate egg development and produce estrogen.
In a male, the seminiferous tubules produce sperm.

NR2. 2, 4, 6, 7

2 is correct because the study found that a high testosterone level increased a woman's spatial test scores and that her spatial skills were weakest during the part of her menstrual cycle when her estrogen level was highest.
4 is correct because a woman's motor and articulation skills are highest when her estrogen level is high, and her estrogen is high during pregnancy.
6 is correct because estrogen is low around day 1 of a woman's menstrual cycle, so her spatial skills should be good.
7 is correct because around day 14 of a woman's menstrual cycle, her estrogen level is high, so her motor and articulation skills should be enhanced.

16. A

We are told that the "dunce" gene is involved in coding for a certain enzyme. As well, we are told that the presence or absence of this gene determines whether or not a fly can learn to associate an odour with an electric shock.
It seems that flies with the mutant form of the gene do not learn that when they smell the odour, they are going to receive a shock.

17. B

The reading explains that DHT may make a man more susceptible to prostate cancer. The altered allele codes for an enzyme that is more efficient at producing DHT. Being heterozygous (having one normal, and one altered allele) would increase the amount of DHT produced. However, if a man is homozygous for the altered allele, he would have the maximum amount of DHT, making him most susceptible to cancer.

18. B

To answer this question, it is necessary to use the data table "Messenger RNA Codons and Their Corresponding Amino Acids" at the back of the exam. It is also necessary to go through a process of elimination as follows:

Amino acid	Possible mRNA codons	Possible DNA triplets
valine	GUU	CAA
	GUC	CAG
	GUA	CAT
	GUG	CAC
leucine	UUA	AAT
	UUG	AAC
	CUU	GAA
	CUC	GAG
	CUA	GAT
	CUG	GAC

Students must be careful to note that the data table gives them the mRNA codons that they then must convert to DNA triplets. Only B has an answer in which the DNA triplet for valine and leucine are both possible.

19. D

If the male experienced a genetic mutation in his gonadal cells, perhaps during fetal development, it is likely that his gonadal cells were mutant but the rest of his body cells were not. As a result, cells produced in his gonads, such as sperm, would lack the *DAZ* gene but other body cells would not. If both his sperm and his blood cells lacked the *DAZ* gene, the mutation could not have been confined entirely to his gonads. It is more likely that such a mutation was inherited through one of the gametes and therefore affected every cell in his body.

20. D

Every time a man has a son, he has provided a sperm with his Y chromosome. Since the *DAZ* gene is on the Y chromosome, any time a man with azoospermia has a son, the son will get the Y chromosome that lacks the *DAZ* gene and will, therefore, have azoospermia. If this man has daughters, he is always providing the X chromosome, so whether or not he has the *DAZ* gene is not relevant to a daughter.

21. A

The term allele means a form of a gene. Sometimes when people, or even textbooks, are discussing ABO blood types, they will mention the type A gene or the type O gene, but that is incorrect. It is correct to say that the gene for ABO blood types has an I^A **allele**, an I^B **allele**, and an *i* **allele**. Another example relates to the gene for height in pea plants: the height gene has a tall **allele** and a short **allele**. It is incorrect to say the tall **gene** and the short **gene**.

22. D

Mendel determined that an organism had two copies of each gene but that during gamete formation, the copies segregated so that gametes, such as sperm or eggs, have only one of each copy. We now know that this process of segregation occurs during anaphase I of meiosis. At that time, the tetrads (homologous pairs of chromosomes) separate, so that the resulting cells each have one of each pair of chromosomes, or one of each pair of genes. This makes the resulting cells N as opposed to their 2N parent cell.

23. C

An example of a genotype that is heterozygous for two genes is *TtRr*. During gamete formation, the *Tt* segregate and the *Rr* segregate. A gamete will have either *T* or *t* and either *R* or *r*. Therefore, it is possible to have a gamete that is *TR*, *Tr*, *tR*, or *tr*. These are the four possibilities.

24. D

To answer this question, it is necessary to work back through the pedigree. The parents of **IV-3** are both deaf-mutes. That means they must be homozygous for the recessive *ee* or *dd*. Since the mother **III-1** has parents who are both *DEe*, she must be *Ddee*. Since the father **III-2** has parents who are both *ddEE*, he must also be *ddEE*. So, we know that the parents of **IV-3** have the genotypes *Ddee* and *ddEE*. They can have children who have the genotype *DdEe* who are not deaf-mutes and *ddEe* who are deaf-mutes. Since **IV-3** is not a deaf-mute, he must be *DdEe*.

25. A

Since individual **III-1** is homozygous dominant for D (DD) and **III-2** is homozygous dominant for E (EE), all offspring will inherit one D and one E, so they will not have the genotype for deaf-mutism.

NR3. 0.44

If a couple is heterozygous for both genes, they both have the genotype $DdEe$. The following Punnett square shows the cross of $DdEe \times DdEE$.

	DE	De	De	de
DE	$DDEE$	$DDEe$	$DdEE$	$DdEe$
DE	$DDEe$	**$DDee$**	$DdEe$	**$Ddee$**
DE	$DdEE$	$DdEe$	**$DDee$**	$ddEe$
De	**$DdEe$**	$Ddee$	**$ddEe$**	$ddee$

7/16 of the children, or 0.44, will be homozygous recessive for one of the two genes and will be deaf-mute. These genotypes are in bold on the Punnett square.

26. A

Since **III-1** has blood type A, he could have the genotype $I^A I^A$ or $I^A i$ for blood. Since he has a father who has sickle cell anemia ($Hb^S Hb^S$) and a mother who does not ($Hb^A Hb^A$ or $Hb^A Hb^S$) and he himself does not have sickle cell anemia, he must have gotten the normal allele from his mother and the disease allele from his father, so his genotype is ($Hb^A Hb^S$) . Only **A** is an answer that has a possible blood type and is heterozygous for sickle cell anemia.

27. A

Individual **II-1** has blood type A so her genotype could be $I^A I^A$ or $I^A i$. She does not have sickle cell anemia, so her genotype for that is either $Hb^A Hb^A$ or $Hb^A Hb^S$. Individual **II-2** has blood type B so his blood genotype could be $I^B I^B$ or $I^B i$. Since he has sickle cell anemia, his genotype for that is $Hb^S Hb^S$. **A** is a possible answer. **B** and **C** are not correct because they provide a blood type that is not possible, and **D** is incorrect because it provides a genotype for sickle cell anemia that is not possible.

28. B

The alleles I^A and I^B are codominant because when an individual is heterozygous $I^A I^B$, both alleles are expressed. Neither dominates over the other. However, if an individual is $I^A i$, the i allele is not expressed, so I^A is dominant over i.

29. B

II-6 is a woman with faulty tooth enamel. Since this is an X-linked dominant trait, she has a genotype of $X^E X^E$ or $X^E X^e$. However, since she had a son with normal tooth enamel, ($X^E Y$) she must be able to provide the normal allele (X^e), so we can conclude that she is $X^E X^e$.

Individual **III-7** is a male with normal tooth enamel. His genotype must be $X^e Y$.

NR4. 0.25

The cross between a woman heterozygous for faulty tooth enamel ($X^E X^e$) and a man with normal tooth enamel ($X^E Y$) will look like this:

	X^E	X^e
X^e	$X^E X^e$	$X^e X^e$
Y	$X^E Y$	$X^e Y$

The boy with normal tooth enamel is shaded. 1/4 of children, or 0.25, will be boys with normal tooth enamel.

30. C

If the man has faulty tooth enamel, his genotype is $X^E Y$. Every time he has a daughter, he provides the X chromosome with the allele for faulty tooth enamel, so all of his daughters with have the trait. If none of the sons have faulty tooth enamel, the mother never provides the faulty tooth enamel allele (X^E), so she must be $X^e X^e$ with normal tooth enamel.

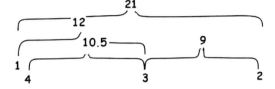

NR5.   1, 4, 3, 2 or 2, 3, 4, 1

Determining the order of the genes on a chromosome is called gene mapping. Cross-over frequency can be used to construct a gene map. Cross-over frequency is the percentage of the time that when crossing over happens, the genes become separated on different chromosomes. The higher the cross-over frequency, the farther apart the genes are on the chromosome. The following is a gene map for these genes:

Thus, the order of the genes is 1432 or 2341.

31. A

Once a gene map has been drawn, such as the one above, it is possible to calculate the distance between genes. The distance between diabetes mellitus gene (1) and Rhesus blood group gene (3) is 12. The distance between ragweed sensitivity gene (4) and Rhesus blood group gene (3) is 10.5. Therefore, the distance between the diabetes mellitus gene (1) and the ragweed sensitivity gene (4) is $12 - 10.5 = 1.5$.

32. D

The diagram and graph show that when estrogen level and ovary size are rising, the behaviour is female-like. Ovulation brings a drop in estrogen level, a reduction in ovary size, and a conversion to male-like behaviour. Answer **D** links female-like behaviour with high estrogen. That is correct and all other possible answers have incorrect linkages.

33. D

In humans, the ovaries do not change in size during the monthly cycle, so **A** and **B** are incorrect. The graph shows estrogen levels increasing prior to ovulation. That is true in humans as well. Therefore, **C**, that estrogen secretion decreases prior to ovulation, is incorrect. **D** is correct. The graph shows that levels of progesterone increases, in the lizards following ovulation.

Levels of progesterone also increase in humans following ovulation, when the remains of the follicle re-form into the corpus luteum and produce progesterone.

34. B

The reading informs us that the offspring form from unfertilized eggs that have undergone chromosome doubling after meiosis. The unfertilized eggs are *n*, but after chromosome doubling, the eggs would become 2*n*. This would provide the same chromosome number as if the egg had been fertilized by a sperm.

35. C

The organ of Corti is the actual hearing organ in mammals. It is the site where the pressure wave that we know as sound is converted into an action potential in the auditory nerve. The organ of Corti is inside the fluid-filled cochlea. A pressure wave in the fluid of the cochlea squeezes the organ of Corti, which then stimulates the auditory nerve fibres. The ossicles are the bones of the middle ear. The oval window is the membrane on the surface of the cochlea that the ossicles press on to create the pressure waves in the fluid, and the semicircular canals are a part of the cochlea that monitor balance, not hearing.

36. C

K-selected populations are ones that try to maintain their population size near *K*, the carrying capacity. Typically, a *K*-selected population is made up of large, slow-growing organisms that have few offspring, provide good parental care, and have a good survival rate of the young. Elephants are a good example of a *K*-selected population. Biotic potential refers to the maximum reproductive rate. Since female elephants are sexually receptive only once every four years, their maximum biotic potential is lower than that of humans.

37. A

At about halfway through a woman's monthly cycle, she has an increase in LH produced by the pituitary. This high level of LH in the blood causes ovulation and the formation of the corpus luteum. The corpus luteum then begins production of progesterone. The progesterone has a negative feedback effect on the hypothalamus and pituitary, shutting down LH production. LH production increases again halfway through the next monthly cycle.

NR6.   1, 4, 5

The question asks us to look for statements that do **not** apply to humans. We do call the human reproductive cycle the menstrual cycle (**2**); whereas the elephant reproductive cycle is called the estrous cycle (**1**). In humans, the endometrium is shed if no pregnancy occurs (**3**); the endometrium in elephants is absorbed if no pregnancy occurs (**4**). In humans, there are no "pronounced" behavioral changes around ovulation (**5**), although there may be some behavioural changes throughout the cycle (**6**).

38. D

Fertilization refers to the fusion of a sperm with an egg. Ovulation occurs halfway through a woman's monthly cycle. Normally, the egg is drawn into the Fallopian tube, which is known as also known as the oviduct, where it can survive unfertilized for about one day. If sperm are in the woman's body, they can fertilize the egg there. The egg could never get all the way to the uterus alive unfertilized because that would take several days.

39. A

A zygote can be described as the cell that results from the fusion of a sperm and an egg.
When the haploid sperm (n) fuses with the haploid egg (really a secondary oocyte), meiosis II takes place, in which the secondary oocyte divides to form a ootid (n) and a second polar body (n).
It is unusual that the zygote does not include the polar body, the zygote at this point is made up of the one cell that formed from the sperm and ootid, thus making it a diploid ($2n$) cell.

40. D

During the cell cycle, DNA replicates during the S phase, so that the two cells formed through mitosis are genetically identical. Each of the eight cells that make up the embryo contain identical DNA because they formed through mitosis.

A is incorrect because two zygotes fertilized by two different sperm produce fraternal not identical twins.
B is incorrect because zygotes undergo mitosis, not meiosis.
C is incorrect because differentiation, the formation of specialized cells such as nerve cells and muscle cells, comes much later than the eight-cell stage.

41. A

The zygote and all somatic (regular body) cells that form from the zygote are diploid, so **B** and **D** are incorrect. Meiosis is a process that occurs only in the gonads (sex organs) during the formation of gametes such as sperm and eggs. There are no gonads yet in this embryo, so **C** is incorrect.

42. A

We are asked to find the evidence that allowed the researchers to conclude that the timber company's strategy was not working.
They found food particles consistent with the food provided in male bears' feces, but that would indicate that the strategy was working. They found bark in the feces of female bears. They would have identified the feces as coming from female bears because it would have contained cells with two X chromosomes. It was this evidence, the bark in the feces of bears that also had cells with two X chromosones, that showed the timber company's strategy was not working, at least with female bears.

43. B

Gel electrophoresis is a process in which particles can be separated by their size and their electrical charge. In the case of DNA, all fragments would have a negative charge, so electrophoresis separates pieces of DNA according to size of particle. The gel is actually composed of a mesh of many tiny fibres with pores. An electric current draws the DNA fragments through the gel. The smaller particles fit through the pores with no difficulty, therefore moving along a rapid rate. Larger particles are slowed as they move through the gel.
The specific of bands of DNA that is formed is sometimes called a DNA "fingerprint."

NR7.   3, 2, 1, 4

Hormone A, which is released from the anterior pituitary and which stimulates the adrenal cortex, is ACTH (**3**) or adrenocorticotrophic hormone. It stimulates the adrenal cortex to releases its hormones. Hormone B causes more water and salt (sodium) to be drawn back into the blood, therefore increasing blood volume and pressure. That is aldosterone (**2**). Hormone C causes an increase in blood glucose (sugar) and the breakdown of proteins and fats for energy.
It also causes swelling to go down. It begins the repair process that follows an injury.
This hormone is cortisol (**1**). The release of hormone D from the adrenal medulla is stimulated by the sympathetic nervous system causing a diversion of blood to brain, heart, and skeletal muscles from the internal organs, and causing an increase in blood glucose, along with increased heart and breathing rate.
This hormone is epinephrine (**4**), which is sometimes referred to as adrenaline.

44. B

The short-term response to stress involves the sympathetic nervous system along with the hormone epinephrine. Using nerve pathways, signals can get from the brain to all parts of the body almost instantly. The prolonged response to stress is an all-hormone response. It takes a while for hormones to travel through the blood to their target organs, so the prolonged response to stress occurs more slowly.

45. A

Mimicry is an adaptation in which an organism appears to be another, perhaps more dangerous, organism. In this case, the defenceless baby owls sound like rattlesnakes. As a result, an approaching predator may back off, thinking that it has stumbled upon a rattlesnake den.

NR8.   5 1 2

This question requires some math. If there are 800 breeding pairs in 1996, and they are declining in number by 20% per year:
20% of 800 is $800 \times 0.2 = 160$, so $800 - 160 = 640$ breeding pairs in 1997.
20% of 640 is $640 \times 0.2 = 128$, so $640 - 128 = 512$ breeding pairs in 1998.

46. D

Since the burrowing owl and the kestrel eat many of the same types of food, they are competitors. Competition between members of different species is interspecific competition, so the answer is **C** or **D**. The badger enlarges the ground squirrel hole for its own purposes, but that provides a subsequent benefit to the burrowing owl. Since the badger gains no advantage from the burrowing owl, the relationship between owl and badger is commensalism. In a commensalistic relationship, one organism benefits and the other is unaffected.

47. C

Limiting factors are all factors that limit a population's growth. Examples could be the food supply, temperature and predators. Limiting factors for bees may well be decreasing in April. During that time, temperatures (unfavourable during the winter) are improving and food supplies are increasing. As a result, whereas the environment could only support a small number of bees during March, many more could be supported by the beginning of May. An increase in parasitism or an increase in environmental resistance would lower the bee population. A decrease in competition is not likely, as the conditions are improving for the bees' competitors as well.

48. A

Parasitism is a relationship in which one organism benefits and the other is harmed.
It is clear here that the mite is benefiting by, having a place to live and a supply of food.
At the same time, the bees are harmed, perhaps even the colony is threatened.
Therefore, the mite is a parasite, and the bee is the host.

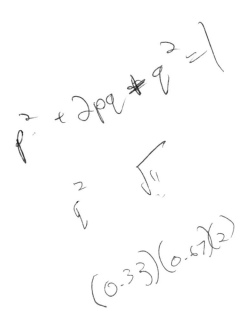

1. **a)** *A gene mutation alters the nitrogen-base sequence of the gene's DNA.* **(1 mark)**

This change in the sequence results in an altered mRNA nitrogen-base sequence that, in turn, can alter the amino acids in the diaphorase enzyme. **(1 mark)**

b) $q^2 = \dfrac{6}{55} = 0.11$
$q = 0.33$ **(1 mark)**

The frequency of the recessive allele is 0.33. **(1 mark)**

c) $P + q = 1$
$1 - 0.33 = p$
$p = 0.67$
$2\,pq = 2(0.33)(0.67) = 0.44$ **(1 mark)**

Theoretically, 44% of the individuals were heterozygous for the allele. **(1 mark)**

d) *The mutation first occurred in an individual in the Fugate family; therefore, more members of this family have the allele than do the general population.*

or

Intermarriage within the Fugate family increased the probability of two carriers mating and producing blue offspring.

or

Because the Fugate family lived in an isolated area, the likelihood of carriers mating and producing blue offspring increased.

e) Any two of the following:

- The population was small, and a large population is required to meet the conditions for Hardy-Weinberg equilibrium.

- There was non-random mating rather than the random mating required for Hardy-Weinberg equilibrium.

- Mutation occurred to produce the defective diaphorase, and Hardy-Weinberg equilibrium requires no mutation.

- Emigration or immigration from the population occurred, and migration does not occur in populations that satisfy Hardy-Weinberg equilibrium.

f) i) *Bb* (*heterozygous*)

ii) *Benjy produced some normal diaphorase and, over time, was able to convert enough methemoglobin into hemoglobin to express a normal skin colour.*

or

Fetal hemoglobin is different than adult hemoglobin. Therefore, the expression of Benjy's phenotype may have changed shortly after birth

or

Any other reasonable explanation.

iii) *Treatment does not change the alleles present in the germ cells of the individuals; therefore they can still be passed on to future generations.*

Written Response—15%

2.

Three Month Old Fetus and Associated Structures

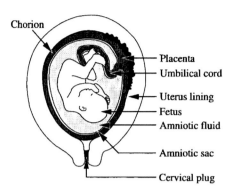

The amniotic fluid surrounding the fetus functions to protect the fetus from physical trauma. The amniotic sac that holds the amniotic fluid provides a protective barrier for the fetus, thereby preventing the entrance into the amniotic fluid of harmful bacteria, viruses, and other harmful pathogens and chemicals that would eventually affect the fetus. It also helps to regulate temperature for the fetus. The placenta acts as a barrier between the fetal blood supply and the maternal blood supply. It is the site of nutrient, gas, and waste exchange between the fetal circulation and maternal circulation. Nutrients and oxygen diffuse into the fetal blood while carbon dioxide and wastes diffuse into maternal blood. The placenta also produces hormones. HCC stimulates the corpus luteum to produce estrogen and progesterone in order to maintain pregnancy in the first trimester. The placenta also acts as a barrier to some pathogens that may be in the mother's body. The umbilical cord contains blood vessels that transport blood between the placenta and the fetus.

A mother's voice produces sound waves. Sound waves are converted to fluid waves in the ears of her fetus within her uterus. These fluid waves stimulate hair cells in the organ of Corti located within the cochlea. This creates action potentials in sensory neurons in the auditory nerve.

The sensory neurons synapse with interneurons. Eventually, stimulation of interneurons occurs in the temporal lobe of the brain where auditory information is interpreted.

or

Any other specific stimuli pathway to the CNS could be described.

One technology that could stimulate appropriate neural development in infants is the use of colourful mobiles and learning centres. These would cause sensory receptors to be stimulated and eventually stimulate neurons in the brain. The stimulation of neurons creates appropriate synapses and helps neurons to develop.

A government policy that would also have a positive influence on fetal development would be the formation of a childhood development specialist team made up of early childhood educators, public health nurses, social workers, child psychologists, and early childhood movement specialists. This specialist team would be available to assess individual home situations, provide information seminars in prenatal classes and to parent groups, and offer assistance in setting up an environment that provides an optimal amount of stimulation for the infant. Appropriate stimulation will develop neuron connections, increase the size of the brain, and help develop appropriate social responses.

Other technologies or government polices that could be described are:

- *any technology that stimulates the senses and therefore increases neural stimulation*

- *any government policy that would help increase appropriate stimulation of a child or appropriate interaction of a child with a significant adult*

- *technologies to investigate genetic causes of abnormal brain development and/or to correct these*

- *government policies or technologies that would protect the fetal environment from conditions that might affect neural development*

Science

Score	Scoring Criteria
	The student
5 **Excellent**	• sketches the fetal environment accurately and correctly labels four parts • clearly describes in detail how the fetal environment supports the fetus at three months of development • clearly describes the pathway for sensory interpretation in a fetus or newborn from a specific stimulus
4 **Proficient**	• sketches the fetal environment accurately and correctly labels three parts • describes how the fetal environment supports the fetus • describes the pathway for sensory interpretation from a specific stimulus
3 **Satisfactory**	• sketches the fetal environment and correctly labels two parts • partially describes how the fetal environment supports the fetus • partially describes a pathway for sensory interpretation
2 **Limited**	• attempts a sketch of the fetal environment and correctly labels one part **or** an accurate sketch is drawn • describes at least one supporting structure in the fetal environment • identifies one step in a pathway for sensory interpretation
1 **Poor**	• only one of the bullets is addressed at a 2 or 3 level

INSUFFICIENT is a special category. It is not an indication of quality. It should be assigned to papers that do not contain a discernible attempt to address the questions presented in the assignment or that are too brief to assess in this or any other scoring category.

Technology and Society

Score	Scoring Criteria
	The student
5 Excellent	• identifies and describes two relevant technologies or government polices that would stimulate neural development • clearly explains how each technology or government policy would affect neural development
4 Proficient	• identifies two relevant technologies or government polices and describes one **or** identifies and partially describes two relevant technologies or government policies • explains how one technology or government policy would affect neural development and partially explains the other
3 Satisfactory	• identifies one relevant technology or government policy and partially describes the other **or** identifies or partially describes two. • explains how one technology or government policy would affect neural development **or** partially explains both
2 Limited	• identifies one relevant technology or government policy or partially describes one • partially explains how one technology or government policy would affect neural development
1 Poor	• addresses one of the two scoring bullets at a 2 level

INSUFFICIENT is a special category. It is not an indication of quality. It should he assigned to papers that do not contain a discernible attempt to address the questions presented in the assignment or that are too brief to assess in this or any other scoring category.

ANSWERS AND SOLUTIONS
JANUARY 2002 DIPLOMA EXAMINATION

1.	C	11.	D	21.	B	31.	C	41.	D
2.	A	12.	D	22.	D	32.	A	42.	B
3.	B	NR3.	4, 3, 1, 2	23.	A	33.	A	43.	C
4.	C	NR4.	1, 4, 3, 2	24.	A	34.	D	44.	A
5.	A	13.	C	25.	C	35.	A	45.	C
6.	C	14.	B	26.	C	36.	C	46.	B
NR1.	4, 2, 3, 1	15.	A	27.	D	37.	C	47.	D
NR2.	9, 0, 4, 0	16.	D	NR5.	1, 3, 4, 2	38.	C	48.	C
7.	A	17.	B	28.	A	39.	B		
8.	A	18.	B	NR6.	6, 4, 3, 2	40.	C		
9.	B	19.	C	29.	C	NR7.	2, 4, 5, 6		
10.	D	20.	B	30.	C	NR8.	6.73		

1. C

If the level of calcium in the blood is too low, it will be necessary to increase blood calcium by getting it from somewhere. The bones contain a lot of calcium, so removing calcium from the bones could provide calcium for the blood. Therefore **A**. and **B**. "increased deposition of calcium in the bones" must be wrong.
D. is incorrect because the reading tells us that calcitonin causes the movement of calcium into the bones, not out of them. PTH is described as a hormone antagonistic to calcitonin.
That means it performs the opposite function. If calcitonin causes calcium to be deposited in bones, then PTH must cause calcium to be removed from the bones.

2. A

All of the alternatives list substances that have some effect on the release of thyroxine, but the question asks us for the one that directly regulates the release of throxine. That is TSH, which stands for thyroid stimulating hormone. TSH is produced by the anterior pituitary gland and stimulates the thyroid to release thyroxine. TRH, thyroid releasing hormone, is produced by the hypothalamus and causes the release of TSH. Iodine is needed for thyroid production, and so, if there is a shortage of iodine, thyroxine production will be hampered.

Thyroxine itself has an effect on thyroxine production because it exerts a negative feedback effect on the hypothalamus. Only **A**, TSH, has a direct effect on thyroxine production.

3. B

Hyperthyroidism refers to an overactive thyroid. As a result, there will be too much thyroxine in the body. Since thyroxine increases the body's metabolic rate, an excess of thyroxine will cause overactive cells and could result in weight loss. All the rest of the symptoms given would result if there were a shortage of thyroxine, which would cause a lower metabolic rate.

4. C

Aldosterone causes salt and water to be pumped from the kidney tubules back into the blood. Cortisol initiates repair of body tissues following injury. In the process, there is an increase of glucose not salt, in the blood.
Thyroxine increases metabolic rate and in so doing, increases blood glucose, not salt. Epinephrine is sometimes referred to as adrenaline. It initiates a "fight-or-flight" response – stimulating the body for action. Epinephrine also causes there to be more glucose in the blood, not salt.

5. A

ADH stands for antidiuretic hormone.
That alone should be a good clue of which
hormone diuretic chemicals counteract.
ADH causes the kidney tubules to become more
porous, so that more water diffuses from the
kidney tubules back to the blood. As more water
diffuses back to the blood, there will be less in
the urine. Therefore, ADH causes there to be a
less-than-normal volume of urine—the opposite
of a diuretic.

6. C

The occipital lobe which is at the back of the
cerebrum (conscious part of the brain),
coordinates visual stimulation. The frontal lobe
(at the front of the cerebrum) is associated with
personality traits, and the parietal and temporal
lobes (on the sides of the cerebrum) are
associated with motor and sensory stimulation,
hearing, and language.

NR1.   4, 2, 3, 1

All reflex responses have this general pattern:
sensory receptor $\rightarrow$ sensory neuron $\rightarrow$
interneuron $\rightarrow$ motor neuron $\rightarrow$ effector
(muscle). The size of the pupils is influenced by
light intensity and is controlled by muscles in the
eye. Therefore, the reflex response will begin
with the light receptors, which activate the
sensory neurons of the optic nerve.

Within the brain, there are interneurons, where a
response is coordinated. Finally, a response is
sent through motor neurons of the motor nerves
that control the muscles of the eye.

NR2.   90, 40

When at rest, the membrane potential is
-90 mV. That means that it is 90 mV more
negative inside the neuron than out. Stimulation
of the neuron causes a flood of positive sodium
(Na^+) ions into the neuron, making it more
positive inside. According to the graph, during
depolarization, the inside of the neuron reaches
$+40$ mV.

7. A

Upon stimulation that exceeds a neuron's
threshold, the membrane of the neuron fibre
becomes permeable to sodium ions and they rush
in. Since sodium ions (Na^+) have a positive
charge, they make the action potential more
positive. Positive potassium ions, which are
originally inside the neuron, rush out from
0.5 ms to 0.8 ms to make the action potential
more negative again.

8. A

Refractory period refers to the time when the
original situation is restored, which is what is
happening from 0.5 ms to 1.0 ms.
Repolarization means that the original polarity of
-90 mV is being restored. Depolarization is
incorrect, as it refers to the period from
0.2 ms to 0.5 ms during which the original
polarity of -90 mV is lost. Threshold is the level
of stimulation required to initiate an action
potential.

9. B

A synapse is the space between the end of the
axon of one neuron and the cell body or dendrite
of another neuron. Neurotransmitters such as
dopamine and serotonin are released from the
presynaptic membrane of the axon and diffuse
across the space or synaptic cleft, binding to
receptor sites on the postsynaptic membrane.
Since MAO breaks down dopamine, it must
function in the synaptic cleft.

10. D

The fight-or-flight response is an unconscious
response through which the hormones
epinephrine and norepinephrine prepare the body
for action. The part of the brain that controls the
hormones is the hypothalamus. The pons is a
relay centre, directing information to various
parts of the brain. The cerebrum is the
conscious, thinking part of the brain, and the
cerebellum coordinates muscle activity.

11. D

RNA is structurally different from DNA in three ways—it is single stranded instead of double stranded, it contains the sugar ribose instead of deoxyribose, and it contains the nitrogenous base uracil (U) instead of thymine (T). Therefore, any of the answers that contains a T is not a possible strand of mRNA. **D** is the only answer that will work.

12. D

The first reading tells us that neural pathways involving dopamine cause pleasurable feelings. When the dopamine is released from the presynaptic membrane, it diffuses across the synaptic cleft, binding to dopamine receptors on the postsynaptic membrane. When enough dopamine receptors have been stimulated, the stimulation has reached a threshold. At this point, depolarization occurs, and a signal travels along the next neuron.

NR3.   4, 3, 1, 2

Following the injection of androgens, there will be a high level of androgens in the blood (4). These hormones will have a negative feedback effect on the hypothalamus/pituitary, causing them to stop releasing the gonadotropins FSH and LH (3). FSH stimulates sperm production in the seminiferous tubules of the testes, and LH causes the release of androgens from the interstitial cells of the testes. Without FSH and LH, sperm production will stop (1). Apparently, this treatment is only effective for a few weeks, so hormone levels return to normal (2).

NR4.   1, 4, 3, 2

Production of sperm by the process of meiosis occurs in the seminiferous tubules (1). The epididymis, in which sperm mature (4), is a coiled tube at the edge of the testes. The vas deferens are two long tubes that transport sperm up from the testes, past the bladder, seminal vesicles, prostate gland, and Cowper's glands, to the urethra (3). FSH and LH are stimulated to be released from the anterior pituitary by releasing hormones produced by the hypothalamus (2).

13. C

Testosterone is a hormone. All hormones travel through the blood. Swelling of the prostate would affect the movement of material from the vas deferens or bladder into the urethra. Urine, sperm, and seminal vesicle secretions must all travel to the urethra and so could be affected by BPH. Testosterone could not.

14. B

The label 2 is pointing to the prostate gland, where cancer occurs if the protein coded by the *p27* gene is absent. Label 1 is the seminal vesicle, 3 is the Cowper's gland, and 4 is the testis.

15. A

In the process of transcription, DNA unzips and RNA nucleotides attach to the coding side of the DNA to form a long strand of RNA called mRNA ("m" is for messenger). Translation occurs when the ribosome "reads" the mRNA and assembles a protein from amino acids that are attached to tRNA.

16. D

Sperm production occurs in the seminal tubules of the testes. The sperm finally mature in the epididymis, but it is clear from the diagram that the mitotic proliferation stage is occurring long before the sperm are mature. The vas deferens is a tube leading from the testis that transports away mature sperm, and the seminal vesicles add fluid to the sperm to make semen.

17. B

The human diploid number is 46. That means that a normal somatic cell contains 46 chromosomes in 23 pairs. At stage A, the cells are diploid because they have not completed meiosis I. During meiosis I, the chromosomes pairs are split, resulting in haploid cells that have 23 chromosomes, one chromosome of each pair. At stage B, meiosis I is complete and meiosis II is almost complete.

18. B

Because the diagram shows us that the Dionne quintuplets formed from a single egg and a single sperm, they must be identical, not fraternal quintuplets. It is not likely that fertility drugs were involved because they cause multiple ovulation—the production of many eggs, and we can see from the diagram that only one egg produced all five babies.

19. C

The diagram shows us that this individual has three chromosome 18s, which the reading identifies as Edward syndrome.
The sex is male because the last pair of chromosomes, the sex chromosomes, are different, an X and Y, not two Xs.

20. B

CVS stands for chorionic villus sampling. It involves taking a sample of cells from the chorion, the outer layer that surrounds the embryo or fetus. At about two months' gestation, part of the chorion has developed into the placenta. CVS can be used to determine the genetic health of the fetus.

21. B

The structure numbered 2 is the placenta. It is commonly thought of as the site where there is an exchange of materials between mother and fetus. However, the fetal portion of the placenta also produces the hormones progesterone and estrogen, and, early during fetal development, HCG. These hormones are important in maintaining the endometrium, the lining of the uterus.

22. D

When blood glucose is too high, insulin is released from the β cells of the islets of Langerhans in the pancreas. Insulin causes glucose to be taken out of the blood, primarily by the liver and the skeletal muscles. When blood glucose is too low, glucagon is released from the α cells of the islets of Langerhans in the pancreas. Glucagon causes stored glucose to be released back into the blood, raising blood glucose.

23. A

A zygote from which an individual is formed is composed of the nuclear material of a sperm and the entire cell of the egg. Therefore, the mitochondrial DNA, including the mutation that causes KSS, comes from the mother.
In the example given, the mother does not have the mutant DNA in her own somatic (body) cells, therefore, the mutation must have occurred during the production of the egg (her oocyte).

24. A

The sperm is very tiny, and the egg is very large. The sperm provides only nuclear material in the formation of the zygote. The egg contains a large amount of cytoplasm, along with its nucleus. There is enough energy and cell "machinery" for the zygote to make the one-week trip down the Fallopian tube while it is becoming a blastocyst.

25. C

The ribosome reads the mRNA strand in groups of three bases called codons. For each codon read, a tRNA molecule with its complementary anticodon is set into place. Attached to the tRNA molecule is an amino acid. As the tRNA molecules are fitted into place, the adjacent amino acids attach together to form a protein.

26. C

From the coding DNA, a strand of mRNA is assembled that has the following sequence: UGG AGG GAG UGG UUU. Since the ribosome reads codons (segments of three bases), the mRNA codon for the third amino acid is GAG. Using the chart "Messenger RNA and their Corresponding Amino Acids" at the back of the exam, you will find that the mRNA codon "GAG" codes for glutamate.

27. D

In a cause-effect relationship, the manipulated variable represents a possible cause.
For example, if there were an experiment to determine if smoking caused cancer, whether or not a person smoked is the manipulated variable. In the experiment described here, differences in mitochondrial DNA are being used to determine when continents were populated. Therefore, the geographic location of the subjects (whose sample of mitochondrial DNA was tested) is the manipulated variable.

NR5.   1, 3, 4, 2

Often people use the words gene and allele as if they mean the same thing, but they don't.
A gene is a segment of DNA that codes for a specific characteristic, such as coat colour (1). Allele refers to a specific version of a gene. Here, the gene for coat colour can be expressed as *T* or *t* (3). Phenotype refers to how an organism appears. These horses can appear as tobiano or not tobiano (4). The genotype refers to the alleles that make up the gene in a certain organism. In this case, the genotype can be *TT*, *Tt*, or *tt* (2).

28. A

The following Punnett square shows that a cross of *Tt* × *tt* will yield a 1 : 1 genotypic ratio in the offspring. A cross of *Tt* × *Tt* will yield a 3 : 1 ratio. Tobiano and not tobiano are phenotypes, not genotypes.

Tt × *tt*

	T	*t*
t	*Tt*	*tt*
t	*Tt*	*tt*

The genotypes of the offspring are 50% *Tt* and 50 *tt*.
(a 1:1 ratio)

NR6.   6432

A somatic, or regular, body cell is diploid. That means that the chromosomes are in pairs. The first part of the answer is 64. A gamete is a sex cell; in animals, that means a sperm or an egg. Gametes are haploid cells; their chromosomes are unpaired. So, the second part of the answer is 32.

29. C

The black allele is dominant over the chocolate and cinnamon alleles. That means that when there is a heterozygous condition involving the black allele and a different allele (*Bb* or *Bb^l*), the individual appears black—the other colours do not appear. When there is a heterozygous condition involving the chocolate and cinnamon alleles (*bb^l*) the chocolate allele dominates, and the cinnamon allele does not appear.

30. C

We know from the information given that since the female is blue, she is *B_dd* and the male, being cinnamon-coloured, is *b^l b^l D_*. From the information provided about the offspring, we can work out the unknown parts of the genotypes. Since some of the offspring are *dd*, we know both parents had to be able to give a *d*. Therefore the male is *b^l b^l Dd*. We know the female has one B—we have to determine if her other allele is *B*, *b^l* or *b*. If the female is *BB*, then half of her all of her offspring will be either black or blue, and they aren't. If she is *Bb^l*, then half of her offspring will be either cinnamon or fawn, and none is. Therefore, she must be *Bbdd*.

31. C

The following Punnett square shows the cross between a *BbDd* (black-coloured female) and a fawn-coloured male (*b^l b^l dd*). Of the offspring, 25% will be chocolate coloured.

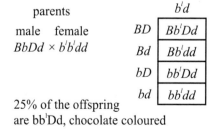

25% of the offspring are *bb^l Dd*, chocolate coloured

32. A

Female cats can be *X^R X^R* orange, *X^r X^r* black or *X^R X^r* orange and black (tortoiseshell). Since this cat is *X^r X^r*, with no *X^R*, she will have no orange colour. Therefore, she will be black.

33. A

The following Punnett square shows that for this cross there is only one phenotype of male offspring and one phenotype of female offspring. Only answer A indicates two possible phenotypes of the offspring.

parents		$X^R B$
male female		
$X Y b^l b^l \times X^R X^R BB$	$X b^l$	$X^R X B b^l$
offspring –	$Y b^l$	$X^R Y B b^l$

50% orange male cats and
50% tortoiseshell female cats

34. D

Because the cat has at least one large B, she will have full colour, and because she is $X^R X^R$, she will be orange. Since she has dd, the colour will be dilute, appearing cream or light orange.

35. A

Carriers are individuals who are heterozygous. Since sickle cell anemia is an autosomal (not sex-linked) recessive trait, we can give the carriers the genotype Ss. If two individuals are Ss, the genotypes of the offspring are 25% SS (normal), 50% Ss (carriers), and 25% ss (with sickle cell anemia).

36. C

Currently, a person who is a carrier of sickle cell anemia has some ability to withstand malaria. If scientists were to eliminate malaria, the sickle cell allele will have lost its survival value. It is likely that the allele will reduce in frequency as it is removed by natural selection. In the short term, it will not disappear, since it can easily exist in heterozygous forms without resulting in the death of the individual.

37. C

Process 1 is gamete formation, (from a diploid ($2n$) cell to a haploid (n) cell). Therefore, this process is meiosis. During process, there is an increase in numbers and it appears that the cells were $2n$ to begin with because they came from a zygote, so process 2 must be mitosis.

38. C

The first stage shows gametes, the plasmodium equivalent of human sperm and eggs. The gametes will fuse to form a zygote. The zygote would be $2n$ (chromosomes in pairs). The two gametes would be n. Each gamete provides one of each pair of chromosomes, to the zygote. From the zygote, a multicellular structure forms (labelled stage 2). The cells of stage two would be $2n$ like the zygote from which they formed.

39. B

A hypothesis is a possible answer to a question or problem. These two suggestions are possible answers to the problem, "How have some strains of *Plasmodium* become resistant to chloroquine?" A theory is an answer that has been well tested by experiments and has gained wide acceptance. Neither of these suggestions appear to have been based on direct observation and either of these suggestions could only be considered a conclusion if they were well supported by observation.

40. C

If the *cg2* gene codes for a protein that transports the drug out of the *Plasmodium*, then any organism that has that gene has some resistance to chloroquine. If researchers found a way to block transcription of the *cg2* gene, the transport protein could not be made. A mutation of the *cg2* gene would be a good thing in this case, so we would not want to prevent it, although that is not something we could control anyway. Stimulating translation of the *cg2* gene would cause the transport protein to be made so we would not want to do that. As well, replicating the *cg2* gene may help make more of the transport protein, so we would not want to do that.

NR7.   2, 4, 5, 6

K selected populations try to maintain their population size as close as possible to K the carrying capacity. They want to have a stable population size. These organisms tend to be slow growing (2), reproduce a small number of offspring (4 and 5), and are relatively large animals (6).

NR8.   6.73

There are 3 500 Komodo dragons and they live in an area of 520 km^2. To determine the population density, divide the population size by the area the dragons occupy.
3 500 ÷ 520 = 6.73 animals / km^2. We are asked to give an answer to two decimal places in the units dragons/km^2.

41. D

Humans have two types of light receptors in our retinas. Our rods can detect low light levels, but cannot see in fine detail and cannot see in colour. In contrast, the cones require bright light to work, but they can see in fine detail and can detect colour. If the Komodo dragons only have cones, then they have a limited ability to see in low-intensity light.

42. B

In humans, sound waves in the air cause the tympanic membrane (eardrum) to vibrate. This vibration causes the three ossicles of the middle ear – the malleus, incus, and stapes – to vibrate. The last ossicle, the stapes causes the oval window of the cochlea to vibrate, which causes vibrations of the fluid of the inner ear. (The entire cochlea does not vibrate.) The eustachian tube equalizes air pressure between the pharynx at the back of the mouth and the middle ear. The eustachian tube does not directly affect hearing at all.

43. C

Mutualism is a relationship in which both organisms benefit. Apparently, the bacteria produce chemicals that poison the prey of the Komodo dragon. That helps the Komodo dragon. The bacteria get an environment to live in and probably a constant supply of food so they are helped as well. Parasitism is a relationship in which one organism benefits and the other is harmed. The bacterial infection of the deer obviously harms the deer, but the deer flesh is a supply of food for the bacteria.

44. A

A climax species can be defined as one that is so dominant that it keeps other organisms at bay, and so, puts successional changes on hold. A pioneer species is one such as moss or lichen that begins a new community where there was not one before. Seral stage species and intermediate species refer to organisms such as poplar trees that invade an area, perhaps dominating for a while, but are eventually pushed out themselves.

45. C

In the reading, native grasses are described as competitors. Interspecific competition is competition between organisms of different species, as in the case here. Intraspecific competition exists between members of the same species; for example, the elk in an area competing for the same food supply. Commensalism is a relationship in which one organism benefits and the other is unaffected. An example would be a bird building a nest in a tree.

46. B

Having a high biotic potential means that it has a high reproductive capacity so that it can increase its population size quickly. Insects, whose populations can explode in a short time, have a high biotic potential. The Norway maple is not really "on steroids," that is just a figure of speech, so **A** and **C** are incorrect. Having a strong root system certainly helps the tree, but this is not directly related to reproductive rate. The tree reaches sexual maturity early, which means that it will start to reproduce at a young age, and it has a large number of seeds —two points that suggest that a tree will have a large number of offspring.

47. D

The hormone JH prevents the pupa from becoming an adult. The hormone ecdysone causes the pupa to become an adult in the spring. One way to keep the insect numbers down would be to keep them from becoming adults, so if the release of ecdysone could be blocked, then the pupae would not become adults and therefore could not reproduce.

48. C

It appears that during the spring ecdysone is released, not JH. In the spring, there is a lot of light. Therefore, it makes sense that the presence of a lot of light stimulates the release of ecdysone.

Written Response—15%

1. a) *Population pressures may have resulted in a search for new food sources or living space and stimulated the change to a greater migration area in 1750 from the pattern prior to 1700.*

or

Lack of food due to climatic changes (or overhunting, death of buffalo, etc) may have caused the tribe to migrate farther south in 1750 to seek new food sources.

or

Any reasonable answer related to an increased migration area or a more southern migration area.

b) The graph shows that from 1750 to 1817, the population of the Blood Tribe was stable. Describe two factors that might have contributed to this stability. **(2 marks)**

Any two of the following:

- *food supply was constant and supported that number of individuals*
- *no new diseases changed mortality*
- *survival rate of offspring (or birth rate) was constant*
- *environmental conditions such as weather were relatively constant so the population could move freely since it was not restricted to a reserve*
- *any other reasonable answer*

c) Describe two possible explanations for the population change from 1920 to the present. **(2 marks)**

Any two of the following:

- *better health care resulted in lower mortality*
- *increased food supply from new agricultural practices resulted in higher natality and/or lower mortality*
- *less mortality from disease occurred as the resistant individuals increased in the population (less death from smallpox)*
- *less warfare occurred after signing the treaty, therefore, mortality was lower*
- *improved shelter reduced winter mortality*
- *any other reasonable answer*

d) Explain how it is possible that a male fetus with OTC deficiency could develop and the infant be born alive, yet become ill and die shortly after birth. **(2 marks)**

Wastes (including ammonia) produced by the fetus diffuse across the placenta and the mother's liver (OTC enzymes) processes the wastes. **(1 mark)**

After birth the child's own liver (OTC enzymes) needs to function or ammonia will accumulate and the infant will die. **(1 mark)**

e) *Assume that individuals **III-2** and **III-3** are expecting another child. **Construct two** Punnett squares to illustrate the two possible crosses, based on the mother's (**III-2**) two possible genotypes. **Calculate** the probability of this child being a son with OTC deficiency. (Provide a legend to identify the symbols used for the two alleles.)* **(4 marks)**

Mother Heterozygous (III-2)	Mother Homozygous Dominant (III-2)

Probability of an OTC deficient son: or	$0.50 \times 0.25 = 0.125$ (combined) 0.25 or 0.00 (separate)

Marks:
1 mark: identifying two genotypes for mother (III-2)
2 marks: (1 mark each): two Punnett squares
1 mark: correct probability calculated

f) Explain how this viral therapy could be used to treat OTC deficiency in a patient. **(1 mark)**

The DNA in the virus for the OTC gene would be incorporated into liver cells.

A correct OTC protein would be manufactured.

This would convert ammonia to urea for the individual.

---

2. Write a unified response that addresses the following aspects of the use of herbal remedies in modem medicine.

Sample Answers

• **Compare** *the scientific validity of the two sources given.*

Source 1: Wild Yam Cream
The conclusions drawn are not valid because they are based on personal accounts of the effects of Wild Yam Cream over a very short period of time: one menstrual cycle. Beth Rosenthal did not set up a scientific investigation, complete with fused variables. There was no control group that received a placebo cream, and there were not enough participants in the study to produce accurate statistics necessary to draw accurate conclusions. There was no corroboration of her results by other independent researchers. The article is written by a person who is selling the product and may have a conflict of interest.

Source 2: Ginkgo biloba
The conclusions drawn from the Ginkgo biloba study are more valid than the conclusions drawn from the Wild Yam Cream study. Some of the reasons for this are as follows. A placebo pill was given to one of the groups to act as a comparison for the experimental group who received the Ginkgo biloba. A pre-test of all three tests of memory-related mental abilities was administered to act as a comparison for test results after the administration of Ginkgo biloba. All patients in both the control groups experimental group, were Alzheimer patients. The study was double-blind, which means that the researchers did not know which group was the experimental group and which group was the control group. A high number of participants were involved, which provides statistics that can be used to draw conclusions. A number of controls were used in the study so the effects of the Ginkgo biloba could more accurately be attributed to Ginkgo rather than to uncontrolled influences. The study took place over a long period of time (one year), which would act to control daily, weekly, or even monthly fluctuations in memory ability associated with uncontrolled influences. The results (27% improvement for Ginkgo group versus 14% improvement for control group) are significantly different. The study was published in a scientific journal, indicating that peer review of the results had taken place.

- **Describe** *the normal roles of estrogen and progesterone in the human female reproductive system.* **Hypothesize** *how Wild Yam cream would have to interact with a woman's hormones if it were to produce the benefits attributed to it by the source 1 article.*

  ### Roles of Estrogen:
  In the female reproductive system, estrogen stimulates growth and maturation of all reproductive structures such as the ovaries, uterus, and breasts. Estrogen produces secondary sexual characteristics in adolescence and adulthood including female-type hair distribution, widened hips, and lengthening of the long bones. Estrogen stimulates the thickening of the endometrium during days 6 to 26 in the menstrual cycle. Estrogen stimulates growth of the uterus and mammary glands during pregnancy.

  ### Roles of Progesterone:
  In the female reproductive system, progesterone (along with estrogen) causes thickening of the endometrium from day 1 to day 26 of the menstrual cycle. Progesterone is also responsible for maintenance of the endometrium and prepares the endometrium for implantation of the embryo by increasing glandular development and blood vessel development. Progesterone prevents the contraction of uterine muscles during pregnancy.

  ### Possible Hypotheses:
  - *Wild Yam cream would have to increase the level of progesterone in the body thereby playing a role in causing increased thickening of the endometrium (or preventing the contraction of the uterus,) which would decrease menstrual cramping.*

  or

  - *Wild Yam cream would have to increase the level of progesterone in the body, which may interact with areas of the brain causing an increased sense of well being or an increased sex drive.*

  or

  Any other appropriate hypothesis.

- **Describe** *one advantage and one disadvantage of the current regulation of herbal therapies.*

  ### Possible advantages:
  - *Consumers can obtain herbs without a prescription from a doctor. This saves both time and money for the consumer and for the medical profession.*
  - *Consumers can attempt to test the benefits of herbal remedies on their own without a doctor's consultation.*
  - *Many people come from cultural backgrounds in which herbs are incorporated into cultural and religious ceremonies. The people can obtain the herbs without the interference or consultation of the medical profession.*

  ### Possible Disadvantages:
  - *The active chemicals in herbs are not explicitly stated on packaging, even though they may cause serious side effects or perhaps interact negatively with other medications.*
  - *The drug companies may know that a certain herb is useful for treatment of a specific illness but do not release this information because it is not financially advantageous for them to do so.*
  - *Because it is not financially advantageous for drug companies to research herbs, the action of certain herbs remains unknown even though some herbs may provide cures or remedies for specific illnesses or diseases.*
  - *Herbs sold in health food stores may be contaminated and cause illness because the sale of herbs is not tightly controlled in terms of purity and/or concentration.*
  - *Consumers may not try herbal remedies because the cost of obtaining the herbs is not covered by health plans. The herbal remedy route may have fewer side effects than prescribed drugs, but because prescribed drugs are covered by provincial health plans, consumers may choose prescribed drugs over herbal remedies.*
  - *Companies may make unproven claims about the effectiveness of herbal remedies without proper scientific testing.*

- **State** *a revised regulation for herbal therapies, and* **explain how** *this revision would address the disadvantage(s) of the current regulations.*
    - *All herbs should be reclassified as drugs. This would result in testing of the herbs to determine their effects (purity, concentration, side effects, health effects, etc.) and protect consumers.*

        or

    - *Companies should be allowed to patent herbal remedies produced from plants. This would result in increased research into the possible benefits of herbal remedies because of possible increased profits for the company.*

        or

    - *Herbal remedies should be covered by provincial health-care plans. This would encourage the use of alternative health remedies by consumers.*

        or

    - *Any other revision to the regulations.*

Science

Score	Scoring Criteria
	The student...
5 **Excellent**	• clearly compares the scientific validity of both sources • fully describes the roles of estrogen and progesterone in the human female • writes a clear hypotheses of how Wild Yam cream would interact with a woman's hormones **and** links it to the effects of the herbal remedy
4 **Proficient**	• compares the scientific validity of both sources • describes the roles of estrogen and progesterone in the human female • writes a hypothesis of how Wild Yam cream would interact with a woman's hormones **and** suggests a link to the effects of the herb remedy
3 **Satisfactory**	• describes one factor relating to the scientific validity of each source **and** suggests a comparison • partially describes the roles of both estrogen or progesterone • writes a partial hypothesis of how Wild Yam cream would affect a woman's hormones **or** describes an effect of the remedy that is linked to a physiological function
2 **Limited**	• identifies one factor relating to scientific validity of one of the sources or makes a comparison statement • identifies a role of estrogen or progesterone • identifies a benefit of the herbal remedy
1 **Poor**	• addresses only one of the bullets at a 2 or 3 level

INSUFFICIENT is a special category. It is not an indication of quality. It should be assigned to papers that do not contain a discernible attempt to address the questions presented in the assignment or that are too brief to assess in this or any other scoring category.

Technology and Society

Score	Scoring Criteria
	The student...
5 **Excellent**	• clearly describes one advantage and one disadvantage of the current regulation of herbal remedies • clearly states a revision to existing herbal remedy regulations **and** clearly explains how this will address disadvantages of the current regulations
4 **Proficient**	• describes one advantage and one disadvantage of the current regulation of herbal remedies • states a revision to existing herbal remedy regulations **and** explains how this will address disadvantages of the current regulations
3 **Satisfactory**	• describes one advantage or one disadvantage of the current regulation of herbal remedies and partially describes one advantage or one disadvantage **or** describes an advantage and disadvantage of herbal remedies • states a revision to existing herbal regulations **or** explains how disadvantages of the current regulations could be addressed
2 **Limited**	• describes one advantage or one disadvantage of the current regulation of herbal remedies **or** describes one advantage or one disadvantage of herbal remedies • states an existing herbal remedy regulation **or** partially explains how disadvantages of the current regulations could be addressed
1 **Poor**	• addresses one of the two scoring bullets at a 2 level

INSUFFICIENT is a special category. It is not an indication of quality. It should be assigned to papers that do not contain a discernible attempt to address the questions presented in the assignment or that are too brief to assess in this or any other scoring category.

Data
Tables

z

a

b

x

c

y

BIOLOGY DATA

Symbols

Symbol	Description
D_p	population density
N	number of individuals in a population
A	area occupied by a population
V	volume occupied by a population
t	time
Δ	change in
K	carrying capacity
gr	growth rate
cgr	per capita growth rate
$>$	greater than, dominant over
$<$	less than, recessive to

Symbol	Description
$\male$	male
$\female$	female
n	chromosome number
B, b	alleles: upper case is dominant, lower case is recessive
I^A, I^B, i	alleles, human blood type (ABO)
P	parent generation
F_1	first filial generation
F_2	second filial generation
p	frequency of dominant allele
q	frequency of recessive allele

Equations

Subject	Equation
Hardy–Weinberg principle	$p^2 + 2pq + q^2 = 1$
Population density	$D_p = \dfrac{N}{A}$ or $D_p = \dfrac{N}{V}$
Change in population size	$\Delta N =$ (factors that increase pop.) − (factors that decrease pop.)
Growth rate	$gr = \dfrac{\Delta N}{\Delta t}$
Per capita growth rate (time will be determined by the question)	$cgr = \dfrac{\Delta N}{N}$

Abbreviations for Some Hormones

Hormone	Abbreviation
Adrenocorticotropic hormone	ACTH
Antidiuretic hormone	ADH
Follicle-stimulating hormone	FSH
Gonadotropin-releasing hormone	GnRH
Human chorionic gonadotropin	hCG
Human growth hormone or growth hormone (somatotropin)	hGH or GH (STH)
Luteinizing hormone	LH
Parathyroid hormone	PTH
Prolactin	PRL
Thyroid-stimulating hormone	TSH

Pedigree Symbols

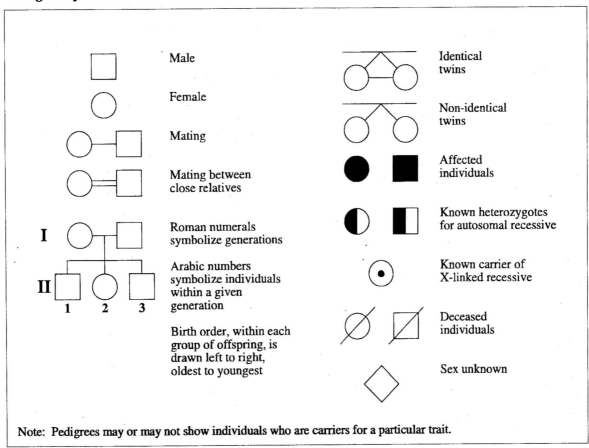

Male	
Female	
Mating	
Mating between close relatives	
Roman numerals symbolize generations	
Arabic numbers symbolize individuals within a given generation	
Birth order, within each group of offspring, is drawn left to right, oldest to youngest	

Identical twins

Non-identical twins

Affected individuals

Known heterozygotes for autosomal recessive

Known carrier of X-linked recessive

Deceased individuals

Sex unknown

Note: Pedigrees may or may not show individuals who are carriers for a particular trait.

Messenger RNA Codons and Their Corresponding Amino Acids

First Base	Second Base				Third Base
	U	C	A	G	
U	UUU phenylalanine	UCU serine	UAU tyrosine	UGU cysteine	U
	UUC phenylalanine	UCC serine	UAC tyrosine	UGC cysteine	C
	UUA leucine	UCA serine	UAA stop**	UGA stop**	A
	UUG leucine	UCG serine	UAG stop**	UGG tryptophan	G
C	CUU leucine	CCU proline	CAU histidine	CGU arginine	U
	CUC leucine	CCC proline	CAC histidine	CGC arginine	C
	CUA leucine	CCA proline	CAA glutamine	CGA arginine	A
	CUG leucine	CCG proline	CAG glutamine	CGG arginine	G
A	AUU isoleucine	ACU threonine	AAU asparagine	AGU serine	U
	AUC isoleucine	ACC threonine	AAC asparagine	AGC serine	C
	AUA isoleucine	ACA threonine	AAA lysine	AGA arginine	A
	AUG methionine*	ACG threonine	AAG lysine	AGG arginine	G
G	GUU valine	GCU alanine	GAU aspartate	GGU glycine	U
	GUC valine	GCC alanine	GAC aspartate	GGC glycine	C
	GUA valine	GCA alanine	GAA glutamate	GGA glycine	A
	GUG valine	GCG alanine	GAG glutamate	GGG glycine	G

* Note: AUG is an initiator codon and also codes for the amino acid methionine.

** Note: UAA, UAG, and UGA are terminator codons.

Information About Nitrogen Bases

Nitrogen Base	Classification	Abbreviation
Adenine	Purine	A
Guanine	Purine	G
Cytosine	Pyrimidine	C
Thymine	Pyrimidine	T
Uracil	Pyrimidine	U

Credits

The publishers wish to thank all those who assisted in the creation of this publication.

Some of the original graphics used in the Alberta Diploma Exams have been adapted, modified or replaced for this publication. Some images used in this publication are © Corel Corporation.

Examination questions, preambles and most graphics appearing in this booklet have been reproduced from the Biology 30 Grade 12 Diploma Examinations for January and June; 2000, 2001 and January 2002 with the permission of Alberta Education. Some of the information, graphs, illustrations or photographs that appeared in the examinations were obtained from other sources. The following is a list of the original sources of items that appear in the exams and this book.

Unit Review

Unit 1 - Nervous and Endocrine System

2 Zabludoff, M. 1996. The origin of syphilis. Discover 17(10): 23

4-6 Lemonick, M.D. 1997. The mood molecule. Time, 29 September, 55-62.

9 Page, S. 1997. The pursuit of pleasure. The Edmonton Journal, 10 August.

10-11 Mihill, C. 1996. Memories are made of whiffs. The Edmonton Journal. 9 June.

15/29/33 Strauss, S. 1997. Kisses and chemistry linked in rats. The Globe and Mail, 12 September.

20-21 Curtis, H. 1983. Biology. New York: Worth Publishers.

24/32 Raloff, J. 1996. Eyes possess their own biological clocks. Science News 149(4): 245.

25 Lemonick M.D. 1994. A terrible beauty. Time, 4 December, 54-58.

26 Diagram from Biology by Neil A. Campbell; Copyright © 1987, 1990, 1993 by The Benjamin/Cummings Publishing Company.

28 Glausiusz, J. 1996. How cholera became a killer. Discover 17 (10): 28

32 Norman, W. and G. Litwack. 1997. Hormones. San Diego: Academic Press.

Unit Test 1

3 Guyton, A.C. and J.E. Hall. 1996. *Textbook of Medical Physiology*. Philadelphia: W.B. Saunders Company.

5-6 Hall, J. 1996. Pinpointing people's panic buttons. *The Edmonton Journal.* 9 January.

9 Greene, M. 1993. Spinal cord research: Making nerves grow. *today's Science on File.* January 1993: 82.

10 Cheng, D.H., H. Ren, and X.R. Tang. 1996.Huperzine A, a novel promising acetylcholinesterase inhibitor. *Neuroreport* 8(1): 97–101.

17 Schmidt, F and G. Thews. 1983. *Human Physiology*. New York: Springer–Verlag

18 Graph from *Textbook of Medical Physiology* by A.C. Guyton and J.E. Hall, (W.B. Saunders Company, 1996). Reprinted with permission of W.B. Saunders Company.

Unit 2 - Reproductive Systems, Hormones, Differentiation, and Development

1-2/9/18 Vergano, D. 1996. The trouble with condoms. Science News. 150 (37): 165

4 Zabludoff, M. 1996. The origin of syphilis. Discover 17(10): 23

5/27-28/NR1 Fackelmann, K.A. 1994. Male rats find alcohol a fertility downer. Science News 146(1): 6.

6/10/NR3 Pringle, H. 1992. The sex difference. Equinox, September/October, 84-86

16-17 Bay Area Fertility and Gynecology Medical Group "Clomiphine citrate." hito://www.ihr.corn/baferti/Varticles/clotninhe. html

19-22 No author. 1992. Brain-deciding to be born. Discover 13 (5): 10-11

30 McInnis, D. 1996. Birth control reins in wild horses' foaling around. Edmonton Journal, 14 April.

NR4 Photograph by Lennart Nilsson. From A Child Is Born (Delacore Press/Seymour Lawrence, 1990)

Unit 2 Test

17 Hedegard, L. 1993. Amalgam-related illness FAQ. *Handbook for victims of mercury-Poisoning from Dental Amalgam.* November.

18 Shirk, M. 1994. U.S., Belgian doctors pioneer method to cure male infertility. *Winnipeg Free Press.* 11 July.

Unit 3 - Cell Division, Medellian Genetics and Molecular Genetic

1 Curtis, H. 1983. Biology. New York: Worth Publishers.

2 Pearson, W.R., et al. 1983. Increased synthesis of glutathione S-transferases in response to anticarcinogenic antioxidants. Cloning and measurement of messenger RNA. Journal of Biology and Chemistry 258 (3): 2052-2062.

3 Glausiusz, J. 1996. How cholera became a killer. Discover 17 (10): 28

4 Campbell, N.A. 1987. Biology. New York: Worth Publishers.

5/38/NR4-5 J.T. 1997. the benefits of mother's milk. Science News 151(5): 322

6 Sternberg, S. 1997. Cystic fibrosis puzzle coming together. Science News 151(2): 85

10-11 Illustration from An Introduction to Genetic Analysis by Griffiths et al. © 1976. 1981, 1986. 1989, 1993, 1996 by W.H. Freeman and Company.

12-14 Seachrtst. L. 1996. "Only the strong survive. the evolution of a tumor favors the meanest, most aggressive cells." Science News 149(4): 216-117

18 Diagram from Biology by Neil A. Campbell; Copyright © 1987 by the Benjamin/Cummings Publishing Company.

19-21 Travis, J. 1996. Mitotic mischief: Can cells divide without chromosomes? Science News 150(8): 140-141

25-26 Photographs by Lennart Nilsson. From A Child Is Born (Delacore Press/Seymour Lawrence, 1990)

27-28/45/NR3 Figures from Biology: Discovering Life by Joseph S. Levine and Kenneth R. Miller. Copyright © 1991 by D.C. Heath and Company. All rights reserved.

29-31 Engels, J.M.M., et al. 1975. Investigations of the inheritance of flower variegation in Mirabilis jalapa. Euphytica 24: 1-5

35-36 Oliwenstein, L. 1993. The gene that knows left from right. Discover 14 (8): 20

37 Pringle, H. 1992. The sex difference. Equinox, September/October, 84-86

39-40 Griffiths, A.J.F., et al. 1993. An Introduction to Genetic Analysis. New York: W.H. Freeman and Company

43-44 Lemonick M.D. 1994. A terrible beauty. Time, 4 December, 54-58.

45-46/NR9 Cummings, M. and W. Klug. 1997. Concepts of Genetics. Toronto: Prentice Hall Inc.

49, NR10-11 Diagram from Biology, Third Edition, by Neil A Campbell © 1987. 1990, 1993 by The Benjamin/Cummings Publishing Company, Inc.

Unit Test 3

7 Hall, J. 1996. Pinpointing people's panic buttons. *The Edmonton Journal.* 9 January.

9, 32 Rimoin, D.L., J.M. Connar, and R.E. Pyeritz. 1996. *Principles and Practice of Human Genetics.* New York: Churchill Livingstone.

10 Poirier, Y. et al. 1997. "Polyhydroxybutyrate, a biodegradable thermoplastic, produced in transgenic plants." http://nightshade.cit.cornell.edu/coursepak/poirier.htm

NR 1 Diagram from *Biology* by Neil Campbell; Copyright (©) 1987 by the Benjamin/Cummings Publishing Company Inc. Reprinted by permission Addison Wesley Longman Publishers Inc.

23, NR 3 Griffiths, A.J. et al. 1993. *An Introduction to Genetic Analysis.* New York: W.H. Freeman and Company.

25 Carney, M., A. Futreal, and J. Lancaster. "BRCA1 and 2—A genetic link to familial breast and ovarian cancer." http://www.medscape.com/Medscape/womens.health/1997/v02.n02/w134.lancaster/w134.lancaster.html

NR 5 Diagram from *Understanding Biology* by P.H. Raven and G.B. Johnson, (Mosby-Year Book, 1991). Reprinted with permission of The McGraw-Hill Companies.

33 Richards, M. 1996. Genetics and health. *Biological Sciences Review.* November: 26–29.

NR 9 Cummings, M. 1994. *Human Heredity.* St. Paul: West Publishing Company.

Unit 4 - Population Genetics and Interaction

1 Klinger, K.W. 1983. Cystic fibrosis in the Ohio Amish: gene frequency and founder effect. Human Genetics. 65: 94-95

2 Gonick, L. 1996. Science classics. Discover 17 (2): 88

NR1 Cummings, M.R. 1993. Human Heredity. New York: West Publishing Company.

4/NR2 Lemonick M.D. 1994. A terrible beauty. Time, 4 December, 54-58.

5 Cummings, M. 1994. Human Heredity. St. Paul West Publishing Company.

7 Vergano, D. 1996. The trouble with condoms. Science News. 150 (37): 165

9 Mech, D. 1996. "Obtaining information from a pristine ecosystem to assess degraded ecosystems and assist in restoration ecology." http://www.pwrc.nbs.gov:80/newhome/mech3.htm (7 Sept. 1996).

13 Breakthroughs. 1996. Killer dolphins. Discover 17(9): 22

17 Graph adapted from The Economy of Nature 3/E by Ricklefs (c) 1993 by W.H. Freeman and Company.

18 Sternberg, S. 1997. Cystic fibrosis puzzle coming together. Science News 151(2): 85

19-20 McInnis, D. 1996. Birth control reins in wild horses' foaling around. Edmonton Journal, 14 April.

21-22/23-24 Naylor, V.J. 1995. Ajo Mountain Drive Road Guide. Arizona: Southwest Parks and Monuments Association.

21-22/23-24 Map and illustration from Ajo Mountain Drive Road Guide by Valerie J. Naylor (Southwest Parks and Monuments Association, Tucson, Arizona, 1995).

Unit Test 4

4-7/NR2 Brodie, J. 1997. The tragic comeback of the snow geese. *The Globe and Mail,* 8 March.

8-10 Nuttall, I. 1995. "Disease sheet: Dracunculiasis (Action)." http://www.who.ch/programmes/ctd/ diseases/drac/ dracact.htm

13 Luttwak, E.N. 1996. Best of all worlds. *The Times Literary Supplement March: pp. 3-4.*

Written Response

WR1. Nichols, M 1996. The sperm scare. *Maclean's* 109 (14): 50-54.

Moomaw, W.R., review of *Our Stolen Future: Are We Threatening Our Fertility, Intelligence, and Survival? A Scientific Detective Story, by* Theo Colborn, Dianne Dumanoski, and John Peterson. *Chemical and Engineering News* 74 (1 April 1996): 34-35.

Stainsby, M. 1996. Shrinking sperm counts linked to Petrochemicals. *The Edmonton Journal,* 1 May.

Raloff, J.1994. That feminine touch: are men suffering from prenatal or childhood exposures to "hormonal" toxicants? *Science News* 145(4): 56-58.

Lambton, C. 1993. Why has human sperm count declined? *Guardian,* 11 February.

WR2. NCBI. "The Human Gene Map. Ataxia Telangiectasia" http://www.ncbi.nlm.nih.gov/cgi-bin/SCIENC E96/gene?ATM (7 April 1997)

Ataxia-Telangiectasia Children's Project. "Home Page" http://ww2.med.jhu.edu/ataxia (5 Nov. 1997)

WR3. Monmaney, T. 1996. Chernobyl's legacy: The stuff of science fiction. *The Edmonton Journal.* 5 May. Shcherbak, Y. 1996. Ten years of the Chornobyl Era. *Scientific American.* April: 44–49

WR4. Lanza, R., D. Cooper, and W. chick. 1997. Xenotransplantation. *Scientific American.* July: 54–59. Cozzi, E. and D. White. 1996. Transgenic pigs—human organ factories? *Biological Sciences Review.* November: 23–25

Figure adapted form *Biological Sciences Review* by E. Cozzi and D. White, Philip Allan (1996) U.K. Reprinted by permission of Philip Allan Publishers.

WR5 Trichopoulos, D., F.P. Li, and D.J. Hunter. 1996. What causes cancer? Scientific American 275 (9): 80-87

WR6 McKusick, V.A., et al. 1997. "Adrenoleukodystrophy; ALD. http://www3.ncbi-nlm.nih.gov/htbinpost/Omim /dispmin?300100

WR7 Day, M. 1997. Third-world human lab rats. New Scientist, 17 May, 36-37

O'Brien, S.J. and M. Dean. 1997. In search of AIDS-resistance genes. Scientific American. 275(9): 44-51

WR7 Map by Laurie Grace. Adapted from Scientific American, 275(9): 49. Reprinted by permission of Laurie Grace.

WR8 Barnard, C.J. and J.M. Behnke. 1990. Parasitism and Host Behavior. New York: Taylor and Francis.

Phares, C.K. 1987. Pleurocercoid growth factor: A homologue of human growth hormone. Parasitology Today 3(11): 346-348.

WR9 OMIM:OnlineMendelianInheritanccinMan. "Diabetes mellitus,juvenile-onset insulin-dependent; IDDM." http://www3.ncbi.nlm.nih.gov/Omim/ National Eye Institute. "Diabetic neuropathy, The nerve damage of diabetes" and "Don't lose sight of diabetic eye disease." http://www.niddk.nih.gov

WR10 Staples, D. 1997. Wolf Boys no freaks, just kids proud of who they are. The Edmonton Journal, 14 May.

Figuera, L.E. et al. 1995. Mapping of the congenital generalized hypertrichosis locus to chromosome Xq24-q27.l. Nature Genetics 10: 202-207.

Pivnick E.K. et al. "Hypertrichosis, facial dysmorphia, pigmentary retinopathy: A new syndrome?" http://www.circ.uab.edu/sergg/f95/neuro8.ht m

WR10 Figure from "Mapping of the congenital generalized hypertrichosis locus to chromosome Xy24-q27.1" by Luis E. Figuera et al. As found in Nature Genetics, vol. 10, June 1995.

June 2001 Examination

3-6 Henahan, S. 1998. "Cloning a treatment for Parkinson's disease." Access Excellence. http://www.gene.com/ae/WN/SU/pd598.html.

13-15/NR2 Graph and excerpt adapted from Sex Differences in the Brain by Doreen Kimura. Copyright 1992 by Scientific American, Inc. All rights reserved.

16 Levin, J. and Suzuki, D. 1993. The Secret of Life. Toronto: Stoddart Publishing Co. Limited.

17-18 Travis, J. 1996. Gene variations sway prostate cancer risk. Science News(150). November 9: 295.

19-20 Travis, J. 1996. Chromosome linked to male infertility. Science News(149). May 18: 310.

24-25/NR3 Adapted from diagram by Robert J. Huskey. From http://wsrv.clas.virginia.edu/~rjh9u/deafmute. html.

29 Author unknown. 1997. Why an elephant in love always grumbles. The Edmonton Journal. 23 November.

32-34 Figure adapted from Biology, Third Edition, by Neil A. Campbell. Copyright 1993 by The Benjamin/Cumming Publishing Company, Inc.

35-38/NR6 Author unknown. 1997. Why an elephant in love always grumbles. The Edmonton Journal. 23 November.

42-44/NR7 Simon, J. 1997. Drug-sniffing dogs hot on the trail of endangered species. The Edmonton Journal. 14 September.

45-46/NR8 Author unknown. 1997. Project aims to save owls. Globe and Mail. 12 July.

47 Graph adapted from Beekeeping: A Practical Guide by Richard Bonney. Published by Storey Communications, Pownal, VT, 1993.

47-48 Bonney, R.E. 1993. Beekeeping: A Practical Guide. Vermont: Storey Communications, Inc.

WR1 Cathy Trost. From "The Blue People of Troublesome Creek" as found on http://wsrv.clas.virginia.edu/~rjh9u/blkysc82. html.

Diagram by Robert J. Huskey. From www.people.virginia.edu/%7erjh9u/diaenz.ht ml.

WR2 Newberger, J.J. 1997. New brain development research-a wonderful window of opportunity to build public support for early childhood education. Young Children. May: 4-9.

Nash, J.M. 1997. Fertile minds. Time. June 9: 46-54.

Hopson, J.L. 1998. Psychology. Psychology Today. September/October: 44-49.

January 2002 Examination

9-12 Glenn Zorpette. From "Extreme Sports, Sensation Seeking and the Brain" as found in Scientific American Presents, vol. 10, no. 2, 1999, pages 56-59.

NR3-4 Nancy J. Alexander. Adapted from "Beyond the Condom: The Future of Male Contraception" as found in Scientific American Presents, vol. 10, no. 2, 1999, pages 80-85.

13-15 Nathan Seppa. From "A protein is pivotal in prostate cancer" as found in Science News, vol. 154, September 12, 1998, page 167. Copyright 1998 by Science Service Inc.

16-17 Figure by John and Judy Waller. From Human Physiology: From Cells to Systems, 2nd edition, by L. Sherwood © 1993.

18 Figure from Human Heredity, 3rd edition, by M. Cummings © 1994.

22-27 Douglas C. Wallace. From "Mitochondrial DNA in Aging and Disease" as found in Scientific American, vol. 227, no. 2, August 1997, pages 40-47.

Page 14 Photograph by Ornestico Ramirez, Painted Pony Horse Ranch, 2000. From http://members.aol.com/famtwins/page4inde x.htm

37-38 Figure from Invitation to Biology, 5/E by Helena Curtis, and N. Sue Barnes. 1972, 1977, 1981, 1985, and 1994 by Worth Publishers.

39-40 John Travis. From "Gene Creates Malaria Drug Resistance" as found in Science News, vol. 152, November 29, 1997, page 340. Copyright 1997 by Science Service Inc.

41-43/NR7-8 Claudio Ciofi. From "The Komodo Dragon" as found in Scientific American, vol. 280, no. 3, March 1999, pages 84-91.

44-46 Brad Cundiff. Adapted from "Invasion of Primacy" as found in Nature Canada, vol. 25, no. 2, Spring 1996, pages 32-38.

47-48 Robert A. Wallace, Gerald P. Sanders, and Robert J. Ferl. Adapted from Biology: The Science of Life, Fourth Edition (HarperCollins College Publishers, 1996), pages 770-771.

WR1 Ross McLeod. Adapted from "Ornithine Transcarbamylase Deficiency in a Blood Indian Family" as found in the Bulletin of Hereditary Disease Program of Alberta, vol. 6, no. 4, 1987, pages 14-16.

Figures adapted from "Ornithine Transcarbamylase Deficiency in a Blood Indian Family" by Ross McLeod, as found in the Bulletin of Hereditary Disease Program of Alberta, vol. 6, no. 4, 1987, pages 14-16.

Adapted from Emery and Rimoin's Principles and Practice of Medical Genetics 3/e, volume 1, edited by Alan E.H. Emery, David L. Rimoin, J. Michael Connor, and Reed E. Pyeritz, pages 620-622, 1888, © 1997, by permission of the publisher Churchill Livingstone and by permission of Dr. David L. Rimoin.

WR2 Beth Ellyn Rosenthal. From "Hot Flash: Wild Yam Cream" on http://www.meltdown.com/pms2.html, 2000. Reprinted with permission from Beth Ellyn Rosenthal.

Article by Pierre L. Le Bars, Martin M. Katz, Nancy Berman, Turan M. Itil, Alfred M. Freedman, and Alan F. Schatzberg. From "A Placebo-Controlled, Double-blind, Randomized Trial of an Extract of Ginkgo Biloba for Dementia" as found in the JAMA Abstracts, October 22, 1997, on http://www.ama-assn.org/sci-pubs/journals/ar chive/jama/vol_278/no_16/oc71278a.htm. Adapted and reprinted with permission from the American Medical Association.

ORDERING INFORMATION

All School Orders

School Authorities are eligible to purchase these resources by applying the Learning Resource Credit Allocation (LRCA – 25% school discount) on their purchase through the Learning Resources Centre (LRC). Call LRC for details.

THE KEY Study Guides are specifically designed to assist students in preparing for unit tests, final exams, and provincial examinations.

KEY Study Guides – $29.95 each plus G.S.T.

SENIOR HIGH		JUNIOR HIGH	ELEMENTARY
Biology 30	Biology 20	Language Arts 9	Language Arts 6
Chemistry 30	Chemistry 20	Math 9	Math 6
English 30-1	English 20-1	Science 9	Science 6
English 30-2	Math 20 (Pure)	Social Studies 9	Social Studies 6
Math 30 (Pure)	Physics 20	Math 8	Math 4
Math 30 (Applied)	Social Studies 20	Math 7	Language Arts 3
Physics 30	English 10-1		Math 3
Social Studies 30	Math 10 (Pure)		
Social Studies 33	Science 10		
	Social Studies 10		

Student Notes and Problems (SNAP) Workbooks contain complete explanations of curriculum concepts, examples, and exercise questions.

SNAP Workbooks – $29.95 each plus G.S.T.

SENIOR HIGH		JUNIOR HIGH	ELEMENTARY
Chemistry 30	Chemistry 20	Math 9	Math 6
Math 30 Pure	Math 20 Pure	Science 9	Math 5
Math 30 Applied	Math 20 Applied	Math 8	Math 4
Math 31	Physics 20	Math 7	Math 3
Physics 30	Math 10 Pure		
	Math 10 Applied		
	Science 10		

Visit our website for a "tour" of resource content and features at
www.castlerockresearch.com

#2340, 10180 – 101 Street
Edmonton, AB Canada T5J 3S4
e-mail: learn@castlerockresearch.com

Phone: 780.448.9619
Toll-free: 1.800.840.6224
Fax: 780.426.3917

2006 (3)

SCHOOL ORDER FORM

Castle Rock Research Corp

THE KEY

THE KEY	QUANTITY
Biology 30	
Chemistry 30	
English 30-1	
English 30-2	
Math30 (Pure)	
Math 30 (Applied)	
Physics 30	
Social Studies 30	
Social Studies 33	
Biology 20	
Chemistry 20	
English 20-1	
Math 20 (Pure)	
Physics 20	
Social Studies 20	
English 10-1	
Math 10 (Pure)	
Science 10	
Social Studies 10	
Language Arts 9	
Math 9	
Science 9	
Social Studies 9	
Math 8	
Math 7	
Language Arts 6	
Math 6	
Science 6	
Social Studies 6	
Math 4	
Math 3	
Language Arts 3	

SNAP WORKBOOKS
Notes and Problems/ Student Notes and Problems

	QUANTITY	
	Workbooks	Solutions Manuals
Chemistry 30		
Chemistry 20		
Physics 30		
Physics 20		
Math 30 Pure		
Math 30 Applied		
Math 31		
Math 20 Pure		
Math 20 Applied		
Math 10 Pure		
Math 10 Applied		
Science 10		
Science 9		
Math 9		
Math 8		
Math 7		
Math 6		
Math 5		
Math 4		
Math 3		

TOTALS

KEYS	
WORKBOOKS	
SOLUTION MANUALS	

Learning Resources Centre

Castle Rock Research is pleased to announce an exclusive distribution arrangement with the Learning Resources Centre (LRC). Under this agreement, schools can now place all their orders with LRC for order fulfillment. As well, these resources are eligible for applying the Learning Resource Credit Allocation (LRCA), which gives schools a 25% discount off LRC's selling price. Call LRC for details.

Orders may be placed with LRC by
telephone: (780) 427-5775
fax: (780) 422-9750
internet: www.lrc.learning.gov.ab.ca
or mail: **12360 - 142 Street NW**
Edmonton, AB T5L 4X9

PAYMENT AND SHIPPING INFORMATION

Name: _____

School Telephone: _____

SHIP TO
School: _____

Address: _____

City: _____ Postal Code: _____

PAYMENT
☐ by credit card
VISA/MC Number: _____ Expiry Date: _____
Name on Card: _____
☐ enclosed cheque
☐ invoice school   P.O. number: _____

#2340, 10180 – 101 Street, Edmonton, AB   T5J 3S4
email: learn@castlerockresearch.com

Tel: 780.448.9619   Fax: 780.426.3917
Toll-free: 1.800.840.6224

www.castlerockresearch.com